SPEECH COMMUNICATION

Sixth Edition

SPEECH COMMUNICATION

William D. Brooks
Friends University

Robert W. Heath

wcb
Wm. C. Brown Publishers
Dubuque, Iowa

Cover design by Jeanne Regan.

The credits section for this book begins on page 363, and is considered an extension of the copyright page.

Library of Congress Catalog Card Number: 88–71226

ISBN 0–697–03043–1

Printed in the United States of America by Wm. C. Brown Publishers
2460 Kerper Boulevard, Dubuque, IA 52001

10 9 8 7 6 5 4 3 2

Contents

Preface

Writing the sixth edition of *Speech Communication* was once again an exciting and rewarding experience. Since both Robert Heath and I have taught from *Speech Communication* for a number of years to a wide variety of students, we are sensitive to the pedagogical marriage of textbook and classroom. *Speech Communication* commonly receives commendations from reviewers who have used it for their own classes, as well as from professors and students who have written letters or have remarked in person that *Speech Communication* is pedagogically helpful. We hope students will find *Speech Communication* exciting, readable, understandable, and relevant to their personal growth as effective communicators.

The basic organizational pattern of *Speech Communication* has been changed slightly for the sixth edition. We begin with a thorough study of the process of communication and then apply the principles and theory that best describe the process across communication levels—intrapersonal, interpersonal, and public. However, the unifying theme of *Speech Communication* is the same as in the first five editions: namely, that effective communication at all levels—intrapersonal, interpersonal, and public—is necessary to full and successful living.

An underlying assumption of *Speech Communication* is that communication skills can be learned. A person of reasonable ability who desires to understand communication and to acquire skills in communication can do so under the guidance of a competent instructor. *Speech Communication* is written with that belief in mind. One of the strengths of the book is that it is based on the strongest and most sound theory and research available today. At the same time it gives the student pragmatic instruction about how to apply the theory.

The book's objectives are (1) a clear understanding of the theory and principles of communication, and (2) an internalization of those principles in behavior. Both knowledge and skill are necessary for effective communication. To that end, we have provided study aids throughout the book that will make it easier to acquire the concepts and principles of communication and to translate those concepts and principles into behavior.

Part openers and *chapter openers* relate units to one another and clarify the purposes and concerns of each. Each chapter has a *Focus page* that serves as a detailed preview of the chapter. It is in brief outline form and allows the student to get a holistic view of the entire chapter. *Summaries* conclude the chapters.

This sixth edition continues the use of *study probes*. These probes, in the form of questions and learning activities, appear several times within each chapter so that students can internalize as they apply what they have read, can review to that point, and can check their comprehension of the explanatory material they have read. At the end of each chapter are *Questions and Exercises for Review, Key Terms,* and an annotated bibliography, *For Further Reading*. At the end of the book is a *Glossary* and author and subject *Indexes*.

In addition, illustrations, examples, graphs, and other visual aids are presented throughout so that the principles and theory will be more easily understood and more easily related and applied to the students' own world. It is our hope that this edition of *Speech Communication* will be interesting and, yes, even enjoyable to read.

The most obvious change in this sixth edition is the combining of material from chapters 2 and 4 into one new chapter. Both chapters dealt with information processing, so we consolidated the material to make the connection more apparent. Other changes or additions to this sixth edition include the following: new material on reducing communication apprehension in chapter 3; prescriptions for better listening in chapter 4; objectives for using power in interpersonal relationships in chapter 6; new material on family communication and in a work setting in chapter 7; and new material on ethics and reasoning in chapter 13.

We are grateful to the many students, instructors, and professors who have used *Speech Communication* and who have written or communicated to us in person their suggestions, recommendations, compliments, and requests to not change various aspects of *Speech Communication*.

We have relied strongly on the unsolicited feedback from these persons. In addition, several users of *Speech Communication* at colleges and universities of various types and sizes were asked for extensive reviews and suggestions for improving this edition. The time and effort given by each of them to these tasks is appreciated; and their suggestions and recommendations, which were in high agreement, have been followed in what was changed and not changed in this edition. Thanks for your help.

Few courses are more directly relevant to one's life and one's world than the basic communication course. Our world is characterized by change and speeded-up interaction. It is our wish that through your study of communication you will acquire not only communication knowledge and skills that are helpful to you, but a basic belief in and attitude toward communication as transaction—the means whereby individuals and groups share, understand, and cooperate to fulfill their mutual needs.

William D. Brooks
and
Robert W. Heath

SPEECH COMMUNICATION

Part 1

Foundations of Communication

Part 1 of *Speech Communication* is concerned with intrapersonal communication, since the individual's ability to communicate with himself or herself is at the heart of interpersonal and public communication. Chapter 1 presents an overview of communication. Attention is given to the process of communication, the major components, and the levels of communication. Chapter 2 is concerned with the individual's communication system and how that system, comprising receptors and the central nervous system, receives and processes information. Perception and symbolization are the major topics with which we are concerned. Chapter 3 is about the self as a variable in communication. What we think about ourselves, who we are, and who we want to be are powerful influences in our communication. We will study how we come to define ourselves and how we can develop better concepts of ourselves. Listening is an important within-the-person process and is investigated in significant detail in chapter 4. Part 1 concludes with the study of nonverbal communication. These five chapters provide a foundation from which to study interpersonal communication and public communication in Parts 2 and 3.

Focus

Implications of Effective Communication Behavior

Personal Growth
Social Growth
Cooperative Action

Definition of Speech Communication

Speech Communication as Process

- *Dynamic*
- *Systemic*
- *Transactional*
- *Adaptive*
- *Continuous*

Major Components in Communication

- *Communicators*
- *Message*
- *Channel*
- *Feedback*
- *Noise*

Levels of Speech Communication

Intrapersonal Communication
Interpersonal Communication
Public Communication
Organizational Communication
Cultural Communication

Introduction
An Overview of Communication

1

Communication is a survival mechanism. We develop as unique persons; we relate to others; and we cooperate with others through communication. Communication is a process that is dynamic, systemic, transactional, adaptive, and continuous, and we engage in it at numerous levels, including the intrapersonal, interpersonal, and public communication levels.

Through sounds, positions and movements, animals communicate.

Human beings are communicators. Our quality of life depends upon communication. Primitive peoples' attempts to make recognizable sounds were undoubtedly motivated by the need to meet threats to survival. They learned to make sounds that were warnings of impending danger, threatening sounds to frighten away intruders, and pleasant sounds to establish friendship and rapport. Such communication, observable also in animal behavior, is called **presymbolic communication.**

The presymbolic communication of animals is amazingly efficient. The signals animals send—through sounds, positions, and movements—can express such definite things as "Get out of my territory!" "Help!" "Build a nest with me," or "Fly straight ahead, keeping about twenty degrees right of the sun, and then, at one hundred yards, there is a patch of clover bloom." Crickets and grasshoppers have an astonishing variety of songs, with accompanying moods that vary from courtship to combat-to-the-death. Mice communicate with high-pitched tones—tones in the ultrasonic range—and ants convey various messages by tapping other ants with their antennae. Some species of butterfly change their color in a fraction of a second and give off an odor as a mating signal. The male unicorn fish, within seconds of becoming interested in a female, signals to her by developing a bright blue spot on his back and light blue stripes down his side, to which she responds appropriately if she is ready to mate.

Perhaps the most interesting animal communication is that of monkeys and apes. Since 1960, more than two dozen excellent studies have described communication among the primates. All describe communication systems that are

Through effective communication one is more likely to live a full life.

elaborate in their establishment and maintenance of intragroup and intergroup relationships and modes of behavior. For example, the leader determines the direction of the group's movements for the day and gives the signals for starting and stopping. The early morning howling of the howler monkeys gives directions for their movements throughout the entire day; thus they can communicate to influence behavior that will occur several hours later. The leader also arbitrates disputes in the group and is responsible for its defense. Elaborate social hierarchies and status positions are defined and maintained.

In human communication, as in animal communication, the purpose is to enable organisms to adjust to their environments.

Implications of Effective Communication Behavior

If communication behavior can be described and understood, then it follows that it can be learned. But why is it important that we acquire better skills in communication? Let us consider three reasons.

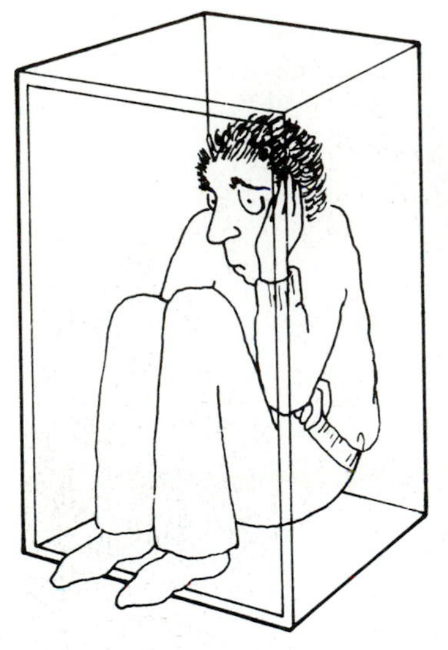

Don't let self-isolation box you in.

Personal Growth

One reason why it's important to learn to communicate more effectively is that through communication I become whoever I am and you become whoever you are. We are more than our physical bodies—more than skin and bones. The mental and the emotional along with the physical make me "me" and you "you." Through communication you and I discover the *names* for things about us and, more importantly, the *meanings* of things about us. Through communication you and I develop language so that we can identify and describe the things about us, even identify and describe ourselves. Through communication our personalities develop. But our mental and emotional development doesn't stop at age five, or age thirteen, or upon graduating from high school—it continues. For each of us, the quality of our communication affects the quality of our living. The link between communication and mental health is clear. Can I think and express my thoughts clearly? Have I learned to be open and to trust? Can I let myself be known by others? Or am I afraid and fearful? Am I withdrawn from others and from my world? These are matters directly related to one's communication development. For these reasons, personal growth is one of the major objectives of the study of communication.

Social Growth

A second objective in the study of communication is social growth. As social beings living with others, we need to communicate effectively with others. No one can live—certainly not live fully—isolated from all other human beings. We are social creatures with strong social needs, and these needs are met through communication.

Most of us have had both successful and unsuccessful communication experiences, some wonderfully wholesome and satisfying and some in which we were hurt or which were unpleasant and less than satisfying. One of the purposes in our study of speech communication, then, is to gain a better understanding of social communication.

Cooperative Action

A third reason why the study of speech communication is important is that, through communication, we cooperate with each other to do things we cannot do alone—things that bring us greater control over our environment and fuller, more satisfying lives. The culmination of such efforts are organizations—businesses, industries, schools, churches, school boards, city governments, county governments, state governments, the national government, and even world political organizations. Organizations enable us to solve mutual problems and to bring order into our environment.

Decisions are made and actions are taken through organizations.

Through communication we organize and operate factories, corporations, and businesses that provide goods and services we could never produce individually; we have religious organizations so we can worship together; and we have sports teams and entertainment organizations so that we can have pleasure together. These and other organizations exist through communication. The jobs that people have in these organizations exist through communication.

Decisions are made through organizations, and actions are taken through organizations. In a free and democratic society, effective communication is required within governmental units as well as among the general citizenry. We share knowledge, information, attitudes, and judgments in informal, on-the-job situations as well as in formal audience situations. We make known our attitudes and try to persuade others; and we listen to others as they express their attitudes and share their insights and knowledge with us. This process of sharing information and viewpoints is necessary to cooperative action in our world, and it is an important reason for studying speech communication. But what is speech communication?

Definition of Speech Communication

Speech communication is the process by which information, meanings, and feelings are shared by persons through the exchange of verbal and nonverbal messages.

There are two basic areas of concern in our definition: (1) the idea of process, and (2) the major components in the **process of speech communication.**

Speech Communication as Process

Speech communication is a process. **Process** implies dynamics and change. It implies parts interacting and influencing each other so as to function as a whole. When we accept the concept of process, we view events and relationships as dynamic, systemic, transactional, adaptive, and continuous.

Dynamic

Anything that is a process is dynamic rather than static. Static things are fixed and unchanging, but dynamic things change constantly. **Communication** deals with change. If nothing changed there would be no need for communication; but our environment changes. Relationships change. Attitudes, desires, goals, understanding of others, knowledge—all of these change, and through communication we adjust to change.

Systemic

Speech communication is systemic. By systemic, we mean that speech communication occurs within a larger system. Communication always occurs within a system.

By system we refer to interrelated and interdependent elements working together to achieve a desired outcome. The major components of the speech communication process are communicators (frequently referred to as source and receiver), message, channel, feedback, and noise.

Transactional

Transaction is the third characteristic of the speech communication process. The essence of the term *transaction* is relationship. Included in the transactional characteristic of communication is the fact that each communication event is a unique combination of people, messages, and situation.

What do we mean when we say that communication is transactional?

Further, no communication encounter is exactly like some prior encounter. Therefore, each communication event must be approached, not with a set of "rules of behaving" but with an openness and willingness to adapt to the specific communication encounter. Throughout this text we will be studying how the various components of communication interact—how each affects others and how each affects the outcome of communication. As you can see, communication is a complex process.

A fourth characteristic of process is adaptation. Any process exists to achieve some outcome. In other words, processes are purposeful and functional. In order for the process to achieve its intended outcome it must adapt to change. **Communication is adaptive.** This means that in communication one must begin to pay attention to the other person, to the topic, to the physical surroundings, to motives and needs, and to other elements that we will study in this text. Effective communication is characterized by an ability to adjust and to adapt to changing situations.

Adaptive

Communication is continuous. It has no beginning and no end. When does a communication process really start and when does it end? One of the authors relates the following illustrative experience: One summer at Grandfather Mountain in North Carolina, I became engaged in a conversation with someone I had never seen before. That was not the beginning of our communication because the habits, perceptions, and language each of us brought to the conversation came from our past experiences. Our small talk was on "safe" subjects like the weather and the beauty of the surroundings. Common experiences and even common acquaintances soon emerged, however, as we brought our past into the communication situation. The places we had been, the things we had done, the people we knew—all these affected who we were and what we communicated. And so this communication encounter did *not* begin with our first words. Neither did it end with our last words. In fact, it has found its way into this book. So it is with any communication encounter between people. Communication is an ongoing process. Our communication moves into our future to affect subsequent communication. Communication has no beginning and no ending.

Continuous

These five characteristics—change (dynamic), interrelatedness of elements (systemic), the uniqueness of each relationship (transaction), adjustment to change (adaptive), and ongoing (continuous)—are important concepts to keep in mind as we study human communication.

Can you explain how communication is a process?

Major Components in Communication

We have noted that communication is systemic and that systems have component parts. What are the basic components of speech communication? They are communicators (sources and receivers), message, channel, feedback, and noise. There are limitations in any model, of course, since models are simplistic and always identify only selected variables while ignoring others. Models are also static (they freeze the process at one point in time as a photograph freezes action at one point), so they cannot portray changes and interactions. Nevertheless, a model can aid us in understanding the communication that occurs between human beings.

Communicators

The models in figures 1.1, 1.2, and 1.3 schematically demonstrate three traditional views of the communication process. The first model illustrates what has been called a linear or stimulus-response view of communication. The

Figure 1.1 Linear (stimulus-response) model. This view assumes that communication occurs when a message is transmitted through a channel from a sender to a receiver. Notice the assumed passive role of the receiver.

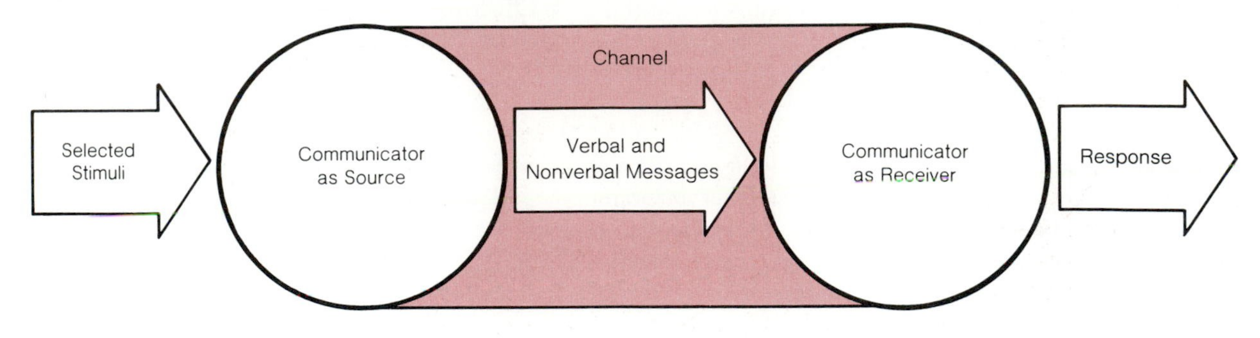

second model focuses on communication as an interaction process and incorporates a more complex set of assumptions. The third model views communication as systemic and includes additional complexities. **Communicators** are those involved in information reception, perception, processing and transmission. In systems terms, communicators are engaged in inputting, transformation, and outputting. Two processes especially important in the transaction process are encoding and decoding. Encoding is the process of selecting a code or language to express intentions, thoughts, and feelings to a specific receiver. It is the process of putting the message into a code. The code might be sign language for deaf persons, oral English for English-speaking persons, or oral Russian for Russian-speaking persons. The process of decoding involves perception and interpretation of the message. Decoding means that the code containing the message is identified and changed into its appropriate meanings.

Message

In the simplest sense, a **message** may be thought of as an idea, concept, emotion, desire, or feeling that a person desires to share with another human being. A message may be in verbal or nonverbal codes. The purpose of a message is to evoke meaning in another person. Not all messages are intentional; some are unintentional. Unintentional messages are transmitted without the source consciously encoding them. Many nonverbal messages are unintentional messages.

Channel

A **channel** is the means by which a message moves from person A to person B. When we communicate face to face, light waves and sound waves are the major channels. These are the two channels identified in figure 1.1. You might also consider how books, films, and television make use of light and sound waves. What channels would one use to evoke responses with cologne, touch, or ESP?

Figure 1.2 Interaction model. This view assumes that communication is a process involving source, message, channel, receiver, feedback, and noise. Notice the active participation of the receiver.

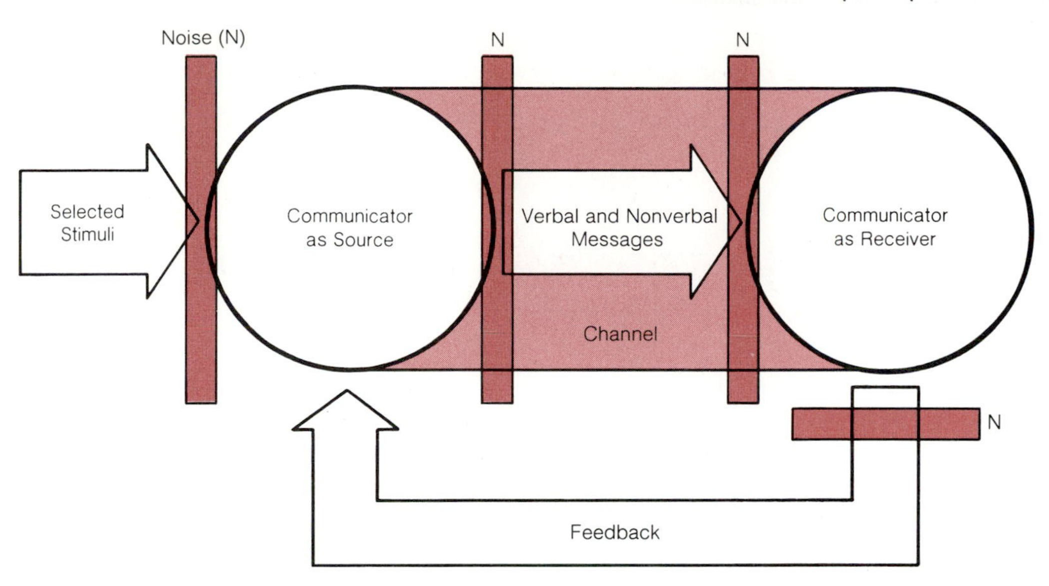

Feedback

Feedback is that integral part of the human communication process that allows the speaker to monitor the process and to evaluate the success of an attempt to get the desired response from the receiver. Of course, feedback, or "return signals," have a regulatory effect upon the speaker since the speaker must adjust to the feedback responses in order to be successful. Feedback can be received from one's own speech mechanism (the sound of one's own voice, the appearance of one's gesture) and from the outside systems of transmission (the verbal and nonverbal responses of the receiver). The responses of acceptance or rejection (inattention, smiles, nods of approval, frowns, and applause) indicate to the speaker the modifications that must be made in subsequent encounters.

Noise

Noise may occur anywhere along the communication line, and it may be physical, physiological, or psychological in nature. Examples of such interferences with speech communication are annoying vocal habits on the part of the speaker (the excessive use of *and-uh,* for example), improper articulation, or lack of adequate projection of the voice. Communication interferences may also include an unfavorable environment (a hot, poorly ventilated room, dim lighting,

Figure 1.3 Transactional model. Notice that this model assumes two mutual, interdependent, and reciprocal influences of two persons.

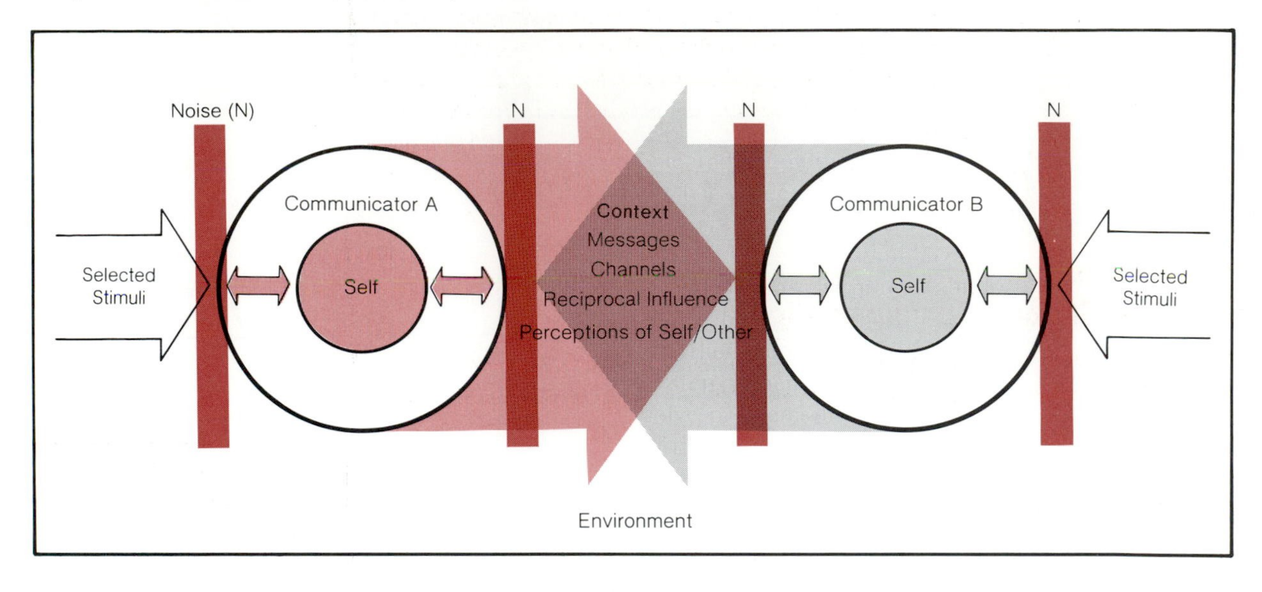

or poor seating arrangements) extraneous distractions (background noises, the shuffling of chairs, people passing outside a door or window, or whispering or coughing among the members of the audience). Poor listening (inattentiveness, lack of proper listener motivation, or physical defects in the hearing mechanism) may also interfere with speech communication. Another powerful "noise" is cultural in nature. One's culture can be an important factor in self-identity and in the differentiation of one group from another. It is not surprising that a potent noise factor in cross-cultural communication is created by the perceived cultural differences. How many short circuits in the communication process occur because we as communicators fail to consider cultural influences upon our communication partner's ways of perceiving, processing, and sending both verbal and nonverbal messages? Do you believe our communication effectiveness is influenced by differences in age, sex, race, nationality, or religion? Can you think of cultural noise factors that have occurred as you communicated with persons from other cultures? These conditions and literally hundreds more, either alone or in combination, may be present as "noise" and may modify adversely or even totally change a message as it travels from source to destination.

These five components are not the only important variables in communication. Beliefs, attitudes, images, values, social roles, and experience are additional variables that determine the content of messages, how they are constructed, by what means they are sent, and to whom they are sent. And all of these variables *operate in the receiver* to determine what messages are selected, perceived, and interpreted. Indeed, the process of communication is comprised of many variables interacting within each communicator. Yet the five basic elements we identified first are present in all types and levels of communication. These elements are selected as our entry points into the study of communication. Together they create the communication system in which one operates.

Levels of Speech Communication

Communication may be categorized in many ways. In this book, speech communication is discussed in terms of intrapersonal, interpersonal, public, organizational, and cultural.

What are the major components in communication?

Intrapersonal Communication

Intrapersonal communication is the communication that takes place within an individual. The individual's communication system may be thought of as a complex, dynamic, open, purposive information-processing, and decision-making system—the basic operations of which are to convert raw data to information, to interpret and give meaning to that information, and to use such meaning as a basis for behavior. Intrapersonal communication is, for the most part, neurophysiological activity. It is also the level upon which an individual "talks to himself or herself" and thus handles events, ideas, and experiences. Intrapersonal communication is the base of operation for all **levels of communication.** The patterns, rules, and skills one uses in interpersonal and public communication are formed on the intrapersonal communication level. Thus this first level provides the base for speech communication behaviors that manifest themselves at the second and third levels.

Interpersonal Communication

Interpersonal communication refers to persons engaged directly in overt and covert transmission and reception of messages.

Interpersonal communication includes dyadic communication and small group communication. Dyadic communication includes situations such as two persons visiting over a cup of coffee, the job interview, the conference between subordinate and superior, or a telephone conversation with one's friend. In each of these, two persons communicate directly with each other. Each is specifically aware of the other; each can send messages overtly to the other.

Interpersonal communication also includes small group communication. The difference between small group communication and dyadic communication lies in the number of participants. The small group may be three persons talking in the backyard, a committee of five persons planning homecoming activities, or a meeting of any problem-solving group. Dyadic communication is communication between two persons only. The essential element in both kinds of interpersonal communication is that of direct, person-to-person interaction.

Public Communication

A third level of communication, **public communication,** is characterized by the sending of a message to a public. The public is an audience of several persons. In public communication, the audience functions primarily as receivers and responders. In public speaking situations, for example, members of the audience may *communicate* with the speaker, but *the speaker* does most, if not all, of the *speaking.*

Public communication includes speaker-audience communication and mass communication. Mass communication refers to the mass distribution of identical copies of the same message to persons or receivers unknown to the sender and unknown to each other in any sense of interaction.

The mass media are television, radio, motion pictures, newspapers, magazines, books, and billboards. Mass communication is directed toward a relatively large, heterogeneous, and anonymous audience. Mass communication can be characterized as public, rapid, and transient.

Organizational Communication

A fourth level of communication is **organizational communication.** Organizational communication includes all three levels previously identified—intrapersonal, interpersonal, and public, but the distinguishing characteristic is that *the communication is from an organization.* The organization "acts like a person" with regard to communication, even as a corporation acts like a person in a legal sense. The organization originates messages, owns messages, and sends messages to numerous receivers, including internal and external public recipients. For example, when you were admitted by the university or college you now attend, the university was the organization admitting you—not the person whose name appears on your letter or document of admission. The person signing the document represents the organization that has admitted you. Organizations are also the intended receivers of numerous messages sent from individuals and other organizations. Thus, organizational communication is an even higher level of communication than are interpersonal and public communication.

Cultural Communication

A fifth level of communication, **cultural communication,** includes organizations in a particular culture as well as its individual communicators.

Each culture has its own identifiable communication needs, objectives, language, channels, problems, skills—in short, each has its own communication system.

When one culture interacts with another culture, intercultural or cross-cultural communication occurs. Thus, intrapersonal, interpersonal, public, and organizational communication are involved. Competence at all levels is important.

The five levels share a common ground in the basic foundations of communication. This book focuses on the first three levels: intrapersonal, interpersonal, and public communication. Part 1 focuses on the foundations of communication, of which several are intrapersonal in nature. Part 2 is concerned with interpersonal communication, and Part 3 presents information on public communication.

Can you explain how communication is a process?

Summary

In this chapter you were introduced to the study of speech communication. Five concerns were given attention. We emphasized the purposes of communication; the relationship between quality of communication and quality of living; the characteristics of process; the major components of communication; and the levels of human communication.

Questions and Exercises for Review

1. In what three ways is communication helpful to us?
2. Communication is transactional. Name at least one implication or guideline for helping one in communicating with another person.
3. What are the implications of the fact that communication is continuous?
4. Write a definition of noise as the term applies to communication.
5. Write your personal definition of communication.
6. What are some implications of your definition of communication for your survival in cross-cultural and organizational environments?

Key Terms and Phrases

presymbolic communication
speech communication
process of speech communication
process
communication is dynamic
communication is systemic
communication is transactional
communication is adaptive
communication is continuous
communicators
message
channel
feedback
noise
intrapersonal communication
levels of communication
interpersonal communication
public communication
organizational communication
cultural communication

For Further Reading

Frings, Hubert, and Frings, Mable. *Animal Communication.* Norman: University of Oklahoma Press, 1977.

The Frings's discussion of communication between various types of animals and creatures is most interesting and informative.

Lilly, John C. *The Mind of the Dolphin: A Nonhuman Intelligence.* New York: Discus, Avon Books, 1967.

This is an interesting study of dolphins and their communicative and problem-solving abilities.

Miller, Gerald R., and Steinberg, Mark. *Between People.* Chicago: Science Research Associates, 1975.

Three approaches to the study of communication—psychological, social, and cultural—are presented in chapter 1.

Sereno, Kenneth K., and Mortensen, C. David, eds. *Foundations of Communication Theory.* New York: Harper & Row, 1970.

Includes discussions of process, systems, transaction, models, information, and definitional considerations of communication.

Williams, Frederick. *The New Communications.* Belmont: Wadsworth Publishing Co., 1984.

Focuses on the rapid changes in our ways of gathering and exchanging information, instructing ourselves and others, moving others to belief or action, and simply entertaining ourselves. Relates human communications to the new communications technologies as well as to the social aspects of these changes.

Focus

Basic Elements in the Individual's Communication System

Perception

Physiological Limitations in Perception

Optical Illusion

Neurological Inhibition

Innate Limitations and Saliences

Psychological Limitations in Perception

Selective Perception

Experience

Psychological and Emotional States

Filtering and Completing

Information Processing—Symbolization

Language and Thinking

The Nature of Words and Meaning

Words Have Many Meanings

Meaning is Arbitrary

Meanings Are in People, Not in Words

Meaning is Learned

The Abstraction Process

Thinking and Reasoning

Emotion and Reasoning

Description, Inference, and Judgment Statements

The Individual's Communication System

The individual's communication system is composed of receivers (sight, smell, taste, touch, hearing), an information-processing unit (central nervous system), and transmitters (neural-physical means for talking, writing, gesturing, and moving). Information reception is affected by perception, and perception is influenced by physiological and psychological factors. Topics included in the discussion of information processing in this chapter are symbolization, language and thinking, the abstraction process, and thinking and reasoning. This chapter concludes with a discussion of the storing and recalling of information.

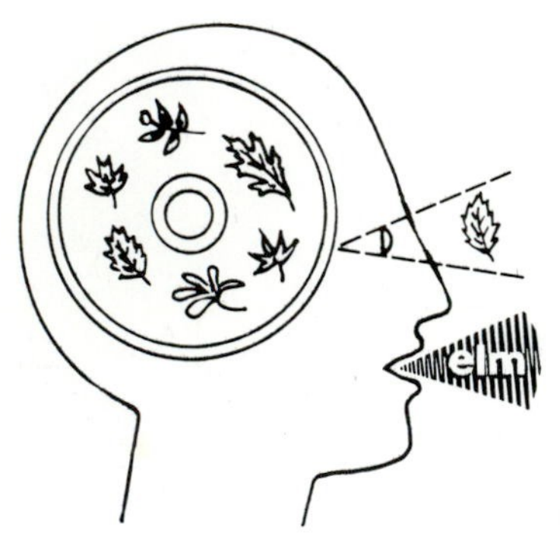

We receive, process, and send information.

When we consider human communication, it is natural that we should think about social situations—a speaker addressing an audience, a committee seated around a table in conference, or persons engaged in conversation. However, at the center of all social communication situations are individuals, each with a personal communication system. If we are to understand and improve our ability to function in social communication, we must first investigate our individual communication systems. The quality of a person's interaction with others is to a great extent dependent upon the skills developed in intrapersonal communication.

The individual is a complete, self-contained communication system, able to receive messages from inside (oneself) or outside (another). The individual can process the information, and then respond by sending messages inside or outside. The individual sees, hears, feels, smells, and tastes; learns, remembers, and thinks; speaks, writes, gestures, moves, and behaves. To understand the individual's self-contained system better, let us consider the elements comprising that system.

Basic Elements in the Individual's Communication System

The basic elements in the process of communication within the individual include receivers, an information-processing unit, and transmitters. The **receivers** with which we are most concerned are the five senses: sight, hearing, smell, taste, and touch. Through these we receive information and other messages. The **information-processing** unit is the central nervous system. The **transmitters** are the organs used in speaking, writing, vocalizing, moving, gesturing, or posturing—the means whereby messages are sent. These three classes of elements—receivers, information processor, and transmitters—function interdependently to make intrapersonal communication possible. If any element is defective or inefficient in its function, the quality of communication is correspondingly lower than it might be otherwise. If one cannot see or hear it is more difficult to receive information about the world—information needed to survive, to enjoy, to plan, and to maximize living.

The process of communication as carried out by the individual's communication system is complex, and there are both natural and acquired limitations upon its efficiency. The information-processing subsystem, in particular, is highly complex. This system—composed of the brain, the hypothalamus, the spinal cord, and the entire central nervous system—processes innumerable messages simultaneously. This system is involved in receiving, interpreting, and regulating numerous internal messages while at the same time it is receiving, processing, and responding to information from the outside environment.

Perceiving, remembering, thinking—these are among the important processes carried out in the brain. This chapter is concerned with the process of receiving and processing information. This process of receiving and processing information involves problems in using language and problems in thinking. Sometimes a person's brain, because of injury or disease, cannot function well and communication is severely affected, such as in the case of loss of speech due to stroke. The problems with which we are concerned in this chapter, however, are problems of poor habits and problems in using language effectively and thinking critically.

Perception

There are two sources of information—internal and external. Information from internal sources may come from the brain or from organs of the body. External information comes primarily by seeing or hearing, but it may come from any of the senses.

Human beings possess five primary senses: sight, hearing, touch, smell, and taste. By means of smell and taste, many lower animals perceive changes in their environment and receive information that influences their survival behavior. A great deal of animal behavior is related to the search for food; smell and taste are extremely important sources of information in the chemical environment of lower animals. Smell and taste are better developed in many animals than they are in humans.

For us, seeing and hearing are the dominant avenues for receiving information. So powerful is sight that it tends to override touch. For example, when a person looks at a raised line through a tilting prism, the line will be "seen" as tilted; if the individual simultaneously touches the raised line, it will "feel" tilted. However, if one feels the line without looking through the prism, it will not feel tilted. In other words, our sight channel is so dominant that the impression yielded by the sense of touch is distorted to conform with the visual information, even if the visual impression is incorrect.

The human eye is, in many ways, the most remarkable biological structure created by nature. It is an optical instrument, a chemical laboratory, and an electrical coder-transmitter. Since so much of our information about the world around us is received through visual stimuli, we need to know the eye's limitations and how it contributes to the way we perceive the world.

Our eyes can be likened to twin television cameras. Each eye has a lens, as does a television camera, and at the back of each eye is a light-sensitive screen (the retina) that responds chemically to form the images of everything we see. Each element of the screen is connected by transmission lines to the brain, with more than a million of such lines available. The signals that travel along these lines are electro-chemical signals. Although the eye is like a television camera in many ways, it possesses even greater complexity and sensitivity. Yet there are limitations in seeing; these limitations (as well as the limitations in hearing or touch) and the reasons for them are matters of interest in our study of intrapersonal communication. We can communicate only the information we receive through **perception.**

The following story illustrates the fallibility of information received visually and aurally. In the middle of a meeting of psychologists and other scientists, a door was suddenly thrown open and in rushed a man wearing a clown's costume. He was followed by a black man wearing a black jacket, red tie, and white trousers. The men yelled at each other and scuffled on the floor. A shot rang out, and both men rushed back through the door and out of the room. The meeting chairperson then asked the scientists to write complete reports of what they had seen and heard, to be used in the police investigation that was sure to follow. Forty scientists wrote reports. None gave a complete description of what had happened; twelve reports missed at least fifty percent of what had happened; and only six reports did not misstate facts. Four reports stated that the black man had no hat. Others wrote that the black man had a derby, a high hat, a cap, and so forth. His suit was described as red, brown, black, striped, blue, and coffee colored. The incident had been secretly planned, rehearsed, and photographed, and the experiment demonstrated dramatically the fallibility of vision and hearing as avenues of information. Similar demonstrations have been made in many college speech and psychology classes since the original experiment was carried out.

We do not perceive all we see, nor do we necessarily perceive accurately what falls on the eye's screen; and yet our intrapersonal communication is limited to the information we get from all the senses. What are some of these limitations in perception—whether from sight, hearing, or the other senses? Limitations in perception are of two kinds—physiological and psychological.

Physiological Limitations in Perception

Optical Illusion

One cause of faulty perception is the **optical illusion.** Optical illusions cannot be explained on the basis of what happens physically on the retina because the retinal image mirrors that which exists objectively. Nor can optical illusions be explained in terms of knowledge and its "derived expectancies." Optical illusions defy knowledge. For example, we know the two line segments in the familiar Müller-Lyer illusion[1] (shown in figure 2.1) are of equal length. We can confirm that knowledge by measuring the lines with a ruler. Yet when we add the arrow-shaped marks to the line segments, the lines are perceived as unequal in length.

All optical illusions attest to possible inaccuracies in receiving information. An example of this is an early experience of one of the authors. As told by him:

> I recall that on hot, dusty summer afternoons, when I was a boy, it was not unusual to "see" pools of water down the dusty farm road. They were mirages—or optical illusions, of course—but they looked real enough. One day, as I walked along the road, I observed several such mirages ahead. The mirages disappeared as I came closer to them. However, one of them (and it was indistinguishable from the others at first) persisted in staying a pool of water.

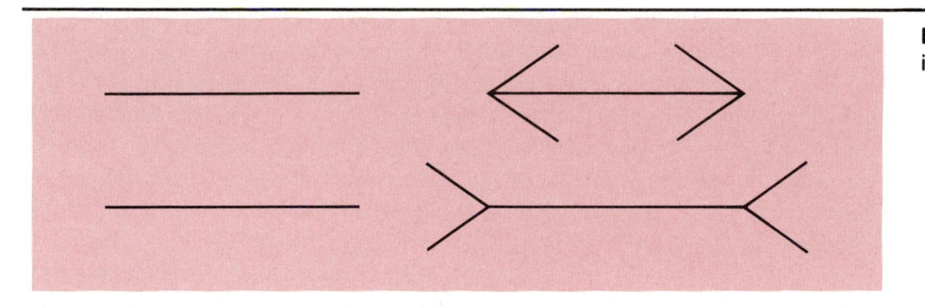

Figure 2.1 Müller-Lyer illusion.

When I got to it, I discovered that it was a real pool of water. A truck hauling water for cattle had accidentally emptied its load of water at that place in the road. I no longer was only "seeing" a pool of water on a dusty road; I now was seeing, feeling, and verifying that it was an actual pool of water that, at a distance, was indistinguishable from the optical illusions.

Neurological Inhibition

A second source of error in receiving information is **neurological inhibition.** The neural networks, composed of many nerve cells, transmit messages to and from the higher centers of the nervous system. The messages, detected in the form of electrical impulses, may travel long distances involving the spinal column and several parts of the brain; or the circuit may be quite short. For example, in the case of the reflex arc, the junction at which nerve cells interact is called a **synapse.** At this junction, the message (electrical impulse) may be stopped or sent on. At each synapse the impulse must be re-created if it is to be sent through the next nerve cell. The electrical impulse must be of sufficient strength to cause the adjoining nerve cell to re-create the impulse. Thus, each nerve cell acts as a relay station, receiving and sending signals. Only signals above a certain threshold of amplitude are received. If the strength of the impulse is not great enough to trigger the next nerve, the message will be stopped. This process operates in the same manner for all five senses.

Some incoming messages are stopped through neurological inhibition. At each synapse in the neural network are special nerve fibers that carry inhibitory impulses. These impulses can act against incoming impulses by raising the threshold of the nerve cell to a point so high that the incoming impulse will not be strong enough to trigger the next nerve cell into re-creating and sending on the impulse. The incoming impulse is inhibited—stopped—and prevented from reaching the brain. This chemical-electrical inhibiting process can act as a control of perception—a "preventer of perception." Because of this the brain is not a repository for all the stimuli available to our sensory organs. Neurological inhibition can prevent information from being received.

Innate Limitations and Saliences

Perception is also governed by innate limitations and prominent characteristics. For example, the ability of a musician to discriminate between tones is determined largely by the inherited structure of the ear. In this way, inherited traits affect perception.

Another example of inherited or natural forces affecting perception is known as the **releaser concept.** Psychologists have discovered that a given behavior is often critically dependent on just one aspect of a stimulus, while other equally perceivable qualities have no effect. The releaser phenomenon is commonly noticed in the animal world, too. The red belly feathers of the male British robin will automatically trigger an attack by another male robin, but a dummy, accurate in all ways except that the belly is not red, elicits no attack. Conversely, a small bundle of red feathers alone will release the attack behavior. There are many other examples of the releaser phenomenon operating in perception. These releasers do not have to be learned, as the releaser phenomenon appears to be innate. There is evidence indicating that some smells are related to releaser mechanisms in humans. The smell of cooked cabbage may have been such a phenomenon for a child we know for whom the smell had quite an automatic effect upon the "stability" of his stomach. Many odors elicit strong emotional responses, with some smells repelling us and others brightening our outlook throughout the entire day. It may be that many of the feelings aroused daily in our odoriferous world are influenced in part by memories recorded in the genes many ages ago.

Another example of seemingly innate tendencies are tastes we have. One of the exercises sometimes used in biology classes is to have students place "taste papers" on the tongue. To some students the taste is bitter; to other students the taste is sweet; and to yet others there is no taste except that of wet paper.

Psychological Limitations in Perception

In our study of communication, the psychological limitations in perception are of even greater importance than are the physiological limitations.

Selective Perception

One psychological limitation in perceiving is that of **selective perception.** Although all the images within range of the lens may appear on the screen of the eye, only some are in fact "seen." Certain stimuli are selected to be seen, while other stimuli are not perceived. Each of us has had an experience in which a single face in a crowd or a familiar voice in a din of noisy conversation suddenly popped into our consciousness. From among the many stimuli we perceived only one. That stimulus was selected. There were other faces as prominent, but we saw one specific face rather than other faces; there were other voices as loud, but we heard that special voice. It is not simply a matter of being especially sensitive to stronger stimuli, for unselected stimuli may be stronger than those selected. Rather, selected stimuli demand our perception because they have special significance and meaning for us. One of the most important sources of this meaningfulness is past experience.

The delicate, but powerful communication possible in the aroma of a flower.

Experience

Experience affects perception. There is a general tendency to see or hear whatever one is already looking for or listening for and expecting to see or hear. People do this all the time unless they have learned about this tendency and check on their perceptions and conclusions. Some people have learned to be careful about the information they use in thinking. They think better; and their higher quality of information processing pays them high dividends in better relationships, better leadership, and greater job success throughout life.

John Wilson of the African Institute of London University related a striking real-life story that illustrates how experience influences what one "sees."[2] Mr. Wilson used a motion picture film one day in his efforts to teach African natives to read. The film was shown at a very slow speed since the Africans were not used to viewing motion pictures. With simple steps, the film demonstrated how persons in an African village could get rid of standing water, drain pools, pick up debris, and the like, so as to improve general health conditions. At the end of the film, Mr. Wilson asked the audience of men what they had seen. Someone said, "A chicken!" Mr. Wilson and his aides were unaware that chickens were in the film, so they carefully scanned the frames one by one. Sure enough, in the bottom right-hand corner of two or three frames, a frightened chicken took flight; it was in their sight for only a fraction

Although all the images may appear on the eye's screen, through selective perception only some are in fact "seen."

of a second. Every one of the thirty-plus Africans saw the chicken but missed the important illustrations of how to stop mosquitoes from breeding. Several theories were suggested to explain this phenomenon, including the Africans' sharp eye for game birds, the religious significance of the chicken, and the fact that persons used to viewing film focus on a point slightly in front of the screen so as to take in the whole frame first while the unsophisticated film viewer does not do this. Regardless of their reason for seeing a chicken and not seeing tin cans being buried, the Africans' experiences and learning determined what information the eye brought into their perception.

For all of us, the principle holds true—experience affects perception. The accomplished chef learns to detect the missing spice in the complex aroma arising from the stew. The musician hears the one flat note. All of us are constantly receiving information colored by our experiences.

Psychological and Emotional States

A third source of error in information reception is the effect of **psychological** and **emotional states.**

How does emotional and psychological stress (such as extreme fear) affect the process of receiving information? Research has suggested that if an experience has intense psychological and emotional discomfort assigned to its interpretation, a neurological circuit may be set in motion so that the brain will be prohibited from receiving such a message again.

These messages will be blocked out entirely or distorted so that the messages will be different. Not only are such messages not received, but other messages may also be unintentionally blocked out in the process. Several incidents have been reported in connection with fires—house fires, hotel fires, and a steamship fire—in which a high proportion of persons caught in the fire experienced such strong emotional reactions that they were unable to receive and act on messages that could have saved their lives. The debilitating effect of intense emotion and intense fear proved fatal. The importance of psychological-emotional effects on perception and communication is that some messages are not allowed to enter the brain, and other messages, when they are allowed to enter, are distorted so that the information received is erroneous. Knowing how this phenomenon operates, you can be alert to it when you find yourself in highly psychological and emotional situations. If the organism can block or modify incoming messages from the senses, then the picture of reality directing one's behavior can be false. Such limitations invite mistakes in intrapersonal communication.

The three psychological factors, selective perception, experience, and emotional state, permit us to engage in two processes directly tied to perception: **filtering** and **completing.**

Can you identify and explain three psychological limitations on perception?

Filtering and Completing

We cannot take in all of the information "out there." There is too much, and such an overload of sensory-intaking would *disorient* us; so we use the process of filtering to block out the excess. Filtering enables us to control how much information we take in, what kind of information we take in, and what that information means.

Can you explain the process of filtering?

Conversely, *we have to have enough* **sensory-intaking** to build a perceptual world. If we don't have sufficient information, we can't orient ourselves. Completing enables us to "add on" and "fill in" abbreviated sensory input so that it is meaningful and useful to us in orienting ourselves. On the other hand, when the input is so limited that it's impossible for us to fill in, to add to, or to make use of it, we suffer from sensory deprivation. **Sensory deprivation** is a state of being deprived of sensory information—information we need in order to know who we are and where we are. This need has been strikingly demonstrated in experiments on the effects of sensory deprivation. In these experiments, the subjects are totally isolated from their environment except for being fed and performing bodily functions. Aside from these activities, they are cut off from receiving information via the senses—no smell, no sight, no hearing, no feeling. Blindfolded and with hands, arms, and legs wrapped heavily, they are placed in soundproof, totally dark rooms. Soon they begin to experience hallucinations; they see odd designs and shapes. Without sensory input, they lose their orientation and their contact with reality.

We have to receive information through our senses. We have to have enough information, but we can't handle too much. And what we get must be usable—must make sense in terms of providing us with a perceptual world in which we can orient ourselves. Filtering and completing are wonderful phenomena because they enable us to create our perceptual world; but when we use them ineffectively, we can build a perceptual world that does *not* resemble our "real world," or the worlds of others, either. In this way, filtering and completing can harm us.

Information Processing—Symbolization

The information-processing unit is composed of the brain and the central nervous system. The primary unit is the brain—the mind. No one has ever seen a mind. Recorded brain waves can show whether the brain is thinking, but they cannot show what is being thought. We cannot see the storing and interpreting of information; nor can we see the information being used in thinking. These information-processing functions have been studied only indirectly. Nevertheless, considerable understanding has been acquired about the brain's processing of information. The single most important characteristic of the brain for information processing is its ability to deal with symbols. Before we can have language or thought, we must have symbolization.

Symbolization can be defined as the brain's ability to represent an experience when the stimulus is absent. Whether the event is in the past or projected by imagination into the future, the ability to represent an experience is an extremely important step. When the brain can think of an object or an event, it can begin to solve problems by reasoning rather than by trial and error. It is the capacity of the human brain to symbolize—to acquire the ability to use words (our primary symbols)—that makes complex information processing possible. The discovery that everything has a name opens a whole new world to the child. With the acquisition of language, the child begins to learn to think.

Words are not the only symbols, however. A **symbol** can be anything perceived, anything that in our mind stands for something else. Symbols may take any form: they may have the form of a material object, a color, a sound, an odor, the motion of an object, or a taste. The meaning of a symbol is never determined by properties intrinsic in its form; the color for mourning might just as well have been red or green instead of black, for example.

By using symbols, we contemplate, make laws, resolve problems, confess sins, observe social and cultural codes, establish governments and institutions, remember the past, and plan for the future. These kinds of behavior are possible because we can symbolize.

The most important symbols we have are words. When we write *tree* on a piece of paper, we are simply making some marks on the paper to represent a particular object. Our symbol for *tree* is an English word, but people who speak and write French have a different word, that is, they make a different set of marks on a paper to stand for the object *tree*. This illustrates another characteristic of symbols—namely, they are arbitrarily assigned to stand for whatever they represent.

By having a name or symbol for the object *tree*, we don't have to carry one around with us or touch one or point to one every time we want to refer to it. Because of symbolization, we can store thousands, even millions, of objects in our brain. We can put past experiences, feelings, and associations into our storehouse in the brain. Not only is our past part of our experience, but the future can also be part of it as we create events in our imagination through the use of symbols.

What is the referent in the process of symbolization?

The thing for which a symbol stands is called the **referent.** In the case of the word *tree,* the referent is the physical object. Of course, the word is *not* the thing it stands for. The word *tree* has no bird nests in it or apples hanging from it. The word tree is *not* the object, but only a set of marks on paper or a set of sounds in the air. Symbolization is the process whereby the world of experience is taken in, named or marked, stored, and available to be brought back into our awareness. Thus, we can have the past with us and we can contemplate the future. We can interpret and evaluate past experiences, and prepare for future experiences through the use of our system of symbols in a process called thinking.

Language and Thinking

Human beings can reason. We can "try ideas in the mind." Wouldn't it be foolish of us to attempt to "test-out" physically every plan or idea we have for tomorrow? For each of the thousands of ideas that come to us during the day, we recall from our experience and knowledge all the information we judge relevant to that idea, and then test it out in our minds. Language is the vehicle for such reasoning, and what a wonderfully fast convenience it is! It short-circuits trial-and-error living.

A second relationship between language and thinking is that words connect and give permanence to nonverbal processes of thought that would otherwise be momentary. This is especially true, for example, in the case of visual images. Such images would appear and then be lost if it were not for the fact that they can be symbolized, stored, and later recalled upon command.

A third advantage that accrues to us through language is that logical thinking permits us to hold in check and to diminish debilitating emotional responses. An animal—and man also, under certain conditions—tends to respond immediately and directly to the emotional aspects of a situation. Through the use of language, however, we can often check our emotional responses, submit them to logical analysis, and then unite emotion and reason in motivated but rational behavior.

Since man's communication (intrapersonal, interpersonal, public, organizational, and cultural) is language-dependent, it is important to learn how we use language and how we can avoid the most common and dangerous misuses of language. We now consider some of the basic principles underlying the use of language and identify some common problems or dangers in using it.

[1]right \'rīt\ adj [ME, fr. OE riht; akin
straight, right, regere to lead straight, c
oregein to stretch out] (bef. 12c) 1 : RIG
accordance with what is just, good, o
: agreeable to a standard b : conformi
⟨the ~ answer⟩ 4 : SUITABLE, APPROPRIA
: STRAIGHT ⟨a ~ line⟩ 6 : GENUINE, RE
ated on, or being the side of the body wh
on which the hand is stronger in most pe
right hand than to the left c : located c
ing the object specified or directed as hi
raised out to the side d (1) : located c
ing in the same direction as the object
cated on the right when facing downstre
: having the axis perpendicular to the b
to, or constituting the principal or mor
⟨made sure his socks were ~ side out⟩ 1
dance with truth or fact ⟨time proved hi
physical or mental health or order ⟨not i
correct or proper state ⟨put things ~⟩
: PREFERABLE; also : socially acceptable
often cap : of, adhering to, or constitute
syn see CORRECT — right·ness n
[2]right n [ME, fr. OE riht, fr. riht, adj.] (be
ence to duty or obedience to lawful auth
the ideal of moral propriety or merit mo
which one has a just claim: as a : the p
is justly entitled b (1) : the interest th
erty — often used in pl. ⟨mineral ~s⟩
possessed under law or custom and agr
esp. of a literary and artistic nature ⟨fil
thing that one may properly claim as c
justice 5 a : the right hand; also :
⟨gave him a hard ~ on the jaw⟩ b : t
right side ⟨woods on his ~⟩ c : the pa
true account or correct interpretation b
factually correct 7 often cap a : the
located to the right of the presiding offic
nental European legislative body occu
holding more conservative political vie
(1) cap : individuals sometimes professi
established order and favoring tradition
sometimes advocating the forced estab
political order (2) : a group or party
favors conservative, traditional, or som
and policies b often cap : a conservati
given stockholders to subscribe pro rat
generally below market price b : the n
such privilege — usu. used in pl. — by
: PROPERLY — in one's own right : by vi
or properties — to rights : into proper o
[3]right adv (bef. 12c) 1 : according to ri
location or position : PRECISELY ⟨~ at h
of the floor⟩ 3 : in a suitable, proper,
wasn't doing it ~⟩ 4 : in a direct line c
⟨go ~ home⟩ 5 : according to fact or
a : all the way ⟨windows ~ to the floo
⟨felt ~ at home⟩ 7 : without delay : IM
: to a great degree : VERY ⟨a ~ pleasan
⟨looked left and ~⟩
usage This ancient and homely adverb
nervous, esp. in senses 4, 6, and 8. Som
and 6 should not be used in formal pro
be much used in the most formal wri
ordinary edited prose. Sense 8 is vario
standard, or regional. None of these c
current good use. It does appear in mos
more common in the Southern and Mi
seems to be more common in speech th
edited prose ⟨it is the man and his Lo
thor] recognizes this right well —Newg
Rev.⟩ ⟨a defender of the language —
right profitably in his earlier [book] —V
— right now : at the present : just now

Meanings are in us rather than in the word or message received. By permission. From Webster's Ninth New Collegiate Dictionary © 1984 by Merriam Webster, Inc., publisher of the Merriam Webster® Dictionaries.

The Nature of Words and Meaning

Words Have Many Meanings

Words are symbols and symbols stand for something else. Consider the word *book.* What comes to mind when we use the word *book?* One person may think of the Bible, another of a textbook, another of a novel, and still another of betting on the horses. This aspect of words causes problems for us as langauge users. We can explain the process of reference—how words and symbols stand for something else—but we cannot easily explain meaning or how a given word happens to be used at a given time in a person's mind. Because the same word generates a variety of meanings, we cannot expect a word to elicit exactly the same response from different persons, or from the same person at different times. If we consider this first characteristic of the use of words, we realize that words are more than symbols; in communication they are stimuli that evoke responses.

Dictionary definitions attempt to be objective. These meanings are called **denotative meanings.** Other meanings—those held in our minds as unique and personal—are called **connotative meanings.**

As a child acquires language and begins to use it, unique and personal meanings are established. Thus a word takes on, in addition to its denotative meaning, connotative meaning—meaning specific to that person because of the associations, feelings, and referents attached to that word. Connotative meanings involve conditions, emotions, and experiences that are unique to a particular person. The referents of denotative meanings are less "person-bound" and more "objective." To denote means to name, designate, or identify, and so denotative meanings are said to be more logical than connotative meanings. For example, we could read a dictionary definition of the word *horse, dog,* or *cat.* The dictionary definition would give us denotative meanings for those words; but for many, and perhaps for you, those words conjure up pictures and thoughts of much loved childhood pets. If so, these words have specific cognitive and affective associations (perhaps clearly positive and happy ones) that impinge on the word *horse, dog,* or *cat* to add new and personal meanings. These are connotative meanings. For all of us, connotative meanings make the word—for good or for ill—truly our own.

Meaning is Arbitrary

A second characteristic of words is that, to an extent, their meaning is arbitrary. " 'When I use a word,' Humpty Dumpty said, 'it means just what I choose it to mean—neither more nor less.' "[3] Whatever meaning a word has is the meaning we arbitrarily give to it.

Meanings Are in People, Not in Words

A third characteristic of words is that they do not mean; people mean. Meanings are not "out there"; meanings are not in words; meanings are in people. A sixteen-year-old remarked to his grandfather that a certain television entertainer was *square.* He was left bewildered when his grandfather acknowledged that he, too, thought the entertainer was a person of honesty. The grandfather had one meaning for the word *square* (square shooter, square dealer, treat you square, i.e., *honest*) and the grandson had another meaning (*simple, old-fashioned,* or *outmoded.*)

Because meanings are in *us* rather than in the word, when we receive messages, we project our own meanings into the words. The story is told of an airline stewardess who looked over a passenger's shoulder as he was deeply engrossed in a book on the game of bridge; as she moved away, she remarked, "That must be a fascinating love story you are reading." Startled, the man looked at the chapter heading and saw that it was entitled, "Free Responses after the Original Pass."

Not all examples of projection and of assuming what a word means are humorous. Some are serious and costly. To avoid miscommunication, it will help to remember that meanings are in people, not in the words.

How can a word have many meanings? Select a word and identify several meanings it could have.

Meaning Is Learned

A fourth characteristic of words is that their meaning is learned. A piece of meat that has been carved from a steer, placed on a charcoal-heated grill, and broiled to a sizzle arouses a desire to eat and perhaps even produces salivation. By pairing the word *steak* with the object just described, the "mouth-watering" response that resulted from the original stimulus can, through association, be elicited by the use of the word *steak.* The simple process of association by itself will not completely explain all meaning, but it goes a long way toward explaining how one word can have a group of associations.

For example, consider the word *mother.* For many of us, the word *mother* produces a warm response. It includes any number of associations: this female parent as a source of comfort; as a provider of wholesome meals; as the one who has been present at our special events; and much more. All of these associations with the word *mother* have been acquired by many of us over time and give the word *mother* many meanings. Do not make the error of assuming the word you use means exactly the same thing to your receiver as it does to you.

The Abstraction Process

An important concern in language is the **abstraction process.** We employ categories in order to classify the stimuli we perceive. For example, there are numerous furry, four-legged animals with tails. It is easier to deal with all these animals if we can classify them and have different words for each of them. One classification we use is *dog*. We can make predictions regarding what members of this category might do on our lawns, what kinds of noises they might make under various circumstances, and whether they might be friendly or not. This is the process of abstraction. In order to conceive of the category *dog,* it is necessary for us to abstract from all furry creatures those whose characteristics identify the ones we have named dogs. This abstraction process includes not only noting similarities but also differences. This process is quite helpful to us.

Essentially, the abstraction process that we employ to handle incoming stimuli in our day-to-day world can also be termed a stereotyping process. It is impossible to handle every incoming stimulus individually and separately. Although the abstraction process is useful, it can create some problems in communication. For example, we may assume that because we have an abstraction of a given category, the characteristics of that category will hold true for each of its members. If our category *doctor* includes people who have a certain amount of training and expertise regarding the human body, then we may be inclined to accept blindly the advice given by any doctor although there are a number of doctors who may be inadequate for our needs.

General semanticists have suggested the devices of **indexing** and **dating,** and the **use of quotation marks** to aid us in avoiding this kind of error.[4] We can index dogs by considering them dog_1, dog_2, dog_3 whenever we see a dog. This should remind us that not all dogs are necessarily friendly. Likewise, we need to remember that the abstraction of *mother* is one we may have developed some years back. *Mother* has probably changed in the intervening years. By employing dating procedures we can remember that people and things change. $Mother_{1989}$ may not be the same as $mother_{1974}$. So we need to respond to the word differently.

Finally, the use of mental quotation marks can remind us that the meaning we have for a word is an abstraction and can be different from the meaning someone else has. When we are discussing the term *democracy,* for instance, it would be of use to keep imaginary quotation marks around that word in the backs of our minds; *democracy* for us may represent something different from that which the word represents for another person. If such is the case, we may stop during a conversation and say, "Wait a minute. Tell me what you mean by the word *democracy* and I'll explain what I mean by it." Better understanding can be achieved through this process.

Thinking and Reasoning

This chapter has focused thus far on perception, symbolization, and language. We now give attention to thinking and reasoning. We will begin by looking at the role our emotions play in our decision-making process.

Emotion and reasoning are both useful in making decisions.

Emotion and Reasoning

One misunderstanding about the process of reasoning is that emotion and feeling are not to be trusted and not to be allowed in logical thought. Actually, we don't experience emotion devoid of reason, nor do we reason absolutely devoid of emotion. Reason and emotion need not be in conflict; they can operate together. It is a mistake for a person to believe that a speaker who shows no emotion or feeling is necessarily logical (he or she may be quite illogical in reasoning) or that a speaker who shows feeling cannot be logical (his or her reasoning may be quite sound logically). The ideal situation is one in which emotion and reason can occur together. In any behavior there is a cognitive and an emotional component—an element of reason as well as an element of emotion. Not only are the two found together, but they seem to be positively correlated; i.e., as intellectual capacity increases so does emotional capacity. As Hebb and Thompson, two psychologists, state it:

> Emotional susceptibility increases with intellectual capacity. . . . [Such] correlations between increasing intellect and increasing emotionality would suggest that thought and emotion are intimately, essentially related.[5]

Of course, an overriding emotional state can be harmful to thinking, but we can use our intellects to control those situations in which our emotional responses become extreme. As long as one's emotional state is not at the level of being debilitating to thought, then emotion and feeling ought to operate with reason to enable one to be most effective in interaction.

Description, Inference, and Judgment Statements

One problem in thinking is failure to recognize the kind of statement one is making. There are three kinds of statements, and each kind represents a different relationship. These statements may be statements of fact or description, of inference, or of judgment (evaluation).

Consider the following statements:

1. The woman next to you is wearing a Mickey Mouse wristwatch.
2. The woman next to you is frightened.
3. The woman next to you is unattractive.

All three of the statements begin with the same words, all use a common subject (women), all have a common verb (is), and there are no significant grammatical, structural, or formal differences among the sentences. Yet each statement is different. The first is a statement of description or fact; the second is an inference; the third statement is a value judgment.

Statements of fact or description are based on observation. The most accurate statements we can make are statements based on observation. Observation is the fundamental source of statements of fact or description, which can be made only after one or more of the senses comes into direct contact with the nonverbal world. The nonverbal world that we see, feel, taste, and hear is the world of facts.

The second sentence, "The woman next to you is frightened," is a **statement of inference**. Fear is not as easily observed as a Mickey Mouse wristwatch; fear manifests itself in more ways than do wristwatches, and fear varies from person to person. Moreover, we conceptualize fear as an internal state, but a wristwatch is an external phenomenon. There are several observable behaviors that can indicate to us that the woman is or is not frightened, but these observed actions are merely indicators. We have to interpret their meaning and their association with a particular internal state in a particular person. We have to infer that the woman is frightened.

The third statement in the example is a **statement of judgment**. Statements of judgement bring our values into consideration. To one person, the woman may be unattractive, but to another she may be quite attractive.

Agreement proves very little about statements of judgment except that there is an agreement on values. Judgment statements have to do with goodness and badness, usefulness and uselessness, desirableness and undesirableness, approval and disapproval. The important characteristic of statements of judgment, as we are using the term, is that they include value. Inferences do not indicate preferences; judgments do indicate preferences, and they are value-oriented. A judgment is an evaluation of an object, event, or person, and it should be used with care.

Table 2.1 provides a summary of the characteristics of the three types of statements.

Table 2.1 Thinking processes involved in logical argument

Statement of Fact or Description	Inference	Judgment
1. Can be made only after observation.	1. Can be made any time—before, after, during, or without observation.	1. Can be made any time.
2. Does not go beyond what can be observed.	2. Goes beyond observation.	2. Goes beyond observation.
3. Emphasizes denotative meaning.	3. Uses either denotative or connotative meaning.	3. Emphasizes connotative meaning.
4. Intends to report.	4. Intends to interpret.	4. Intends to persuade or express an attitude.
	5. May have low or high degree of probability.	5. May have low or high agreement.
		6. Utilizes values and preferences.

Some persons find it difficult to restrain themselves from slipping away from observations and into inferences and judgments. Such persons seldom describe—they infer and judge. They make inferences that are *not warranted*. Probably one of the most difficult tasks for the student of communication is to acquire the attitude and disposition necessary for observing and describing more and jumping to conclusions less.

We can learn to recognize the difference between a statement of fact or description and one involving an inference or judgment. Further, as we learn to distinguish among these types of statements we can, as senders of messages, develop an awareness of our own use of such statements. Moreover, as listeners we can practice recognizing these different types of statements when they are used by others. It is not possible, of course, for us to use only statements of observations and fact. We have to use inferences if we are to communicate, but it is possible to be aware of the type of statement being used, and to treat each type of statement properly. Confusing inferences, judgments, and facts creates the danger that all statements will be acted upon as if they were facts. It is at this point that miscommunication occurs.

It takes relatively no time, energy, or thought to make inferences if one is willing to "leap" to them; but when inferences are made they should be treated as tentative and should be thought of in terms of probability rather than certainty. Descriptive statements, as we have already observed, are more

Figure 2.2 Example of Toulmin's inferential pattern of reasoning.

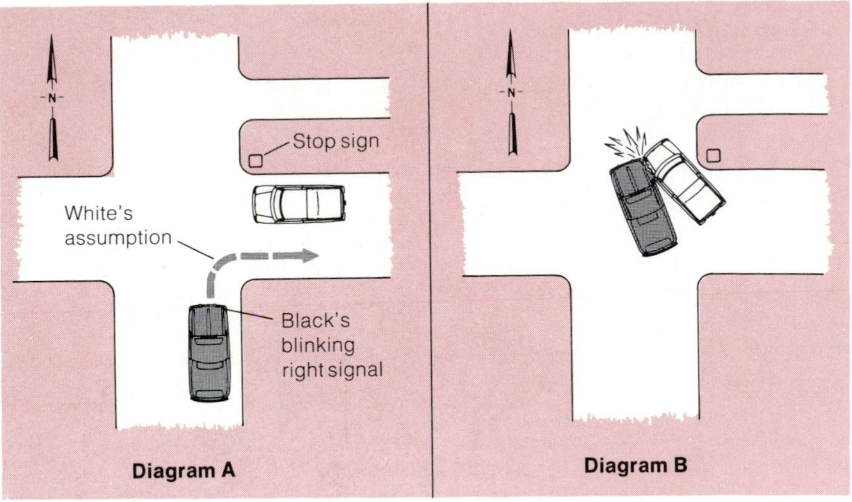

certain, although there can be errors in observing (as we learned in the discussion of perception) and in reporting. Yet given enough capable observers, we can attain a relatively high probability of agreement.

We create problems for ourselves, however, when we treat inferences and judgments with the same degree of certainty as that of the most agreed-upon facts. In figure 2.2, Diagram A shows the driver of the white car stopped at a stop sign as the black car approaches the intersection from the south. White observes Black's right turn signal blinking and assumes Black is going to turn right at the intersection; White starts to cross the intersection. White is acting on the inference he has made as if it were a fact. Black does not turn, however, but continues straight through the intersection. A costly collision occurs (Diagram B). Black intended to turn right into the driveway a few feet beyond the intersection. White was held responsible for the personal injuries and property damage resulting from the accident.

White's behavior illustrates the risks that are run when one acts upon inferences as though they were unquestionable facts. White acted upon an assumption of certainty rather than one of probability. (Haney has raised the question whether accident-prone drivers are unwittingly inference-prone persons.)[6]

Summary

Recognizing that intrapersonal communication is basically involved in all levels and types of communication, this chapter has focused upon the communication system of the individual. The individual's self-contained communication system is composed of receiving units, an information-processing unit, and transmitting units. Receiving elements include sight, hearing, touch, smell, and taste; seeing and hearing are the major avenues for humans to receive information. Information processing is performed by the brain and the central nervous system. Speaking, writing, gesturing, moving, and other nonverbal behavior are involved in the process of sending information.

It has been noted in this chapter that the process of receiving information is subject to error. What one receives in the way of information is influenced by selective perception, the effect of past experiences, and optical illusion, as well as psychological and emotional states. What a given individual "receives" is not necessarily what is present in reality nor is it exactly what another individual "receives." This fact, if we can become sufficiently aware of it to apply it in our thinking (intrapersonal communication) and in our search for shared meanings with others (interpersonal and public communication), can be highly beneficial to us.

We studied how we use language and how we think as we process information in intrapersonal communication. We considered some relationships between language and thinking. We were concerned with words, their nature and meaning; and we discussed the process of abstraction. Finally, we called attention to thinking and reasoning.

Questions and Exercises for Review

1. Can you identify how each of the basic elements in the individual's communication system functions in your life?
2. Can you differentiate between external and internal perceptual fields? Can you give examples of both external and internal messages you have received in the last hour?
3. What is selective perception? Can you relate an example of how selective perception has influenced your interaction with others in the past week?
4. Can you explain the filtering process as it applies to perception? Can you give an example of how you have filtered a message recently?
5. Why is symbolization important to your interactions with others?
6. What are the relationships between thinking and language?
7. Name and explain three characteristics of words and list the implications of these characteristics for communication.

Key Terms and Phrases

- receivers
- information processing
- transmitters
- perception
- optical illusion
- neurological inhibition
- synapse
- releaser concept
- selective perception
- psychological state
- emotional state
- filtering
- completing
- sensory-intaking
- sensory deprivation
- symbolization
- symbol
- referent
- denotative meaning
- connotative meaning
- abstraction process
- indexing
- dating
- use of quotation marks
- statement of fact or description
- statement of inference
- statement of judgment
- experience

For Further Reading

Ashby, W. Ross. *Design for a Brain.* New York: John Wiley & Sons, 1952.
Can a machine think? Mr. Ashby sets forth a design for a mechanical brain. The discussions of the functions that occur in thought are enlightening.

Brewer, R. E., and Brewer, M. B. "Attraction and Accuracy of Perception in Dyads." *Journal of Personality and Social Psychology* 8 (1968): 188–93.

Brown, M. Neil, and Keeley, Stuart M. *Asking the Right Questions.* Englewood Cliffs, N.J.: Prentice-Hall, Inc., 1981.
Excellent treatment of relationship of asking relevant questions to critical thinking.

Chomsky, Noam. *Syntactic Structures.* The Hague: Mouton, 1957.
If you want to read contrasting views of language and you want to tackle difficult material, you will appreciate this book.

Emmert, Philip, and Donaghy, W. C. *Human Communication: Elements and Contents.* Reading, Mass.: Addison-Wesley, 1981.
Discusses the interfacing of perception, motivation, and reasoning in the intrapersonal communication process.

Farb, Peter. *Word Play: What Happens When People Talk.* New York: Knopf, 1974.
An interesting discussion of the role of language in our interactions with others.

Fergus, R. H. *Perception.* New York: McGraw-Hill Book Company, 1966.
This book gives a thorough treatment of perception for the person who wants to explore the topic in depth.

Goss, Blaine. *Processing Communication.* Belmont, Calif.: Wadsworth Publishing Co., 1982.
Explains how research in the cognitive aspects can be applied to human communication.

Gover, Robert. *One Hundred Dollar Misunderstanding.* New York: Balantine, 1961.
A practical and light account of the problem of meaning discrepancy.

Hayakawa, S. I. *Language in Thought and Action.* New York: Harcourt Brace Jovanovich, 1978.
This is a readable book, very informative and interesting. It focuses on general semantics and how we use words and meanings.

Miller, G. R. "Human Information Processing: Some Research Guidelines." In *Conceptual Frontiers in Speech Communication,* edited by Robert J. Kibler and Larry L. Barker. New York: SCA, 1969, 51–67.
This article is for the person seeking an in-depth understanding of information processing.

Notes

1. Camille B. Wortman and Elizabeth F. Loftas, *Psychology* (New York: Alfred Knopf, 1981), 183; or R. L. Gregory, *Eye and Brain: The Psychology of Seeing,* 2d ed. (New York: McGraw-Hill, 1973), 176.

2. John Wilson, "Film Literacy in Africa," *Canadian Communications* 1, no. 4 (Summer 1961): 7–14.

3. Lewis Carroll, *Alice's Adventures in Wonderland, Through the Looking Glass,* and *The Hunting of the Snark* (New York: Modern Library, 1925), 246–47.

4. Alfred Korzybski, *Science and Sanity* (Institute of General Semantics, 1958), 1–18.

5. D. O. Hebb and W. R. Thompson, "The Social Significance of Animal Studies," *The Handbook of Social Psychology,* 1st ed., ed. Gardner Lindzey (Reading, Mass.: Addison-Wesley Publishing Co., Inc., 1944), v. 11, 553–55.

6. William V. Haney, "Are Accident-Prone Drivers Unconsciously Inference-Prone?" *General Semantics Bulletin,* no. 20 (1957).

Focus

How We Come to Think about Ourselves

Through Interaction with Others

Through Our Reference Groups

Through Viewing Self as an Object of Communication

Through the Roles We Play

The Many Selves

How Self-Concept Affects Communication

As the Basis of Self-Fulfilling Prophecy

In Selecting the Messages We Send and Receive

In Developing Attitudes Toward Communication

Communication Confidence

Communication Apprehension

Improving Self-Concept

Through Greater Acceptance of Self and Others

By Dropping False Masks

By Risking Our Real Selves through Disclosure to Build Trust

By Avoiding Silence and Ritual Responses

By Interacting with Trustworthy and Supportive Persons

The Self in Communication

3

Self-concept refers to those perceptions one has of his or her physical, social, and psychological self. We develop a concept of who we are as we interact with others (especially significant others and our reference groups), as we view ourselves as objects of communication, and as we take various roles in our relations with others. We are not *one* self, but many selves. Whatever concept we have of ourselves has an effect on our communication. It is the basis of our behavior. It determines the messages to which we attend in sending and receiving.

It is possible, through the process of self-disclosure and trust-building, to improve self-concept. This chapter focuses on understanding the role of self-concept in communication as well as on how we can develop a healthy concept of ourselves.

How We Come to Think about Ourselves

A person who says, "I just can't meet new people!" is expressing a facet of his or her self-concept. We are becoming increasingly aware that how one sees himself or herself is intimately related to behavior. Research is teaching us that how one handles a problem depends not only on real ability, but also on how able one thinks one is. Indeed, evidence from classroom and clinical research suggests that success in school and in life may depend less on the qualities we inherit or acquire than on how we feel about those qualities.

Speech communication begins within the self. Skill in interpersonal communication, as well as in public communication, is closely associated with a useful and realistic perception of self. According to Jung, this perception of self is the product of intrapersonal communication,[1] but the data used to define one's concept of self is often derived from interpersonal communication.

All of us have certain beliefs about ourselves. You have a perception of your attractiveness, the sound of your voice, your intellectual ability, and your ability to influence others. **Self-concept** can be defined as the physical, social, and psychological perceptions of ourselves that we have derived from our experiences and our interaction with others.

Generally, experiences that do not fit our self-concepts, or to which we cannot adjust our self-concepts, are perceived as personally dangerous; we try to build defenses against them. However, what we often need is a willingness to revise our self-concepts to fit the new experience, rather than defenses that guard against any change. Things around us change, and we must interact with and adjust ourselves to our environment. Persons we have known change, and consequently our relationships with and responses to them change. Similarly, others see changes in us. If we can recognize and accept change in ourselves, then we will become more understanding and accepting of change in others.

How does self-concept develop? The young child's self-concept is relatively undefined, but as the child begins to perceive the world and to discover himself or herself, he or she starts to develop a self-concept. The recognition of one's own voice and of one's face in a mirror mark the beginning of awareness of personal properties and characteristics—of a concept of self. Because one's developing concept of self tends to follow the direction in which it started, early childhood is a critical period. The child learns that words like *cute, smart, good, bad,* or *dumb* are attributed to him or her as a person, and gradually a picture of self is developed.

Can you explain how self-concept is acquired?

Skill in interpersonal communication is closely related to a realistic perception of self.

Self-understanding is the basis of a healthy view of self, and we acquire an understanding of ourselves primarily through our interactions with others—our perceptions and awareness of how others see us and of how they react to us. The first source of influence on self-concept that we will consider, then, is others.

Others

Self-concept develops within a social framework. Personality characteristics such as shyness, extroversion, and introversion develop through social interaction. Our concept of self develops as we incorporate how others, especially significant others, feel about us, react to us, and what they expect of us. **Significant others** normally include parents, brothers and sisters, peers, and any other persons for whom we have esteem and who have influence and power over us. Throughout our lives others affect us—our success, security, happiness, and general well-being. So powerful is the influence of others on the development of self-concept that some scholars maintain that self-concept is the direct result of how significant others react to the individual.[2]

Others, in our interpersonal communication and in our public communication, tell us through their reactions what we are—good or bad, successful or unsuccessful, liked or not liked. We use such data in "talking to ourselves" about who we are. Our deeds, ideas, words, and selves are constantly being evaluated by others through our interactions with them, and their evaluations, in turn, influence the development of our self-concept.

Those groups with whom we have strong affiliation are reference groups.

Reference Groups

A second source of information available to us for defining ourselves is reference groups. **Reference groups** are those groups to which we belong or want to belong. As children our reference groups probably included playmates, our "club," and our athletic teams. As adults, our reference groups may include study groups, clubs and school organizations, and our circle of close friends. Such groups approve certain values, attitudes, and behaviors and disapprove others. If these groups are important to us (and by definition, reference groups are important to us), then the way they evaluate us and react to us can be a powerful determiner of our self-concept. Research shows that how we evaluate ourselves is in part a function of how we are evaluated by reference groups. The group can communicate its evaluation of and response to an individual's behavior by ignoring a person's presence, giving disapproving glances or approving nods, and making direct statements. Such communication tells one "who he or she is" as perceived by the group.

Viewing Self as an Object

A third source of information through which we develop our self-concept is that of viewing our "self" as an object—as a physical object. Each of us has a view of himself or herself as a physical being. We see ourselves in the mirror; we feel the movement of ourselves as we walk; we see ourselves as attractive or unattractive, tall or short, well-proportioned or ill-proportioned. The perception you have of your physical self is directly related to your concept of yourself.

Role Playing

A fourth way in which we develop our self-concept is **role playing.** We learn to "role play" early in childhood. We imitate the behavior of others, part of which is their behavior toward us. Mother makes sounds to the baby and the baby begins to imitate these sounds. The father smiles and makes facial movements, and these too are imitated. Through imitation the infant begins to act toward himself or herself as others act toward him or her. This is the beginning of role playing. Throughout childhood we engage in role playing by imitating the behavior of others. And we are rewarded or punished for the "roles" we play. Thus, more and more children see themselves and act toward themselves in the same way that other people see them and act toward them. By such a process children come to understand what roles they can take.

As adults, we hypothesize about the behavior of others. We take their roles in our minds instead of playing their roles physically. In our minds, we play others and ourselves interacting with them. You probably played such scenes in your mind before you asked a new classmate to go out with you, or before you asked your parents for a loan. If you did a good job of playing the role in your mind, your predictions were validated. If you did a poor job, your request was unsuccessful, and you were then faced with the problem of redefining who you are.

Through role playing, self-assessment, interacting in reference groups, and interacting with others, each of us develops a concept of who we are—and from these experiences we develop several selves.

The Many Selves

In order to understand your "self" better, you should look at yourself from several viewpoints. Each person's existence has several dimensions, and any personality has several facets. In a manner of speaking, there are many different selves.

There is the self as a physical object. Each of us has a view of himself or herself as a physical being. A second dimension of self is the dimension of ideas, feelings, and beliefs. All of us have a perception of ourselves as certain types of intellectual and emotional beings.

A third dimension of self grows out of our relationships with other people. We have perception of ourselves in terms of how we get along with people and how we function in each group to which we belong. In the family, you play one role and occupy a certain position; in the communication class your role may be different.

Another dimension of self is private versus public self. In each of us there is the self that no one sees. There may be a part of your private self that even you do not know; this part may be withheld and not disclosed to others. On

We all have a view of ourselves.

the other hand, each of us has a public self—that self intentionally or unintentionally disclosed to others. All of these aspects of self—the public, the private, the known, and the unknown—are important selves we need to understand if we are to discover, expand, and improve our many selves.

How Self-Concept Affects Communication

Communication is affected by self-concept in at least three ways: (1) in terms of **self-fulfilling prophecy,** (2) in terms of the selection of messages to be sent or of messages to be received and processed, and (3) in terms of attitudes toward communication situations.

Self-Fulfilling Prophecy

Can you list and explain some effects of self-concept on communication?

People behave in a manner as consistent as possible with their self-concepts; they act as they perceive themselves to be. The student who perceives himself as a "failure-type student" can find plenty of excuses to avoid studying, reading, or participating in class discussion. And at the end of the term he usually receives the low grade he predicted. Similarly, the student who sees herself as a person nobody likes will usually find that she is not liked, and may not understand that behaving in a manner consistent with her self-concept (sour

expression, hostility, refusal to be friendly or to participate) invites rejection by others. Our positive or negative self-concepts are quite important, since we tend to fulfill our own prophecies.

Negative self-concept (low self-esteem) is developed as the result of many negative experiences over a long period of time. Some of the characteristics or symptoms of negative self-concept are (1) sensitivity to criticism, (2) over-responsiveness to praise, (3) hypercritical attitudes, (4) a feeling that "nobody likes me," and (5) a pessimistic attitude toward competition.

Labels identify, define, and shape us.

You may be able to think of someone you know who has these characteristics. Such persons are supersensitive to any criticism, and so you have learned to "handle them with kid gloves" because they explode, pout, or cry very easily. Or, perhaps you know someone who has only negative orientations to everything. Such a person seldom has a happy word, a good word, a word of praise, or an expression of appreciation for anything; rather, such a person tends to gripe, complain, criticize, and debase everything and everyone. These are characteristics of persons with a negative self-concept.

On the other hand, individuals with a positive self-concept may be characterized as (1) being confident of their abilities to deal with problems; (2) feeling equal to other persons; (3) accepting praise without embarrassment; (4) admitting that they have a wide range of feelings, desires, and behaviors, some of which are socially approved and some of which are not; and (5) being able to improve themselves: for example, discovering an unlikable aspect of themselves and then setting out to change it.

Because a person has many selves, it is unrealistic to attempt to classify each individual entirely in one or the other of the categories described above. Actually, an individual may fall on middle ground between the extremes of the two categories. It is a good objective, nevertheless, for anyone to move away from the traits of negative self-concept toward those of positive self-concept, since self-concepts tend to be fulfilled.

Acceptance of self: an interactive process.

One aspect of self-fulfilling prophecy is "living up to the label." We have a tendency to live up to our labels whether they are given to us by others or selected by and for ourselves. If you label yourself "no good in music" or a "poor public speaker" you may prove this to be so. For example, if you label yourself as unfriendly you will probably behave in an unfriendly manner. You will avoid opportunities to talk; you will refrain from smiling; and you will seek seclusion rather than the company of others.

Your expectation of another's behavior will often become a self-fulfilling prophecy for the other person. Such an expectation is communicated to the other person who then comes to define himself or herself in that way and to fulfill that expectation. Even when there is no verbal communication of that expectation, it is communicated. We know, of course, that nonverbal communication does take place between persons, and thus expectations are communicated. Rosenthal has discussed an interesting experiment in which elementary teachers were told that one group of children (an experimental group selected randomly from the classroom) had scored exceptionally high on a test for the "intellectually blooming." In reality, the children in the experimental group were no different from the control group in regard to their scores on the test, but the teachers believed they were different.[3] The teachers labeled the students as having a high intellectual potential; apparently the students attached the label to themselves, for the experimental group fulfilled the prophecy. Other similar experiments, reviewed by Rosenthal, have produced the same findings. Labels become self-fulfilling prophecies.

Selection of Messages

A second effect of self-concept on communication is that one tends to select messages to be sent or received that are consistent with one's self-concept. The kinds of messages one sends and the treatment given them are influenced by "who the sender is." Similarly, "who one is" creates selective attention and selective perception. Persons who choose to watch only soap opera television shows probably have self-images different from those persons who watch only documentaries. And subscribers to *Forbes* and *Time* may have self-images different from those of subscribers to *Reader's Digest*.[4] As senders and receivers, our self-concepts direct our behavior as it is related to encoding, decoding, and responding to messages. The message that is inconsistent with our views of self and the world is often distorted, misinterpreted, or ignored entirely. Similarly, the process of encoding is influenced by self-concept because we are limited in encoding to our experiences in life. It is not surprising, then, that the messages we send identify our perceptions of ourselves and the world.

Developing Attitudes toward Communication

Communication Confidence

A third way self-concept affects communication is through *concept of self as a communicator*. Since birth you have existed in a communication environment. You have been communicating with others and observing yourself as well as observing others' reactions to you in those situations. In short, you have developed attitudes toward various communication situations and toward communication in general. You may enjoy talking with your best friend, but be a little hesitant in talking with a stranger. You may enjoy gabbing with your "gang," but be more reserved in contributing to a problem-solving group or in giving a public speech. How we view ourselves as communicators is manifested in our attitudes toward various communication situations. We call this general attitude **communication confidence** or, its opposite, communication apprehension. Hopefully, we have positive attitudes toward communicating, but some students are fearful of certain communication situations. If you are one of these students, you are in good company. Recent studies indicate that three out of every four college students fear public speaking. For these students even the fear of death is less ominous.[5]

Communication Apprehension

The pervasiveness of this fear of communication captured the attention of communication scholars perhaps more than any other communication-related topic over the past several years. Since 1970, more than two-hundred major research projects, convention papers and professional journal articles have focused on some variation of this concern.[6]

One of the most popular methods for decreasing **communication apprehension** uses a behavioral therapy procedure known as systematic desensitization. In systematic desensitization, participants are taught to identify and relax tense muscles in their bodies. Next, they learn to visualize scenes that in reality would cause them discomfort and anxiety. When the relaxation exercises and the visualization scenes are paired, participants are conditioned to feel more relaxed in certain communication situations. After learning to relax in one imagined scene, the high-communication-apprehensive person proceeds to visualize more difficult anxiety-provoking scenes.

After completing a successful treatment, a person should feel more confident while communicating. This confidence will then become part of his or her self-concept which, in turn, will improve communication. While the desensitization program is one of several proven methods for reducing communication apprehension, at least one study indicates that communication apprehension can be reduced effectively in a communication course that focuses on a blend of communication skills development and the learning of principles and theories relevant to effective communication.[7]

In addition to systematic desensitization, there are some other time-tested methods for reducing and controlling communication apprehension. These apply to giving a speech as well as to other less formal communication situations.

1. *Prepare Well.* Nothing can cause one to fear a communication situation quite as much as not being prepared—not knowing what to say and how to say it. If you prepare well, you are much more likely to believe that your message is important to your audience and that your materials (ideas, slides, illustrations, etc.) will have high interest value. Confidence in the *content* of your speech translates into self-confidence.

2. *Outline Your Message Carefully.* Write down its parts and sequence of points so that you can rely on your notes and prompts rather than just your memory. Fear can make you lose your train of thought, but good notes will allow you to recover.
3. *Practice Your Speech.* Communication experts differ on how many times to practice, but once is not enough. You should feel comfortable and confident that you know what you will say without becoming "wooden" in your delivery.
4. *Plan Your Movements.* Knowing ahead of time how you will work your props and what kind of gestures and physical actions you will use helps give you a sense of confidence when doing it in front of an audience.
5. *Communicate with the Audience.* Force yourself to smile. Select and establish eye contact with a person who you feel is empathetic, friendly, and supportive. When you receive positive feedback from your audience, fear decreases and confidence increases.

Improving Self-Concept

Each of the various factors discussed in subsequent chapters of this text is affected by self-concept. The reception of information is affected by self-concept. Language usage is affected. The reception and processing of non-verbal, as well as verbal, messages are affected. All of the components of interpersonal communication have their roots in the communicator's self-concept. Since self-concept has such a pervasive influence on communication behavior, we need to examine how to improve our own self-concepts.

Become More Accepting of Self and Others

When we begin to accept and like ourselves, our total concept of self begins to improve. One method for developing greater self-acceptance is to increase our awareness of our strengths. Sometimes this process is aided by simply identifying our strengths. Each of us possesses strengths: they may be skills, talents, abilities, or personal traits and characteristics, but they are strengths upon which we can build. The best way to identify our strengths is to make a list of the skills, characteristics, and talents we have. A practical exercise to identify strengths is called "strength bombardment." A small group of acquaintances lists the strengths of each person in the group and then each person reads his or her list for John, then for Mary, and so on. Each person is bombarded with his or her strengths.

A second step toward greater self-acceptance is to be more accepting of others. Acceptance of others is closely related to self-acceptance. There appears to be a reciprocal relationship: accepting others encourages others to accept us, and their acceptance causes us to be more accepting of ourselves.

We can become more accepting of others by expressing warmth and liking, by practicing self-disclosure, by listening with interest—even empathy—and by becoming helpful to others.

Drop False Masks

This second suggestion—dropping false masks and revealing oneself honestly—is an important one to consider. Often, we are hesitant to reveal ourselves and try instead to appear to be something else. We are a success-oriented society and so each of us is taught to appear successful—successful in all the ways important to our society. We come to believe that we must appear intelligent; we must appear to be whatever society, our peers, or advertising choose as our role models.

The result is that a good many relationships are based on contact between two imitation selves. What we need to do is drop our false masks and reveal ourselves more honestly and authentically.

We must learn to run some risk in being open and honest. When we pretend to be what we are not, we waste energy and concentration. Our attention is on our own performances rather than on the other person, and thus we miss the messages and clues as to how others are perceiving us. Secondly, pretending to be who we are not is dangerous because we may not be good enough actors to carry it off. In fact, the truth seems to be that such acts are almost impossible to carry off. A third negative outcome of hiding ourselves, of pretending to be who we are not, is that we engender doubt and suspicion instead of creating confidence and trust.

In human relationships, being vulnerable is a precondition to real communication. We should increase our willingness to be vulnerable—to reveal ourselves. But each of us is made up of various selves; none of us has a single, absolute set of attitudes in our relationships with all persons. We have different relationships and play different roles with our mothers, friends, and bosses. The self we reveal in each of these encounters needs to be an honest one—one that is congruent with our feelings, meanings, and desired behaviors in that specific encounter.

Develop Trust through Self-Disclosure

A third way to improve our self-concept is to develop trust in others through judicious self-disclosure. In **self-disclosure,** an individual explicitly communicates self-information to another person. The **Johari Window** (shown in table 3.1)[8] is a useful schema for seeing how self-disclosure is helpful.

Area I, known to self and known to others, could be called the *public self.* Certainly self-description data are in this category. Area III, known to self but unknown to others, contains self-data that clearly have relevance for self-disclosure. Information in area III is moved to area I in self-disclosure.

Table 3.1 The Johari Window. (From *Group Processes: An Introduction to Group Dynamics* by J. Luft. National Press, 1963. Used with permission.)

	Known to Self	Not Known to Self
Known to Others	I Free Area	II Blind Area
Not Known to Others	III Hidden Area	IV Unknown Area

Area II, unknown to self but known to others, reflects the fact that others may know more about us than we have self-disclosed. They view our words and behavior and make inferences about us—some true and some false. Conversely, we often know more about some aspects of another than that person knows about himself or herself. Information in area II could be involved in self-disclosure only if the self-data were made known by the other, or if—after an accidental slip—attention were called to this new data and the person then acknowledged its disclosure to the other.

Whether or not information in area II or area IV is self-disclosure information depends upon the attitude and willingness of the person to receive self-data, to explore unknown self-material, and to acknowledge the information to others. The Johari Window not only illustrates the different selves, but it shows the various types of self-data that may be discovered and explicitly disclosed. We possess as many Johari Windows as there are specific others who populate our life space at a given time.

One's self-concept can be improved as the information contained in areas II, III, and IV of the Johari Window is diminished and moved into area I. Self-disclosure is a process that places data into area I from area III after it has moved from areas II and IV into area III. It is generally agreed that self-disclosure has a positive value and that it facilitates growth. Culbert, however, has pointed out that whether self-disclosure is beneficial or harmful depends on the state of the receiver and the relationship between the receiver and the discloser: "A more comprehensive position is that 'it depends'; for self-disclosure may also result in bad, negatively valued, growth-inhibiting outcomes."[9] Therefore, the role of the receiver must also be considered in this discussion of self-disclosure.

The receiver may be involved at one of three levels: (1) the receiver may be a close friend who is *directly, closely,* and *empathically involved* and who has asked a specific question which prompts the disclosure; (2) the receiver may be *rather uninvolved* and the self-disclosure represents a "getting-to-know-you" type; or (3) the receiver may be *quite uninvolved,* receiving a disclosure for which no solicitation has been made. The obligations the receiver feels upon receiving self-disclosed information may vary according to the level of involvement and the relationship that exists between the two persons. A *quite uninvolved* receiver may react with little concern, whereas an *empathically involved* receiver will feel obligated to help in supportive ways.

Some of you can talk about yourselves quite openly and freely because you have already discovered this phenomenon in communication and have found it rewarding. Others of you find it more difficult to share things about yourselves with others. Most of us are hesitant to discuss our deepest feelings with others—especially those with whom we are not well acquainted. This is understandable since in disclosure there is an element of risk. Specific guidelines for identifying and disclosing private information is discussed in the final section of this chapter.

Avoid Silence and Ritual Responses

A fourth suggestion for improving self-concept is to break the habit of silence and ritual responses. Although these behaviors can be used constructively in interpersonal communication—for example, silence and small talk often confirm the bonds of friendship and love, they can be used also to withdraw and avoid sharing one's self.

It is the retreat into silence when verbal interaction with others is expected, the use of silence as an escape mechanism, that is counterproductive. Others may see this silence as communicating indifference or an unwillingness to relate. They may react by rejecting us. We may not intend for our silence to be interpreted this way—in fact, we may desire companionship but fear exposing ourselves so much that we sit mute.

Can you recall an instance in which someone used silence or ritual response to stop or prevent communication?

Similarly, we may use **ritualized communication** to avoid real communication. We can hide in ritual. It is an easy way for us to avoid being ourselves. Surely you have participated in ritualized conversations. They are carried on according to a kind of formula—carried on so that we avoid real communication almost entirely.

We should learn to communicate honestly, to avoid the escapes of silence and ritual communication. By ridding ourselves of these self-defeating response behaviors, we will ultimately improve our self-concepts.

Interact with Trustworthy and Supportive Persons

List five of your strengths and five of your weaknesses. How can you eliminate your weaknesses and build on your strengths?

Still another means by which self-concept is improved is through interaction with other persons who are trustworthy and supportive. We observed earlier in this chapter that self-concept develops through living. Self-concept develops through one's interaction with others. To an extent, then, self is related to the quality of the people around you.

Unfortunately, sometimes the adults with whom children interact are neither democratic nor facilitative to self-growth, but are authoritarian and inhibit healthy growth. Sometimes the child's experiences in school are those of being forced to conform because of fear, coercion, or being demeaned. It is little wonder that such a child crawls into a shell and, as Kozol says, "dies at an early age."[10] One of the greatest gifts parents can give a child is acceptance of and interaction with that child.

It is not in childhood alone that facilitative relationships are helpful to the development of a healthy self-concept. In adulthood, too, one may discover persons who, because of their trust, love, and acceptance, contribute to the development of a healthy self-concept.

Summary

Probably few things are more beneficial to a person than those on which this chapter has focused. To see one's self accurately; to understand and know one's self clearly and honestly; to acquire those abilities and characteristics associated with a strong, wholesome self-concept—these objectives are directly related to effective communication. With a healthier and more accurate self-concept, one can function more effectively in intrapersonal as well as in interpersonal and public communication.

Questions and Exercises for Review

1. How does one acquire a concept of oneself?
2. Why are we *many* selves?
3. How does self-concept affect communication?
4. Have you known someone who "lived up to a label"? Explain how living up to the label affected that person.
5. What is self-disclosure? And what are some guidelines relative to such disclosing?
6. What can you do to decrease a friend's communication apprehension?
7. Explain how an understanding of the Johari Window could help to improve your self-concept.
8. Name three persons you know and admire. Now list five things these persons have in common.

Key Terms and Phrases

self-concept
significant others
reference groups
role playing
self-fulfilling prophecy
negative self-concept
communication confidence
communication apprehension
self-disclosure
Johari Window
ritualized communication

For Further Reading

Culbert, Samuel A. *The Interpersonal Process of Self-Disclosure: It Takes Two to See One.* New York: Renaissance Editors, Inc., 1967.

This is an interesting explanation and in-depth treatment of the process of self-disclosure.

Daly, John A., and McCroskey, James C., eds. *Avoiding Communication: Shyness, Reticence and Communication Apprehension.* Beverly Hills: Sage Publishing Co., 1984.

Gordon, Chad, and Gergen, Kenneth, eds. *The Self in Social Interaction.* New York: John Wiley & Sons, 1968.

This book treats the various social interactions in terms of the effect on self-concept.

Jourard, S. M. *The Transparent Self.* New York: Van Nostrand Reinhold Company, 1971.

This is a popular discussion of the process of self-disclosure. It is quite readable and interesting.

McCroskey, James C. *An Introduction to Rhetorical Communication.* 4th ed. Englewood Cliffs, N.J.: Prentice-Hall, Inc., 1982.

An excellent overview of the problems of communication apprehension and stage fright. Includes a discussion of causes, effects, and control.

McCroskey, James C. "Oral Communication Apprehension: A Reconceptualization." In *Communication Yearbook* 6, edited by Michael Burgoon. Beverly Hills: Sage Publications, 1982.

Miller, Sherod et al. *Straight Talk.* New York: Rawson, Wade Publishers, Inc., 1981.

A thorough discussion of the "Awareness Wheel" as a framework for identifying and expressing personal experience.

Miller, Sherod; Nunnally, Elam W.; and Wackman, Daniel B. *Couple Communication I: Talking Together.* Minneapolis: Interpersonal Communication Programs, Inc., 1979, 33.

An excellent discussion of intimate communication.

Pearce, W., and Sharp, S. "Self-Disclosing Communication." *The Journal of Communication* 23:4 (1973): 409–25.

A unique treatment of self-concept that deals with self-disclosure from a transactional perspective.

Zimbardo, P. G. *Shyness: What It Is and What to Do About It.* Reading, Mass.: Addison-Wesley, 1977.

Notes

1. Donald Washburn, "Intrapersonal Communication in a Jungian Perspective," *Journal of Communication* 14 (September 1964): 131–35.

2. See Harry Stack Sullivan, *The Interpersonal Theory of Psychiatry* (New York: W. W. Norton & Company, Inc., 1953); John J. Sherwood, "Self Identity and Referent Others," *Sociometry* 28 (1965): 66–81; and Carl Backman, Paul Secord, and Jerry Peirce, "Resistance to Change in the Self-Concept as a Function of Consensus Among Significant Others," in *Problems in Social Psychology,* ed. Carl Backman and Paul Secord (New York: McGraw-Hill Book Co., 1969), 462–67.

3. Robert Rosenthal, "Self-Fulfilling Prophecy," in *Readings in Psychology Today* (Del Mar, Calif.: CRM Books, 1967), 466–71.

4. David K. Berlo, "Interaction: The Goal of Interpersonal Communication," in *Dimensions in Communication,* ed. James H. Campbell and Hal W. Hepler (Belmont, Calif.: Wadsworth Publishing Co., 1965), 36–55.

5. P. G. Zimbardo, *Shyness: What It Is and What To Do About It* (Reading, Mass.: Addison-Wesley, 1977), 37.

6. James C. McCroskey, "Oral Communication: A Reconceptualization," in *Communication Yearbook 6,* ed. Michael Burgoon (Beverly Hills: Sage Publications, 1982).

7. Carole Lewandowski, Robert Heath, and David Morris, "Oral Communication 101: A Communication Apprehension Reduction Process." Unpublished research report of a project conducted at Oral Roberts University, Spring 1984.

8. J. Luft, *Group Process: An Introduction to Group Dynamics* (Palo Alto, Calif.: National Press, 1963).

9. Samuel A. Culbert, *The Interpersonal Process of Self-Disclosure: It Takes Two to See One* (New York: Renaissance Editions, Inc., 1967), 6.

10. Jonathan Kozol, *Death at an Early Age* (Boston: Houghton Mifflin Co., 1967).

Focus

The Importance of Listening

The Listening Process

Hearing
Identifying and Recognizing
Auding

Purposes of Listening

Enjoyment
Information
Making Decisions Based on Evaluation
To be Supportive

How to Improve Evaluative Listening Behavior

Listen to Difficult Material—Don't Avoid It
Determine the Purpose of Your Listening
Create Interest in the Topic
Adjust to the Speaker—Don't Criticize Appearance or Delivery
Adjust to the Physical Situation
Keep Emotions in Check—Avoid Quick Responses
Listen for Ideas and Patterns in Reasoning
Use Spare Time Wisely—Speaking Rate vs. Listening Rate

How to Improve Supportive Listening Ability

Observe
Acknowledge
Encourage
Check It Out
Interpret

Listening

We spend more time listening than we do speaking, writing, or reading; and yet little time is spent in the study of listening. In this chapter the listening process and the purposes of listening are explained. The chapter concludes with a discussion of some listening problems and some suggestions for helping you to overcome them.

The Importance of Listening

It has been said that as much as 98 percent of speech training emphasizes *sending skills* while less than 2 percent focuses on *receiving skills.* Yet what the listener brings to the communication situation is of prime importance to effective communication. The listener needs to be aware of what is at stake in the communication situation; the sender needs to understand the listening process and the listener in order to achieve the desired response.

Various studies have shown that adults spend about 70 percent of their waking hours engaged in communication activities, with about 10 percent of this communication time spent in writing, 15 percent in reading, 30 percent in talking, and 45 percent in listening.[1] Hence, 75 percent—and later studies show up to 90 percent—of all human communication is carried on by speaking and listening. The extensive use of the telephone, movies, radio, television, and public address systems have amplified the importance of listening. Our democratic form of government is based upon a well-informed public that relies heavily on broadcast media; modern entertainment depends upon a variety of good listening habits; many jobs and positions depend quite heavily upon effective listening; and learning in school relies upon listening ability.

Evidence indicates that without specific training we do not develop listening skills adequate to meet the needs of modern life. The data indicate that most of us are poor listeners. We can accurately recall only 50 percent of the information we hear immediately after hearing it. Confusion, misinformation, and misunderstanding are common products of our communication experiences.

The Listening Process

In a sense **listening** is a combination of what we hear, what we understand, and what we remember. Hearing, the first element, is the detection or perception of sound. A listener does not receive a word or message instantly; rather, the listener accumulates sounds, receiving a word after a brief but measurable interval of time. The listener accumulates sounds bit by bit, identifies short sound sequences as words, and then translates these words and groups of words into meaning. It may be helpful to think of the act of listening as comprising three stages: hearing, identifying and recognizing, and auding. The diagram in figure 4.1 illustrates these three states.

Hearing refers to the process by which speech is received by the ear in the form of sound waves. The second stage, **identifying and recognizing,** is one in which patterns and familiar relationships are recognized and assimilated. Through auditory analysis, mental reorganization, and association, the sounds and sound sequences are recognized as words. The third stage, **auding,** is the translation of the flow of words into meaning. Auding involves one or more avenues of thought—indexing, comparing, noting sequence, forming sensory impressions, and appreciating.

Figure 4.1 Three stages of listening.

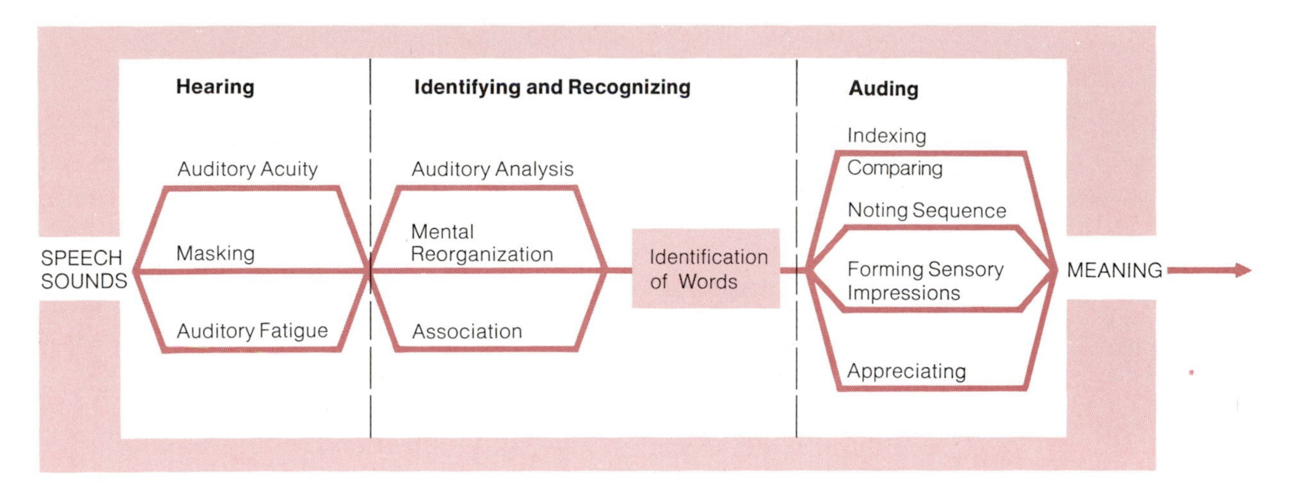

Hearing

As hearing is identified in figure 4.1, one of the first factors to affect the hearing of sound is auditory acuity—the ability of the ear to respond to various frequencies (tones) at various intensities (levels of loudness). Human speech frequencies range from 125 to 8,000 cycles per second, although most words fall between 1,000 and 2,500 cycles per second—the critical range of auditory acuity.

The loudness of sound is measured in decibels and ranges for speech from fifty-five decibels (soft talking) to eighty-five decibels (loud conversation). A person is said to have a hearing loss when he requires more than the normal amount of intensity in order to hear sounds of certain frequencies. A requirement of fifteen to twenty decibels over normal would be considered a significant hearing loss. Any loss of this amount in the critical range of 1,000 to 2,500 frequencies is especially serious since it affects the intelligibility of speech.

Another factor that influences hearing is masking. When background noise, especially competing conversation, enters the ear in the same frequency range as the speech one is intending to receive, the extraneous noise is said to mask the intended oral message. When the extraneous sound is composed of all frequencies it is called **white noise.** White noise is sometimes produced when a large number of persons (a roomful) talk in loud voices—all at the same time.

Auditory fatigue is yet another factor that can affect hearing. Continuous exposure to sounds of certain frequencies can have the effect of causing a temporary hearing loss. A monotonous tone or a droning voice can frequently create auditory fatigue. Studies today are showing that hearing losses, some of an

The white noise of a cacophony of talk.

enduring nature, result from prolonged exposure to noise in urban communities. Some researchers have suggested also that music played at high-volume levels for prolonged periods can cause a hearing loss.

Identifying and Recognizing

The second stage in listening—identification and recognition of patterns and relationships—can be affected by the quality of auditory analysis, mental reorganization, and association. Auditory analysis refers to the process of comparing the incoming sounds with sounds that are already familiar to the individual. Sounds are recognized in terms of their likenesses and differences.

The second process in this stage is mental reorganization. In mental reorganization the listener applies some system that will aid retention and will structure the incoming sounds. The listener may syllabify a word, for example, as he or she pronounces it. If it is a series of numbers, the listener may place the numbers in groups of three, or repeat the series several times. Whether the listener group recodes, or rehearses, he or she is engaged in mental reorgnization.

Finally, sounds are associated with prior experiences. Words used in speech may be entirely strange to the listener—for example, a foreign language—or they may have become associated with subjective meanings quite different from those the sender had in mind. In any event, there is a process for identifying words in which the listener's experience, background, and memory are used to create associations in regard to the incoming sounds.

Auding

The third major stage of listening is auding, the process of assimilating the continuous flow of words and responding to them with understanding or feeling. Again, the listener's experiential background is brought into play along with various thinking skills to make sense of the stream of words received. The listener may index; make comparisons; note sequence; react by forming sensory impressions or appreciating what is heard.

Indexing, as it is used in auding, refers to the outlining or ranking of information according to importance. It is the searching for main ideas and supporting or secondary ideas; it is the separating of the relevant from the irrelevant; and it is the structuring of bits and pieces into more meaningful wholes. Some persons who are exceptionally skilled in indexing apparently have an unusual ability to visualize an outline of incoming information.

Another aid to the assignment of meaning is arranging the material according to time, space, position, or some other relationship; that is, by noting sequence. This function aids the listener in creating a framework into which information can be placed and related. Material is easier to remember when the order of events and placement of parts are noted.

Sometimes the listener reacts with the senses to incoming information. Probably the sensory response most frequently used in association with incoming information is sight—the ability to add a visual dimension to the information. Some persons are apparently highly skilled in forming sensory impressions so that they taste words describing tastes, smell descriptions of smells, and generally translate words into sensory images; this adds meaning to the verbal message.

A final function that may be performed during the auding stage is appreciating, that is, responding to the esthetic nature of the message. Appreciation can play an important role in listening to ceremonial public speeches, as well as in the reception of messages intended to activate the feelings and emotions.

All these elements and more are used to carry out the process of listening—the process by which information is assimilated; ideas are received and reacted to; and interpretations, judgments, and applications are made to derive meaning from the messages received.

A billion-dollar recording industry is only one of many industries that exist because much of our listening is for enjoyment.

Purposes of Listening

The development of good listening ability involves recognizing that there are specific purposes in listening, each with defined requirements and skills. The most important purposes are (1) listening for enjoyment, (2) listening for information, (3) listening in order to evaluate critically, and (4) listening to be supportive and empathic to another person. You may listen, of course, with all four purposes in mind, but the most effective listening appears to occur when you know for what you are listening and listen with that specific purpose in mind. This is called purposive listening. Purposive listening leads to effective listening, because no matter what the social situation, you are focused on the message and its sender.

Listening for Enjoyment

Appreciative listening can increase our enjoyment of life, enlarge our experience, expand the range of what we enjoy, and decrease the tension of daily life. Much of the daily conversation in which each of us engages serves a social purpose—the enjoyable function of sharing feelings and responses to build and maintain positive, supporting relationships. In addition, we engage in listening to satisfy our desire for appreciating and experiencing art and beauty. In the adult world, listening for enjoyment is composed of listening to music, listening to stories or drama on television, engaging in social conversation, and, for some persons, listening to live drama, oral interpretation, or literature read aloud.

Many people miss much pleasant and beneficial listening because they have a limited, narrow experience in appreciative listening. You should attempt to expand your experiences in appreciative listening; to limit yourself to a diet of "soap opera" listening is to miss the opportunity to live more richly, deeply, and pleasantly through expanded esthetic stimuli.

Listening for Information

Another purpose for listening is to receive information—to acquire an answer to a definite problem or question, to listen for direction, to listen to the news of current interest, or to acquire the opinions and views of others. We have noted previously the important contribution that listening makes to learning in general, and the important relationship between listening ability and the acquisition of a viable picture of the world and ourselves. Further, as a college student, you are keenly aware of the central role listening plays in the acquisition of information and understanding. In fact, if you can learn to listen well in your classrooms, you will have acquired a skill that will pay high dividends throughout your life. Following are some guidelines for effective classroom listening.

Guidelines for Effective Classroom Listening

1. *Listen Purposefully.* What is the general topic? What is the specific point being discussed?
2. *Focus on the Message.* Shut off the distractions (noise) and your tendencies to wander mentally. Concentrate on the particular communication situation in which you are involved.
3. *Work at Listening.* Effective listening skills can be developed only through continual practice and ongoing self-evaluation. A willingness to work at listening and expend the necessary energy is the first step toward improving your listening ability and gaining the benefits that go with it.
4. *Suspend Judgment.* Learn to delay judgment and wait to evaluate what you hear until after the speaker has finished.
5. *Be Data Based.* What is the information? What is the evidence? What methods has a speaker used to make the case and what issues or information have been left out?
6. *Listen to the Whole Message.* Listen with your ears and your eyes. Go beyond the words to hear the buried messages, the unspoken messages and the meta-communication cues. Listening involves feelings, actions, and attitudes. It involves gestures, intonations, eye movement, pauses, and . . . silences.

7. *Appear Attentive.* Show speakers that you are listening carefully and thoughtfully. Be responsive to what they say through your facial expressions and body language. Take notes if you can in order to focus on their message.

Listening to Make Critical Evaluations

The word *critical* can be a source of confusion. We use the term here to refer to careful evaluation rather than to negativism, aggressive attack, or the constant challenging of statements. The antagonistic, challenging aspect of criticism can be the antithesis of effective listening. Even critical listening (as we use the term here) can have dire consequences if it interferes with the objective of receiving information accurately by inappropriate timing of the evaluative process. If, during a speech meant to transmit information, you attempt to examine carefully each sentence and idea, the efficiency of listening for information will be seriously decreased. We need to stress again that the purpose for which you listen must be considered if you are to listen effectively. We need to have evaluative assimilation in informational listening, but it should be *withheld* until you have fully comprehended the entire message. We are usually well repaid for postponing evaluation.

On the other hand, if the purpose of our listening is to make a decision—a judgment—then we profit by adopting an evaluative attitude more immediately. We evaluate the strength of each main point advanced by carefully testing the reasoning used and the quality of the evidence used in supporting the point. Such weighing and evaluating is most effectively done point by point rather than at the end of a message. Critical listening makes us aware of prejudices in ourselves and in others. It forces us to judge on the basis of facts and information rather than on emotions and falsehoods. It calls for patience, objectivity, and the testing of thinking and reasoning.

Listening to be Supportive

When you are listening to be **supportive** your primary interest is total awareness of what is happening. The empathic listener's primary goal is to understand the speaker and to express an openness to the totality of the other's communication. When your purpose is to be supportive, you do not listen with just your ears. You listen with your eyes, with your sense of touch, and with an awareness of your own feelings and emotions. The total listener listens to words; but also listens to the messages buried in the words and to the cues (metacommunications) that surround the words.

The important point is that one may have various purposes in mind when listening, but the specific purpose for which one listens ought to determine the skills called into play. The major concern of any listener is to discover the purpose and nature of the message involved and to make one's own adjustment to it.

Individualized learning systems often utilize informational listening.

How to Improve Evaluative Listening Behavior

If you want to improve your listening behavior, you should try to eliminate poor listening habits and develop the basic skills and attitudes essential to good listening. The following eight suggestions can be helpful in achieving this objective.[2]

Learn to Listen to Difficult Material

Too many of us listen only to material that is easy, comfortable, and entertaining. If the material becomes difficult, we decide not to listen. This habit, of course, deprives the individual of opportunities to learn and to acquire new insights.

The poorest listeners are inexperienced listeners, listeners who are unacquainted with lectures, documentaries on radio or television, panel discussions, interviews on television, or public speeches. Before college, many students have not experienced difficult oral discourse; they suddenly find themselves listening to lectures in which new and sometimes complex concepts are presented. Their bad listening habits become a severe handicap.

Good listeners, on the other hand, develop an appetite for a variety of spoken messages. They have learned to enjoy the challenge of difficult subjects. They like intellectual stimulation and growth. If you want to become a better listener, you should make a planned effort to listen to difficult material, including news commentaries, panel discussions, and lectures.

We listen to learn in classes.

Determine the Purpose behind the Communication Situation

Another part of improving listening behavior is to acquire the habit of determining why you are listening. If the communication is persuasive in purpose, you know that you will be engaged in critical listening. If the communication is to inform or instruct, you will be concerned with receiving the ideas and concepts as clearly, accurately, and fully as possible. Determining the purpose of the communication situation improves listening.

Create an Interest in the Subject

Speakers do not always clearly point out how the information they are presenting is relevant to your needs. You should purposefully seek ways to make the information interesting and beneficial to you. Research studies are unanimous in their discovery that if you can create an interest in the subject, your concentration and learning efficiency will increase.

How do you create an interest in the subject? Look for an immediate reward. Information tends to be interesting when it has immediate application. If necessary, you should determine how the information will be useful to you at a later time and place. Ask yourself, "Why am I here? What initial motive brought me to hear this speaker?" and "What uses can I find for this material?" Questions like these usually help you to discover a genuine interest in the topic.

"What did he say?"

True listening involves taking in all of the cues of another and expressing an openness to the totality of what that person communicates.

Adjust to the Speaker

Your listening will also be improved if you learn not to allow the speaker's distracting appearance or delivery to dominate your attention and thinking. Your goal must be to listen to the message. Your aim is to receive what the speaker is saying.

Every speaker has peculiarities, and if you allow yourself to be bothered by a droning voice, a shrill pitch, a persistent cough, or socially inappropriate dress or unusual hair style, you will not concentrate fully on the message. It is possible for you, the listener, to adjust to the speaker's eccentricities by telling yourself that it is the message you want and that the idiosyncrasy of the speaker is unimportant. Listeners can learn to adjust to the speaker, and when that adjustment becomes a natural part of their behavior, they will be more effective listeners.

Adjust to the Physical Situation

The good listener fights distraction and adjusts to the physical environment of the communication situation. Sometimes problems in the environment are easily solved by closing a door, turning off the television, moving closer to the speaker, shifting so as to see the person, or asking the speaker to speak louder. If the distraction cannot be eliminated easily, it becomes a matter of concentration on the part of the listener. You should, of course, do everything possible to control the physical situation. In face-to-face communication and in public communication you should make a habit of sitting where you can easily hear and see the person with whom you are communicating.

Keep the Emotions in Check

Our emotions act as filters to what we hear. Thus, when a speaker is using terms that are "purr" words for us, we are apt to react with positive emotions and accept everything that is said—truths, half-truths, or pure sham. When we hear something that is opposite to our convictions, we tend to react quickly and emotionally, arguing mentally with the speaker or planning rebuttals.

When our emotions are aroused, we create "deaf spots" that impair our ability to perceive accurately and to understand. A single emotion-laden word or argument may trigger this blockage, and when it occurs, our listening efficiency drops toward zero.

Effective listeners keep an open mind and attempt to withhold evaluation until comprehension is complete. They try to identify the words or phrases to which they respond most strongly and to purposely "cool" their reactions. When you hear something that upsets you, make a list of the most disturbing words or phrases. Then analyze why each word influences you as it does. You may find it helpful to discuss each of these words with a friend or classmate. You may discover that these words carry unique and purely personal connotations for you that are without foundation. In any event, getting these words into the open will greatly help cool your reactions to them.

Listen Primarily for Ideas and Patterns of Reasoning

The seventh objective for effective listening is to attain the ability to recognize main points and central ideas. Good listeners focus on ideas; they have acquired the ability to discriminate between fact and principle, idea and example, and evidence and argument. They are able to recognize conventional patterns of organization. They know that it is important to grasp the main idea as quickly as possible and to comprehend the underlying structure of the message or the particular argument being given.

Poor listeners tend to be unable to make these distinctions. They fall into the habit of listening only for facts. Lee has found that only about 25 percent of the persons listening to a speech could identify the central idea of the speaker.[3] Focusing on "getting the facts" can hinder listening. You can become so busily engaged in listening for and trying to remember facts that the ideas are missed entirely. Facts are useful in constructing and understanding ideas; as such, they should be considered secondary to the idea. When people talk, they want you to understand their *ideas,* and grasping ideas is a basic skill in effective listening.

Use Spare Time Wisely

The final objective suggested for a self-improvement program in listening is to make the wisest possible use of the spare time created by the difference between speaking rate and thinking rate. The good listener acquires the ability to capitalize on thought speed. Most of us can think easily at about four times the average rate of speech. The speed of thought can be our greatest listening asset.

We should not attempt to synchronize our thought to the rate of speech; rather, we should use the spare time purposefully to enhance our understanding of the message. Listening specialists suggest that the following mental activities be used to fill this spare time: (1) anticipate what the speaker will say; (2) note the adequacy with which each point is supported; (3) after each point, mentally review the portion of the talk covered so far; and (4) listen "between the lines" for additional meaning. Listening between the lines includes listening for hidden or unstated meanings, for new meanings (other than those we assign initially), and listening for what is not said as well as for what is said.

These are the four ingredients of concentration in listening. The listener has time to engage in these "extra thoughts" while listening to the speaker. We can gain a great deal of knowledge about the speaker's competency, integrity, and creative ability from careful study of the speech. Great gains in understanding or comprehending lectures can be made if we continually practice the four skills of concentrating so as to use spare listening time efficiently.

How to Improve Supportive Listening Ability

Miller outlines five skills for supportive listening: observe, acknowledge, encourage, check out, and interpret.[4]

Observe

1. *Listen for sense (descriptive) data.* By carefully observing nonverbal cues and vocal variations, the listener can more accurately interpret the verbal messages.
2. *Listen for interpretative (inferential) statements.* When a speaker says "I think," "I believe," or "It's my opinion that," the speaker is making a statement that goes beyond sensory observation. Any statement that goes beyond descriptive, observable data is considered to be an inference. It is the speaker's interpretation of what was seen, heard, touched, smelled, or tasted.
3. *Listen for feeling statements.* You may hear someone say, "Ever since the professor assigned the seven-minute speech, I've had knots in my stomach. I'm scared!" Notice that this person is not describing an observable sensation or an interpretative inference; rather, we are hearing a disclosure of internal feelings or emotions.

4. *Listen for intention statements.* In addition to expressing what they want, speakers frequently express what they do not want. "Want" or "intention" statements may express one's intention for oneself, or one's wants, hopes, or goals for the listener, or even for their relationship.
5. *Listen for action statements.* You might hear someone say, "I'm going home during break," or "I'm going to ask Sharon out." These statements are expressions of commitment to specific actions.

Acknowledge

A supportive listener acknowledges. Acknowledging can be done by paraphrasing. When paraphrasing, it's usually best not to simply parrot what you have heard, but to put what you've heard into your own words and mirror it back to the speaker. Paraphrasing is an art that requires practice. Once you become skillful, however, paraphrasing reaps many benefits.

Encourage

A supportive listener encourages. Whereas the evaluative listener may come across as a fact finder and take-charge person, the encourager uses phrases like "I'd really like to hear more about this," or "I'm really interested in knowing how you felt when he told you. . . ."

Check It Out

Supportive listeners check it out. When you are not sure that you correctly interpreted the speaker's intended message, check it out. Ask questions such as, "What do you think? How do you feel? What do you want to happen? What do you plan to do about it?"

The purpose of checking it out should be total communication accuracy and understanding. It tells the speaker you have been listening and that you understand the intended message. Notice the absence of "why" questions—they frequently contribute to defensiveness.

Interpret

Supportive listeners interpret. Occasionally you will hear what the speaker thinks, feels, and wants, but sometimes you will notice conspicuous absences of references to the person's original sensory experience. In other words, what did the person see or hear that resulted in that feeling and intention?

If your goal is to be an effective listener, you will also seek to become aware of the "adaptation" behaviors ingrained deeply in your personal interaction patterns. Extensive research indicates that listeners adopt rather predictable patterns of listening behavior. These behaviors include regulation of speaking turns, involvement, dominance, eye gaze, gesture, posture, distance, language choice, and use of intimate questions.[5]

As a supportive listener, you can ask questions and lead the speaker into areas of particular concern to you. This interpreting of messages can bring improved understanding and acceptance to the speaker and to yourself.

Summary

In this chapter we have emphasized the importance of listening and explained the listening process. The various purposes of listening have been identified, and the most common problems encountered in listening have been discussed along with specific suggestions for how you can improve your listening behavior. Throughout your course in communication, you will be using your listening skills as a primary means of learning about communication. It is hoped that you will apply the things you have learned in your own listening behavior.

Questions and Exercises for Review

1. Can you identify the stages of the listening process?
2. What are the purposes of listening?
3. How do emotion-laden words affect listening for some persons?
4. How can one be supportive in listening?

Key Terms and Phrases

listening
hearing
identifying and recognizing
auding
white noise
auditory fatigue
supportive listening

For Further Reading

Barbara, Dominick A. *The Act of Listening.* Springfield, Ill.: Charles C. Thomas, Inc., 1958.
This is a very readable book by a person well known for his concern with listening as it relates to psychiatric practice and to mental health.

Barker, Larry L. *Listening Behavior.* Englewood Cliffs, N.J.: Prentice-Hall, 1971.
This is perhaps the clearest, most concise treatment of listening.

Davis, A. Jann. *Listening and Responding.* St. Louis: The C. V. Mosby Company, 1984.
Focuses on communication in health care and other helping professional environments. Emphasizes communication from listener's perspective.

Johnson, Wendell. *Your Most Enchanted Listener.* New York: Harper & Row, 1956.
This book, too, is well known for its ease of reading and its interesting presentation of listening theory.

Miller, Sherod et al. *Couple Communication I: Talking Together.* Minneapolis: Interpersonal Communication Programs, Inc., 1981.
A basic communication skills book for couples desiring to improve their ability to talk through issues important to their relationship.

Miller, Sherod et al. *Straight Talk.* New York: Rowson, Wade Publishers, Inc., 1981.
Expands on concepts introduced in *Talking Together.* Explains and illustrates use of the Awareness Wheel as an instrument for improving listening ability.

Nichols, Ralph G., and Stevens, Leonard A. *Are You Listening?* New York: McGraw-Hill Book Company, 1957.
This is an excellent introductory book by the person who is Mr. Listening in this field because of his early research and study in listening.

Steil, Lyman K. et al. *Effective Listening: Key to Your Success.* Reading, Mass.: Addison-Wesley Publishing Co., 1983.
An excellent general treatment of listening.

Stewart, John, ed. *Bridges Not Walls: A Book about Interpersonal Communication.* 4th ed. New York: Random House, 1986.

Wolf, Florence I. et al. *Perceptive Listening.* New York: Holt, Rinehart & Winston, 1983.
Combines an explanation of current listening theory with numerous research-based principles that guide the learner endeavoring to improve personal listening.

Wolvin, Andrew D., and Cookley, Carolyn Gwynn. *Listening.* 3d ed. Dubuque, Ia.: Wm. C. Brown Publishers, 1988.

Notes

1. Paul T. Rankin, "The Importance of Listening Ability," *English Journal* 17 (October 1928): 623–30.
2. Ralph Nichols and Leonard Stevens, *Are You Listening?* (New York: McGraw-Hill, Inc., 1957).
3. Irving J. Lee, *How to Talk With People* (New York: Harper & Row, 1952), 60.
4. Sherod Miller et al., *Straight Talk* (New York: Rowson, Wade Publishers, Inc., 1981), 191.
5. Joseph N. Capella, "Interpersonal Communication: Definitions and Fundamental Questions," in *Handbook of Communication Science,* ed Charles R. Berger and Steven H. Chaffee (Newbury Park, Calif.: Sage Publications, Inc., 1987), 216–17.

Focus

The Importance of Nonverbal Communication

Types of Nonverbal Communication

Paralanguage
Action Language
Object Language
Tactile Communication
Space as Communication
Time as Communication
Silence

Differences between Verbal and Nonverbal Communication

Three Principles of Nonverbal Communication

One Cannot *Not* Communicate
Nonverbal Channels Are Effective for Communicating Feelings, Attitudes, and Relationships
Nonverbal Communication Can Have High Validity

Nonverbal Communication

5

Actions speak louder than words! And the other forms of nonverbal communication, which are identified and discussed in this chapter, are also rich in their communication of meaning—especially affective meanings such as attitudes, feelings, and interpersonal relationships.

Like verbal communication, nonverbal communication makes use of a language, codes, and rules. At the same time, however, there are interesting differences between verbal and nonverbal communication. Those differences are discussed in this chapter along with three important principles of nonverbal communication.

The Importance of Nonverbal Communication

Every message is put into a code. The codes to which we direct most of our attention are the spoken and written codes—verbal communication. Actually, verbal signals carry only a small part of the information that people exchange in everyday interaction. Harrison has estimated that in face-to-face communication no more than 35 percent of the social meaning is carried in the verbal message.[1] However, Mehrabian and Wiener have found from their studies that as much as 93 percent of social meaning is attributable to nonverbal communication.[2] Still, we sometimes slip into the error of thinking that *all* communication must be verbal. Another code does exist, however—the nonverbal code, a much-used vehicle of communication.

Nonverbal communication includes the full range of human communication: tone of voice, gesture, posture, movement, and other signals. A good deal of this nonverbal communication goes on around us; it is important because we make decisions based on it and relate to each other through it. From nonverbal communication cues we make decisions to argue or agree, to laugh or blush, to relax or resist, to continue or end a conversation. Many, and sometimes most, of the critical meanings in communication are transferred through the nonverbal codes. Although we do not always realize that we are sending and receiving messages nonverbally, the influence of nonverbal communication is always present in face-to-face communication situations. We gesture with our hands, raise our eyebrows, meet someone else's eyes and look away, and shift positions in a chair. Although the actions may seem random, researchers have discovered in recent years that there is a system to them. Messages come across not only in words but also in body language, and such nonverbal messages often get there faster than do the verbal messages.

Every culture has its own body language, its own nonverbal code. The difference that may exist between cultures was at one time dramatically illustrated in Japan's public baths. Japanese girls traditionally express their approval of male guests with shy and subdued laughter. This behavior unnerved many male tourists from Europe and America. In order to overcome the cultural differences in meaning, Geisha girls had to be trained to reserve their giggles for Oriental men. One's ethnic background, social class, and sex all influence body language. Research has also shown that persons who are truly bilingual are bilingual in body language as well as in words. New York's famous mayor Fiorello La Guardia is said to have been able to campaign in English, Italian, and Yiddish. When films of his speeches are run without sound, it is not difficult to identify from his nonverbal communication the language he is speaking.

In this chapter we will describe the types of nonverbal communication, compare nonverbal with verbal communication, and identify some tentative principles of nonverbal communication. The direct relationship and application of nonverbal communication to specific forms of interpersonal and public communication will be discussed in later chapters. As you read this chapter, you will notice that nonverbal communication has a close relationship to topics discussed in the earlier chapters on communication foundations.

Types of Nonverbal Communication

Nonverbal communication falls into seven categories: paralanguage, action language, object language, tactile communication, space, time, and silence.

Paralanguage

We have recognized for a long time that there is information in the tone of voice, the emphasis or inflections given certain words, and the pauses inserted in the sentence. We know from experience that a simple "Yes" may express defiance, resignation, acknowledgment, interest, enthusiasm, or agreement, depending upon tone and emphasis. Most of us, at one time or another, have remarked, "It wasn't *what he said* but *how he said it* that made me angry!" We were referring to the nonverbal vocal phenomena—intonation, emphasis, and stress. These vocal phenomena, often referred to as **paralanguage,** consist of vocal qualifiers, differentiators, and a general category called voice quality.

Vocal Qualifiers

Vocal qualifiers are usually thought of as *tones of voice.* Increasing **loudness or softness** is one type of vocal qualifier. The part of the utterance bearing the increasing loudness or softness may be a single syllable, word, sentence, or a group of sentences. Increasing loudness often expresses anger, hostility, or alarm. If you listen to persons in the midst of a heated argument, you may notice that the loudness of the speaking voices increases. On the other hand, increasing softness is often used to express disappointment. Loudness or softness is seldom used alone as a qualifier of the verbal message, but each is used along with other techniques (pitch, tempo, and voice quality) to convey the message.

A second vocal qualifier is **pitch.** A raised pitch often accompanies loudness and can be used to communicate alarm, annoyance, and anxiety. The whining, high-pitched voice may tell a story of tenseness, fear, and anxiety that is as revealing as the verbal message itself; or the relaxed, low-pitched voice may communicate calm and relaxation. We use pitch to differentiate declarative and interrogative messages. By using certain pitch patterns of inflections, we can utter as a question a statement constructed declaratively ("That was a *basketball game?*"). Such is the capacity of pitch to qualify the meanings of verbal messages.

Tempo, increased or decreased, is a third vocal qualifier. Increased tempo or rate of speaking sometimes (especially as it is associated with other vocal qualifiers) indicates annoyance; at other times it may indicate anxiety; and it is sometimes associated with energy and intelligence. Conversely, an extremely slow tempo often signals uncertainty.

Many psychiatrists and others skilled in communication rely heavily on the information in nonverbal messages. Through experience they have come to have confidence in the validity of the information received from vocal qualifiers.

Vocal Differentiators

Among the most commonly used **vocal differentiators** are *crying, laughing,* and *breaking.* These types of communication are used according to the rules of each culture. In America, for example, women have more freedom to use crying to communicate than do men. Laughing and crying may mean quite different things in different cultures. Custom dictates who can and cannot cry, how much they can cry, and what things can be meant by crying.

Breaking refers to speaking in a broken, halting voice, or to some rigid and intermittently interrupted speech. The nervous giggle is considered to be a form of breaking. The quavering voice of emotion is another example of breaking. In our culture, breaking in any form communicates insecurity and loss of control. Laughing, crying, breaking—any one of these vocal differentiators—could be applied to the same verbal message at different times and under different circumstances to create totally different messages.

Vocal Quality

A third phenomenon is **voice quality.** Meanings are conveyed and understood through voice quality. Anxiety, calm, hostility, and other emotional states have been identified with voice quality as a general characteristic of a particular emotional state. Psychiatrists, medical doctors, counselors, and teachers who are skilled in and sensitive to nonverbal communication make use of voice quality in interpreting messages.

Although each type of vocal communication has been discussed separately, it would be a mistake to think in terms of each operating separately and individually to communicate nonverbal messages. In practice, these phenomena are combined with one another in many different ways. Hence, people who attempt to purposefully receive, interpret, and understand nonverbal messages focus on the *general* or *multiple nonverbal factors* rather than on a specific factor. Loudness, high pitch, increased rate, hollowness, and crying are more meaningful when considered together than is any one of these when considered by itself.

Action Language

Action language[3] includes all facial expressions, movement, gestures, and postures that are *not* used exclusively as substitutes for words. Walking, for example, gives one mobility, but it can also communicate. Similarly, eating can be action language. Eating rapidly may communicate something about the person's hunger, upbringing, or emotional state.

It is useful to divide action language into two categories: (1) expressive actions which are unintentional, and (2) purposive actions which are intentional. The former are often subliminal, while the latter are overt and identifiable by either the listener or the talker. **Expressive actions** are constantly adaptive, responding to feelings and needs of the moment, while overt actions are specifically communicative and instrumental. Expressive actions result in the message that is "given off," while **purposive actions** result in a given message.

Purposive actions are actions one *does on purpose*. One knows one is doing that action. Expressive actions are *not* overt. One does not realize one is doing that action. The action or behavior is just slipping out automatically without the sender knowing it. These two categories are not absolute; they do overlap at times. Some expressive actions are noticeable, and some communicative gestures become so habitual that we use them almost unconsciously. It is not uncommon for a person to develop certain habituated movements and gestures and to use them regardless of whether they have any connection with the verbal message or not. Most public officials and entertainers have their idiosyncratic, habituated gestures, and these are often used by comedians who impersonate well-known public figures. For example, Rich Little has built his identification on his impersonation of popular persons, especially political personalities such as Richard Nixon, Jimmy Carter, and Ronald Reagan.

As overt, intentional actions, gestures are used to locate, to describe, to emphasize, and even to express abstract concepts. As expressive, unintentional actions, gestures, facial expression, posture, and movement reveal the personality and emotional states. In twitching, blotching, dilated pupils, rising hair, and so on, we can observe the fear, nervousness, anger, joy, and other emotional states of the individual. We may not notice each individual cue, but we observe the total visible pattern. We perceive the visual meaning as a configuration and interpret it almost instantly.

There is little doubt that we differ in our abilities to send and interpret messages in the action language channel—both intentional and unintentional messages. Some persons are very expressive in their visible behavior, while others are more reserved. Again, some persons are keenly sensitive and accurate in understanding nonverbal signs, while others ignore them. Coleman found that there is not only a difference in individuals' abilities to send and receive nonverbal messages, but there is also a difference between men and women in using nonverbal communication. Generally speaking, women seem to be better than men in sending nonverbal messages, but men seem to be better than women in interpreting them.[4]

Various types of human encounters have been filmed in order to study the use of action language. We have discovered that action language is better studied in specific social contexts and in relationship to all other nonverbal communication cues if it is to be accurately understood. We have to learn to attend to facial expressions, movements, gestures, body positions, and tonal qualities of the voice—in short, all of the nonverbal messages.

Expressive actions can produce a message that is "given off."

The most readily observed of all action language are **facial expressions.** We focus on the face more often than on any other part of the body. Especially, we focus on the eyes. Americans are careful about how and when they meet one another's eyes. In normal conversation, we allow each *eye contact* to last only about a second, then one or both of us will look away. Avoidance of eye contact is often interpreted as hiding, dislike, or an effort to escape. On the other hand, prolonged eye contact often indicates interest and liking.

Movement is another type of action language. Pace, length of stride, and walking posture vary with the emotional state and the personality of the individual. Our personalities are so much reflected in our manner of walking that it is not difficult to identify people you know well by hearing their step. Some persons have a light, rapid walk, while others shuffle along with heavy feet.

Walking may also indicate leadership or power in a group—the leader "sets the pace." Pace setting seems to be associated with power, control, and status. It seems that in every society (human and animal), the leaders set the pace. This principle has been used by the FBI, Kremlinologists, and others to successfully identify the leaders among groups under surveillance.[5]

Through our actions, we communicate inner feelings and attitudes. Openness, approachability, and acceptance are communicated nonverbally just as are closedness, withdrawal, and defensiveness. Nierenberg and Calero observed negotiation situations and reported a significantly higher frequency of

The eyes and facial expressions are powerful vehicles of communication.

agreement among men whose coats were open than among those whose coats were buttoned. Open hands, open arms, uncrossed legs, and unbuttoned coats seem to go with acceptance and openness; while folded arms, hidden hands, crossed legs, and buttoned coats go with defensiveness and negative attitudes.[6]

If you have attended a baseball game and the team manager has rushed out to argue with the umpire, you have probably observed a classic demonstration of closedness. Usually, the umpire crosses his arms, and may even turn his back, in stubborn defensiveness that says, "I'm closed to negotiation!" It is generally believed that crossed arms are indicative of defensiveness nearly everywhere in the world.

Salespersons, teachers, executives, and lawyers associate certain **gestures** and **posture** with evaluating, thinking, or preparedness for action. These include sitting on the edge of the chair, leaning forward, supporting the head or chin with one hand to the cheek (as portrayed by Rodin's *The Thinker*), and tilting the head to one side. Also, stroking the chin or pulling the beard is said to be associated with considering and decision making.

Crossed arms can indicate fear, uptightness, or rejection among other nonacceptive and negative orientations.

Can action tell you when a person is *lying or being secretive?* There are those who answer yes. They say the best indicator is incongruity among nonverbal messages (smiles, but clasps hands nervously; crosses legs and points the feet toward the door) or between a verbal message and a nonverbal message. Touching or rubbing the nose, rubbing the eye, crossing the legs, covering the mouth with the hands—these, also, are said to suggest strong rejections of the verbal message.

There are nonverbal signals for *reassurance and reinforcement.* When we want our ideas accepted and confirmed, we often emit signals that are calls for such reassurance. Our anxiety and lack of confidence is revealed through hand clenching, cuticle picking, pen or pencil chewing or nail biting. A woman may bring her hand to her throat or play with her necklace. All these signs may indicate anxiety over being accepted.

Frustration, which is different from anxiety over being accepted, may be revealed by rubbing the back of the neck, running the fingers through the hair, handwringing, and short breathing.

Fear or nervousness may be shown by rapid movements, rapid speech, selecting the furthest chair, crossing the arms or legs, continual shifting of the body, turning the body away from the other communicator, turning so as to point toward the door, clearing the throat, suddenly expelling air ("Whew!"), and cigarette smoking. It has been found that the lighting and smoking of cigarettes do not indicate fear or tension. In fact, smokers usually light up after the threat has passed—after the tension subsides. Rather, it is the putting out of the cigarette or letting it burn without smoking it that indicates nervousness.

Aggressiveness can be expressed by the pointed finger.

When someone wants to interrupt, he will often pull an ear, or place the index finger on the lips. The index finger—*the pointing finger*—is also used in another way. If someone has jabbed you with a finger and said, "Know what I mean?" you know how the pointed finger can be symbolic of a bayonet or weapon, indicating aggressiveness and dominance. Some persons have refined the gesture by using their eyeglasses in the same way. If you want someone to become hostile toward you, wave your pointed finger in his face. It may seem natural to use this gesture when we are communicating forcefully, but we ought to be aware of the danger of arousing antagonism in others.

Whether it is the locked ankles, the tapping of fingers, doodling, toe-tapping, clicking a ballpoint pen, the smoothing and arranging of hair, smoothing of the dress, balancing a shoe half on and half off, the steepling gesture (making a church steeple by putting the fingertips of one's hands together), erect posture, or shoulders back—action language is rich in the communication of intended and unintended messages. If we could develop skill in reading action language consciously—to verify meanings in a given encounter—we might prevent some of the communication breakdowns and misunderstandings we experience day after day. We might also learn more about our own action language and the effect we have on others through our nonverbal communication.

Object Language

Object language[7] comprises the display of material things—art objects, clothes, the decoration of a room, hairstyle, implements, machines, and the human body. Engagement and wedding rings are objects of communication, as is the American flag, a peace decal, and the sports-letter jacket. It is well known that the clothing one wears and its style and condition tell something about the person. We make inferences from the shine of the shoes, the cut of the hair, and other material things that reveal another's social sensitivity, associations, preferences, and values. Personal apparel represents deliberate choices and is a guide to personality. How we dress, for example, shows sexual attraction and sexual interest, group identification, status, identification of role, and expression of self-concept. Compton's study is one of several that has found a close relationship between selection of clothing and expression of self, particularly personality and status.[8] Among the books currently found in bookstores that attest to the importance of clothing and dress as object language are *Dress for Success* and *Woman's Dress for Success Book.*[9]

Tactile Communication

Tactile communication is communication by touch, the earliest and most elementary mode of communication for the human organism. Tactual sensitivity is the most primitive sensory process in lower organisms. Many of the lower organisms orient themselves to the world by their feelers or antennae. They literally *feel* their way through life.

Tactile communication is of special significance to human beings. It is the first form of communication experienced by the infant, and we know that these early tactile experiences are crucial in the later development of symbolic recognition and response. The *infant's need for tactile contacts*—nuzzling, cuddling, patting, feeling—and the quick response to and acceptance of tactile messages are well-known facts. Parental care and love through infancy and childhood are largely matters of tactile communication—contacts that comfort, reassure, express acceptance, give encouragement, and build confidence. Moreover, the kind and duration of early tactile experiences wherein the infant or child can send and receive messages have an effect on early personality development.

Can you identify the touching behaviors that are normal in courtship in our culture?

Sometimes a small child will transfer tactile communication to objects other than the mother or father. A baby may become attached to the feel of a specific blanket, a soft cuddly animal, or a toy and begin to enjoy these textures and tactile contacts. Denial or deprivation of early tactile experiences may impair future learning, such as speech, cognition, and symbolic recognition, or limit the individual's capacity for more mature tactile communication. Through early tactile experiences the infant begins to communicate, and gradually enlarges communication as capacities for other sensory perceptions are developed. The foundation for these other forms of communication, both verbal and nonverbal, is tactile communication.

A second developmental stage in tactile communication is also related to subsequent adult tactile communication. This is the stage where the child learns that there are *social curtailments* and *prohibitions* connected with tactile communication. The child learns to define some things (property, sacred places, forbidden objects, persons, etc.) as untouchable except under certain conditions (when one has permission, has performed certain rituals, has made a purchase, etc.). Sometimes the child's naive use of tactile communication is prohibited by strong and painful punishment. The process of socializing the child according to the rules of tactile communication may vary from successful to unsuccessful, that is, it may be accompanied by fears and strong inhibitions. Nevertheless, the tactile communication experiences of the infant and the child are directly related to the effectiveness of adult interpersonal communication. Through the early tactile experiences of child and parents, as well as child and others, the first patterns of interpersonal relations are established. They will affect subsequent patterns. These early tactile experiences are related to the individual's confidence in the world and trust in people.

For adults, tactile communication is a potent form of nonverbal communication. Tactile communication has at least *four distinguishing characteristics:* (1) tactile experience is ordinarily limited to two persons; (2) tactile experience is immediate and transitory, operating only as long as contact is maintained; (3) tactile communication is reciprocal in the sense that who or what we touch also touches us; and (4) tactile communication takes place on the level of signals (direct stimulation through the sense of touch) rather than through symbolic mediation. Tactile experiences, as emotional and attitudinal messages and responses, are powerful, clear, and capable of an amazing variety of transformations in human communication. Through the touch of a hand one can feel fear, coldness, and anxiety, or love, warmth, and security. Tactile communication plays a pervasive role in human communication.

Space as Communication

Anthropologist Edward T. Hall has pointed out that cultures establish meanings that are related to distance or **space.**[10] In the United States, the comfortable and appropriate distance to stand for conversation is about an arm's length. The Brazilian, as he talks with an American, moves in closer; the American is apt to interpret that space violation as pushy, overbearing, or aggressive; and, if the American backs away, the Brazilian is apt to think the American is being standoffish or cold.

Space between Persons

The American and the Arab are even less compatible in terms of the space defined as appropriate for conversation. The Arab may stand quite close and look intently into the American's eyes as they talk. This space element and eye-contact behavior may be associated with sexual intimacy by the American, who consequently may find it disturbing in a nonsexual context. Hall

"Do you think you could back it off a bit, Soldier?"

believes that the space or distance between persons in communication is related also, to the nature of the messages. He has identified eight distances that may be indicative of certain types of messages. They include (1) very close (3 to 6 inches)—soft whisper, top secret, or intimate information; (2) close (8 to 12 inches)—audible whisper, very confidential information; (3) near (12 to 20 inches)—soft voice, confidential; (4) neutral (20 to 36 inches)—soft voice, personal information; (5) neutral (4½ to 5 feet)—full voice, nonpersonal; (6) public distance (5½ to 8 feet)—full voice; (7) and (8) stretching the limits of distance (up to 100 feet) and hailing and departure distance.[11] The first two distances constitute the intimate zone; numbers three and four are the personal; five and six make up the social zone; and further distances are called the public zone.[12]

The **intimate distance** (under 12 inches) in American culture is used by lovers, husband and wife, children or other members of the family, and very close friends. This distance is acceptable for two American women talking together, but it is not acceptable for American men at present. For Arab men, intimate distance is acceptable. It is quite acceptable, for example, for two Arab men to stroll along hand in hand as they visit. Generally, we do not want our intimate space boundaries violated by those with whom we are not on intimate relationships. You can observe people become tense in a crowded elevator because of the necessary violation of the intimate zone. You can easily observe the many nonverbal messages that people send to each other as they cope with this situation—messages that say, "I'm not doing this intentionally; I have to." "I apologize for being so close to you." or "Get away! There is room enough to permit you to stand farther away." You have probably noticed that when two or three people are in an elevator, they often stand at opposite ends so as not to invade each other's intimate or personal zones. As the elevator becomes crowded, people pull themselves in and stand stiffly, trying not to touch anyone. If they do touch, they may verbally apologize for it. And if they are forced to touch, they usually tense their muscles in the touching area so as to be "cold." To be relaxed and "warm" against a stranger will probably elicit cold and harsh looks or even verbal reprimands.

Even the **personal zone** (1½ to 3 feet) has many restrictions attached to it. It is a normal and acceptable distance for conversation at a party, for many work relationships, for talk with your classmates, and for chatting with close friends on the street, but it assumes a well-established acquaintance and a trusting relationship.

The **social zone** (4½ feet to 8 feet) is said to be the distance at which American business is transacted. It is the distance between the housewife and the appliance repairman, the salesperson and the customer, the boss and the secretary, and those only casually acquainted at social gatherings.

Public distance is often used for public speaking, for acting (distance between actor and audience), and for certain business situations.

Personal Territories

Birds, animals, and people mark out the territory on which they stand as their own personal space. They let others approach, but not too closely. In one experiment, a person deliberately intruded on the personal space of female college students seated at study tables in a library. The intruder sat down right next to any coed sitting alone at a library table. Each of the victims tried to restore an appropriate distance by moving her chair farther away, turning sideways, and by building a barrier of books, purse, and coat. The experimenter then pursued by moving his chair closer to the retreating victim. When all avoidance mechanisms failed, the victim took flight. Only one of the eighty students whose personal space had been invaded asked the experimenter to move. Personal space, like sex, seems to be one of those things we react to but do not acknowledge in words. The amount of space a person needs is influenced by personality. Introverts, for example, seem to need more elbow room than extroverts.

Mood is also indicated by space. We put more space between ourselves and those we dislike than between ourselves and those we like. Drawing away can communicate avoidance, rejection, or fear; while drawing closer can communicate acceptance, admiration, and liking. Space speaks.

It is said that we practice **territoriality**—each of us has a personal space that we carry around with us. Like a bubble enclosing us, it is our personal territory, our "body buffer zone." Others may not enter it without permission or invitation. Studies by Dr. A. F. Kinzel with federal prisoners indicate that prisoners with histories of violence against other persons have body buffer zones at least four times larger than those without histories of violence.[13] Several of the violent prisoners he studied referred to their "not being able to stand invasion of their buffer zone." They lashed out violently when such violations occurred.

This is my space and my territory.

Kinzel and others have raised a question concerning the effect of urban overcrowding upon human behavior. We know that animals have clearly marked territories and personal space needs; experiments have shown that overcrowding and destruction of their minimum space requirements cause animals to become hostile, aggressive, and even self-destructive at times. We have yet to determine whether humans can adjust satisfactorily to overcrowding or whether we too have certain space requirements for psychological survival.

We do know that we can easily observe people staking out and holding their territories. The person who puts his feet on the desk while you talk is saying very clearly, "This is my territory!" This person may say the same thing by pulling a desk drawer out and putting a foot on it; by throwing a leg over the arm of the chair; by leaning back and placing both hands behind his or her head; or by standing up after inviting you to be seated. You have probably observed students staking out and holding their space in the library. Barriers and lines of demarcation are built with books, pencils, and coats. Often, students drop their books on the cafeteria tables to "hold" them while they wait in lines to get their meals. One of the authors recalls one time when he went into the cafeteria and saw only a half-a-dozen or so tables with people seated at them, but every one of the remaining tables was "taken." It was a room all staked out, with all territories claimed, and yet it was practically empty of people!

It has been discovered that placing physical barriers between persons to ensure their territorial space improves morale in certain situations. Protective counters between waitresses and cooks have served this function. Waist- or shoulder-high partitions in a large office have had a similar effect. We recognize the integrity of personal space in ways other than through the erection of partitions, however. The butler or waitress does not listen to the conversations of guests, and the pedestrian avoids staring at an embracing couple.

Furniture Arrangement

The arrangement of furniture and the distance between chairs utilizes space to communicate certain messages—messages having to do with rules, relationships, and status. For example, patients are more at ease if the doctor is not behind a desk. Executives have added easy chairs, sofas, and coffee tables to their office furnishings; now they can communicate status, power, and aloofness by staying behind the desk, they can invite the caller to sit at a table with them, or they may suggest sitting in easy chairs—thus communicating informality, warmth, and equality.

In discussion groups, committee meetings, or other business meetings, the chairperson will generally assume the head-of-the-table position, and other places around the table may have special status meanings. For this reason, many of us like to work in discussion groups in which everyone is seated in a circle. King Arthur made famous the use of a "round table" to indicate the equality of his knights.

Pay special attention to how professors, deans, and others arrange and use furniture in their offices. What are they communicating to you? Do you suppose it is intentional or unintentional nonverbal communication? Is their furniture arranged to keep you at a distance? to show roles and status? Is the furniture arranged to form primarily a "work office," a "social office," or a "counseling office"?

The use of furniture and space to communicate status, role, and power is an interesting phenomenon in nonverbal communication. Studies have shown, for example, that persons of low status, when entering the office of a superior, stop just inside the door and talk across the room to the seated superior; a person of intermediate status walks halfway to the desk; one whose status is equal to that of the seated person walks right up to the desk; and one of superior status walks behind the desk and stands over the seated person. These movements are space-oriented. They are penetrations into the territory of the person in whose office they occur.

Space in Interrogation

One other facet of "space-speaks" principles is that of police interrogation. Police investigators are advised to keep moving closer to the person being interrogated and to allow no object—table, chair, or desk—to come between themselves and the subject. Such an object gives the subject a buffer or shield to confidence and security. One of the detectives in a police communication class taught recently by one of the authors told how he holds the subject's knees together tightly with his own knees; he holds the subject's wrists and arms tightly, too. With "no place to go," the personal and intimate space dominated, the subject's superior confidence and resistance is lost. Unable to escape physically or nonverbally, the subject cannot escape the question psychologically, and tends to spill out the truth.

Space does speak and it can speak powerfully. We ought to become aware of what we communicate with our own use of space and distance, and of what others are saying through their use of space.

Time as Communication

As with space, **time** is a form of nonverbal communication. Time talks. In American culture, punctuality communicates respect and tardiness can be an insult. In other cultures, however, timeliness is an insult. In America, a late message, whether term paper, business report, or press release, is likely to have undesirable consequences. Tardiness often communicates a low regard for the receiver and for the message. Many persons use only air mail for their letters; they believe that it builds credibility and respect by communicating a high regard.

Time is used to communicate role relationships and status. The "boss" may walk right into the subordinate's office, while the subordinate knocks before entering the boss's office. A secretary may have to phone the boss to gain entry for the subordinate; then the subordinate may have to "wait to see the boss." Studies have verified that the lower the status of the visitor, the longer the visitor must wait before getting into the office.

Can you provide an example from your experience of how someone—perhaps you—used space, objects, time, or silence to communicate?

The element of time can also communicate alarm. Remember the last time your phone rang at 2:30 A.M.? You probably felt some sense of urgency and importance, perhaps even danger. The element of time alone communicated the alarm.

Silence as Communication

Silence can be used to communicate. It is not unusual that what is *not* said is as important or more important than what *is* said. Silence can have message value. Silence can influence others. We need not be exceptionally sensitive to silence to be aware of its clarity and power as a vehicle of communication. Surely most of us have been rebuffed with silence. We have been "told" clearly by someone through silence, avoidance of eye contact, and lack of response that he or she wished to be left alone. Such treatment by the "silence-user" is quite insulting and provokes hostility, but there is no question that it communicates. We "get the message" easily.

In summary, we have identified seven kinds of nonverbal communication—vocal characteristics, action language, object language, tactile communication, communication through the use of space, time communication, and silence. Any of the codes, singularly or in combination, may be used to modify verbal messages—to reinforce, validate, or complement the verbal message, or to contradict and negate it. Nonverbal communication may also be used in its own right, without accompanying verbal messages, to establish bonds and relationships necessary for survival.

Differences between Verbal and Nonverbal Communication

The two communication systems, verbal and nonverbal, constitute *different languages* and operate according to different laws. When we talk face-to-face with another person we send *discrete, digital, verbal symbols,* while at the same time we are sending *continuous, analogical, nonverbal cues.* One of the differences between analogical and digital information, according to neurologists, is that the human nervous system handles the two kinds of cues differently; they travel over different neural pathways in the brain. The analogical information travels over the older portions of the brain—the portions that develop in the early years before words and numbers (digital information) are learned. Digital pathways lie in those parts of the brain that develop late in the child.

We receive and process analogical and digital information at different speeds. **Analogical messages** are received rapidly, while **digital messages** reach us more slowly and are processed more slowly. This means that the message sent by one's body is perceived and reacted to before the meaning of verbal messages are perceived. Hence nonverbal messages often create a set that acts as a filter affecting our perception of and reaction to verbal messages.

There are other differences between digital and analogical messages than those of perception. Words can and do represent abstractions (such as love and hate), but nonverbal messages observed in one's behavior (expressive messages) are more likely to be directly related to the feeling of the moment. Most verbal messages are governed by one's will—are constructed intentionally—while many nonverbal cues are not under one's control. One cannot so easily govern body movements and psycho-physiological responses. Table 5.1 further compares verbal and nonverbal communication.

Table 5.1 Verbal and Nonverbal Codification Differences*

Nonverbal Communication	Verbal Communication
Nonverbal communication is based on continuous functions; the hand is continuously involved in movement.	Verbal communication is based on discontinuous functions; sounds or letters have a discrete beginning and ending.
Nonverbal communication is regulated primarily by principles governed by biological necessity.	Verbal communication is governed primarily by arbitrary, man-made principles.
Nonverbal communication influences perception, coordination, and integration, and leads to the acquisition of skills.	Verbal communication influences thinking and leads to the acquisition of information.
Understanding of nonverbal denotation is based upon the participants' emphatic assessment of biological similarity; no explanation is needed for understanding what pain is.	Understanding of verbal denotation is based on prior verbal agreement.
Nonverbal communication uses the old structures of the central and autonomic nervous systems.	Verbal communication uses younger brain structures, particularly the cortex.
Nonverbal communication is learned early in life.	Verbal communication is learned later in life.
Action and objects exist in their own right.	Words do not exist in their own right. They are arbitrary symbols representing abstractions or events.
Nonverbal communication is emotional to a great extent.	Verbal communication is intellectual to a greater extent.
Nonverbal communication represents an intimate language.	Verbal communication represents a distant language.

*It should be recognized that these differences are *not* absolute. There are exceptions and qualifications, but we are interested in calling attention to differences frequently found between verbal and nonverbal communication.

Three Principles of Nonverbal Communication

Because of the differences between nonverbal and verbal communication—nonverbal communication has several unique characteristics—it is possible to suggest some tentative axioms or principles of nonverbal communication.

One Cannot *Not* Communicate

All observed behavior has message value. Behavior has no opposite; there is no such thing as non-behavior. Hence it follows that we cannot avoid communicating. We can avoid communicating verbally, but nonverbal communication cannot be avoided—even inactivity and silence have message value.

All observed behavior has message value.

Sigmund Freud once wrote: "No mortal can keep a secret. If his lips are silent, he chatters with his fingertips; betrayal oozes out of him at every pore."[14] Thus, an individual may appear calm and self-controlled—unaware that signs of tension and anxiety are leaking out in the tapping of a foot or the tenseness of the fingers.

Nonverbal Channels Are Especially Effective in Communicating Feelings, Attitudes, and Relationships

Humans communicate verbally to share cognitive information and to transmit knowledge, but they rely heavily on nonverbal communication to share emotions, feelings, and attitudes. In fact, some nonverbal communication (tactile communication, for example) is used almost entirely to communicate noncognitive information. Watzlawick has stated that when relationship is the central concern of communication (superior-subordinate, leader-follower, helper-helped, etc.), verbal language is almost meaningless.[15] In courtship, love, or combat, nonverbal communication is the effective mode. One can, of course, verbally profess love or trust, but these are most meaningfully communicated through the nonverbal codes. The verbal channel has a high potential for carrying semantic information, while the nonverbal channel has a high potential for carrying affective information. The emotional side of the message is very often expressed by the nonverbal elements. When we express a liking or disliking for a person, we often express it, not only through what we say, but through how we say it.

Through the nonverbal codes (all the types we have identified) we communicate power, trustworthiness, status, affection, hostility, acceptance, and the full range of attitudes and feelings. From the student in conversation with a professor who holds the professor's eyes with his own a little longer than usual to communicate admiration and affection, to the student who narrows her eyes and sharpens her voice as she communicates hostility to the professor, nonverbal communication makes its impact on interpersonal transactions.

Recent studies tend to show that attitudes are communicated nonverbally. Posture, for example, often reflects our attitudes toward the people with us. One experiment indicates that when a man is with another man whom he dislikes, he is either very relaxed or very rigid, depending on how threatening he perceives the other man to be. Women, in this experiment, always signaled dislike with a very relaxed posture. Several other studies have identified strong relationships between posture (particularly trunk and head positions) and attitudes, as well as between body movement (turning away or toward, moving nearer to or further from, etc.) and attitudes.[16] Four general postural attitudes have been identified—withdrawal, approach, expansion, and contraction. Therapists, psychiatrists, and others sensitive to nonverbal communication use these postures along with other verbal cues to diagnose and understand persons whom they try to help.

Expressive gestures, facial expressions, and vocal cues also communicate inner states and emotion. Autistic gestures (interlaced fingers, closed fist, finger on the lips, nose rubbing, ear pulling, etc.) have been found to be related to states of inner conflict.[17] Other signals such as clearing the throat, closing the eyes, scratching, tapping the fingers or feet are related to specific attitudes and emotions.

The face (smiles, frowns, etc.) is often used to express affiliation, liking and approval, or disliking and disapproval. Nods of the head may be social reinforcers. A continued exchange of glances may indicate a willingness and desire to be involved in ongoing interaction, while avoidance of eye contact is often an indication of lack of interest and a desire to break away from interaction.[18]

Involuntary Nonverbal Messages Are Often of High Validity

When people interact, they rarely trust in words alone. They observe the shifting forward, withdrawing, frowning, smiling, speaking in strained or serious tones; the straightening of clothing; the manipulation of a cigarette, coffee cup, or pencil. Nonverbal cues are often used to determine the authenticity of verbal messages. Thus the blush or the frown is likely to be taken as more reliable than the accompanying verbal reassurances. When verbal and nonverbal cues conflict, the nonverbal story tends to be believed. Words can be chosen with care, but expressive nonverbal cues cannot be chosen; the body is not so easily governed. Further, because we are trained primarily in verbal communication and often disregard nonverbal communication, we are far less guarded in even our instrumental nonverbal behavior than in our verbal behavior; hence we may reveal information nonverbally that we carefully control or censure in our verbal messages.

When we are able to communicate honestly we do not send out contradictory messages. Some of the social games we play, however, force us to send verbal messages that are inconsistent with our true feelings revealed through nonverbal cues. We say, "Delighted that you could come," "We had a wonderful time," "Glad to meet you," and so forth, regardless of our feelings. When our nonverbal message contradicts the verbal, people tend to believe the nonverbal.[19] It has higher validity. Actions *do* speak louder than words. We rely on the nonverbal cues to gain our *real* impression of others. In one experiment, perfect strangers described their impressions of each other based on observing the visual nonverbal cues (posture, movement, facial expression, clothing, etc.) without verbal communication. Not only did each believe he or she could describe the other person after observation, but an analysis of their descriptions revealed exceptionally high agreement on many factors, including submissiveness, assurance, friendliness, psychological state, and extroversion.[20] The validity of nonverbal messages that express feelings, emotions, and relationships has been demonstrated by a number of scientists.[21] Labarre has noted that successful psychiatrists, artists, anthropologists, and teachers rely on the validity of nonverbal communication.[22]

Can you explain the three principles of nonverbal communication as you might observe them in the waiting room of a doctor's office?

Summary

In this chapter we have noted that nonverbal communication plays a significant role for us in exchanging meanings with other persons. We hope you will become more aware of the nonverbal messages sent by those with whom you communicate, more aware of your own nonverbal communication with others, and better able to send and receive messages clearly.

We have identified and described seven of the most important kinds of nonverbal messages. They include paralanguage; action language; object language; tactile, spatial, and time communication; and silence as a means of nonverbal communication. We should remember that paying attention to several cues from many or all of these sources, rather than one or two single cues, will allow us to be more accurate in knowing what the person is communicating to us.

We have emphasized that the nonverbal channels often seem to be especially effective channels for messages relating to feelings, attitudes, and interpersonal relationships. And we have emphasized that involuntary nonverbal messages are often of high validity. Because of their validity, they can help receivers to interpret the accompanying verbal messages more accurately.

Questions and Exercises for Review

1. How is nonverbal communication related to culture?
2. Can you name and explain seven types of nonverbal communication?
3. What are the differences between verbal and nonverbal communication?
4. Can you identify the three principles of nonverbal communication and explain each?

Key Terms and Phrases

nonverbal communication
paralanguage
vocal qualifiers
loudness or softness
pitch
tempo
vocal differentiators
voice quality
action language
expressive actions
purposive actions
facial expressions
movement
gestures
posture
object language
tactile communication
space
intimate distance
personal zone
social zone
public distance
territoriality
time
silence
analogical messages
digital messages

For Further Reading

Goffman, Erving. *Relations in Public.* New York: Harper & Row, 1972.
A popular treatment of public interaction through nonverbal communication.

Hall, Edward T. *The Silent Language.* New York: Doubleday & Co., 1973.
A popular treatment of the various types of nonverbal communication.

Harrison, R. P. *Beyond Words.* Englewood Cliffs, N.J.: Prentice-Hall, 1974.
A readable and interesting introduction to nonverbal communication.

Knapp, Mark L. *Essentials of Nonverbal Communication.* New York: Holt, Rinehart & Winston, 1980.
A thorough summary of theory and supporting research. Written for the college student.

Knapp, Mark L. et al. "Nonverbal Communication: Issues and Appraisal." *Human Communication Research* 4 (Spring 1978): 271–80.
Discusses the emergence of and the current state of affairs in the area commonly known as nonverbal communication.

Mehrabian, Albert. *Silent Messages.* Belmont, Calif.: Wadsworth Publishing Co., 1971.
An excellent overview of the use of nonverbal communication to express feelings and attitudes.

Montagu, Ashley. *Touching.* New York: Harper & Row Publishers, 1978.
An in-depth treatment and review of research of tactile communication.

Notes

1. Randall Harrison, "Nonverbal Communication: Exploration into Time, Space, Action, and Object," in *Dimensions in Communication,* eds. J. H. Campbell and H. W. Hepler (Belmont, Calif.: Wadsworth Publishing Co., 1965), 161.

2. A. Mehrabian and M. Wiener, "Non Immediacy Between Communication and Object of Communication in a Verbal Message," *Journal of Consulting Psychology* 30 (1966).

3. Jurgen Reusch and Weldon Kees, *Nonverbal Communication: Notes on Visual Perceptions of Human Relations* (Berkeley: The University of California Press, 1956).

4. James C. Coleman, "Facial Expressions of Emotion," *Psychological Monographs* 63 (1949): 1–36.

5. Gerald R. Nierenberg and Henry Calero, *How to Read a Person Like a Book* (New York: Pocket Books, Inc., 1973), 38.

6. Nierenberg and Calero, *How to Read a Person,* 46.

7. Reusch and Kees, *Nonverbal Communication.*

8. N. Compton, "Personal Attributes of Color and Design Preferences in Clothing Fabrics," *Journal of Psychology* 54 (1962): 191–95.

9. For further study of this phenomenon read John T. Molloy's *Dress for Success* (New York: Warner Books, 1976); and *Woman's Dress for Success Book* (New York: Warner Books, 1978).

10. Edward T. Hall, *The Silent Language* (New York: Doubleday & Co., Inc., 1959), 163.

11. Hall, *Silent Language,* 163–64.

12. Hall, *Silent Language,* 163–64.

13. A. F. Kinzel, "Body Buffer Zones in Violent Prisoners," *American Journal of Psychiatry* 127 (1970): 99–104.

14. Sigmund Freud, "Fragment of an Analysis of a Case of Hysteria" (1905), *Collected Papers,* vol. 3. (New York: Basic Books, 1959) 13–146; M. L. Knapp, *Nonverbal Communication in Human Interaction* (New York: Holt, Rinehart, & Winston, 1972).

15. Paul Watzlawick, Janet Helmick Beavin, and Don D. Jackson, *The Pragmatics of Human Communication* (New York: W. W. Norton & Company, Inc., 1967), 63.

16. See W. James, "A Study of the Expression of Bodily Posture," *Journal of General Psychology* 7 (1932): 405–36; F. Deutsch, "Analysis of Postural Behavior," *Psychoanalytic Quarterly* 16 (1947): 195–213; Howard M. Rosenfeld, "Instrumental Affiliative Functions of Facial and Gestural Expressions," *Journal of Personality and Social Psychology* 4 (1966): 65–72; and R. Taguiri, R. R. Blake, and J. S. Bruner, "Some Determinants of the Perception of Positive and Negative Feelings in Others," *Journal of Abnormal and Social Psychology* 48 (1953): 585–92.

17. See M. Krout, "An Experimental Attempt to Produce Unconscious Manual Symbolic Movements," *Journal of General Psychology* 51 (1954): 93–120; and S. Feldman, *Mannerisms of Speech and Gesture in Everyday Life* (New York: International Press, 1959).

18. Ralph Exline, David Gray, and Dorothy Schuette, "Visual Behavior in a Dyad as Affected by Interview Content and Sex of Respondent," *Journal of Personality and Social Psychology* 1 (1925): 201–9.

19. Albert Mehrabian, "Orientation Behaviors and Nonverbal Attitude Communication," *Journal of Communication* 17 (December 1967): 331.

20. R. Barker, "The Social Interrelations of Strangers and Acquaintances," *Sociometry* 5 (1942): 169–79.

21. See Charles Darwin, *The Expression of the Emotions in Man and Animals* (New York: D. Appleton & Company, 1862; reprint ed., Chicago: University of Chicago Press, 1965); Dr. Duchenne, *Micanisme de la Physionomie Humaine* (folio edition, 1862); Paul Ekman and Wallace V. Friesen, "Nonverbal Behavior in Psychotherapy Research," in *Research on Psychotherapy,* vol. 3, ed. J. Schlien (Washington, D.C.: American Psychological Association, 1967); and Clyde L. Rousey, *Diagnostic Implications of Speech Sounds* (Springfield, Ill.: Charles C. Thomas, Publisher, 1965).

22. Weston Labarre, "The Cultural Basis of Emotions and Gestures," *Journal of Personality* 16 (1947): 64, 65.

Interpersonal Communication

This unit focuses on interpersonal communication. As Part 1 was concerned with elements within the individual (perception, symbolization, information storage and recall, language, thinking, and self-concept), so Part 2 is concerned with elements between individuals; that is, with elements that cannot exist with only one person but exist only when two or more are involved in communicating.

Although there are many such elements that we might study, we have selected five of the most common and important to consider in this chapter. The five major topic areas are (1) interpersonal attraction (affection versus alienation and hostility); (2) interpersonal trust and interpersonal acceptance of the other person (supportiveness versus suspicion and defensiveness); (3) role; (4) control and the sharing of power; and (5) feedback.

Chapters 7 and 8 are concerned with two specific types of interpersonal communication—dyadic communication and small-group communication. The major components of interpersonal communication discussed in chapter 6 are applied in these two chapters.

Focus

Interpersonal Attraction and Affection versus Alienation and Hostility

Factors Related to Interpersonal Attraction and Affection

Accidental Happenings
Unjust Treatment
Rewards
Stress
Social Isolation
Proximity
Homophily and Heterophily

Factors Related to Alienation

Being Ignored
Anomia

Factors Related to Hostility

Withdrawal
Adjustive Techniques

Interpersonal Trust and Acceptance (Supportiveness versus Suspicion and Defensiveness)

Factors Related to Trust and Acceptance

Characteristics within One's Self
Characteristics, Reputation, and Intentions of the Other Person
Nature and Quality of Communication
Presence of a Third Person

Factors Related to Suspicion and Defensiveness

Evaluation versus Description
Control versus Problem Orientation
Deceptive Strategy versus Spontaneity or Openness
Neutrality versus Empathy
Superiority versus Equality
Certainty versus Provisionalism

Influencing the Development of Trust

Role as a Factor in Interpersonal Communication

Role Expectations
Appropriate and Inappropriate Roles
Assigned and Assumed Roles
Stereotyped Roles

Power as a Factor in Interpersonal Communication

Definition and Perspectives
Sources of Power
Objectives for Using Power

Feedback

Types of Feedback

Internal or External
Positive or Negative
Direct or Indirect
Immediate or Delayed
Verbal or Nonverbal

Using Feedback Effectively—Guidelines

6 Basic Components in Building Relationships

The major components of interpersonal communication with which we are concerned in this chapter are (1) interpersonal attraction and affection versus alienation and hostility; (2) interpersonal acceptance of the other person, that is, trust and supportiveness versus suspicion and defensiveness; (3) interpersonal control, that is, the sharing of power with another; (4) role playing and expectations; and (5) feedback. These components are present in dyadic and small-group communication, in formal and informal communication, and in instrumental and social communication. How these components operate and how you can acquire skills that relate to them are the topics of discussion in this chapter.

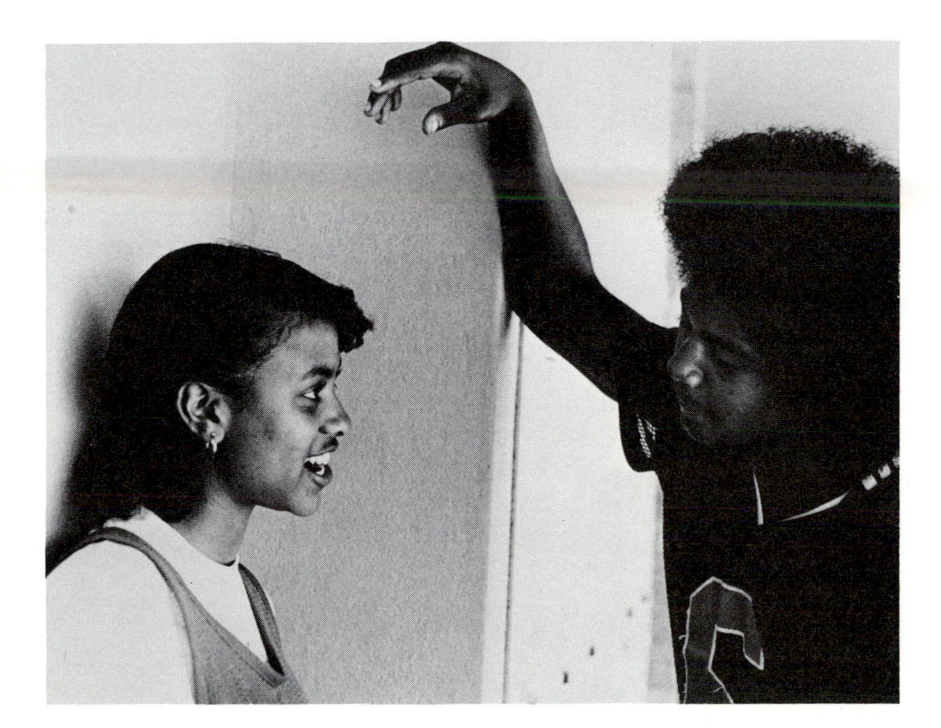

Interpersonal communication occurs when two or more persons are involved in an interaction that allows all participants to send overt verbal messages. Conversations, interviews, committee meetings, telephone conversations, and group discussions are examples of interpersonal communication situations. In public communication, as contrasted to interpersonal, there is an audience, which is primarily a listening group and does not perform in the medium that the speaker uses. Interpersonal communication tends to occur in a "private setting," while public communication occurs more often in a "public setting." The continual planned nature of discourse in public settings contrasts sharply with the episodic, impulsive, and fragmentary character of interpersonal interaction; and the impersonality of public communication situations, the rigid control of channels, the calculated use of message cues, and the restrictions on communication roles create a highly structured social situation in which there is an expectation of unidirectional influence.

In this section we are concerned with some of the factors that appear to be extremely important in face-to-face communication. The concepts discussed in Part 1 should be kept in mind as we move to another level of communication, from intrapersonal to interpersonal communication. In this chapter we investigate some general factors that apply to *all* interpersonal communication situations and that influence the outcomes of interpersonal communication significantly.

The components of interpersonal communication are best identified by Schutz's paradigm of interpersonal communication effectiveness.[1] From this paradigm Schutz developed a test to measure interpersonal communication effectiveness. The test is called FIRO-B. This test is widely used to measure interpersonal communication. Hundreds of colleges and universities have used this test in studies, theses, and dissertations in departments or schools of communication, psychology, education, and business. Businesses and industries also use the test widely. FIRO-B is clearly the most widely accepted identifier of what constitutes effective interpersonal communication.

The three major factors in interpersonal communication represented in FIRO-B are affection, inclusion, and control. To these three factors we have added two more variables that have been shown to be related to interpersonal communication effectiveness—role-expectations and feedback.

Interpersonal Attraction and Affection versus Alienation and Hostility

The first component we consider is affection. By affection we mean "liking," positive feelings toward or interpersonal attraction. Opposites of affection and attraction are alienation, hostility, dislike, and even anger. Interpersonal attraction exerts a powerful influence on interpersonal communication. When there are strong, positive relationships between persons, a high probability exists that communication between them will be successful; but when there is a strong dislike between persons, communication will be severely handicapped.

When we talk of **interpersonal attraction** and **affection** we are referring to the positive attitudes persons share, the moving toward, or the liking one person has for another. Not all of the determinants of our liking for another person lie within the other person; some of the causes lie within ourselves. Although the characteristics and behavior of another person play an important role in determining whether we find that person attractive, researchers have found that liking does often lie in the eye of the beholder. Therefore, our consideration of interpersonal attraction and affection includes qualities of the attracted as well as of the attractor.

Factors Related to Interpersonal Attraction and Affection

Accidental Happenings

Accidental happenings are an important element in interpersonal attraction. They might better be termed "good" happenings and "bad" happenings. Good happenings cause us to like the person, but bad happenings cause us to draw away from that person. Even when the thing that happens to another is beyond that individual's control, it can affect our attitude toward the person. There is evidence that we tend to like those who have succeeded (everybody likes a winner) and dislike those who have failed. One explanation of this phenomenon is that we want to believe that people get what they deserve, that people are responsible for their own fate and that the world is a predictable place. Walter's research reveals that persons who hear about an accident, for example, want to blame someone (preferably the victim) for the accident. Moreover, his research shows that the desire to hold the victim responsible increases proportionately with the severity of the accident.[2]

Good happenings to another can cause us to like that person; everyone loves a winner.

A dramatic illustration of this phenomenon occurred in the flooded Wabash River at Lafayette, Indiana. Five men left Logansport in two small boats. The boat with three men in it ran out of gas, and began to take on water. In the attempt to transfer one of the men to the other boat, both boats were upset, dumping all five men into the 46° flood waters. Although people were on the scene of the accident almost immediately, only two of the men were saved. It was a terrible tragedy, but more shocking to many was the reaction of some persons with whom we talked. They blamed the victims for errors in judgment (standing in a boat, being out on a flooded river, overloading a boat and so on). Lerner has conducted several experiments indicating that people convince themselves that chance occurrences to others are deserved.[3] So it is that persons who win, who are successful, and to whom good things happen are valued higher and admired more than persons who lose, who fail, and who have suffered unfortunate events.

Unjust Treatment

A second factor in interpersonal attraction has to do with **unjust treatment** of one by another and the effect produced by that treatment. Tacitus stated centuries ago: "It is a principle of human nature to hate those whom you have injured." Several recent experiments have demonstrated that we tend to change our attitudes toward another so that our attitudes are consistent with our behavior toward that person. If we harm another, we tend to develop a dislike for the person harmed; and if we do a favor for another, we tend to increase our liking for the other.

Rewards

Rewards may also be related to attraction. We like those who reward us and dislike those who punish us. Several researchers have suggested that interpersonal relationships always cost us something along with giving us something, and that liking is conditioned by comparing the cost to the reward (reward − cost = profit). If the relationship is profitable—if mutually satisfying rewards are obtained—interpersonal attraction is high. When someone praises us, our liking for that individual increases. If we find interpersonal communication with a person to be socially rewarding, enjoyable, or exciting, we will experience greater attraction to that person. Conversely, if we make no effort to enjoy talking with others, we should not be surprised that we are not liked by others. Again, we see the direct relationship between being likable and interpersonal communication. By improving our skills in interpersonal communication, we can discover and be discovered by another, and a mutually satisfying and rewarding situation can be created.

Stress

Stress is another factor related to interpersonal attraction. There is now considerable evidence indicating that persons under stress prefer to be with those who are in the same situation or with whom they have had significant previous interaction. These persons are often in a position to comfort and reassure each other. The mere presence of others appears to produce psychological and physiological responses helpful in reducing anxiety. Combat studies of bomber crews have shown that the presence of others reduces the anxiety created by severe battle stress.[4] Anxiety and stress motivate us to seek and to be attracted to others.

Social Isolation

Isolation can create a powerful desire for interpersonal contact and is a strong facilitator of interpersonal attraction. We are social creatures, and **social isolation** for any prolonged period of time is a painful experience. The autobiographical reports of criminals in solitary confinement, religious hermits, prisoners of war, and castaways clearly reveal that isolation is devastating. We can, through sheer physical presence, provide a reward to another who is lonely or isolated.

Social isolation is a painful experience.

Proximity

Proximity has been shown to influence one's choice of friends. Other things being equal, the finding is that the closer two individuals are to one another geographically the more likely it is that they will be attracted to each other. Studies supporting this finding are numerous and consistent. They have shown that proximity is directly related to friendship formation, to mate selection, and to a decrease in prejudice. For example, increased contact between whites and blacks results in a reduction of prejudice, whether the contact is on the job, in an integrated housing project, in a university classroom, or on a police force.

In classrooms, apartment houses, college dormitories, housing projects, and similar situations, the findings of numerous studies are consistent—proximity is directly related to liking. Persons in closer proximity to others tend to interact more, form social bonds more quickly, and experience greater attraction and liking. Conversely, persons on boundaries, or isolated from others, tend to experience less interaction and less popularity. The implication of these findings ought to be clear. Liking and attraction come more easily as we are in closer proximity to others, and it is more difficult to establish those relationships when we are isolated from others. If you find it a little difficult to get acquainted with others or to talk with others, you should place yourself in the "middle of the action" when you can. Certainly, going into the corner or far away from people will only serve to intensify your problem.

Studies have also indicated that liking and proximity tend to adjust themselves so that they go together; that is, as liking increases, persons come into closer proximity. As an example, perhaps you or someone you know has moved from one floor to another in your dormitory, or from one house to another so as to be nearer to a special person.

Proximity: a factor in interpersonal attraction.

Homophily is a strong similarity of attitudes, interests, values and personality.

Proximity is not the "whole story" of course, but other things being equal, proximity can determine interpersonal attraction. It is clear that proximity is a powerful influence in bringing about liking, and liking is related directly to interpersonal communication.

Homophily and Heterophily

Homophily refers to the degree of similarity of attributes of two persons. **Heterophily,** its opposite, is the degree to which two persons are unlike. Persons may be alike or opposite in a number of areas—education, socioeconomic status, age, religion, politics, values, and attitudes. Since homophily and heterophily can include all attributes—and since any two individuals have thousands of attributes—it is probable that any two persons are both homophilous and heterophilous at the same time. They may enjoy the same kind of vocation but have opposite political or religious preferences, for example. Nevertheless, the greater the degree of homophily between two persons, the greater the likelihood of strong interpersonal attraction.

The relationship of homophily to communication is that of interpersonal attraction to communication; that is, the greater the homophily, the more effective the communication. Of course, if there were *total homophily* (an impossible situation, we might note) then the two persons would be exactly alike and in complete agreement, and there would be nothing to talk about. Or, if two persons were *totally heterophilous,* they would lack the common vocabulary and experiences necessary to communicate with each other. Experts say the best homophily-heterophily situation is one in which there is slight dissimilarity but high overall likeness.[5] In this situation, there will be common ground and mutual interpersonal attraction—factors that facilitate dynamic, cooperative interpersonal communication.

Figure 6.1 Model of Heider's P-O-X balance theory.

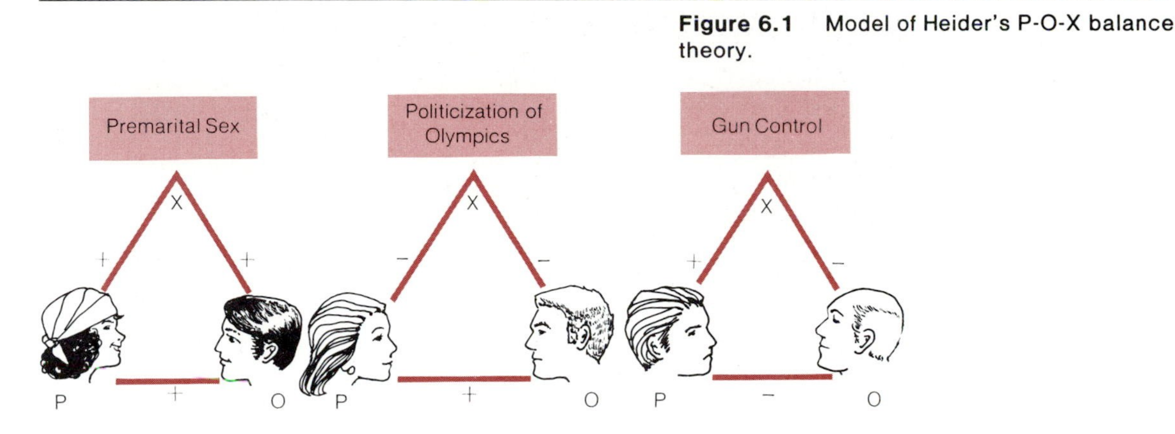

Among the attributes that seem to be quite important in terms of homophily or heterophily are attitudes. We do not know whether persons are attracted to each other because they have similar attitudes and beliefs or whether, as a result of their attraction and association, they come to develop similar attitudes and beliefs. Perhaps it is some of both. We do know, however, that there is a tendency to make attitudes toward objects and ideas congruent with attitudes toward the other person. One explanation of this phenomenon has been given by Heider.[6] His **P-O-X balance theory** explains how the orientation held by each person toward the other is related, in a balanced way, to the orientation each holds toward the object of communication. In figure 6.1, "P" is talking to "O" about "X," an object of communication. The symbol "+" indicates a positive attitude toward the object of communication or a liking for the other person, and "−" indicates a negative attitude toward the object of communication or a dislike of the other person. Figure 6.1 illustrates three "balanced situations." If the relationship between P and O is positive (+) and P has a positive attitude (+) toward capital punishment (X), then O will probably have a positive attitude toward capital punishment, too (left); or if the persons have a positive relationship and one of them has a negative attitude toward the object, then the other will probably have a negative attitude toward the object also (center); or if the relationship between P and O is negative and P has a positive evaluation of X, then P assumes that O has a negative evaluation of X (right). The theory suggests that there is a tendency for people who like each other to agree on likes and dislikes and for people who dislike each other to disagree.

Heider's balance theory recognizes that attitudes between people as well as their attitudes toward common objects are important factors in interpersonal communication; it also recognizes that the two factors are interrelated.

However, unbalanced orientations do occur, and they would include situations such as those illustrated in figure 6.2. The model at the left in figure 6.2 shows two persons who relate positively to each other (P and O); P has a

Figure 6.2 Examples of unbalanced orientations.

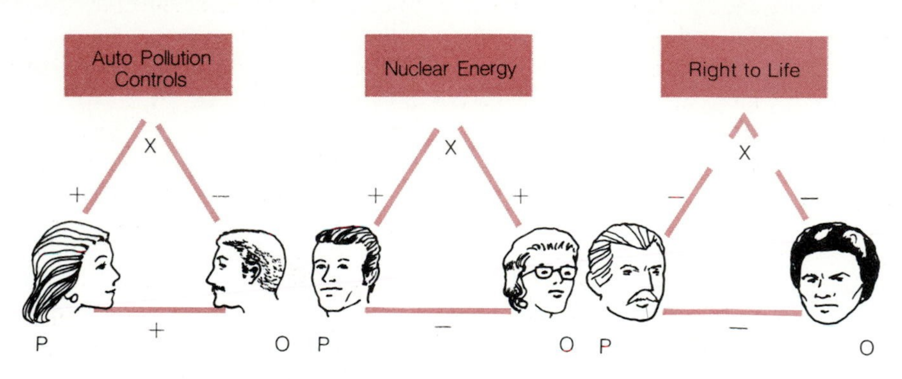

positive attitude toward X (auto pollution controls) while O does not. The middle illustration, as well as the one on the right, shows persons who do not like one another but have the same attitude toward the topic of conversation. In all three examples, things are not the way they are "supposed to be" as far as the people involved are concerned. Through communication, persons attracted to each other tend to bring their attitude and belief systems into balance, to preserve states of balance, or to resolve states of imbalance. For example, one couple had opposite orientations toward bowling. She liked to bowl, but he did not. Interestingly enough, today he too enjoys bowling and participates in a bowling league. A situation of imbalance was turned into one of balance.

Most of us have had the experience of hearing someone we liked very much say something with which we could not agree. Maybe your friend spoke out for the Equal Rights Amendment (ERA), while you were against it. You probably experienced what is called *dissonance*—a state of imbalance. What feelings were created in you, and what did you do or think to resolve the situation for yourself? You may have found it very difficult to maintain your previous attitudes toward both that person and the ERA. In a case like this, research findings indicate that we cannot maintain our previous attitudes exactly as they were since they would be in a state of imbalance. In the preceding example, it would be possible for you to change your attitude toward your friend or you could change your attitude toward the ERA. Another option is to get your friend to reconsider his or her orientation toward the ERA, or, other options are to forget it, repress it, or remember to avoid bringing this subject up when talking with your friend. In some instances, we may have learned indirectly of a friend's attitude toward an object of communication; or by inference from various related cues, we may suspect that our friend has an attitude opposite to ours on some topic, and we may purposely avoid the topic in such situations.

Similarity of attitudes, values, interests, personality, and other attributes determines the degree of homophily. Dissimilarity of attributes determines the degree of heterophily. Interpersonal attraction and, subsequently, interpersonal communication, thrive on homophily. What can you do about a situation in which your relationship with another is heterophilous? You can increase attraction and homophily by frequent interaction. You can develop empathy so as to project yourself into the other person's role and come to understand that person better. You can be openly supportive, nonmanipulative (development of trust factors that we will discuss next), and you can pay more attention to feedback (another topic to be discussed in this chapter).

All of these factors (accidental happenings, treatment of each other, rewards, stress, isolation, proximity, and homophily/heterophily) affect interpersonal attraction and affection. Although some of these factors are outside our control, we can work toward creating a relationship of mutual attraction and affection by controlling those we can.

Compare yourself and a recent acquaintance in terms of homophily and heterophily.

Factors Related to Alienation

Not all relationships are mutually attractive and filled with affection. Sometimes alienation and hostility emerge.

Alienation refers to being estranged or withdrawn from other persons. An alienated person holds negative attitudes toward other persons and has a feeling of "aloneness." Alienation does not mean simple disagreement with another person. Disagreeing with another is communication, but alienation is nonparticipation. It is withdrawing from purposeful interaction. It is being apart from others. Alienation cannot occur between a person and someone the person has never known. Rather, it is a withdrawing from a relationship—an estrangement. It can happen between one person and another, or between a person and a group (family, for example). The alienation in which we are most interested here is that between two persons—that which results in the breakdown of a relationship or changes a positive relationship into a negative one. There are at least two types of alienation—one caused by a person or persons who ignores the one becoming alienated, and the second type caused by the one becoming alienated simply avoiding or refusing communication.

Being Ignored

Being ignored, being denied access to another person, is a dominant causal factor of alienation. Often such alienation is partial; that is, one feels denied the right to communicate with the other on certain topics—not on all topics. Sometimes one has been made to understand that he or she cannot communicate at certain times or under certain conditions. If one is denied the opportunity to communicate on certain topics or at certain times, then withdrawl from the relationship is a natural consequence. Thus alienation can be the result of being denied or of being ignored. If this happens often enough and with many persons with whom one normally interacts, then anomia-alienation sets in.

Anomia

Anomia-alienation, the second type of alienation, is a general unwillingness, avoidance, or refusal to communicate. One can easily understand how such alienation works against effective interpersonal communication. Besides the obvious—the nonoccurrence of effective communication—this type of alienation is counterproductive to trust, supportiveness, self-disclosure, helpfulness to others, the enhancing of one's self-concept, and virtually all of the other variables related to interpersonal communication that we have discussed in this text. This aspect of alienation—anomia-alienation—has been shown to severely affect other variables directly related to interpersonal communication.

Can you explain why some people sometimes avoid communication?

According to many writers today, alienation is quite widespread. So widespread, in fact, that even today's comics have altered their heroes to identify with their readers. No longer are heroes necessarily the protectors of virtue and the objects of praise and adulation. Today's heroes are pelted with bottles, insulted, and put down. The superhero of yesteryear is today's antihero. Howe wrote:

> . . . the $50-million-a-year comic book industry is changing. No longer do heroes fly around zapping just any old lawbreaker. The new hero frets over social problems, like pollution, slum control and civil rights, and he often suffers from identity crises. . . .Even Superman is in for a change. In future issues he will come to feel that he is a stranger in an imperfect world, his editors say. Surveying ant-like hordes of human beings from a skyscraper, he muses in one forthcoming issue. "For the first time in many years, I feel that I'm alone."[7]

Similarly, mass communication—television in particular—can foster alienation. The average citizen is aware of or is knowledgeable of dozens of TV personalities who come smiling into the family living room, but the TV personality is seldom "known."

Factors Related to Hostility

Out of competitiveness, mistrust, frustration, and fear comes anger; and from anger comes **hostility.** Anger is warm and immediate, while hostility is cold and calculated. When we become aware of hostility in another person—hostility directed toward us—most of us respond in kind or at least with a potential for hostility. Further, the blocking of any goal-directed behavior may arouse hostile and aggressive tendencies that are reflected in interpersonal communication. Statements indicating a wish or intention to commit a destructive act, statements attributing undesirable qualities or unfavorable characteristics to another person, and statements denying another person desirable qualities or favorable characteristics are examples of direct hostile communication. Hostility can take any number of forms: one-upmanship, squelching, or the nasty comment disguised as a joke. If you can recall hearing any of these forms of hostile communication in the last few days, you will note how very calculated they were. Angry remarks, on the other hand, are hot, immediate, directed specifically to the person, and a call for heavy involvement. The hostile person is easily identified by the "coolness" that accompanies the cutting remarks.

Withdrawal

One of the major difficulties in handling hostility in interpersonal communication lies in providing opportunities for the person to release hostility. Unless some provision is made for their release, hostile feelings tend to be perpetuated so that the ultimate result is a total breakdown in communication. The problem is that as hostility against us increases, we tend toward **withdrawal,** or leaving the scene; thus the opportunity for reducing this hostility is lost.

Adjustive Techniques

If we do not withdraw from the communication situation, some **adjustive techniques** for reducing hostility may be available. In primitive times hostile and aggressive feelings led to physical attack. People today disapprove of fighting as a means of handling hostility, although apparently there is still a social norm of physical attack in the lower socioeconomic strata. This norm is not generally characteristic of other classes. For the most part, **physical aggression** as an adjustive technique is socially and legally rejected. There are other adjustive techniques available, however, including verbal aggression, rationalization, and negativism.

The fact that physical aggression is banned does not mean that acts of aggression are not available as a release for hostile feelings. Aggression can take the verbal form. Consider the following: He: "Where have you been?" She: "Well, I got here as soon as I could." He: "Yeah? You didn't even leave until it was time to be here! Really care, don't you?" She: "What's caring got to do with it? I told you I was busy." **Verbal aggression,** like hostility, is avoided by the good communicator. Nevertheless, when hostility occurs and the individual resorts to verbal aggression, you, as a knowledgeable communicator, can understand that the verbal aggression is an adjustive behavior—an outlet for hostility. Further, you also know that the verbal aggression can have a cathartic, cleansing effect; it can result in reduced hostility. Your understanding of this process can permit you to help in the solution of the problem rather than "feed the fire" that leads to further communication breakdown.

When people find that they cannot achieve desired goals, they become frustrated and hostile. Sometimes they restructure the situation so that they desire a different goal. In other words, if a goal is blocked, we adjust to the situation by rationalizing—by speaking of the unattainable goal as an undesirable one. Such a public commitment of our thinking tends to validate our inferences. *By verbalizing the change of goals* we convince ourselves that we are right; those statements that we *want* and *need* to believe actually come to be believed. This is the process of **rationalization**—one of several processes whereby we adjust to feelings of frustration, hostility, and aggression.

Although rationalization may allow us to reduce tensions and to allay hostility, it carries some dangers. We can do two things related to rationalization that will improve our communication effectiveness: (1) if we observe another engaged in rationalization, we can be wary of accepting the evaluations that are made; and (2) we can learn to identify our own rationalizations so that we break the habit of saying things we later regret.

Another way to react to hostility is to reject all or any part of proposals made. Some persons assume a general attitude of hostility and mistrust. They often give negative responses to almost all messages because that kind of response has become habitual. Such behavior indicates a general attitude of rigidity and fear of any new idea. There is some indication that extreme rigidity and **negativism** are associated with low intelligence, low ability in role playing, and high generalized anxiety. Most of us, of course, react negatively once in a while because of a temporary mood or because the specific topic arouses fear. Sometimes a frozen evaluation underlies such fear. We need to identify our frozen evaluations continually, and we need to update and constantly adjust our evaluations of the world about us.

Interpersonal Trust and Acceptance (Supportiveness versus Suspicion and Defensiveness)

As attraction, affection, and hostility exist only in relation to another person, so trust, supportiveness, suspicion, and defensiveness also exist only in relation to another person.

The importance of acceptance of the other person in interpersonal relations has been emphasized in the teachings of philosophers and religious leaders for hundreds of years. This characteristic of trust has received renewed attention in our lifetimes.

Little progress can be made in interpersonal communication unless there is a climate of trust and acceptance. From the first meeting (the acquaintanceship process) through ongoing relationships, the basic factor involved in communication is the ability of the communicators to accept each other. The establishment of such a climate is necessary to effective communication. Once a trusting climate has been created, fears of rejection, betrayal, and harm disappear and feelings of supportiveness, acceptance, openness, and safety emerge. The absence of such supportiveness ultimately fosters an atmosphere of suspicion and defensiveness that is dangerously destructive in interpersonal communication.

Trust has been defined as "reliance upon the behavior of a person in order to achieve a desired objective."[8] This means that you are in a situation in which the behavior of the other person can help you or hurt you in terms of your needs and goals. You run that risk when trusting another. The trusting and accepting person is confident that the other will behave in such a way that beneficial consequences will result.

Factors Related to Trust and Acceptance

Why does one trust? The reasons for trusting seem to lie in two areas—within the person and within the situation.

Characteristics within One's Self

Any person possesses a number of characteristics, determined by either genetics or experience, that influence behavior in general and psychological orientations, such as trust and acceptance. If one has developed a concept of self that is one of merited high esteem, then trusting and accepting seem to be facilitated. According to Deutsch, *self-esteem* and *authoritarianism* are the two intrapersonal factors most related to trust.[9] Authoritarianism is negatively related to trusting and accepting (authoritarian persons tend to be more suspicious and defensive than nonauthoritarians). Self-esteem is related positively to trusting (persons of high self-esteem tend to be more trusting and supportive than persons of low self-esteem).

In addition to these intrapersonal factors, there are at least three situational factors, identified by Deutsch, that appear to be related to trust.[10] They are (1) characteristics and intentions of the other person, (2) the nature and quality of the interpersonal communication, and (3) the presence or influence of a third person. These situational factors probably interact with the intrapersonal factors to determine the degree of trust. The intrapersonal factors probably give one an inclination to respond defensively or supportively, or to trust or not trust, but the specific situation itself may trigger the response and influence the intensity of the response. Many of us can become quite defensive or quite supportive given certain situational factors. You yourself may have experienced surprise at finding yourself so defensive in some specific incident; something about the situation seemed to exert strong pressure toward defensiveness.

Characteristics, Reputation, and Intentions of the Other Person

Some situations possess characteristics that invite defensiveness, while other situations facilitate trust. One factor in such situations is the other person, including his or her **characteristics, reputation, and intentions.**

The first factor in trust is the other person's expertise. If the other person is an expert on the topic being discussed, you will have confidence in him or her and be more trusting.

A second factor in trust is the other person's reliability and reputation. Reliability may be perceived as dependability, predictability, honesty, or consistency; but your trust is based upon the other's reputation for these qualities, rather than his or her possession of them. When the other person's reputation is perceived as high, you are encouraged to be more trusting.

Finally, the intentions of the other person have an effect upon trust. Each person engaged in communication has his or her own goals. The other's intentions are perceived, generally, as being either congruent with or contradictory to one's own intentions. As congruent intentions or goals are evidenced, trust is engendered. Congruent goals foster cooperative behavior. Competitive goals foster competitive behavior.

Interpersonal trust is related to the persons involved and the situation.

Brooks conducted a study in which forty-five pairs of persons were asked to solve problems by communicating under different goal relationships.[11] One of the three goal relationships established for each pair was competitive in that one person could win only if the other lost; the second was congruent in that the two persons could win only if both cooperated and aided one another; and the third was one of independent goals—either individual could win or lose regardless of the cooperation or participation of the other. The results indicated that when the goals were congruent, cooperative behavior did follow. The efficiency of problem solving was higher in the **congruent goal** situations than in either the **competitive goal** situation or the **independent goal** situation. The amount of communication was highest in the congruent goal situation, as was honesty of communication. The study indicates that goal relationships are related to honesty, amount of communication, and efficiency in communication. Although the experiment was a game situation, its findings are in agreement with other studies and confirm that the goal relationship is an important factor in the creation of trust.

One example of a competitive goal situation is the **"prisoner's dilemma"**—a communication simulation game—which the following situation illustrates.

Two suspects are taken into custody and separated. The district attorney is certain that they are guilty of a specific crime but he does not have adequate evidence to convict them. His strategy, then, is to point out to each prisoner the alternatives open to him, that is, to confess to the crime or not to confess. The district attorney points out that if he confesses and the other prisoner does not, then the confessor will receive lenient treatment for turning state's evidence, whereas the latter will get "the book" thrown at him. Shall he confess and guarantee his getting minor punishment, or shall he run the risk of full punishment because his partner confesses? If neither would confess perhaps neither could be found guilty.

The prisoner's dilemma—the competitive goal situation—was used to gain confessions from Hickock and Smith in the Clutter family murder case, a multiple murder made infamous by Truman Capote's *In Cold Blood.* Alvin Dewey, Kansas Bureau of Investigation agent and former FBI agent, and three FBI agents used the competitive goal situation in the interrogation of Richard Hickok and Perry Smith. Capote relates in his book, which is based upon interviews with Hickok and Smith, that each prisoner feared his partner would confess and escape blame; this fear grew and grew. Hickok and Smith were held separately from the outset. Perry Smith, according to Capote, wanted to "talk to Dick, was fearful that Dick's guts were unreliable, that he panicked too easily; that he'd give an arm, a leg to talk to Dick for just five minutes."[12] And Dick was equally eager to converse with Perry. "Perry, if he lost his nerve and let fly! . . . I should have silenced Perry on a mountain road in Mexico!"[13] In the end, after hours of interrogation and the repetition of alibis, Richard Hickok admitted they had carried out the whole thing, but that Perry Smith was guilty of all four murders. Only after hours of talk with Perry, in which parts of Hickock's tape-recorded confession were repeated, was Smith convinced that his partner had turned on him. Then Smith unloaded all the gory details of the multiple murders. The competitive goal situation—the prisoner's dilemma—had worked for the investigators. It destroyed Smith and Hickock's climate of trust.

It is clear from numerous research studies and from actual incidents that goal relationships are related to cooperative and competitive strategies; and it is also quite clear that cooperation versus competition is a powerful element in fostering or destroying trust. Any of these factors in the other person—goals or intentions, reputation or reliability, expertise—are situational factors that relate directly to trust or suspicion.

Nature and Quality of Communication

A second situational factor that can affect trust is the **nature and quality** of the communication between the persons involved in the encounter. When the communication is open, and when intentions and goals are identified, trust is encouraged. For example, when you can talk freely, rather than guardedly, with a person because that person is a close friend, trust grows and interpersonal communication with that person is enhanced. If, however, one you thought was a friend, or one with whom you are building a friendship, is not open in talking with you and his or her intentions seem to be unclear and hidden, then trust is weakened and the quality of communication with that person tends to deteriorate.

Presence of a Third Person

Finally, a third situational factor related to trust is the **presence of a third person,** or the knowledge that the communication will be given to a third person. **Trust is greater if there is no third party involved!**

Factors Related to Suspicion and Defensiveness

Defensive communication is the opposite of trusting communication. For many people, defensiveness is the overriding psychological orientation taken toward interpersonal communication. The basic reason for defensive communication lies, probably, in the unfulfilled interpersonal needs of an individual. As discussed in chapter 1, we communicate in order to survive—in order to satisfy our needs, needs that go far beyond food and shelter. Communication is our primary vehicle for satisfying these needs. Consequently, as our communication is successful in helping us, we develop confidence in our communication; we view communication positively; and we develop positive relationships with others. (This phenomenon has been discussed from another perspective—that of self-concept development as it was discussed in chapter 3.)

However, when we are not able to meet our needs through communication with others, we may lose confidence in our coping ability and become less confident of others, even to the point of becoming defensive and guarded in our interpersonal communication. Such behavior, of course, can become counterproductive—the more defensive we become, the less effective our communication becomes. We become anxious about getting along in the world, and a general feeling of anxiety results. (This concept of anxiety was discussed in chapter 3 when we considered communication apprehension.) Unresolved anxiety then leads to more defensive tactics in interacting with others. Fear, anxiety, doubt—these feed defensive communication behavior. You have probably observed defensive communication in others: the fear in their posture, eyes, facial expressions, and body movement; their withdrawal behavior—turning away from you, avoiding eye contact, shifting their weight backwards, stepping backwards, or hesitating verbally.

Not only is defensive communication the result of unmet interpersonal needs and the absence of factors conducive to trust, but it can be influenced by factors outside oneself as well. Among the most powerful outside factors are the communication behaviors of the other person. In other words, it is possible for some of your communication behaviors to stimulate defensiveness in the other person, just as some of your communication behavior might stimulate trust. Unless we understand that certain communication behaviors tend to elicit defensiveness, we may find ourselves in situations in which the other person becomes defensive without our understanding why. Gibb has identified both communication behaviors that tend to stimulate defensiveness and those associated with a supportive climate and subsequent reduction in defensiveness. There are six pairs of behaviors in Gibb's category system.[14] Let us consider each pair of behaviors in greater detail.

Evaluation versus Description

It appears that when one is *evaluative* of another person, there is a tendency for the other person to become anxious and defensive. Through verbal or nonverbal codes we communicate evaluation of another. Each of us, of course, makes judgments about and forms attitudes toward others; but we can attempt to reduce the number of blunt and strong evaluative messages we send others—messages such as "That's dumb!" "That's not a workable plan," or "You've not yet dropped that silly idea?"

We ought to be *descriptive* rather than evaluative if we want to be supportive. When we complain about another, we know that the other person is likely to become fearful and defensive. Knowing that, we are foolish to complain to others about themselves, to call attention to their weaknesses, to tell them how bad they are, or to put them down. It should not be surprising that children who are subjected only to evaluative communication by their parents become anxious and defensive; or that a spouse constantly "put down" by the mate acquires defensive communication strategies rather than trusting and supportive ones. Gibb has observed that as we communicate more descriptively, defensiveness decreases. If we can remove the evaluative labels, we will foster supporting climates.

Rather than communicating negative evaluations to another by either verbal or nonverbal means (you can shake your head, roll your eyes, or in other nonverbal ways communicate negative evaluations to another), you should learn to be descriptive. Instead of saying, "You're crazy!" you could say, "I disagree with that idea," or "That idea has one problem I'd like to talk about." "You're all confused" can be replaced with "I don't understand."

Control versus Problem Orientation

This set of behaviors relates to your intentions. If your intentions are to *control* the other person—to change the other person's mind, to get the other to do something, or in some way to influence the other—the other person will be come defensive. We resent being dominated by another person. We want to be responsible for ourselves and not controlled by others. When another tries to control us, we resist—we become defensive. If the other person wants to make our decisions for us, it means that person believes we are ignorant, unwise, uninformed, or in some way inadequate to make our own decisions.

On the other hand, when the other person cooperates on our mutual problem, works with us, respects our abilities to work on the problem, we respond positively. We see that *problem-oriented* behavior as supportive and helpful. That behavior, consequently, engenders trust rather than defensiveness.

Deceptive Strategy versus Spontaneity or Openness

When we perceive the other person as having a hidden plan, we become defensive. Hidden motives and *strategies* arouse suspicions. Gibb has found from his analyses of training group sessions that persons often do perceive the strategies of their colleagues,[15] and when they do, they become defensive. On the other hand, behavior that appears to be free of deception and that is *spontaneous, or open,* tends to reduce defensiveness.

Neutrality versus Empathy

The fourth set of behaviors related to suspicion and trust is *neutrality* and *empathy*. Neutrality often appears to be the same as disinterest. It is frequently interpreted as a lack of concern. Communication with "low affect," as Gibb calls it, sometimes communicates "not caring"; and if the other does not care about us, we tend to become more guarded. If, however, one communicates warmth and caring, trust is encouraged. Empathy indicates caring and engenders a climate of trust. An honest statement of "I understand how you feel" can go a long way in establishing trust and supportiveness.

Superiority versus Equality

The communication of *superiority* in wealth, power, social position, intellectual ability, or in any other way arouses defensiveness in the receiver. The communication of *equality* reduces defensive behavior. True or absolute equality seldom exists, but the person who values others, respects them, and likes them does not see the differences as important. Consequently, that person does not communicate superiority, but respect and admiration—communicates equality. Such messages tend to elicit trust from the receiver.

Certainty versus Provisionalism

The final set of behaviors identified by Gibb are certainty and provisionalism. *Certainty* can be equated with dogmatism, and *provisionalism* can be roughly equated with flexibility and openness.

As the following example shows, nonsupportive behaviors—evaluation, control, strategy, neutrality, superiority, and certainty—on the part of one communicator cause defensiveness in the other. Supportive behaviors—description, problem orientations, spontaneity, empathy, equality, and provisionalism—engender trust. Learning to avoid communication behavior that destroys trust and to respond in ways that facilitate trust are good steps toward improving your interpersonal communication skills.

Can you contrast your supportive and defensive communication behaviors?

Influencing the Development of Trust and Reducing Defensiveness

Now that we have identified the factors conducive to trust or defensiveness, we need to learn how to apply those factors to improve our interpersonal communication: to become trusting rather than defensive, to develop a trusting climate, and to help others become less defensive.

Statement:

Ken: I can't get my car started and I need to get to my appointment!

Defensive Behaviors	(These behaviors tend to cause defensiveness in the other person.)
	Five statements Jim can make that cause defensiveness in Ken.
Evaluation	1. "Your car's a mess!"
Control	2. "Get it fixed!"
Certainty	3. "I know exactly what's wrong with it!"
Strategy	4. "Maybe you ought to buy another car. I'll give you $300 for this one"!
Superiority	5. "I never have these problems. I know how to keep my car running!"

Jim

Supportive Behaviors	(Supportive behaviors tend to encourage and help the other person.)
	Five statements Jim can make that are supportive.
Problem Orientation	1. "When is your appointment? How much time do we have?"
Empathy	2. "Say, I can really understand."
Spontaneity	3. "Let me look at your car. Maybe I can help fix it quickly."
Equality	4. "You're a little uptight, like I was on my job interview last week."
Provisionalism Flexible	5. "I'll be glad to take you to your appointment, if you want me to!"

Jim

A part of being trusting rather than suspicious lies with one's self, as we have already observed. As with self-concept, the development of a psychological orientation toward communication—trust or suspicion, for example—has been going on for a long time. Change may require some good, hard thinking about one's self. Also, like self-concept, the development of trust has a reciprocal component to it; that is, as you learn to behave so as to reduce defensiveness in others and to stimulate trust from others, you increase your trust for others. What can you do to influence the development of trust in another? Giffin and Patton have said you can demonstrate expertness, reliability, and dynamism.[16] In other words, you can be concerned and involved (dynamism), honest and predictable (reliability), and have something to offer another by

Can you explain what behaviors might cause the other person to become defensive?

way of helping (expertise). Then according to Gibb, you could aid the development of trust in another by being descriptive, problem oriented, spontaneous, emphatic, equal, and flexible in your communication with the other person. Also, **interpersonal trust** is built between persons who disclose more and more of themselves and their reactions to each other. You can then have an influence upon the development of a trusting climate. Rejection, ridicule, the put-down—these and other communication patterns can destroy trust and stimulate fear, anxiety, and defensiveness. Reciprocal behavior is again observed as a powerful determiner of interpersonal communication behavior. You can influence trust through your own behavior with others. Trust, like its opposite—suspicion—is a powerful factor in interpersonal communication.

Role as a Factor in Interpersonal Communication

Communication creates norms, rules, and roles that in turn affect subsequent communication. In the chapter on dyadic communication, we shall see roles in the interview that impose certain expectations; however, any human communication situation includes roles and expectations if the participants are to send the messages required of them and if they are to correctly interpret the messages of others. One always speaks or listens from a particular position within a social system—buyer, seller, parent, child, employer, employee, male, female, friend, stranger, spouse, and so forth. To know what the other person's role is—in what capacity that person speaks—is to enhance the possibility for understanding the communication. That two persons understand the role does *not* mean that they will agree and that the communication will be successful, but they will be more likely to interact with minimal confusion.

Role Expectations

A person may occupy several different roles and have an assortment of behavior patterns associated with each role. There may be certain **role expectations** associated with being male and others associated with being female—although this is not as true as it was a few years ago. With one person you are in a subordinate role, with another you are in a superior role, and with yet a third you enjoy a close, coequal position. In one situation you are a jokester, and in another a serious participant. Not only does each of us play different roles in different interpersonal situations, but our roles may change during the communication situation as others and the roles they play constantly influence the demands and duties of our roles. Each role requires the execution of complementary functions. There is no teacher role without students, no buyers without sellers, no interviewer without a respondent.

When you are unacquainted with your role, you may be anxious and unsure of what is expected; if the role requirements or prohibitions are too demanding and rigid, you may find the role difficult and uncomfortable. Some persons try to get by in life with a few unchanging, rigid roles. Other persons err in the other direction; that is, they try to manipulate themselves to fit any and all of the expectations others have for them. Others follow a wiser course. They choose their roles with care and perform them as creatively and productively as possible. If you want to improve your interpersonal communication behavior, you should understand that roles are important "influencers" of communication.

Even an act such as public speaking has role expectations associated with it. An interesting study was made researching the role expectancies of maleness and femaleness in the persuasive speaking situation.[17] The study showed that the characteristics associated with the role of persuasive speaking are "masculine" characteristics. In their study, Zellman and Connor tested stereotypical sex roles and their relationship to the persuasive speaking role. The speaker they chose to play the "appropriate female role" was a woman in her late twenties who was introduced as a housewife with two preschool children. She wore a frilly dress and spoke quietly, softly, and nonaggressively. The same woman then gave the same persuasive speech to a second audience, but this time she was introduced as a journalist from a large metropolitan newspaper, unmarried and very successful in her career. Instead of a dress, she wore a strictly tailored suit; and she wore her hair pulled back severely. She carried a briefcase and spoke in a confident, strong, forceful voice, with vigorous gestures and movements. The experimenters reasoned that if a woman adopted traits that are considered masculine, she would fit the persuasive speaking role better. In the same study, a man in his late twenties presented the same speech that the woman had given, once in the "appropriate role" (a junior executive who was career minded, married with two children, wearing a business suit and tie, and speaking in a loud, assured, forceful voice); and later in an "inappropriate role" (unmarried primary teacher, wearing a flowered shirt, with weak gestures, who spoke in a soft voice).

Appropriate and Inappropriate Roles

The results of the study showed that the male in the *appropriate role* and the female in the *inappropriate role* persuaded the audience more (significantly so) than did the male in the *inappropriate role* and the female in the *appropriate role*. The study demonstrates how powerful *role* is as an interpersonal communication variable. The stereotyped roles of male and female, as related to persuasive speaking, interacted to produce significantly different results in the communication situation. Another interesting finding that emerged from the study was that both the male and female in their *inappropriate roles* were thought to be less happy than in their *appropriate* roles.

Group identification through dress, style, and behavior.

Assigned and Assumed Rules

Roles are sometimes assigned to you. By the fact that you hold a certain office or position, you have an **assigned role.** Your expected behavior is clear and evident. On the other hand, some of your roles are **assumed roles.** No person or organization has assigned the role to you; you voluntarily assumed it because you wanted to enact the values that accompany that role. In fact, Glasser says the young people of a society are more prone to adopt roles than are older persons.[18] Older persons are more interested in goals than in roles. It is evident that our society encourages role adoption.

Another term for role adoption is *status portrayal.* Clothing, for example, is an important vehicle of role or status. Consider the preppy look and the dress-for-success look. The western clothes and cowboy attire are strong role identifiers today. For example, western hats were worn by all our Olympic participants in the opening ceremonies of the 1984 Olympics in Serejevo. The make of automobile and kind of furniture can also be used to indicate role. Undoubtedly you can think of countless other objects and activities that portray roles.

Can you recall and describe a person you saw at a party recently who had assumed a role?

The process of growing up and learning the kinds of behavior society expects of one in different situations is called *socialization.* We learn not only society's roles but also a plethora of roles that are uniquely ours for use in our interaction with specific other individuals. These roles are acquired in our interactions with others much as self-concept is developed (chapter 3).

Role behavior makes our interactions with others more predictable and smooth. If we had no learned or expected behaviors (roles), we would not know what to expect of those with whom we interact. Without learned behavior, we could not come to *know* another person, or group, or a culture. If every person with whom we interacted were *exactly alike,* and if every group needed only *one kind of participation* from all members, then we would have no need for different roles. Or we could be the opposite; that is, rather than having learned and varied roles, all our behavior could be random and totally unpredictable. Roles enrich our communication with each other and enhance our ability, whether in dyads or groups, to solve problems and to satisfy our mutual needs. Persons who lock themselves into one role for interacting with all others at all times, or who perceive others as being in a single, frozen role pattern, take the flexibility and adaptability out of interpersonal communication.

Stereotyped Roles

If we forget the principle we studied earlier (the principle that all things change), then we may tend to "freeze" our role behavior or the expected role behavior of others. This stereotyping can cause us to lose touch with reality: we may find that the role behavior we try to use or that which we expect others to use is inappropriate. And, if we persist in an inappropriate role, we will deter the flexibility and adaptability we need. You will recall that the study we reported earlier illustrated role expectancies in persuasive speaking. It is an example of how a **stereotyped role** can be harmful. Our culture can be enriched if we change this stereotyping. We want to be able to predict, to understand, to know the qualities essential for the persuasive speaking act, but the behavior expected for it (the role) ought to be redefined. We need to recognize change and adapt to it.

Power as a Factor in Interpersonal Communication

The fourth major factor in interpersonal communication is **power.** Power is probably most often experienced in the organization where you work; but power is in every organization—schools, churches, service clubs, military organizations, and all others. Power exists in families and in all interpersonal relationships, but we most often associate it with organizations.

Definition and Perspectives

Organizations could not exist or maintain themselves without a "power structure" or "power network." Power is especially pronounced at the top of every organization where much of it rests on one person, the president or chairman. Power, however, exists at all levels. Any time two persons interact, power is a part of that relationship. It may be shared or not shared. It may be constructive or destructive. It may be abused or used effectively. It is seldom thought about and we seldom assess our own ability to use power well; but power is always one of the most dynamic positive or negative factors in relationships.

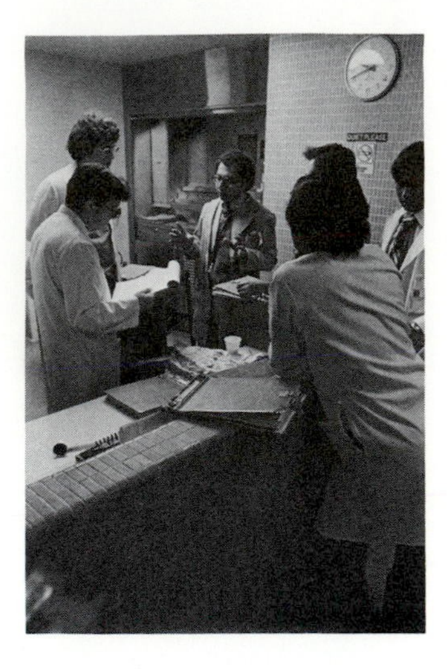

Power is a variable in all relationships.

The question is *not* whether power is bad or not. There *must be control and responsibility* in any compatible and satisfactory relationship. The question is whether or not the use of power is effective, constructive, evidences concern for the other, and facilitates a healthy relationship.

In some situations we will gladly give control (power) to one person. For example, if after a plane crashes, I am left on a windy, blizzardy mountain with four or five other persons, and one of them happens to be an expert mountain climber and former member of a special mountain rescue team, it will be no problem for me to give a lot of power and control over our relationship to that person. In other situations for me, power and decision-making need to be shared. Marriage is such a relationship.

Sources of Power

Power comes to persons in numerous ways. It may come from the *authority* that goes with the position. When one is elected or appointed to a position, that person automatically is given the power placed in that office.

Sometimes power is given to a person by peers because that person has *expertise* that is important to the group's functioning. An expert mountain climber climbing with four novice climbers would be given influence (another word for power) simply because of his or her "expertise."

Power may come from force, *coercion,* or fear. A person may simply take control. This is sometimes the case when a repressive government is overthrown by a rebel faction. The leader of the new government gains power by force and retains it by coercion and fear.

Power may also come from strong *character* and strong personality. Others just see that person as a leader and accept a subordinate position to that individual's strong personality.

Often power comes with being able to hand out *rewards* and punishments. It is easy to see how power is a factor in the classroom with the teacher and students, on the job with the boss, at home with parents and children, or in small children's play groups with the "big bully." Power is often a factor in social groups in college, too.

Finally, *information control* can represent the power of one person over another. When one controls information or functions as a gatekeeper or filter for information, one has the capacity to exert a powerful form of control over the other person.

Power is one of the most important factors influencing interpersonal communication. We talk differently to the boss than to the person we supervise; and we talk differently to the various "power persons" with whom we interact depending on how each of those persons uses power.

Objectives for Using Power

No person can satisfactorily perform in a leadership role, or in any interpersonal relationship for that matter, without facilitating a constructive, moral, and other-directed use of power. The truly effective and successful person will give attention to the use of power. Sharing power, giving responsibility and influence to others, helping others to learn to use influence and power with love and respect—these will become important goals to the person who wants to improve relationships at home, at work, or at play.

If your intentions are to control the other person—to change the other person's mind, or to get the other to do something your way—the other person will not like it and will not be motivated to build a positive, mutually helpful relationship. We resent being dominated by another person. We want to be responsible for ourselves and not controlled by others. When another tries to control us, we resist. If the other person wants to make our decisions for us, it means that person believes we are ignorant, unwise, uninformed, or in some way inadequate to make our own decisions.

On the other hand, when the other person cooperates on our mutual problem, works with us, and respects our abilities to work on the problem, we respond positively. Our goal should be the sharing of power and influence, and an "other directed" use of our influence.

Feedback

Feedback is the fifth and final factor discussed in this chapter on interpersonal communication. If the purpose of communication is to exchange meaning accurately, to influence another person so as to satisfy one's needs, and to respond so as to meet the needs of the other person, then some means of correcting faulty messages, misconceptions, misunderstandings, and incorrect responses is necessary. That "means" for correcting our shared meanings and responses is **feedback**— a vitally important part of the communication process. The corrective function is the heart of the feedback process. Without feedback there is no way to monitor the communication process, no way to seek integration and agreement. We are left with a haphazard or chance system of influencing and cooperating with others.

Effective communication exists between two persons when the receiver of a message gives it the interpretation intended by the sender. Effective communication results from the ongoing corrective process made possible by feedback. Of course, one of the primary means of receiving feedback is listening (seeing, touching, and the other senses are other means). The listening skills identified in chapter 4 are directly involved in feedback.

One point should be made clear in our discussion of feedback: both communicators are senders and receivers simultaneously. We have discussed feedback as though it came from one person (the receiver) to another person (the sender) in a linear manner. Actually, as we have indicated earlier, the process

Observing the behavior of the other person is a source of external feedback.

is complex and characterized by simultaneous interaction. Feedback flows both ways. It is transactional; it comes from both communicators and exerts a mutual influence. Sometimes people are so preoccupied with themselves and their message that they do not listen to or observe the feedback of others. They do not seek feedback from the other person to check on the other's interpretation of the message. Communication without sensitivity to feedback leans toward one-way communication. Two-way communication occurs when both senders obtain feedback concerning how the other, as receiver, is decoding the message.

Types of Feedback

There are a number of ways of categorizing the different types of feedback. We will look at five of those ways.

Internal or External Feedback

Feedback can be classified as either internal or external. When you monitor your performance and think about what you are saying as you encode the message, you are using **internal feedback;** but when you are listening to the verbal response of the other person, or observing the other person's nonverbal response you are using **external feedback.** You may also hear what you are saying as you say it (external feedback) and rephrase it to give it added meaning (internal feedback). You have probably rehearsed a speech or a conversation you were going to have. You tried out phrases to see if they sounded right. This is an example of internal feedback. Internal feedback is constantly taking place as we communicate with others. As we speak, we get set for certain responses; these expected responses result from internal feedback. We hope that our internal feedback matches the external response of the other person. When a person does respond as we anticipate, the internal and external feedback match quite closely. Both kinds of feedback are necessary to effective communication. Reliance on either one alone decreases the efficiency of the adjustive process.

Positive or Negative Feedback

Another classification system for feedback is positive or negative, a system focusing on the reinforcement aspect of feedback and one that has been used extensively in feedback research. This kind of feedback tells the sender whether the message is received correctly or not, and whether the message is accomplishing its objective. As Berlo states, "If the public buys more (positive feedback), the advertiser keeps his messages. If the public quits buying the product (negative feedback), the advertiser changes his messages."[19] A person receiving **positive feedback** tends to continue the behavior—to produce the same kind of message, that is, to send more messages similarly encoded and similar in their purposes; but the person receiving **negative feedback** tends to cease or modify the behavior—to change the message. Both kinds of feedback are important to the communication process since negative or positive feedback provides the source with information as to whether or not the message is successful in accomplishing the objective—in satisfying the need that motivated the communication.

Direct or Indirect Feedback

Feedback may also be classified as direct or indirect. In other words, some response messages are purposefully constructed by the receiver and sent directly to the sender. Other responses may be beneath the awareness level—they are not purposefully constructed, but are simply "given off." These are indirect responses.

Direct feedback is purposive. It is originated by the receiver and sent directly to the source to provide information relative to the primary message. It is intentional feedback communication. **Indirect feedback** is nonpurposive and unintentional. Let's look at some examples.

Our local newspaper, like many newspapers, features a Letters to the Editor section. Each day, from among the letters appearing in the column, can be found one or more "Angry Reader" letters. Such letters are dramatic examples of purposive and direct feedback.

A common example of indirect and unintentional feedback is the situation in which a person sends one feedback message verbally, but also sends a nonverbal message that clearly contradicts the verbal. The nonverbal feedback message may have been communicated by posture, tension, movement towards or away from the speaker, facial expression, breaking or refusing eye contact, tone of voice, or rate of speech. The person responding did not intend to send a contradictory message, but it was "given off" nonetheless.

A letter can be an example of delayed feedback—a quite necessary and sometimes happy form of feedback, even if it is delayed.

Immediate or Delayed Feedback

Feedback may be immediate or delayed. In face-to-face communication—whether formal or informal, public speaking or group discussion—**immediate feedback** is possible. Such feedback gives face-to-face communication great adaptive and corrective potential; but in mass communication feedback is **delayed.** Immediate feedback is not possible in mass communication since the sender of the message is not in the physical presence of the receivers. Only delayed feedback in the form of letters, phone calls, a decrease or increase in number of viewers, and a decrease or increase in sales of products advertised provide feedback information.

Verbal or Nonverbal Feedback

Finally, feedback may be classified according to the channel used, that is, as either **verbal** or nonverbal. **Nonverbal** cues such as facial expression, posture, gestures, sighs, tone of voice, and other bodily movements or physical responses may provide important feedback to the sender. In fact, nonverbal messages are often used as much or more than verbal messages by police, medical doctors, psychiatrists, therapists, and others in investigative or interviewing situations.

Guidelines for Effective Use of Feedback

Many of the principles or guidelines we are going to suggest have been verified in feedback studies. All are commonly cited for effective interpersonal communication in various settings—instruction, social communication, instrumental communication, and problem-solving discussion, for example. They are:

Can you list four types of feedback you have used today?

1. One should use both positive and negative feedback.
2. Effective feedback is descriptive rather than evaluative. By describing, the individual is left free to use feedback in any way deemed appropriate, or not use it at all. And descriptive and problem-oriented language does not provoke as much defensive behavior.
3. Immediate feedback is more effective than delayed feedback. Generally, it is most useful if provided at the earliest opportunity.
4. Unless feedback is interpreted accurately, it is of little value. So, meanings should be checked by translating, paraphrasing, and questioning.
5. Effective feedback is specific rather than general.
6. Effective feedback is constructive rather than destructive. It is motivated by the desire to help the sender. It is directed toward increasing fidelity in the exchanges of meaning.
7. Effective feedback does not overload the communication channels. One should not overload the channels by imposing all of one's own evaluations and interpretations on the message received. Rather, the objective is to provide only necessary feedback—enough information, but not too much.

Summary

In this chapter we have discovered that attraction and affection facilitate interpersonal communication, while hostility and alienation are severe handicaps to solving problems through interpersonal communication. We have noted that trust and supportiveness are essentials of the transactional process, while suspicion and defensiveness inhibit our coming to know each other. And role has been shown to be a dynamic factor in interpersonal communication. The expectancies we have for certain roles become powerful influences in the process of interpersonal communication. Power was discussed as a factor, and finally we examined feedback and its place in the communication process. We have identified the various types of feedback, and we have suggested some guidelines for using feedback more effectively.

Questions and Exercises for Review

1. What can you do to increase your attractiveness to another person?
2. Certain behaviors on your part tend to be supportive of others. What behaviors are these?
3. How are assigned roles different from assumed roles?
4. What can you do to use feedback in communication more effectively?

Key Terms and Phrases

interpersonal attraction
affection
accidental happenings
unjust treatment
rewards
stress
social isolation
proximity
homophily
heterophily
P-O-X balance theory
being ignored
anomia-alienation
hostility
withdrawal
adjustive techniques
physical aggression
verbal aggression
rationalization
negativism
characteristics, reputation, and intentions
congruent goal
competitive goal
independent goal
"prisoner's dilemma"
nature and quality
presence of a third person
interpersonal trust
role expectations
assigned role
assumed role
stereotyped role
power
feedback
internal feedback
external feedback
positive feedback
negative feedback
direct feedback
indirect feedback
immediate feedback
delayed feedback
verbal feedback
nonverbal feedback

For Further Reading

Altman, I., and Taylor, D. A. *Social Penetration: The Development of Interpersonal Relationships.* New York: Holt, Rinehart & Winston, 1973.
An interesting and comprehensive explanation of the social penetration process.

Byrne, D. *The Attraction Paradigm.* New York: Academic Press, 1971.
An excellent summary of attraction research.

Gardiner, J. C. "A Synthesis of Experimental Studies of Speech Communication Feedback." *Journal of Communication* 21(1971): 17–25.
The different types of feedback are discussed in terms of experimental research findings.

Rokeach, M. *The Open and Closed Mind.* New York: Basic Books, 1960.
This is a classic book on openness and dogmatism and how they affect communication.

Spitzberg, Brian H., and Cupach, William R. *Interpersonal Communication Compe-*

Spitzberg, Brian H., and Cupach, William R. *Interpersonal Communication Competence,* Beverly Hills: Sage Publications, Inc., 1984.
Discusses communication competence in school, on the job, and in other relationships.

Notes

1. William C. Schute, *The Interpersonal Underworld* (Palo Alto, Calif.: Science and Behavior Books, Inc., 1966), 18–25.
2. E. Walster, "The Assignment of Responsibilitiy for an Accident," *Journal of Personal Social Psychology* 3(1966): 73–79.
3. M. J. Lerner, "Evaluation of Performance as a Function of Performer's Reward and Attractiveness," *Journal of Personal Social Psychology* 1 (1965):355–60.
4. D. G. Mandlebaum, *Soldier Groups and Negro Soldiers* (Berkeley: University of California Press, 1952), 45–48.
5. Everett M. Rogers and F. Lloyd Shoemaker, *Communication of Innovations: A Cross-Cultural Approach* (New York: Free Press, 1971), 14.
6. Fritz Heider, *The Psychology of Interpersonal Relations* (New York: John Wiley & Sons, 1958).
7. Richard J. Howe, "Updating Superman: Comic Book Heroes Are Being Modernized; They Struggle with Alienation and Social Ills," *Wall Street Journal,* April 15, 1970.
8. K. Giffin, "Interpersonal Trust in Small Group Communication," *Quarterly Journal of Speech* 53(1967): 224–34.
9. M. Deutsch, "Trust and Suspicion," *Journal of Conflict Resolution* 2 (1958): 270.
10. Deutsch, "Trust and Suspicion," 270.
11. William D. Brooks, "An Investigation of Three Goal Relationships Upon Communication Efficiency, Amount of Communication, and Honesty in Communication" (Unpublished manuscript, University of Kansas, 1967).
12. Truman Capote, *In Cold Blood* (New York: Random House, Inc., 1965), 226–27.
13. Capote, *In Cold Blood,* 228.
14. Jack R. Gibb, "Defensive Communication," *Journal of Communication* 11 (1961): 141–48.
15. Gibb, *"Defensive Communication," 145.*
16. Kim Giffin and Bobby R. Patton, *Fundamentals of Interpersonal Communication* (New York: Harper & Row Publishers, 1971), 164.
17. Gail L. Zellman and Catherine L. Connor, "Increasing the Credibility of Women: Role Appropriateness and Communicator Effectiveness," paper presented at the Annual Meeting of the Western Psychological Association, April, 1973, Anaheim, California.
18. William Glasser, *The Identity Society* (New York: Harper & Row, 1972).
19. David K. Berlo, *The Process of Communication* (New York: Holt, Rinehart & Winston, 1960), 113–14.

Focus

Family Communication

Marital Communication

Disclosure

Freedom to Grow

Parents and Children in Communication

Babies and Young Children

The Generation Gap and Parent-Child Communication

Adult Children and Elderly Parents

Social Communication: Friends and Friendships

Initiating and Forming a Friendship

Demographic Exchanges

The Instantaneous General Impression

Maintaining a Relationship

Affection or Intimacy

Dominance or Control

Appropriate Responsiveness or Inclusion

Appropriate Emotional Tone

Exiting a Relationship

Communication at Work: Conflict

Developing an Attitude toward Conflict

Causes of Conflict

Perceptual Differences

Different Goals

Value Differences

Status Differences

Role Pressures

Personality Differences

Types of Interpersonal Conflict

Nondivisible or Nonsharable Goals

Objectives of Conflict that are Sharable

Fully Sharable Objectives

Categorizing Conflict in Terms of Level of Intensity

Controversy

Competition

Combat

Conflict Management: Possible Outcomes

Victory and Destruction

Cessation

Shared-Goal Resolutions

Integrative Unity—Congruent and Fully-Shared Goal Resolutions

Facilitating Cooperative Behavior: Selected Variables in Conflict Management

Amount of Communication

Accuracy in Communication

Content of Communication

Structuring Cooperative Action

The Interview

Informational Interview

Persuasive Interview

The Question-Answer Process

Interview Structure

Opening, Body, and Closing

General Pattern

Sequencing of Questions

The Employment Interview

What the Typical Employer Wants to Know about the Applicant

What the Applicant Should Know about the Position

Specific Suggestions for the Applicant and the Interviewer

Dyadic Interpersonal Communication: Contexts and Application

In chapter 6, we studied the five basic factors that operate in interpersonal communication—interpersonal attraction, interpersonal trust and acceptance, role, control and the sharing of power, and feedback. Now, in this chapter, we look at the application of these variables to selected interpersonal situations. It is not enough to be able to define, identify, and understand these five variables; one must also be able to translate that knowledge into behavior in specific interpersonal situations. To facilitate that growth, we select some specific problem areas in the interpersonal communication contexts that are most common to all of us, and discuss how good interpersonal communication skills can help alleviate those problems.

You recall that we emphasized the *relationship* aspect of interpersonal communication throughout chapter 6. Interpersonal communication is person to person, direct, and transactional. The one word and concept that best encompasses all those things and more is *relationship.* In this chapter, we investigate how relationships are formed; how they are maintained, if they are; and how they are terminated. We select three types of relationship areas in which many of us spend most of our time—family, friends, and work. These three interpersonal contexts account for most of our communication time. And, these three situations clearly have the most influence on our survival and quality of life.

Dyadic communication is often informal.

All three interpersonal communication contexts—family, friends, work—are examples of dyadic communication. **Dyadic communication** is two-person communication. We usually think of it in terms of an informal interpersonal situation involving face-to-face verbal interaction. In dyadic communication, two persons initiate messages and responses as they mutually influence each other. Each person simultaneously sends and receives information so as to create shared meanings. This free interchange gives to dyadic communication a high potential for information sharing and effective integration. It is not surprising, then, that some of the most influential and satisfying communication experiences for each of us are dyadic.

Each of us is involved in numerous dyadic communication situations daily. Sometimes we are seeking information; sometimes we are attempting to secure someone's agreement or approval; sometimes we are making a new acquaintance; sometimes we are just visiting with a friend or a social acquaintance; and sometimes we are engaged in intimate talk, disclosing and sharing with another our deepest feelings and concerns.

Dyadic communication represents a basic or "foundation" phenomenon in interpersonal communication. The ability to establish and maintain a relationship with another person on a one-to-one basis is the foundation upon which all other forms of interpersonal communication rest. It is important, then, to take a close look at the dynamics of dyadic communication. Not only is it our most-used type of communication, but through dyadic communication group and cultural communication come into being. In dyadic communication, as in other forms of interpersonal communication, each person creates the other person as the transaction process occurs. You may want to reread our discussion of the transactional process nature of communication in chapter 1. Person A is not the same person to the stranger in an elevator that person A is to a class friend, or to A's boss, or to any other person with whom A establishes a relationship. Each person is a unique personality, and each relationship is a unique relationship. The relationship is established via the transactional process—the process of each creating the meaning of each other in their relationship.

Care and trust are established through reciprocal disclosure.

Family Communication

Among the situations included in family communication are marital communication and parent-children communication. These communication situations are characterized chiefly by intimacy and the comparative permanence of the relationships. Cooley refers to such groups as the "springs of life, not only for the individual but for social institutions."[1] With one's children (or parent) or one's spouse, one can communicate in a trusting and supportive environment. In interaction situations such as those, communication can be fuller and more accurate than in many other interpersonal communication situations. Although the opportunity for such communication development is provided, there is no absolute guarantee that such development will actually take place. There are communication inadequacies in marriage, and there are parents and children who do not communicate with each other well.

Marital Communication

One of the essential elements in successful marital communication is trust. One cannot be truly intimate without being vulnerable, without opening oneself, sharing oneself, and trusting oneself to another. Trust is necessary for the growth, development, and existence of the marital relationship.

Trust is established through disclosure to a loving, caring, responding person, coupled with reciprocal disclosure by that person. Building a strong relationship depends upon both persons being self-disclosing. When each discloses to the other, trust is built if the other responds with acceptance and support. Trust is destroyed when the risk-taking disclosure behavior of one is rejected, ridiculed, or betrayed. Two elements, then, are especially important in intimate communication—risk-taking through self-disclosure, and the acceptance and support of the responding person. Inclusion, control, affection, and responsiveness are necessary to good family communication.

Let us look specifically at **marital communication** in terms of two topics—disclosure (openness and closedness, honesty and duplicity), and freedom to grow (to adapt to change and to retain one's individuality while being one with the other).

Disclosure

If we want to be loved, we must disclose ourselves. If we want to love someone, that someone must permit us to know him or her. This is one of the most common difficulties in marital communication. Jourard and Whitman, psychologists and marital counselors, say:

> We discovered that even with those they cared most about, people shared little of their true feelings or their most profound longings and beliefs; revealed little of what they really thought on such touchy subjects as sex, self-image, religion. . . . As a therapist and research psychologist I often meet people who believe that their troubles are caused by things outside themselves—by another person, bad luck or some obscure malaise—when in fact they are in trouble because they are trying to be loved and seeking human response without letting others know them. . . . Even in families—good families—people wear masks a great deal of the time. Children don't know parents; parents don't know their children. Husbands and wives are often strangers to each other.[2]

This concealing of self and wearing of masks often begins in courtship—at a time when masks ought to be coming off and the acquaintance ought to be deepening. The story is told of one couple whose refusal to be open with each other about an incident that occurred on their honeymoon resulted in unnecessary misunderstanding and hurt for eight years. On their honeymoon, in the restaurant where they took their first meal, she started up a conversation with a strange couple. He refused to participate in this conversation. Both became quite angry and a fight ensued. Eight years passed, with each probably recalling the incident and experiencing renewed anger again and again. It was revealed in counseling sessions why each had behaved as he or she did. He thought the honeymoon was a time to be alone with his new wife—a time to purposefully close out other people. For his wife to seek out strangers was perceived by him as an insult to his masculinity and to his role on the honeymoon. She saw her husband's refusal to join in the conversation as an insult and rejection of her. She began the conversation with the strange couple because she "had never had a conversation as a wife" and wanted to try out this new role. The honeymoon seemed to her the ideal time to try this aspect of her new role. Eight years of pain and misunderstanding resulted from two persons' inability or refusal to communicate openly.

Each of us has been guilty, perhaps, of unnecessary closedness and concealment. We say that we feel things we really don't feel, and that we believe things we really don't believe. We try to present our best selves, sometimes false selves. We hide in order to protect ourselves from change because change is so frightening. But often these behaviors are counterproductive. They produce an effect exactly opposite to what we intend.

Although disclosure of feelings, attitudes, and beliefs is a necessary characteristic of intimate and satisfying dyadic relationships, the disclosure must be intelligent and benign. We cannot and should not be brutally open concerning every feeling, attitude, and thought. McCroskey, Larson, and Knapp make this point well. They say:

> Disclosure is a particularly important concept in our discussion of interpersonal communication in marriage. Much writing in the popular literature suggests that open communication on all aspects of marital life leads to greater understanding and adjustment. However, there are serious limitations that one should place on that generalization. We have all encountered situations in which individuals in particularly playful or rueful moods give in to momentary impulses to make intense personal disclosures. We sometimes regret these disclosures, even beyond the point where we can derive any comfort from the convenient cop-out, "I'm telling you this for your own good." From the marital situation, the effects of such intense disclosures are long-range and cumulative and may even be destructive. The intensity of the involvement and the commitment which characterizes the marital situation are such that the married couple experimenting with "truth sessions" may discover that their momentary experimentation will have consequences that go far beyond their expectations. The critical questions which should be asked are "Is the disclosure necessary or likely to have productive consequences?" "Can the other person handle it?" The second question implies an almost moralistic assertion. The assertion is that when we disclose personal information to another, we are in effect "messing with his mind." If what we say has deep personal implications for the other, then the responsibility for the consequences clearly lies with the person who is doing the disclosing.[3]

What do openness and concealment have to do with courtship?

Failure to disclose and to be open is especially dangerous to a close and meaningful sexual relationship. Jourard and Whitman state:

> Given a reasonable lack of prudery, a lusty sex life grows best out of a relationship between two persons who can disclose themselves to each other in all areas of their lives without fear of being hurt. . . . Sex deteriorates when a couple cannot establish a close, mutually revealing, *nonsexual* relationship; the very defenses one uses to keep from being known and possibly hurt by the spouse one cannot understand are the same defenses that impede spontaneity in sex.[4]
>
> Indeed, disclosure, openness, and honesty are important interpersonal communication skills in both courtship and marriage.

Freedom to Grow

The second topic we want to consider in marital communication is freedom to grow—the freedom to adapt, to change, and to retain one's individuality. Jourard and Whitman, again speaking of marital communication, say, "Once we have formed our image of who and what we are, we proceed to behave as if that were all we ever could be. We 'freeze,' as though we had taken a pledge to ourselves that even if we did change, we'd try not to notice it. And we don't want the other person to change either." In fact, sometimes one person tends to smother the other, to absorb the other person so as to destroy individuality, and to deny the other person the freedom to grow and to change in response to an ever-changing world. Again, the same authors say:

> Freedom and the right to grow are a difficult and painful gift for a couple to give each other, but there is no alternative. People outgrow the roles in which they have been cast by their partners, and when they have grown and changed, each must be able to let that fact be known so that the partner he or she loves can take it into account. . . . Husbands and wives need tough and candid talk aimed at dispelling misunderstandings. They need to understand how they differ, what they respect and love in each other, what they hold in common—yes, and what enrages them in each other. If we speak honestly, we must be able to say, "What you are doing right now makes me angry."[5]

Too often the members of intimate dyads become locked in habitual behavior patterns so that change is virtually impossible. As McCroskey, Larson, and Knapp say, "One important implication of this observation must be pointed out, however obvious it may already be to you. We tend to develop habitual ways of responding to others. And these habitual response patterns may be more characteristic of marital communication than of other interpersonal contexts. . . ."[6] They point out that when change is responded to by one partner and the couple varies from the "locked-in patterns," the other member of the dyad often does one of two things—either of which is counterproductive. The person simply dismisses the other as unreasonable, messed up, unintelligent, or in need of professional help, or the person tries to resolve the difference by "correcting" the faulty thinking of the other, that is, by enthusiastically embarking on a crusade to convert the other.

Not only do we become slaves to habitual behavior, thus denying change and growth, but sometimes the marital relationship acquires an even more counterproductive characteristic—that of one's "ownership" of the other. All of the marriage liturgy, either religious or civil, urges the couple to become one; and indeed, there is a "oneness" in an integration as deep and close as marriage. However, our earlier discussion of control in this chapter indicated that while there is a "me" in relation to the dyad there is also a "me" separate from the dyad. To become "one" in marriage and never be "me" and "you" is directly counter to an important concept in interpersonal communication, the concept of self. When oneness is the only perception either or both members of the marriage dyad have, undue and unhealthy control usually results. One person, the controller, begins to determine all of the outcomes of their interaction. This "ownership" has a stifling effect on the marriage or on any other intimate dyadic relationship in which that phenomenon exists. In such a situation there is no freedom for the "owned" to grow and to respond to an ever-changing world.

Observing the principles of disclosure and freedom to grow does not of itself guarantee a satisfactory interpersonal relationship. It may mean only that two persons agree to disagree, easily, smoothly, and clearly—that each member of the dyad has his or her own goals, values and needs. More "talk" cannot compensate for genuine incompatibility in these areas. Substantive differences must be resolved as they relate to the specific dyadic relationship or the relationship will have no reason to exist.

Parents and Children in Communication

The most important help in learning a behavior is what happens immediately following the behavior. What happens following a behavior can be good or bad. It can be rewarding to the person behaving or *not* rewarding. There may even be punishment or pain for the behavior. The consequence of a child's behavior is subject to control, or at least influence, from the parent. The parent, however, can ignore behavior. That also is a consequence. That consequence frequently follows much of the random behavior of a baby or small child. Such a consequence may leave the behavior meaningless, and growth or learning is virtually nil. Parents who wish to be a positive influence in their child's development in communication will understand the importance of consequences immediately following behavior.

Consequences and their effects on children can be readily seen by observing children. The child who pushes the tricycle peddle soon notices the consequence, that is, that the tricycle moves. It does not take long, then, to learn to ride a tricycle. A child cries and the mother picks up the child. That consequence soon teaches the child to cry in order to be held. The child draws a picture and the parent praises the child. There are examples of consequences or reinforcement and learning. This principle is basic to parent-child communication during the first few years of the child's life. It is always important to communication interaction, but especially so for the baby and young child. Learn to use reinforcement to help children acquire good communication skills, communication attitudes, and communication values.

Babies and Young Children

What attitudes, skills, and values in communication are important to facilitate in children? What communication needs do children have? Among several are the following:

1. *Children need the security and warmth of communication, and they need to learn that communication is an enjoyable and need-satisfying activity.* Children need communication, verbal and especially nonverbal, from birth on. They need the touch and the vocal sounds of affection and security. The first codes the child learns are the nonverbal codes. The first needs include security, comfort, love, and happiness. Parents who understand the relationship between communication and the child's development provide verbal and nonverbal communication in abundance to their children.

2. *Children need to acquire a positive attitude toward communication.* This means that parents ought to encourage the communication efforts of the child by providing positive consequences and reinforcements. Parents will understand the early high ego and me-centered communication of the two- and three-year old, and not kill off communication by punishing or ignoring "too much" communication from a child or using communication that is "too dictatorial."
3. *Children need to be validated.* They need to be confirmed as having value or worth. From birth through the early years of elementary school this is an especially important need. Treating children in ways that show they have worth and value, accepting them rather than rejecting them, praising them rather than criticizing them, and giving them attention rather than ignoring them—all these parental behaviors validate and confirm the child as being worthy, good, and capable.
4. *Children need to acquire vocabularies, syntax, and grammar as they use language.* The larger the vocabulary, and the more accurate the language usage, the more intelligent and teachable the child is. Parents, then, need to provide a rich and stimulating communication environment for the child. The child that is ignored, left out of conversations, not held, not talked with, not read to, not responded to, not rewarded and praised, not taught the names of many things—that child is dwarfed and injured in ways that may be debilitating for a lifetime. At best, that child will need to relearn, even as an adult, the communication principles and attitudes that are needed for successful living in the home, with friends, or at work. Such re-learning is difficult. It involves dramatic, basic changes in knowledge, attitudes, and behavior.
5. *Children need to acquire healthy, strong, and positive self-concepts as communicators.* Parents have great influence in self-concept development. They can facilitate such development as they meet the communication needs of their children and provide healthy and intelligent response behavior in interaction with their children.

There are other needs and objectives that are equally important to the five we have discussed. There is the need for consistency, for honesty, for providing exemplary role models, for providing an intellectually and emotionally stimulating environment, for providing standards of excellence, for providing moral and spiritual development, and for facilitating the development of an integrated value system. They are essential foundation skills, attitudes, and values for effective communication development.

The Generation Gap and Parent-Child Communication

Probably one of the most difficult communication times for parents and children is the generation-gap time. Generation gap is not a good name for this time, but it is popular in the media.

The generation gap refers to the junior- and senior-high-school members of the home and how they seem to be at odds with adults, particularly their parents. The difficulties in communication between parents and their high-school or junior-high-school sons and daughters is not common to all parents and high schoolers. Nor is the problem unique to just high schoolers and their parents. Some college students have continuing problems in communication. Of course, the problems can continue through various ages and stages. Generally, however, these problems go away as sons and daughters reach college age. This is why the problem is referred to as a generation-gap caused problems, and why the term usually refers to a specified time in children's growing up. Folklore knowledge recognizes its temporariness. We all know the jokes about how much a high school or college student's parents have learned between the student's matriculation and graduation.

The purpose of this section is not to resolve the problem *directly* nor to *blame* the parent or the student. The purpose is to call attention to some common causes of the communication difficulty. Actually, some of these causes can and will exist at later stages of life and between persons other than parent and child.

Among the factors related to the generation gap problem in communication are the following:

1. *Differing modes of interaction.* The student is moving into adulthood. Sometimes the time schedule of such growth or movement is different for the student than for the parent. The parent is yet in a parent-child mode of interaction. The student wants to be in an adult-adult mode of communication and interaction. Parents in a parent-child mode scold, chastise, correct, offer fatherly or motherly advice, and generally interact as parent to child. The son or daughter may respond by condemning that mode of interaction as inappropriate because they are adults. They may put these points more colorfully, more dramatically, than the way in which they are described here, but these are the arguments made.
2. *Different goals and lifestyles.* Coming into adulthood is not an instantaneous moment of insight. It is a learning process that may be gradual or fitful in leap-outs and leap-backs. Parents who have worked toward goals for their children are greatly disappointed when those goals are overthrown for others. Certainly these deep-seated problems (goals, values, and life-styles) are among the most difficult at any age. They are especially potent in the generation-gap stage. What is called for is the very best of communication principles, skills, and

Parent-child communication needs no special content or theme to give pleasure.

attitudes—those things this textbook and your speech communication course and instructor focus upon to bring new cognitive, affective, and behavioral learning and development to you. If time permitted, we could go through the topics of this book: use of nonverbal communication, language processing, thinking well, being other-directed, and conflict management skills to show their direct relevance to generation. Some parents and students have acquired these understandings, attitudes, and skills and can use them to rise above the challenges of the so-called generation gap.

Adult Children and Elderly Parents

Parent-child communication would not be complete without a look at elderly parents and their fifty-to-seventy-year-old children. One of the stages of life for many persons is that time when roles are reversed and children become responsible for supporting their parents who are elderly. The children may need to become responsible in various degrees for the welfare of their parents. But some basic needs of the parents ought to be met, even as the parents some fifty or sixty years earlier met the needs of the children through the children's years of growing into adulthood.

The fifty- or sixty-year-old child can, with good communication understanding, meet the needs of his or her parents and take care of the business that needs to be done without really reversing roles so that the parent is child and the child is parent as far as the communication-mode is concerned. Important communication variables with which one should be concerned are role reversal in terms of communication-mode and the variable of power. A servant-role or servant-perspective, in the best sense, is what is called for in the use of power. One must be cautious of slipping too easily into a strong and pronounced use of power.

Social Communication: Friends and Friendship

Conversation is the most characteristic behavior of sociability. Social conversation as distinguished from other talk is consummatory talk (of primary value at the moment only) and quite different from instrumental talk (used to accomplish a specific goal or to solve a specific problem). In social conversation, talk is its own purpose. The identifying characteristic of social conversation is its sociability—its existence for its own sake.

The purpose of social conversation is to give pleasure. Thus no content, idea, or theme need be dominant. As soon as the talk becomes instrumental, its purpose changes and it ceases to be social communication. In social conversation we seek to achieve harmony, a consciousness of being together, an enjoyment of one another.

For some persons it is difficult to make new friends. Such persons find it quite difficult to move into a new community, a new school, or a new organization. To some degree, making friends either is or has been somewhat difficult for many of us. It is the initial "getting acquainted" that is sometimes slow and uncomfortable. Certainly without the acquaintance process occurring, there can be no friendship relation established. So, we now consider the getting-acquainted process.

In a manner of speaking, a friendship has a life. It is born, grows, and ends. Some friendships last a lifetime, while others are short-lived. Some friendships grow strong and deep, while other are occasional and light. Whether they are old or young, long-lived or short-lived, deep or shallow—all the friendships of which you are now a part once had a beginning. There was a period of becoming acquainted with the other person and forming a relationship.

Initiating and Forming a Friendship

The formative period of an interpersonal relationship has at least two stages—an initial exploratory stage and a "getting-acquainted" stage. The first stage might be called the **entry phase,** while the second stage might be called the **acquaintance process.** Our discussion at this point focuses on the entry phase. The entry phase has been described by Zunin, by Altman and Taylor, and by

Berger,[7] and occurs in the first few minutes, while the second stage occurs over a more extended period of time. The second stage has been described in detail by Newcomb in *The Acquaintance Process,* by Byrne in *The Attraction Paradigm,* and by Jourard in *Self-Disclosure: An Experimental Analysis of the Transparent Self.*[8]

The entry phase—the initial contact phase—is an extremely unstable encounter. Each member of the dyad must rely exclusively on the reactions of the other. Either member of the dyad can terminate the continuation of the interaction—each holds virtual veto power. This initial encounter situation is usually characterized by verbal fencing, a process in which each person "sizes up" the other person—each tries to find out who this other person is. Each seeks to discover the other's identity, attitudes, and values. If you discover that the other person has attitudes, values, and beliefs like your own, and if you feel "safe" with the other person, you will tend to reveal yourself more freely. If, however, you feel threatened or insecure with this stranger, you will reveal as little of yourself as possible. Newcomb calls this process **reciprocal scanning,** and says that it is a "crucial part of the interactional behavior that goes on between persons who are getting acquainted."[9]

Those who have studied this entry phase in becoming acquainted believe that the first few minutes (two, three, or four minutes) may determine future interaction patterns and influence the development, or lack, of a subsequent relationship. Through the research of scholars such as Berger and Zunin we have some idea of what happens during the initial contact phase.[10] Zunin claims that by analyzing the first four minutes of strangers' communication, one can predict with relatively high probability whether or not the persons involved will interact in the future. Jourard reports that persons who are willing to disclose personal information to others in initial contact tend to induce others to engage in self-disclosure. He calls this tendency the "dyadic effect." The research of Altman and Taylor and of Berger, however, indicates that the disclosure occurring during the first two or three minutes is of a particular type—it is relatively shallow, safe, conservative, nonevaluative, and demographic. Altman and Taylor describe the talk during this initial contact phase as "light, undertaken at a superficial and noncommittal level, including areas such as whom one knows, where one lives, where one has traveled, what one's profession is, where one works, etc.[11] Although these topics are dealt with overtly at a superficial level, Berger's research leads him to believe that these data serve as bases for making inferences about the individual. He says:

> By knowing a person's age, one might be able to accurately infer the person's musical preferences. The kinds of topics covered in initial interaction do help to generate a network of propositions about the persons revealing the information. The propositions or predictions generated from the initial data may be in error; however, the fact that such "theories" are generated on the basis of "superficial" interaction is indeed significant. For if the inferences made on the basis of data obtained in the first few minutes of the encounter suggest that persons may be dissimilar on other, more salient, attributes, the probability that

they will continue to interact might well be lowered. By contrast, if the inference pattern suggests a high level of similarity on attributes not yet sampled, the probability that the interaction will continue will be increased. Thus, inferences based on "superficial" interaction may well determine whether persons will continue their relationship.[12]

Berger's research has given us a detailed account of the communication patterns in the initial interaction situations he studied. He wanted to know what kinds of information were exchanged and when patterns shifted in this phase. Zunin postulated a **"four-minute barrier,"** that is, information exchange patterns shifted after four minutes.[13] Berger found that the talk of thirty-six persons (strangers who were interacting) could be classified into seven categories: (1) Demographic Information: having to do with background characteristics of the person, such as hometown, major family characteristics, and year in school; (2) Attitudes and Opinions: information concerning the person's attitudes and opinions toward any object or person; (3) Future Plans: information about future plans of any kind, such as summer jobs, career plans, and plans for school; (4) Personality: having to do with one's own or the other person's personality; (5) Past Behavior: concerning the antecedent conditions for the person's present behavior; for example, why the person came to this school; (6) Other Persons: any references to persons other than those involved in the interaction, such as whether the person knows Jane Smith; and (7) Hobbies and Interests.[14]

Demographic Exchanges

Some of Berger's dyads were given two minutes to talk, some five minutes, and some ten minutes. Berger's results showed that the first four to five minutes were characterized by requests for and the giving of demographic information. In fact, this preoccupation with demographic concerns seemed to suppress the passing of other kinds of information until after the first four or five minutes. Berger's first category dominated the initial interaction. The pattern then shifted to attitudes and opinions (second category) and to other persons (sixth category). The third, fourth, fifth, and seventh categories were "rare conversational topics during initial interaction." Berger points out that one of the prime functions served by **demographic exchange** is to reduce uncertainty about the other or others in the interaction.[15] Specifically, by exchanging demographic information, clues may be gained about a person's possible attitudes and opinions. Thus, by ascertaining into which "categories" a person falls, one can begin to make inferences about the person's attitudes and opinions without directly asking for them. Demographic scanning may aid in attaining smooth social conduct because it enables persons to predict and avoid areas of probable opinion discrepancy.

Closely related to the "uncertainty-reduction function" is the "search-for-similarity function" demographic exchange might also serve. For example, if two persons discover that they are from the same hometown, they will probably pursue the topic in an attempt to determine whether they are from the same part of town and/or whether they know the same people. The search-for-similarity function of demographic exchange is analogous to Newcomb's notion of reciprocal scanning of "orientations."

The Instantaneous General Impression

These studies (Berger, Zunin, and others) have added to our understanding of the kinds and patterns of information exchanged in the entry phase of becoming acquainted. But even before the verbal fencing and innocuous exchanges, there is a general and immediate perceived "image" of the stranger that provides an almost instantaneous "definition" of who this stranger is. In research studies, two-second glimpses have been sufficient for a person to develop an image and general expectation of the person glimpsed. Immediately the stranger is perceived as a unit, as a whole. Specific traits fit together to form the almost instantaneous general impression.[16] Moreover, this impression exerts a powerful influence on subsequent communication with the person. A single dominant or striking factor may heavily influence the general impression. One of these factors is the warmth of the person.[17] If the person is perceived as "warm," that person is also likely to be perceived as sincere, honest, generous, wise, and happy.[18] Physical traits influence our impression of psychological traits, and psychological traits influence our perception of physical ones. First impressions are extremely important; therefore those things first noticed are of special significance. Social psychologists have found that physical appearance, what one first says, and what one first does are important determiners of another person's first impression—hence gestures, posture, and rate of speech are important first indicators. Similarly, some unusual or especially significant physical appearance factors—unusual clothes or inappropriate dress—may also be a powerful determiner of the immediate image. The first impression is an important determinant of the interaction that follows, and the verbal interactions of the first few minutes influence subsequent interaction which leads to the establishment of a dyadic relationship. From such initial encounters fledgling relationships are born. During subsequent encounters in the early stage each person becomes more fully acquainted with the other and the relationship is clarified and established. Once established, the task then is to maintain and sustain the relationship.

Can you describe what happens during the first four minutes of the getting-acquainted process?

Maintaining a Relationship

The second phase in the life of a relationship is its maintenance and support. One might think that once a relationship is worked out during the early stage, all problems are forever solved. However, life is a process, and virtually nothing is static. Change is the one thing we can count on, and so specific action is necessary to maintain any relationship. One must make adjustments that maintain the relationship as mutually satisfying to both participants. Goals and role relations will be redefined many times in order to maintain a relationship.

"Think they'd panic if we stopped to help?"

Four specific factors seem to open up significant areas in which balance must be maintained. These factors have been identified and discussed by numerous writers under various labels. For example, as learned in chapter 6, Schutz identifies three factors especially important to relationship maintenance: inclusion, control, and affection.[19] Inclusion (the acceptance of the other person by each member of the dyad), control (the dominance of one person by the other, or the sharing of power and non-dominance), and affection (the liking between the two persons) represent needs that must be met if a good friendship is to be maintained. The factors identified by Argyle include intimacy dominance, appropriate response behavior, nonverbal responsiveness, and emotional tone.[20] It is clear from his discussion of each that they are closely related to Schutz's factors. Argyle's intimacy parallels Schutz's affection; his appropriate responsiveness is quite similar to Schutz's inclusion factor; and his dominance factor is clearly parallel to Schutz's control. If we put these two lists of factors together, we have the following four factors that are especially important to the maintenance of friendships: (1) affection or **intimacy,** (2) **dominance** or control, (3) **appropriate responsiveness** or **inclusion,** and (4) **appropriate emotional tone,** which to a large extent is communicated through nonverbal responsiveness.

If a friendship is to be maintained, the needs and desires of each member of the dyad, as they are related to these four factors, will have to be met. Cooperative behavior between the persons involved helps fulfill the needs of each.

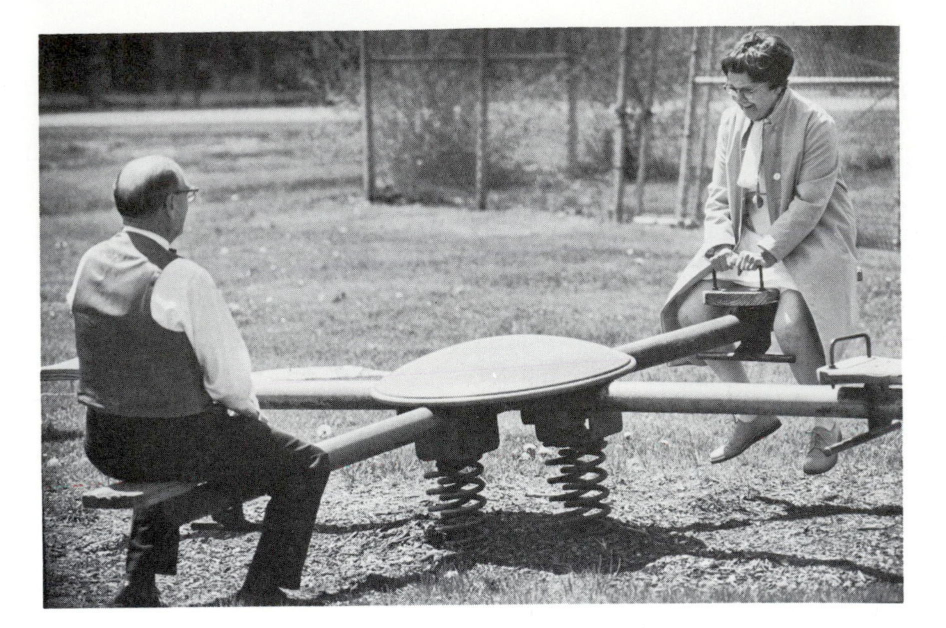

Successful dyadic relationships satisfy the affection and intimacy needs of each person.

Affection or Intimacy

Whether the dyad is boss and secretary, teacher and student, or co-workers, one of the areas in which agreement will be worked out is intimacy. This factor has been observed in studies of interpersonal behavior in the field and in the laboratory. Argyle states:

> If two people seek different degrees of intimacy there will be incongruity and awkwardness. . . . If A uses social techniques such as standing nearer, looking more, and smiling, to a greater extent than B, B will feel that A is intrusive and over-familiar, while A will feel that B is cold and standoffish. Clearly A is seeking an affiliative response from B: It is not enough for him to be able to look B in the eye—B must look back and with the right kind of facial expression. The Argyle and Dean model postulates that each person tries to maintain his own equilibrium level of intimacy.[21]

If a satisfactory dyadic relationship is to be maintained, the affection and intimacy needs of each member of the dyad must be met at the level defined by the members of the dyad as appropriate and necessary for that dyad.

Dominance or Control

A second area of concern is dominance or control. Again there must be agreement between the members of the dyad. There must be a balance or agreement as to who will control whom, and when. If the two persons have different ideas about who will make a decision, who will talk most, or who will command, then compromise will have to be worked out. And throughout the life of the relationship, it will be necessary to maintain "agreed upon" dominance behavior. Argyle states that "the commonest source of conflict in dyadic interaction is where each wants to dominate."[22]

Appropriate Responsiveness or Inclusion

As Argyle explains his concept of appropriate responsiveness, "each response of A's must be followed by a response of B's which is 'appropriate' in terms of the various principles described earlier. In a conversation, question should lead to answer and jokes to laughter."[23] One can easily see how inappropriate response has the effect of excluding the dyadic partner. The maintenance of satisfying dyadic relationships requires **appropriate responsiveness,** that is, appropriate inclusion. Even in the area of nonverbal responsiveness, which Argyle lists as a separate factor, appropriate participation with the other is necessary. If you recall the discussion in the chapter on nonverbal communication, you can easily see how nonverbal responsiveness is especially effective in expressing feelings and acceptance toward another person.

Appropriate Emotional Tone

Appropriate emotional tone is the fourth area of concern. While interaction can proceed between two persons who are in different emotional states, it is not a stable state of affairs. In all probability, either the interaction will cease or there will be a change in the emotional state of one member of the dyad.

When needs are satisfactorily met in the four areas just identified, effective dyadic interaction or friendship can occur. Argyle says, "It may take some time to establish a steady state. . . . When it has been established, it appears to have some of the properties of a system in equilibrium. A system is said to be in equilibrium if it remains in a steady state and if deviations are met with forces to restore conditions to normal."[24] The idea that a stable equilibrium develops in successful dyads as well as in larger groups seems to be borne out by several studies.[25] The inability to develop a harmonious balance that provides a mutually satisfying relationship should be apparent during the formative stage of the dyadic relationship. If, however, relationships and roles are worked out and defined satisfactorily over a period of time—during the formative stage—then the task of maintaining the relationship is to perpetuate the balance and thus satisfy the needs of each other through reciprocal behavior. When harmonious, mutually agreed upon and mutually satisfying interaction occurs relative to affection, control, inclusion, and emotional needs, then friendships are maintained.

Exiting a Relationship

Toffler, like several other writers, has written poignantly about the "speeded-up pace" of life today in technological societies. He calls this ever-increasing pace of living "the accelerative thrust," and points out that the result of accelerative thrust is transiency, or a temporariness in all our experiences, including friendships. He describes the situation as follows:

> The acceleration of change shortens the duration of many situations. . . . To survive, to avert what we have termed future shock, the individual must become infinitely more adaptable and capable than ever before. . . . He must understand in greater detail how the effects of acceleration penetrate his

Graduation Day—the end of many interpersonal relationships.

> personal life, creep into his behavior, and alter the quality of existence. He must, in other words, understand transience. . . . Transcience is the new temporariness in everyday life. . . . Our relationships with people seem increasingly fragile or impermanent. . . . Relationships that once endured for long spans of time now have shorter life expectancies. . . .[26]

If Toffler's observations are true, exiting relationships is an important problem with which we ought to be concerned. In fact, the inability of persons to handle this problem has led, in part, to shallow relationships, even to the avoidance of meaningful relationships and to consequent general alienation. Exiting relationships is as much a part of the real world as are initiating and maintaining relationships.

First, it seems clearly evident that to maintain an ongoing relationship with every person one meets and knows is impossible. Too many persons flow in and out of our lives yearly, weekly, and even daily. We must accept the fact that many relationships will terminate.

At the same time, it is helpful to have some relationships that are long lasting; if so, then a second principle is that we must learn to discriminate clearly and carefully among types of interpersonal relationships. This principle is in accordance with the concepts of change and process. We dare not lock ourselves into a narrow, frozen pattern of behavior in our interpersonal relationships. Each relationship is unique. Some will terminate quickly; others need to be relatively permanent.

Third, we must not avoid forming relationships because impermanence is so pronounced. Such behavior is contradictory to our basic social nature and to our most important means of survival—integration through communication. The attempted avoidance of all relationships is pathological.

Communication at Work: Conflict

The work setting in America today is within organizations. We are no longer an agrarian society. Rather, we are a dynamic, industrial, and communication society. There are few jobs, if any, that do not involve communication heavily. From the application process of seeking employment through on-the-job interaction with customers and fellow workers, communication is critical to succeeding in the world of work.

Moreover, it is not lack of technical skills or of knowing how to do the job that gives people trouble in securing good jobs and keeping them. Rather, it is the inability to communicate—specifically, the inability to get along with people. "Getting along with people," of course, is relationship communication. Interpersonal communication competence is a major need in the work setting.

A serious problem in communication in the work setting is conflict. No organization, group, or dyad is free of it. Moreover, the results of conflict between groups or persons in organizations can be costly when production is adversely affected and wastefulness results. The energy of highly trained people can be used up in nonproductive conflict, and relationships can be soured and ruined. These negative relationships sometimes remain as pathological influences in the organization.

Conflict, however, also has its positive outcomes. It is not something to be "avoided at all costs"! In fact, it cannot be avoided entirely and to attempt to avoid it reveals an unhealthy attitude and a misunderstanding of conflict.

Whether conflict is harmful or helpful depends on how it is used, and on how constructively one copes with it. We will consider the following topics in this area: (1) developing an attitude toward conflict, (2) causes of conflict, (3) types of conflicts, (4) the components of conflict, (5) possible conflict outcomes or resolutions, and (6) facilitating cooperative behavior and conflict management.

Developing an Attitude toward Conflict

Challenge and conflict bring about productive change, as long as the conflict is handled creatively and constructively. Simmel's thesis, expressed in both of his classic works, *Conflict* and *The Web of Group Affiliations,* is that conflict is a form of socialization—that no organization or group could exist without conflict.[27] Johnson tells us:

> Moreover, every interpersonal relationship contains elements of conflict, disagreement, and opposed interests. Interpersonal conflict exists wherever an action by one person prevents, obstructs, or interferes with the actions of

> another person; there can be conflicts between goals, ways of accomplishing the same good, personal needs, and expectations concerning the behavior of the two individuals. It is inevitable that you will become involved in conflicts whenever you have a relationship with another person. A conflict-free relationship may only be a sign that you really have no relationship at all, not that you have a good relationship.[28]

The total and permanent absence of conflict, even if it were possible, would not be a desirable situation. However, many of us have assumed that controversy, confrontation, and conflict are automatically undesirable, that they are to be avoided at all times and at all costs. This is not true. We should develop an attitude that recognizes the inevitability of conflict and facilitates its beneficial potential.

Causes of Conflict

What causes conflict? There are many causes of conflict on the job or elsewhere. Probably no list would include all of the causes, but some causes are so well known and frequent that they can be easily identified. Among such are the following.

Perceptual Differences

Perceptual differences can cause conflict. The research is quite clear in showing that we *do perceive* things, even objects, differently. It is not surprising, then, that conflict can arise from those differences in perception.

Different Goals

Different goals can be a cause of conflict. The contradictory goals may each be legitimate, but if they are divergent, conflict can result. Each goal requires money, time, and personnel—all scarce and valuable resources in organizations.

Value Differences

Value differences are a third cause of conflict. Values are strong, often emotion-laden, beliefs one has. When a person's values relative to a policy, practice, or decision are threatened, conflict can easily arise. The sales department may want fast production on a new product because they can sell all they can get of it now, but engineering or the production shop may value carefulness and correction more than speed and may see deadlines aimed at stepped-up production as threatening to quality control.

Differences in values may arise from procedural, philosophical, ideological, or moral concerns. They are often rooted in religious orientation, ethical-personal standards, education, culture, and upbringing.

Status Differences

Status differences also cause conflict. Pecking order is a characteristic of all groups. You may have already learned how careful one needs to be with some superiors in making suggestions or initiating new ideas or new activities. Status is carefully guarded in many organizations and probably finds its most pronounced emphasis in military organizations. To threaten status, to not observe expected rules relative to status, to go outside the chain of command, can give rise to conflict.

Role Pressures

Role pressures and role expectations can cause conflict. Sometimes the "office" has expected behaviors that go with it, but the office holder or subordinates of the office holder disagrees with those expectations.

Moreover, some jobs require certain acts or support from an office or position above or even below. If those offices or persons do not adequately provide what is needed for the office or person, then pressure relative to that role is created and conflict may result. Conflicts often arise over roles people are expected to play as compared to the roles they really do play.

Overlapping assignments and unclear assignments, including poor job description, are other examples of role-caused conflict.

Personality Differences

Finally, **personality differences** can cause conflict. People have different styles of interacting. Some shout, some argue, some are mild, some compliment and reinforce a lot and others hardly at all. Some want things neat and others do not. Some are risk-takers and others want security, safety, and high predictability. Personalities vary and personality is a strong influence on behavior. It is not surprising that conflict arises from personality differences.

Types of Interpersonal Conflict

Interpersonal conflict can be categorized in two ways other than by cause: by the type of goal about which the conflict revolves, and by the level of conflict intensity.

There are at least three types of goals with which interpersonal conflict may be concerned: (1) goals or objectives that are nondivisible or nonsharable; (2) goals or objectives that may be divided and shared in various proportions between the parties in conflict; and (3) goals or objectives that may be fully claimed and possessed by both parties in the conflict.

Nondivisible or Nonsharable Goals

Some objects of conflict are nondivisible. Both contestants cannot win; if one wins, the other must lose. In the contest of basketball, for example, the game's rules are such that there are **nonsharable goals.** One team must win and the other must lose. Similarly, if two men are competing to "win the hand" of a woman they both want to marry, both cannot win. Win-all-or-nothing conflicts can be extremely difficult and dangerous situations. Such conflicts, if carried out fully to the end, result in total loss for one; they are then life-or-death struggles.

Objectives of Conflict that are Sharable

Sometimes conflict objectives are sharable. Although each participant may desire to win all, it is possible to win some and lose some, while the adversary also wins some and loses some. Deutsch, as well as most other scholars who have studied conflict, states that most conflicts are of this type—they have **sharable goals,** or objectives that can be redefined to make sharing possible.[29] In such conflict situations, there can be a cooperative interest in reaching an agreement since both parties can win some, and that may be preferable to losing all.

Conflict may consist of various levels: controversy, competition, or combat.

Conflicts of this type present a particular difficulty because they may not be perceived as conflicts with sharable goals. They may be misperceived as win-lose conflicts, and the resolution of the conflict becomes more difficult. Conflict with sharable objectives may escalate into a conflict whose goals are nonsharable through inappropriate communication behavior. We will return to a discussion of these problems later in this chapter, but let us now consider the third type of conflict objective.

Fully Sharable Objectives

Fully sharable objectives are congruent goals—goals that may be possessed by both parties to the conflict. Such conflicts cease to be conflicts as soon as they are perceived correctly by the persons involved. When participants understand that they both can win fully, a natural, cooperative situation is created.

Categorizing Conflict in Terms of Level of Intensity

Interpersonal conflicts can be categorized according to the level of intensity: controversy, competition, and combat.

Controversy

As we use the term in this context, **controversy** refers to a disagreement that is perceived by the parties as resolvable to at least the partial satisfaction of both. In controversies, the parties desire a solution beneficial to both. They do not want to destroy each other.

This spring, as every spring, teachers' associations and boards of education will be locked in controversy. Neither desires to destroy the other. Both are necessary for the production of services (education for children and youth) they both desire. There are specific, rational, and peaceful procedures through which they engage in the conflict; hopefully, the resolutions will permit both parties to fulfill their desires and to function at some satisfactory level.

Competition

Competition, as used here, refers not to a disagreement over values, policies, or facts, but to a course of action on the part of each party that can enable each to win. Competition involves winning and losing. The parties may engage in the competition according to a defined set of procedures or rules (as in basketball, baseball, or poker) or they may compete without written or agreed-upon rules to govern their behavior (as in the situation of two fellows trying to win the same girl). The prize may be all or nothing (as in basketball) or may be proportionate to the success of the competitors (as in track in which one wins first, another second, etc.). In any event, in competition there is a commitment to winning the prize at the expense of the opponent, whereas in controversy each party seeks to remove controversy (the disagreement, misunderstanding, misinterpretation of facts, etc.) so that they may cooperate rather than compete.

Although there is a strong motivation to win in competition, it stops short of destruction of the other party. Winning the goal is enough. Many games exist to fulfill the functions of competition. And undoubtedly, competition and controversy play important roles in the growth of persons, groups, or societies.

Combat

The highest level of conflict intensity is **combat.** Combat may grow out of competition just as competition may emerge from strong controversy; but regardless of its origin, combat involves action against one's opponent with the intent of harming or destroying that opponent.

Conflict Management: Possible Outcomes

Now we turn to management of conflict. We will consider the possible resolutions to conflict in a sequence that is the reverse of that used to discuss types of conflict.

Victory and Destruction

One possible end to conflict is the **total victory** of one party and the **total destruction** of the other at the combat level. This is called a win-lose situation. In the case of games and competition-type conflicts, the conflict terminates when the winner has been determined and the prize, or portions thereof, awarded according to the rules.

Cessation

Some combat situations are resolved without total victory and total defeat. Sometimes one contestant (or both contestants) perceives that there is nothing that can be done to bring victory. With no way to carry the combat to a victory for either party, both decide to cease. Neither wins and neither is destroyed. They have fought to a draw and decide to stop.

A combat can also be resolved by **cessation**—by agreeing not to resolve it—when one party (or both) decides that the cost of continuing the conflict is greater than what can be won. When the cost of the conflict outweighs what can be gained in victory, contestants will often decide to cease the conflict.

In combat, the conflict will be resolved by winning, by cessation, or by de-escalating the combat into competition where one can win without the destruction of the other, or each can win some and lose some—a "shared-goal resolution." Ideally, combat might even be de-escalated to the level of controversy, or congruent goals, so that both parties can enjoy mutually beneficial solutions.

Shared-Goal Resolutions

In a **shared-goal resolution,** conflicts are managed by all parties agreeing to partial victory and partial defeat for each. The object to be won is divided so that each contestant wins some and loses some. Half a pie is seen as better than none at all. Some games have this type of resolution built into the rules. In the Indianapolis 500 auto race, for example, each of the thirty-three contestants wins some money; even the person taking last place receives some money. The winner receives more, of course, but each contestant in this very competitive game (conflict) wins part of the total pot. The goal is shared. The shared goal is probably the most-used technique for the management of interpersonal conflict. It involves compromise and bargaining or negotiating. If these two procedures fail to produce a satisfactory share-the-goal resolution, contestants may turn to mediation, or even to arbitration, rather than attempt to resolve the conflict by either destruction or cessation. Let us, then, consider these four procedures: compromise, bargaining, mediation, and arbitration.

Compromise refers to a procedure of **conflict management** in which the parties are willing to give up certain goals or values in order to preserve goals or values of higher priority. Each party settles for something less than what it wanted. Each gives up lesser goals so that both can have part of the important goal—the shared value. However, even when there is a basic agreement on the important goal, that agreement may be destroyed or purposely ignored because of negative interpersonal relationships such as those discussed in earlier chapters—lack of trust and closed-mindedness. Some of the most important variables that operate to help or hinder the process of conflict management will be discussed toward the end of this chapter.

Bargaining or negotiating involves exchange—trade between contestants. Bargaining or negotiating can be dynamic and exciting; it may involve argument, threats, proposals, and counterproposals. Communication variables become extremely important in the bargaining process.

Reiches and Harral have written specifically about one of these techniques in negotiation—the role of argument. They state, as we emphasized above, that argumentation does not occur in a "total-conflict situation," an all-out victory or defeat effort. Rather, in argumentation "one wins relative to his own goals and value system; satisfaction with the bargaining outcome does not necessarily imply crushing one's opponent."[30]

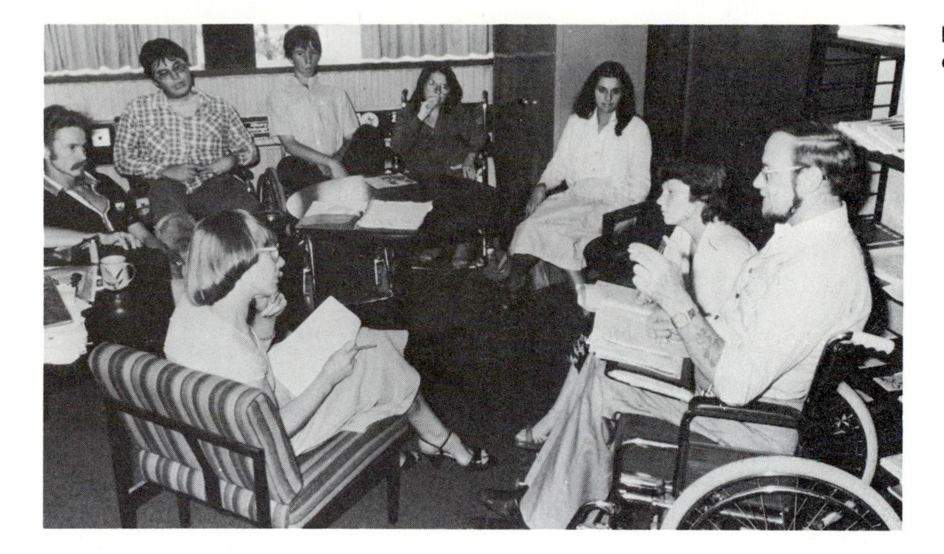

Negotiating involves exchange.

Mediation is a third technique used in conflict management. **Mediation** refers to the use of a third party in the negotiation or bargaining process. The contestants agree to allow a third party, an outside party, to assist them in the process. The mediator has no power to make decisions. The mediator cannot make trades or compromises for the contestants. The mediator simply serves as a catalyst to reason, persuade, provide data, and manage procedures, as agreed to by the parties. Mediators are used frequently in our society to manage interpersonal and intergroup conflicts. From marital difficulties to labor-management conflicts, mediation is a commonly used tool.

Arbitration is a final process in the sense that it often follows unsuccessful attempts at conflict management through personal compromise, bargaining, and mediated bargaining. **Arbitration** is characterized by giving the power of decision to an "outsider"—the arbitrator. The parties to the conflict give up their right to make decisions in the management of the conflict. The arbitrator functions as a judge and jury, hearing the arguments, considering the evidence and the cases presented, and deciding how to award the goal sought by the contestants. Arbitration is used most often when general public interest demands that certain conflicts be resolved.

Integrative Unity—Congruent and Fully-Shared Goal Resolutions

A fourth type of conflict management is that in which both parties win—an **integrative resolution,** wherein both parties share the goal fully and full integration and satisfaction of both parties are the outcomes. Once data has been provided, interpretations verified, values agreed upon, or misunderstandings cleared up—the parties involved in the controversy perceive their goals or desires to be compatible and congruent. There is no inherent basis for conflict; there is no conflict.

It is with the last two types of management of conflict (shared goals and integrative unity) that we are most concerned. These are wholesome growth-promoting kinds of conflict management. They differ from the first two types of conflict management (victory/destruction and cessation) in a very significant way—they require moving toward cooperative action rather than competitive or hostile combative action.

Facilitating Cooperative Behavior: Selected Variables in Conflict Management

Although there are many variables that operate in the process of conflict management, we will focus on four that seem to be especially significant in this type of interpersonal communication.

Amount of Communication

Studies seem to indicate that the opportunity for **full, free communication** and the use of that opportunity are related positively to cooperative behavior and subsequent conflict management. As a result of their experiments in conflict management, Steinfatt, Seibold, and Frye state: "When full communication is allowed, real reward produces more cooperation than does imaginary reward. This apparent interaction is in addition to an apparent main effect for communication across reward conditions."[31] They were studying the effects of imagined reward (visualized in the mind) and real reward (actual reward received) in cooperation for conflict management, as well as the effect of communication on cooperation. They found that communication by itself had an effect on cooperative handling of the conflict. Steinfatt and others concluded, "Communication, the opportunity to exchange information concerning the possibilities of the situation, is necessary; without communication no creative solutions occur.[32] Unless the communication lines are open and used, conflicts go unresolved. It ought to be apparent, then, that pouting, "clamming up," and fleeing from the conflict are counterproductive behaviors. Rather, one of the most important variables in conflict management is willingness and opportunity to engage in full communication.

What would one do to facilitate cooperative behavior in a conflict situation?

One of the problems in marital conflict often encountered by marriage counselors is that the couple has closed all lines of communication. Opening the channels of communication, restoring the opportunity for communication, and getting the couple involved to communicate with each other are among the counselor's first tasks. An increase in the number of channels used, a simultaneous redundancy of multichannel messages, and open face-to-face communication—all serve to increase cooperative behavior; and cooperative behavior is necessary for shared goals or integrative conflict management.

Accuracy in Communication

In addition to opportunity for full communication, a second important variable in inducing cooperative behavior and managing conflict satisfactorily is **accuracy in communication.** Just as it is common for individuals in conflict to close communication channels instead of moving toward fuller and freer communication, so too it is common for individuals in conflict to communicate inaccuracies and threats rather than objective and accurate information. The studies of Pilisuk and Skolnick show that when intentions are communicated with integrity, increases in cooperative behavior follow; but when one person is deceptive, there is a decrease in trust and cooperative behavior and an increase in competitive behavior.[33] Shure, Meeker, and Hansford have found that as competition increases in conflict situations, subjects think their opponents are trying to deceive or trick them.[34] As honesty is revealed, however, cooperative behavior increases.

Honesty and accuracy seem to be necessary to increase cooperation in attempts to manage conflicts.

Content of Communication

A third variable found to be important in conflict management is the **content of the messages.** When the message content is primarily substantive and orientational rather than emotional or affective, cooperative behavior is induced. You will recall that we made this point in chapter 6 when we discussed supportive and defensive communication behavior. Research by Bales indicates that threats, although common in conflict communication, are detrimental to consensus seeking, whereas high-orientation statements are helpful.[35] Similar effects of threat statements have been found by Deutsch and Krauss.[36]

Threats communicate potential harm. High-threat verbal behavior is characterized by a large number of statements reflecting antagonism toward the person or ideas. High-orientation verbal behavior includes statements of procedural suggestions, relevant facts, and conciliation or willingness to consider other alternatives and ideas. As bargaining communication increasingly allows for the honest expression of intentions, expectations, and conditions of reconciliation, it will be more successful in inducing cooperative behavior.

The content of the messages, then, has an important effect on the process of conflict management. When messages are orientational and substantive, when they clarify and emphasize expectations, procedures, sanctions, and promises of reward, cooperative behavior is likely to be facilitated. When deception, antagonism, and threat characterize the bargaining communication, competitiveness rather than cooperation tends to result, and escalation into combat is encouraged.

Structuring Cooperative Action

When we want to induce cooperative behavior in conflict management, we need specifically to create situations that tend to **structure cooperative action.** Johnson states:

> Perhaps the surest way of resolving a conflict constructively is to involve yourself and the other person in a situation where you have to cooperate with each other to achieve mutually desired goals. Cooperative interaction means that you and the other person will engage in joint action to accomplish a goal you both desire. Two individuals who both wish to build a sandcastle and help each other to do so are in cooperative interaction. . . . Cooperative interaction has very powerful, positive effects upon the relationship between two individuals. Cooperation produces increased liking for one another, increased trust, and a willingness to listen to and be influenced by each other. . . . In a conflict situation, the primary way to ensure a constructive resolution is to work out a cooperative solution. . . .[37]

Numerous studies have verified the positive relationship between cooperative interaction and conflict management. If cooperative interactions can be created or structured, conflict may be resolved constructively.

The Interview

The interview completes the spectrum of types of dyadic communication—from intimate interaction through social communication to serious or instrumental communication. All are settings of dyadic communication, but each is different from the others in terms of purpose and in terms of salient variables. The interview involves two parties, at least one of whom has a preconceived and serious purpose and both of whom speak and listen from time to time. The interview is different from other dyadic communication because one person, and perhaps both, has a preconceived and serious purpose. Two persons talking, with neither having thought in advance about the objective to be accomplished, does not constitute an interview. The words *serious purpose* differentiate the interview from social conversation for enjoyment. The interview is a form of instrumental communication.

The interview has been widely studied and we have a wealth of data and knowledge about it. In fact, several books have been written on the subject of interviewing. Because interviewing has been studied extensively from a scientific standpoint, we are able to treat dyadic instrumental communication in somewhat more detail and with more precision than we are able to do in the cases of intimate interaction and social communication.

Virtually hundreds of empirical studies underlie the theory and principles of interviewing. And although we could discuss numerous of those principles, we are going to focus on only two areas—the question process and the interview structure. This does not mean that other areas, such as nonverbal communication, are not important. They are, in fact, quite important, but we have discussed them elsewhere in this text. All those variables previously covered—

self-concept, person perception, feedback, feelings, behavior patterns, and conflict phenomena—are directly applicable in the interview setting. Similarly, the factors we highlighted in our discussion of intimate and social communication are important in interviewing. It would be helpful for you to recall those variables and to apply them to the interview; but in addition, we must consider the interview structure and the question process if we are to have a useful understanding of the interview as a form of dyadic instrumental communication. Before discussing these two topics, however, let us consider the types or purposes of interviews.

Informational Interview

The two most common types of interviews are informational and persuasive. **Informational interviews** aim to acquire information about beliefs, attitudes, or feelings; or to obtain objective data from the interviewee; or to explain, instruct, or appraise the interviewee. Public opinion polls and research surveys are typical well-known examples of the "information-getting" interview, while explaining the procedures and policies of an organization to a new employee is an example of the "information-giving" interview. Also in the informational category are counseling, reprimand and appraisal interviews, problem-solving conferences, police and insurance investigations, the receiving of complaints, and informative interviews of celebrities or experts for newspapers, radio, or television.

Persuasive Interview

Sometimes, however, a person wishes to modify the beliefs or attitudes of another and attempts to do so through the **persuasive interview.** The sales interview is a typical example: the interviewer (the salesperson) attempts to get the interviewee (the customer) to buy the service or product. Another example of the persuasive interview is a subordinate's attempt to persuade the chairperson or boss to accept a proposal. Similarly, when you try to convince your instructor to raise your grade, you are engaged in a persuasive interview or conference. Throughout life, we engage in interviews in which we try to persuade another person to agree with us. The employment interview, for example, is a special type of interview that utilizes information getting, information giving, and persuasion as each party tries to get information from the other and, perhaps, tries to persuade the other party. Regardless of the purpose of the interview, however, the question-answer process is the primary vehicle for the communication. Let us consider the question-answer process.

The Question-Answer Process

In the question-answer process, the questioning skill of the interviewer is called into play. One of the first steps in the development of that skill consists of becoming acquainted with the various types of questions and their applications. The major types of questions to be used in the interview follow.

Open Questions

Open questions call for a response of more than a few words. One type of open question, the open-ended question, may do nothing more than specify a topic and ask the respondent to talk. "What do you think about life?" and "Tell me a little about yourself," are examples. A second kind of open question is more direct—it identifies a more restricted topic area and asks for a reply. In some classification systems this question is known as the direct question, rather than a form of open question. "What did you do on your weekends last winter?" is an example.

Closed Questions

Closed questions, a second category, call for a specific response of a few words. One type of closed question is the yes-no, or bipolar, question. It calls for a "yes" or a "no" answer—or, perhaps "I don't know." "Did you attend the last home basketball game last winter?" is a closed question. Similarly, "What two courses did you like most, and what two courses did you like least in high school?" is a closed question, though not a yes-no question.

It is important to note that the use of either open or closed questions influences the length of the interviewee's responses. Open questions encourage the respondent to talk at greater length, while closed questions inhibit participation by the respondent.[38] Since one of the problems in most interviews is getting the interviewee to become freely involved and to participate in the interview, it is unwise for the interviewer to use only closed questions. Generally speaking, open questions are more likely to be used in the early part of the interview or at the introduction of each new topic area, while closed questions are used as follow-ups for the responses to open questions.

Mirror Questions

Mirror questions are nondirective techniques. A mirror question encourages the interviewee to expand on a response that the interviewer believes was incomplete. Mirror questions are usually restatements of what the interviewer has just said. If the interviewee has said, "I don't approve of legalizing abortion," a mirror question might be, "You say that abortion should not be legalized?"

Probing Questions

Probing questions are asked in order to probe more deeply into the reasons or an attitude or belief, or to elicit more specific information. Not all probes are questions of why or how, although these are the most common probing questions. There are a variety of other vocalizations that act effectively as probes and encouragements. Brief sounds or phrases such as "Uh-huh," "I see," "That's interesting," "Oh?" "Good," "I understand," and "Go on," have the effect of requesting further comment from the respondent. Probes and encouragements are introduced at any time—during pauses or while the interviewee is speaking. They indicate careful attention and interest, and are intended to encourage the respondent to "tell more" without the interviewer's specifying the further response. It is important, however, that an interviewer avoid the habit of relying on only one reinforcing or probing word.

Silence is fully as important as direct probing questions and sounds. As indicated in chapter 5 (in the discussion of nonverbal communication), silence communicates. The inexperienced interviewer is often afraid of pauses and silences. He tends to fill every silence, and by so doing, to rush through the interview. If the respondent is slow in answering a question, the inexperienced interviewer may rush in to rephrase the question or to ask a new question. With experience, interviewers can learn when to use silence as a means of communication—as a probe. Research findings indicate that silences of three to six seconds are most effective in getting the respondent to provide more information.[39]

Leading Questions

Leading questions strongly imply or encourage a specific answer. They "lead" the respondent to an answer the interviewer expects. The leading question can be detrimental to the interview when used for the wrong reasons. If the interviewer wants straightforward, valid, and reliable information from the respondent, leading questions should be avoided. Cannell and Kahn state, "Questions should be phrased so that they contain no suggestion as to the most appropriate response,"[40] and Bingham, Moore, and Gustad say, "Avoid implying the answer to your own question."[41] If, however, the interviewer wishes to test the respondent, to see if the respondent really understands or is genuinely committed, then the leading question may be quite useful. For example, when the speech therapist asks the mother of a stuttering child, "You are slapping his hands every time he starts to stutter, aren't you?" he is leading her to an incorrect answer unless she clearly understands that slapping the child for stuttering is inappropriate behavior. The interviewer, when using this technique, is sometimes referred to as the devil's advocate.

One type of leading question is the yes-response or the no-response question. "Naturally, you agreed with the decision, didn't you?" is an example of a yes-response question. One of the components of leading questions is expectation. If the interviewer asks, "Are you twenty-one years old?" the question is direct and closed, but it is not leading. If, however, the interviewer asks, "Of course, you are twenty-one years old, aren't you?" an expectation is indicated. Expectations can be identified by the syntax and logic of the question, but, as noted in chapter 6, intonation can also communicate expectation. Through intonation and emphasis one might make the question, "Did you agree with that decision?" a leading question—by implying surprise and incredulity at anything other than the expected answer.

Another form of the leading question is the loaded question, which uses loaded words and has high emotional connotations. It reaches "touchy spots" and strikes strong feelings. It may present a dilemma from which it is difficult for the respondent to escape. Questions that are not stated objectively are considered loaded. Various techniques are used to indicate the bias or expectation. Prestige may be used: "The President of the United States believes that the problem is serious. Don't you agree?" The interviewer may also associate positive stereotypes with responses that are desired or negative stereotypes with responses that are not desired.

To gain an understanding of the question-answer process, we need to become familiar with and be able to recognize the various types of questions that may be used. Through guided practice, we can develop skill in using questions.

Interview Structure

Interview structure can be thought of in two ways: (1) as the composition of the interview in terms of opening, body, and closing; and (2) as the organizational plan of the body of the interview.

Opening, Body, and Closing

First, let us consider the structure of the interview in terms of its parts—**opening, body, and closing.** The initial stage—opening the interview—is quite important, for during this time the relationship between the interviewer and the respondent is established. The objectives of the opening are to establish confidence, trust, purpose, and to identify mutual goals. Rapport, an important element throughout the interview, is largely established in the opening stage. Some pre-interview acts also relate to the establishment of rapport. The request for an interview should be made in terms that do not alarm or threaten the interviewee; and the place selected for the interview should be private, comfortable, and conducive to a smooth and satisfactory interview.

The second phase of the interview is the substantive part, which relies heavily upon the question-answer process previously discussed. Structure, as it relates to this part of the interview, will be discussed shortly.

The final stage of the interview is the closing. Some interviews come to a natural close as a result of the discussion's progress or as a result of the participants' inclinations. Other interviews really need to be continued, but circumstances dictate that they must be closed. Still other interviews could be continued profitably, but time dictates that they must be ended. Regardless of the reasons or conditions, the interview closing ought to contain a short summary by the interviewer, an opportunity for the interviewee to make additions and corrections, and an indication of the next steps.

General Pattern

Now, let us consider the second way structure is used in interviewing—as the organizational plan or strategy. The interview can be structured *in terms of general pattern* so as to be directive or nondirective, and in terms of **sequencing patterns of questions.**

With the **directive structure** the interviewer decides what questions will be asked, what topics will be covered, the sequence of the topics and questions, and the overall procedure that will be followed in the interview. Using the

When you try to convince your instructor to raise your grade, you are engaged in a persuasive interview or conference.

nondirective structure, the interviewer allows the interviewee to make most of these decisions. The interviewee is reinforced and encouraged to talk about whatever he or she wishes. If one is using a nondirective structure, open questions, mirror questions, and indirect probes will be used; but if one is using a direct approach, closed questions and direct probes may be used.

The direct structured interview may be described further in terms of degree of directness. The most highly structured interview pattern is the **standarized interview.** In this type of structure each question in the interview is precisely worded; each question is carefully ordered in the sequence of questions. In other words, every question is asked in exactly the same words and at the same place in the interview for every person interviewed. All of the interviewer's verbal content, as well as the sequence of the content, is rigidly controlled. Such an interview structure is most frequently used in research interviewing, so that interviewee responses to common or standardized stimuli can be compared.

Some direct interviews, on the other hand, are not so rigidly standardized. They may use a directive structure and cover a specified number of areas, but the interviewer is free to move into one area or another as the situation seems to warrant. The interviewer is also free to add questions, to probe on a given topic, or to shorten the investigation of a given topic. The structure is basically directive rather than nondirective, but it gives the interviewer a great amount of flexibility to adjust to the interviewee.

Sequencing of Questions

Structure may also be examined according to the sequencing of questions. The more common sequencing types are the funnel, inverted funnel, tunnel, covert, and quintamensional. The **funnel sequence** involves moving from broad, open questions to more narrow, closed, and delimiting ones. The **inverted funnel sequence** progresses from closed, restricted questions to open and broad ones. The **tunnel sequence** employs a series of similar questions that are all open or all closed. The **covert sequence** normally involves placing individual topics at the most advantageous position in the interview. Journalists frequently use covert sequencing when they place the most threatening questions in the heart of the interview. The **quintamensional sequence,**[42] primarily used in survey interviews, has one or more questions in each of five areas:

1. Filter dimension—questions to assess the extent to which interviewee is informed.
2. Free answer—permits discussion of the topic in the interviewee's own words.
3. Dichotomous—the interviewee is asked to respond to dichotomous questions: yes-no.
4. Reason why—interviewee may explain his or her answer.
5. Intensity—the intensity of each opinion is probed.

The different structures vary in value and efficiency according to the purpose of the interview. Counseling and therapy interviews are often nondirective since it is desirable to reduce the threat to the interviewee, to give the interviewee control over information sharing, and to make the interviewee responsible for information acquisition and growth. On the other hand, the employment interview often utilizes a direct approach, but with considerable flexibility built into it. Research interviews, as indicated, are normally structured so as to be standardized. Skill in structuring the interview and skill in the questioning process are necessary for the successful interviewer. In addition, the interviewer and the interviewee will be more successful if they are also adept in the utilization of the other interpersonal communication skills.

Let us now consider the employment interview as an illustrative vehicle.

The Employment Interview

The employment interview's purpose is to inform, to get information, and to persuade. Moreover, the employment interview is unique in that both the applicant and the employer share the power of decision. Generally, the employment interview places the applicant in the position of persuading the prospective employer that he or she represents a good investment for the employer. But sometimes situations arise in which the procedure is reversed and the primary burden is upon the employer to sell the job to the applicant.

Initial messages are important in an employment interview.

The employment interview represents a communication situation in which almost every college student will participate sooner or later—an extraordinarily important communication situation. An understanding of and skill in interpersonal communication can enhance one's performance in the interview.

What the Typical Employer Wants to Know about the Applicant

The results of several studies of employment interviews indicate that the major areas of concern to the interviewer are the applicant's ability, desire to work, socioemotional maturity, and character. An applicant, knowing that these areas are important to the interviewer, would be wise to give some thought to these questions so as to provide full and accurate information in an effective manner.

In terms of **ability**, interviewers are especially interested in the applicant's vocational and avocational experiences. It is wise for the applicant to know how these experiences contribute toward providing expertise needed for the position. It is to the advantage of the applicant to point out such relationships rather than leaving them to be "assumed" by the interviewer.

Education and training, both formal and informal, are part of one's ability and should be fully explored in the employment interview. Similarly, intelligence—as revealed through grades in school, activities, honors, recognitions, and conduct during the interview—is related to ability. The questions asked by the interviewee, as well as the responses made to the interviewer's questions, are used to evaluate intelligence and general ability.

A second area of major concern is **desire to work**. Studies of interviewing show that questions and information relating to three areas—past record of changes in jobs, applicant's reasons for wanting the particular job, and the applicant's knowledge of this company or organization—are used to evaluate the applicant's desire to work.

The employer's third area of concern is the **socioemotional maturity** of the applicant. The typical interviewer may attempt to discover the applicant's personal goals, independence, self-reliance, creativity, imagination, and ability to exercise authority, to take orders, or be corrected.

Finally, the **applicant's character** is of importance to the interviewer. Character may be judged on the basis of personal behavior, honesty, history of financial responsibility or irresponsibility, and the accuracy and objectivity of self-reports. As we shall note again later, dishonesty, sham, and boastfulness are extremely detrimental and even disastrous in the employment interview.

What the Applicant Should Know about the Position

The applicant should be prepared to satisfy the employer's questions and be able to answer one's own questions also.

One of the most important areas of concern for the applicant is that of job expectation or requirements. There are many sad stories about jobs that were not what the applicant assumed or understood them to be. Careful thought and effort should be given to understanding fully what the job entails.

The applicant should also discover who the co-workers will be. A common background in education, values, philosophy, and training will enhance the relationship one has with co-workers and increase the potential job satisfaction.

The applicant should also be concerned with the opportunities and policies for advancement, benefits, hours, pay, job security, and working conditions. It is helpful for the applicant to have these areas clearly in mind during the interview in order to secure the information necessary for an informed decision.

Specific Suggestions for the Applicant

The following list of suggestions should be considered as general guidelines for interviewers and interviewees in the employment interview.[43]

Suggestions for the applicant:

1. Clarify the job requirements.
2. State why you are applying for this job with this company.
3. Present your qualifications as something of value to the company. As much as possible, deal in specific details and examples—job experiences, avocations, travel, activities, offices held, organizations, and school work.

4. Do not hesitate to *admit potential "weaknesses."* Under no circumstances should you attempt to bluff or fake on these, but wherever possible, *make a transition from a "weakness" to a strength;* or at least, when the facts justify it, show some good *extenuating circumstances* for the "weakness."
5. Do not depend merely on a "smooth front" to "sell yourself." Provide full information to the prospective employer.
6. Get as much information as possible on such matters as *salary*—usually in terms of a *range,* or of the *"going average."*
7. Let the employer set the tone of the interview. Be a *little* more formal than usual—but don't be a stuffed shirt! Be cautious about jokes, wise cracks, and sarcastic asides.
8. Watch the opening moments of the interview. Avoid making remarks that create a *"negative set"* for the rest of the interview. Avoid starting the interview with a remark such as "I'm really not sure that my background will be appropriate for your company or for this job." Or "I'm sorry to say I haven't had any experience along these lines."
9. *Be informed on the company*: its history, geographical locations, general methods of doing business, and reputation.
10. Conclude the interview with an understanding of what is to happen next and who is to contact whom.

Suggestions for the employer:

1. Take the initiative in getting the interview under way; don't just sit back and stare at the applicant. Offer your hand first. Ask the applicant to be seated. Establish rapport *before* probing for information.
2. Make an easy, casual, smooth *transition* from opening greetings to the first serious topic of the interview.
3. *Start off with "easy" questions* on the applicant's background. Encourage the applicant to talk freely about something which, from information that appeared on the application, should be easy to discuss with specific details and examples.
4. Don't give a "sales pitch."
5. Do more listening than talking. Encourage the applicant. Listen carefully between the lines. Insert "prompters" to encourage more talk and use "mirror" techniques.
6. Don't exaggerate the benefits of the company or the job. Create confidence and trust by being honest about potential or actual drawbacks.
7. *Avoid evaluative comments on the applicant's answers* such as "that's too bad," or "I'm certainly glad you said that!"

8. *Without being mechanical,* try to cover topics in a *systematic* order. Your objective is not only to avoid hit-and-miss jumping around but also to avoid giving the impression you're engaging in an oral examination.
9. Be alert to "cues" in the applicant's answers and behavior. Adapt immediately to what is said so that you can *follow up a promising lead.* Probe suspected weaknesses.
10. Ask questions that will reveal the applicant's *attitudes* and *personality* in terms of the job's *total* requirements.

The employment interview is a give-and-take process, highly dynamic and rich in its informational and persuasive potential. The communication skills involved are varied and include those examined in this text in the sections, *Foundations of Communication* and *Interpersonal Communication.* Whether it is an employment interview, survey interview, exit interview, journalistic interview, research interview, or investigative interview, the person who desires to improve behavior as an interviewer or interviewee must learn to be perceptive and accurate in observing and understanding the other person.

Summary

In this chapter we have discussed how a relationship comes into existence—how the acquaintance process works, how important first impressions are, and how carefully persons proceed in coming to know each other. We identified the factors that influence the maintenance of satisfying relationships—affection, control, appropriate responsiveness, and emotional tone. We then discussed how and why relationships are terminated.

The second concern of this chapter was the application of interpersonal communication variables, such as we studied in chapter 6, to specific interpersonal relationships—family, social, conflict, and instrumental relationships, such as the interview. We observed how communication can be effective or ineffective in each of these interpersonal communication settings, and we identified those communication behaviors, attitudes, and skills that are needed for effective participation in these communication situations.

Questions and Exercises for Review

1. Describe the three stages in the life of a relationship.
2. What are the four primary objectives in maintaining a satisfactory interpersonal relationship?
3. How does role, as an interpersonal communication factor, operate in social communication?
4. What are the characteristics of the various types of interpersonal conflicts?
5. How can one facilitate cooperative behavior in conflict resolution?
6. What are the different kinds of questions one might use in interviewing?

Key Terms and Phrases

dyadic communication
marital communication
generation gap
entry phase
acquaintance process
reciprocal scanning
"four-minute barrier"
demographic exchange
intimacy
dominance
appropriate responsiveness or inclusion
appropriate emotional tone
perceptual differences
different goals
value differences
status differences
role pressures
personality differences
nonsharable goals
sharable goals
fully sharable objectives
controversy
competition
combat
opening, body, and closing
sequencing patterns of questions
directive structure
nondirective structure
standardized interview
funnel sequence
total victory
total destruction
cessation
shared-goal resolutions
conflict management
mediation
arbitration
integrative resolution
full, free communication
accuracy in communication
content of the messages
structure cooperative action
informational interview
persuasive interview
open questions
closed questions
mirror questions
probing questions
leading questions
inverted funnel sequence
tunnel sequence
covert sequence
quintamensional sequence
socioemotional maturity
applicant's character

For Further Reading

Bingham, W. V. D.; Moore, B. V.; and Gustad, J. W. *How to Interview.* New York: Harper and Brothers, 1959.

A rather thorough treatment of various types of interviews with a research orientation.

Downs, C. W.; Smeyak, G. Paul; and Martin, Ernest. *Professional Interviewing.* New York: Harper & Row Publishers, 1980.

A thorough treatment of a range of various types of interviews including employment, broadcast, and research.

Jourard, S. M. *The Transparent Self.* New York: Van Nostrand Reinhold Co., 1971.

An excellent discussion of self-disclosure.

Newcomb, Theodore M. *The Acquaintance Process.* New York: Holt, Rinehart & Winston, 1961.

A readable and interesting discussion of the acquaintance process.

Pearce, W., and Sharp, S. "Self-Disclosing Communication." *The Journal of Communication* 23:4 (1973): 409–25.
This is a synthesis of research findings. The findings are discussed in terms of five characteristics of self-disclosing communication.

Sincoff, Michael Z., and Goyer, Robert S. *Interviewing.* New York: Macmillan Publishing Co., 1984.
A broad range of interviewing types. Includes a discussion of equal employment opportunity and legal aspects of the employment interview.

Stewart, Charles J., and Cash, William B., Jr. *Interviewing: Principles and Practices,* 4th ed. Dubuque, Ia: Wm. C. Brown Publishers, 1985.
An excellent discussion of the important variables in communication in the interview situation.

Notes

1. Charles H. Cooley, "Primary Group and Human Nature," in *Symbolic Interaction,* ed. Jerome G. Manis and Bernard N. Meltzer (Boston: Allyn & Bacon, 1967), 156.
2. Sidney M. Jourard and Ardis Whitman, "The Fear That Cheats Us of Love," *Redbook,* October 1971, 83.
3. James C. McCroskey, Carl E. Larson, and Mark L. Knapp. *An Introduction to Interpersonal Communication* (Englewood Cliffs, N.J.: Prentice-Hall, 1971), 175–76.
4. Jourard and Whitman, "Fear That Cheats Us," 157.
5. Jourard and Whitman, "Fear That Cheats Us," 158.
6. Leonard Zunin, *Contact: The First Four Minutes* (Los Angeles: Nash Publishing Co., 1972); Irwin Altman and Dalmas A. Taylor, *Social Penetration: The Development of Interpersonal Relationships* (New York: Holt, Rinehart & Winston, 1973); and Charles R. Berger, "The Acquaintance Process Revisited: Explorations in Initial Interaction" (Unpublished manuscript, Northwestern University, 1973).
7. Theodore M. Newcomb, *The Acquaintance Process* (New York: Holt, Rinehart & Winston, 1961); Donn Byrne, *The Attraction Paradigm* (New York: Academic Press, 1971); and Sidney M. Jourard, *Self-Disclosure: An Experimental Analysis of the Transparent Self* (New York: John Wiley & Sons, 1971).
8. Newcomb, *Acquaintance Process,* 261.
9. Berger, "Acquaintance Process Revisited," 4; and Zunin, *Contact,* "Preface."
10. Altman and Taylor, *Social Penetration,* 11.
11. Berger, "Acquaintance Process Revisited," 4.
12. Zunin, *Contact,* 6.
13. Berger, "Acquaintance Process Revisited," 7.
14. Berger, "Acquaintance Process Revisited," 14.
15. See S. E. Asch, "Forming Impressions of Personality," *Journal of Abnormal Social Psychology* 41 (1946): 258–90. Also, you may recall our discussion of person perception in chapter 3 in which the traits theory of impression formation was explained in detail.
16. H. C. Smith, "Sensitivity to People," in *Social Perception,* ed. Hans Toch and H. C. Clay (Princeton, N.J.: D. Van Nostrand Co., 1968), 14.
17. Smith, "Sensitivity to People," 14.
18. W. C. Schutz, *FIRO: A Three Dimensional Theory of Interpersonal Behavior* (New York: Holt, Rinehart Company, 1958); Michael Argyle, *Social Interaction* (New York: Atherton Press, 1969).

19. Argyle, *Social Interaction,* 190–203.

20. Argyle, *Social Interaction,* 201.

21. Argyle, *Social Interaction,* 201.

22. Argyle, *Social Interaction,* 201.

23. Argyle, *Social Interaction,* 203.

24. See, for example, Henry Lennard and Arnold Bernstein, *Patterns in Human Interactions* (San Francisco: Jossey-Bass Publishers, 1969); Erving Goffman, *Relations in Public* (New York: Harper & Row, 1972).

25. Alvin Toffler, *Future Shock* (New York: Random House, Inc., 1970), 33–35, 45, 46.

26. George Simmel, *Conflict,* trans. Kurt H. Wolff, and *The Web of Group Affiliations,* trans. Reinhard Bendix (Glencoe, Ill.: Free Press, 1955).

27. David W. Johnson, *Reaching Out* (Englewood Cliffs, N.J.: Prentice-Hall, 1972), 203.

28. M. Deutsch, "Conflicts: Productive and Destructive," *Journal of Social Issues* 25 (1969): 7–8.

29. Nancy A. Reiches and Harriet B. Harral, "Argument in Negotiation: A Theoretical and Empirical Approach," *Speech Monographs* 41 (1974): 36–48.

30. Thomas M. Steinfatt, David R. Seibold, and Jerry K. Frye, "Communication in Game Simulated Conflicts: Two Experiments," *Speech Monographs* 41 (1974): 34.

31. Steinfatt et al., "Game Simulated Conflicts," 34.

32. M. Pilisuk and P. Skolnick, "Inducing Trust: A Test of the Osgood Proposal," *Journal of Personality and Social Psychology* 8 (1968): 121–33.

33. G. H. Shure, R. J. Meeker, and E. A. Hansford, "The Effectiveness of Pacifist Strategies in Bargaining Games," *Journal of Conflict Resolution* 9 (1965): 106–17.

34. Robert F. Bales, *Personality and Interpersonal Behavior* (New York: Holt, Rinehart & Winston, 1970).

35. Morton Deutsch and Robert M. Krauss, "The Effect of Threat Upon Interpersonal Bargaining," *Journal of Abnormal and Social Psychology* 61 (1960): 181–89.

36. Johnson, *Reaching Out,* 215–16.

37. Stephen A. Richardson, Barbara S. Dohrenwend, and David Klein, *Interviewing: Its Form and Functions* (New York: Basic Books, 1965), 147.

38. See R. L. Gordon, "An Interaction Analysis of the Depth-Interview" (Ph.D. diss., University of Chicago, 1954); G. Saslow et al., "Test-Retest Stability of Interaction Patterns During Interviews Conducted One Week Apart," *Journal of Abnormal Social Psychology* 54 (1957): 295–302.

39. C. F. Cannell and R. L. Kahn, "The Collection of Data by Interviewing," in *Research Methods in the Behavioral Sciences,* ed. L. Festinger and D. Katz (New York: Dryden Press, 1953), 346.

40. W. V. D. Bingham, B. V. Moore, and J. W. Gustad, *How to Interview* (New York: Harper and Brothers, 1959), 74.

41. George Gallup, "The Quintamensional Plan of Question Design," *Public Opinion Quarterly* 11 (Fall 1947), 385.

42. Adapted from Robert S. Goyer, W. Charles Redding, and John T. Rickey, *Interviewing Principles and Techniques* (Dubuque, Iowa: Kendall/Hunt Publishing Co., 1969), 23–25.

Focus

The Nature of the Small Group

Why People Join Groups

Types of Groups

Primary Groups
Casual Groups
Educational Groups
Support Groups
Problem-Solving Groups

Issues Related to the Individual

Belonging
Taking A Role
Task Roles
Maintenance Roles
Status and Identity
Affection
Cohesiveness
Social Climate
Understanding of and Sensitivity to Group Processes

Issues Related to the Group

Leadership Skills
Decision-Making Skills
Problem-Solving Skills

Planning for Productive Meetings

Need for the Meeting
Goals of the Meeting
Agenda
Participants
Facilities

Participant Skills

Small-Group Communication

8

In this chapter, we study several types of small groups, including primary, casual, educational, support, and problem-solving groups. The two areas of concern in small-group communication are "people issues" (climate) and "task issues." A healthy group climate is one in which the members have a sense of belonging, discover a satisfying and needed role, achieve identity and status, develop affection and cohesiveness, and understand the process of communication in the small group. Task issues have to do with leadership skills, problem-solving and decision-making skills. Productive meetings don't just happen. Rather, the careful planner assesses the need for a meeting, sets clear goals, prepares an agenda, selects appropriate participants, and fits the meeting room and facilities to the meeting. The final section of the chapter focuses on participant skills.

The small group has become one of the most common settings for speech communication. Small groups operate in every organized human activity. As a student, you have participated in many problem-solving small groups. The average professional person attends as many as two or three luncheons or dinner meetings a week, in addition to many conferences and committee meetings during regular working hours. Government representatives conduct most of their problem solving and decision making in small groups. Most people participate in small groups, formally and informally. Since it is virtually impossible for an educated person in a responsible position to avoid such participation, understanding how small groups function is essential.

In order to understand how small groups function, we must examine the nature of the small group. The small group has a powerful potential for action. When people come together in a group, friendships can develop, decisions can be made, and problems can be solved. Many people, however, are not able to effectively participate in decision making because they do not understand the nature of the small group or their role in it.

The Nature of the Small Group

Homans has defined a **group** as "a number of persons who communicate with one another, often over a span of time, and who are few enough so that each person is able to communicate with all the others, not at second hand, through other people, but face-to-face. . . . A chance meeting of casual acquaintances does not count as a group for us.[1] Neither does the collection of people at a basketball game constitute a group. That is an **aggregation,** not a group in our sense of the term. Congregations, aggregations, audiences, and other collections of a large number of individuals are not groups.

Each small group (committee, coffee klatch, task force, project team, cell group, etc.), regardless of its type, shares some common characteristics with all other types of small groups. Among the most important of these characteristics are the following.[2]

Purpose. Every group has a purpose. It exists for some reason. It came into being to fulfill some purpose or need and, if it continues to function as a viable and healthy group, it is because its members know why it exists and because it is fulfilling that purpose.

Procedures. Every group has its ways of operating—of doing whatever has to be done to fulfill its purpose. Group procedures vary from quite strict adherence to specific rules to informal, nonspecified procedures. However, even in the most informal coffee klatch social group that meets at the same time each week, or each day, procedures become standardized. Ways of operating come into existence without being written down or printed in a book of rules.

A great deal of business is conducted in small groups.

Roles. The members of groups have roles they fill as each person makes an individual contribution to the group. The group comes to expect certain people to do certain things and not to do other things. In other words, the group, through its establishment of roles, regulates who contributes what and when so that the group functions smoothly as a whole or as a unit.

Climate. Each group develops a climate that reflects the nature of the interpersonal relationships among its members as well as the purpose the group fulfills. The climate may be primarily intellectual. It may be formal or informal. It may be warm and acceptive or tense and threatening. It may be lively and fun-filled or dull and boring. Whatever the dominant characteristics of the climate, a climate will evolve in every group, and it becomes an important and influential characteristic of how that group functions. The increasing importance of the concept of climate to group and organizational satisfaction and effectiveness is evident in recent research among group and organizational communication scholars. In essence, they are focusing on "what it feels like to work here or to be a participant in this group."

Size. A fifth characteristic of groups that has a strong effect on its proficiency is size. Throughout this chapter, the phrase *small group* is purposefully used because the small group is most efficient in solving problems or in fulfilling whatever purpose exists for that group's reason for being. Four to seven members is the optimum number for participation in problem-solving groups. The group needs to be small enough to allow its members to speak directly to each other. Generally speaking, groups larger than seven almost always develop subgroups. In the larger groups, it is more difficult to retain unity, and the role each member can play is diminished. Interaction is extremely important to group productivity and the small group best facilitates adequate interaction.

Why People Join Groups

Need Satisfaction

People join groups to satisfy needs. Early in this book, we observed that humanity is basically a social creation. None of us is made to live in isolation. It is natural, then, for us to form groups to satisfy our needs. And because our needs vary, so do our groups. We form different types of groups to satisfy our various needs.

Among our needs are those of solving problems. Many of our problems cannot be easily resolved by us, so an easier and more effective way to solve the problems is through group involvement. Undoubtedly, you can list a number of groups to which you belong because they help you accomplish things you would not be able to accomplish alone. Our use of the word *belong* is not meant to imply only formal membership but the process of bonding to a group for whatever personal or social purposes might apply.

Affiliation

People join groups to satisfy their need for affiliation. We enjoy others, and we select and join certain groups because they are fun and we like socializing with the people in those groups.

Security

We join some groups to satisfy our need for security. There is safety in numbers and in the voice of established groups that will speak for their members. Neighborhood watch groups, for example, provide protection, safety, and security for their members. Other examples of such groups are campus groups to protect students from intruders, environmental groups, or specific groups organized to meet any sudden challenge to the members' health, wealth, employment, education, convenience, or other state of being.

The most common and most important security group is the family. It is the family as a social group that provides the initial security required for survival of the human infant. But the security provided by the family unit goes far beyond the initial security and protection required by an infant. Through childhood, adolescence, young adulthood, and even into grand and great grandparenthood, the family is one's primary source of security.

Esteem

People frequently join groups for esteem. Groups have status even as do individuals, and when a person is an accepted member of a high status group, that person enjoys that status and esteem, too. In fact, it often seems that the more difficult it is to obtain membership in a group, the higher the status or esteem given to its members. Many high status groups have severe limitations on and difficult requirements for membership.

The most important security group is the family.

Identity

A final need that is often satisfied in joining groups is identity. The groups to which we belong provide a valid index of our identity. Group memberships tell the world who we are. If you list the dozen most important groups in which you are a member, someone can have a good idea of who you are. We join groups to identify and define ourselves—to fulfill interests, needs, and goals. We may well be what we eat, but we are also the groups to which we belong.

Types of Groups

In order to meet our needs, we join many types of groups. There are essentially five kinds of groups: primary groups, casual groups, educational groups, support groups, and problem-solving groups. Let us briefly consider each of these five types.

Primary Groups

Primary groups, the first that every human being experiences, are *primary* in the sense that they give an individual the earliest, most basic, and most complete experience of social unity. The individual's first primary group is the family. It is one of the most elaborate, complex, intimate, and influential groups we experience, and it gives us our first training in social behavior and interpersonal relationships.

During early preschool years, each of us probably began to play with other children, and a second primary group was formed—the peer group. As we grew older, we became involved with other peer groups; even now we belong

The purpose of the educational group is to instruct, to teach, or to learn. Belonging is important to the small group.

to peer groups composed of friends, colleagues, church acquaintances, and so forth. These primary groups exert a strong influence upon our lives. Primary groups are among the most important groups to which we belong.

Casual Groups

The coffee group, informal rap sessions, and social gatherings are examples of **casual groups.** These groups do not exist to solve specific problems, although they may, from time to time, hash out problems or hold heated discussions on important issues. Rather, they exist to exchange ideas, to enjoy interacting with one another, and to extend the warmth of companionship. Conversation may ramble over many topics. There is no specified agenda; no requirement to stay on the subject. The members of such groups have as their goal friendly companionship. These groups are sometimes called friendship groups. They serve a social function for us.

Educational Groups

A third type of group is the **educational group,** the purpose of which is to instruct or to learn. There are any number of adult study clubs—the League of Women Voters is one. In classrooms, the small-group format is often used as a vehicle for instruction and learning. Scientists, business people, and professionals find it helpful to meet in conventions, to have seminars or workshops, or to organize programs that utilize a panel discussion, symposium, or forum. These are essentially information-sharing groups; they educate and inform members of the audience.

Some educational groups are more or less private (the classroom and conferences), while other information-giving groups are public in that they have audiences and the audience is the target of the group's communication efforts. Participants in these groups are usually experts or persons particularly involved with the topic of discussion. The purpose of such public discussion groups is not to solve a problem before onlookers, but to inform and educate. These public discussion groups can be organized into any of several patterns, including the panel, symposium, and forum.

A **panel-discussion group** usually has from four to six informed participants plus a chairperson. They sit in full view of the audience and carry on a public conversation among themselves. It is not unusual for the discussion to be carefully planned in advance as to topics, issues, and their sequence and development. Either the chairperson, or the chairperson and panelists, determine the outline or agenda, but the discussion is extemporaneous.

The **symposium** is characterized by two to four speakers, each of whom gives a prepared presentation to the audience. These speakers focus upon a common topic or problem. Each speaker may address a different part of the problem, or each may present a different viewpoint toward the problem as a whole. The chairperson may ask questions of the participants following their presentations, allow them to question each other, or invite the audience to ask questions.

The **forum** is a discussion in which the audience directs questions and enters into the discussion of the topic. The forum may follow a panel discussion and be a panel forum, or it may follow a symposium and be essentially a lecture forum. On occasion, a single speech, or film, or dramatic presentation is given and a public forum follows.

Support Groups

The small group is widely used for support, personal growth, and therapy. Social workers, psychiatrists, psychologists, and churches, in increasing numbers, are employing small-group techniques. The therapeutic group, or **support group,** is interested in personal improvement—changes in behavior, values, or attitudes of the individual. The support group then is a vehicle used to aid in the discovery of solutions and new insights, and to facilitate mutual support.

Of course, not all support groups are formal groups. Informal groups exist by the score. Wherever there is a need for an outlet of tensions and irritations, or a need to enjoy and share with others of like interests and experiences, support groups come into being. Such groups are cathartic. They exist in stores, factories, schools, and other organizations. Your student union is probably a common site for many such groups.

Today, it is increasingly common to institutionalize some such groups. Parents Without Partners, Tall-Girls Club, Weight Watchers, Alcoholics Anonymous, and Campus Life are examples. As the groups are institutionalized, they take on more rules, traditions, and procedures and so become more formal in their organization and functioning.

Problem-solving groups, educational groups, or casual groups may also have therapeutic effects on the individual, but, unlike support groups, that is not their primary purpose.

Problem-Solving Groups

Most of us belong to groups that have specific tasks assigned to them. Unlike the casual group or the support group, the **problem-solving group** has a particular *group goal* involving some anticipated action. Although the difference in goals distinguishes the five types of groups, all five contain the essence of the group process—face-to-face interaction that is relevant to all members.

Some problem-solving groups are ongoing in the sense that they have permanent membership, and their objectives—administrating, decision making, policy making—are continuously moving forward. The staff meeting is ongoing, for example. Standing committees are also examples of ongoing groups. Other small, problem-solving groups are on a temporary or ad hoc basis. They are appointed to accomplish a specific task and cease to function when the task is complete. The decorations committee for the homecoming dance is an example of such a small group.

In order to understand how small groups function, we must examine the agenda behavior of individuals in groups and the agenda behavior of the group as a whole. We are using the term *agenda* in a broader sense than one might be accustomed. On the individual level, **agenda** may refer to a range of conscious or unconscious personal goals. Individual goals may be referred to as "personal agenda." On the group level, the agenda may include not only a list of items to be covered in a meeting but the full range of leadership, decision-making and problem-solving skills required in task-oriented groups.

One essential goal of group problem-solving is to reach **synergy,** or the potential bonus effect inherent within the group. When a group's solution becomes more than the sum total of the input of the group members or is better than the most capable person could have achieved alone, synergy has taken place. If a group fails to solve a problem better than could the most capable group member working alone, the group has failed to work at its optimum level. Perhaps this is the reason many people in business, industry, and education feel that time and money is often wasted in committee work. Organizational communication specialists are increasingly calling attention to the need to monitor not only what topics are discussed in problem-solving groups

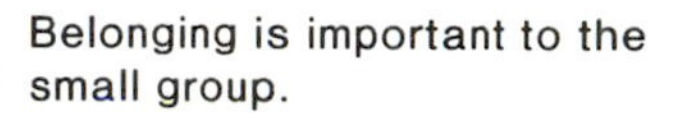

Belonging is important to the small group.

but the processes by which group members are encouraged or restrained as participants. Should concern for synergy be an agenda item for every decision-making and problem-solving group?

Issues Related to the Individual

If you are to become an effective participant in small groups, you need to develop a sensitivity to your behavior as a member. Each person, when joining a new group encounters common agenda issues: belonging, taking a role, gaining identity and status, developing affection, commitment and cohesiveness, social climate, and developing a sensitivity to group processes. These seven issues are important to each group member. Members should understand them and successfully implement each in the small group setting. Leaders as well as participants must pay attention to these factors, which constitute the socioemotional climate of the small-group process.

Belonging

One of the first issues you face on becoming a member of a small group is "Do I want to be a member of this group?" Sometimes, of course, you are arbitrarily or automatically a member of a group. You are born into the family and appointed to the committee; yet even in such groups you can decide that you would rather not belong, or you can decide that you are glad to belong and to be involved. That decision, to want to belong and to become genuinely involved, is a critical factor in the individual's ability to become a constructive member of the group. If this question is not resolved affirmatively, the individual may contribute nothing more than a name on the membership roster. Even worse, interpersonal problems that sabotage the best efforts of other group members may be created. If, on the other hand, the person perceives that personal needs can be met by **belonging** and by becoming involved—if this person wants to contribute to the group—then time, energy, and best motives will be dedicated to the work of the group.

Taking a Role

Taking a role represents a second issue to be confronted when joining a group. There are many roles that must be filled in the small group and every person in a group has a role to fill. We normally think of the leader's role, but there are numerous "task" and maintenance roles.

Some individuals want to be the leader in every group and other individuals do not want the leadership role in any group. Neither of these extremes represents a good attitude toward group participation.

The first view represents a dominant attitude that can have a negative effect on democratic group participation. That view of role taking can prevent an individual from developing a wide repertoire of role-taking skills. Every individual would be a more valuable group member by adapting to the specific role needs of the group.

Of course, the second attitude—that of not wanting to fill any role—is equally harmful. When one perceives oneself as lacking in the skills or competence necessary to fill a leadership role, or any other task or maintenance role, the group's potential for productivity is endangered. Groups have many roles to fill if synergy is to take place. Successful groups attempt to maximize the potential contributions of all members in order to achieve synergy.

As group members we need to be flexible. We need to be able to vary our roles or contributions to the group according to the needs of the group.

The primary roles found in groups can be classified as either task roles (leader, information-provider, clarifier, etc.—roles related to the substantive functioning of the group) or maintenance roles (roles related to the climate or interpersonal relationships of the group).

Task Roles

Task roles in formal groups include chairperson (leader), secretary, treasurer, program chairperson, and similar roles that are normally referred to as officers of the group. In addition, there are some roles, found in most groups, that are informal task roles. Although persons are not elected to these roles, they are necessary task roles that need to be filled if the group is to accomplish its task.

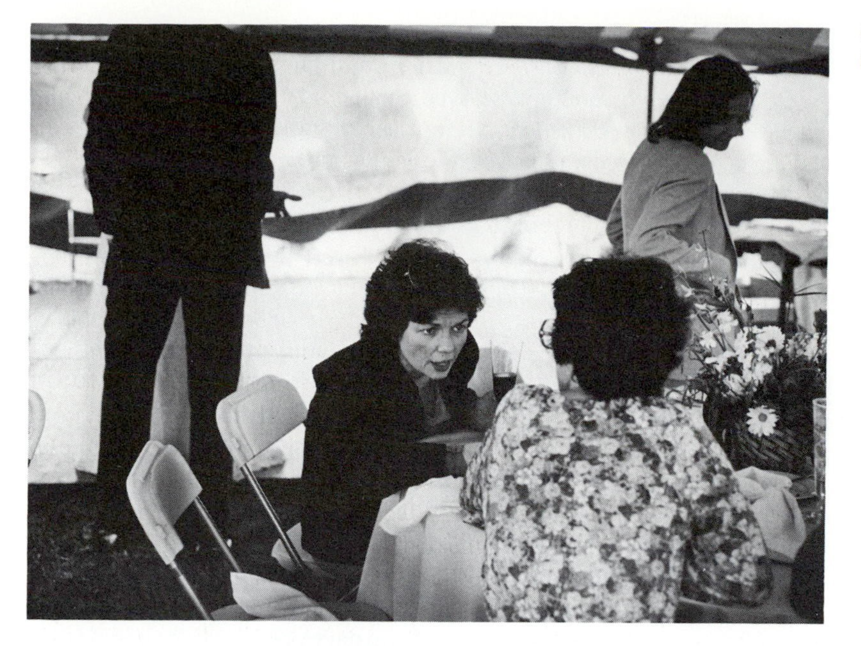

One group role is that of information-giver.

Some informal task roles that Benne and Sheats list are initiators, information-seekers, opinion-seekers, information-givers, opinion-givers, clarifiers, coordinators, evaluators, and concensus-testers.[3] These "tasks" need to be performed especially in problem-solving groups.

The *initiator* is an idea person who is rich in suggestions, defines clearly, shares ideas, and offers possible procedures and solutions. The good initiator can fill this role without being authoritarian, close-minded, or defensive.

The *information-seeker* probably stimulates the initiator and definitely opens the door to other resource persons. The information-seeker has the ability to know when a group needs information, knows what kind of information is needed, and knows how to get it. This person generally does not have the information but is a well-informed, clear thinker who knows how to ask the right questions at the right time. Also, the effective information-seeker insists on valid information, on facts and evidence, rather than jumping to conclusions or engaging in wishful thinking not grounded in reality.

The *opinion-seeker* is needed to elicit feelings, values, and judgments relative to evidence, procedures, and opinions concerning the group's discussion.

Information-givers are resource persons. Many of us have more information than we are sometimes willing to share with the group, but what is essential is that in areas where we do have knowledge, whether by experience formal education or training, we willingly provide that information to the group in a nondefensive and open way.

Opinion-givers are willing to tactfully reveal their values, beliefs and interpretations to the group. They are resource persons of a type much needed.

Clarifiers are another role-type needed in the small group. The clarifier asks sincere and pertinent questions concerning either the information being discussed or the procedures being followed in the discussion process. The role of the clarifier is an important role. Clarification frequently saves valuable time, reduces misunderstandings and brings about answers to questions that other group members wondered about but were afraid to ask.

Coordinators summarize and relate the various contributions in an integrative way.

Another task role is *evaluator.* Every problem-solving group needs an evaluator. This person keeps the group on track by keeping the criteria for judgment ever in the fore. If the discussion wanders too far away from criteria-based evaluation, the evaluator helps the group focus again on the criteria.

The *consensus-tester* is sensitive to assessing agreement and disagreement in the group.

This is not an all-inclusive list of task-roles. Groups may create additional roles, but these nine, as identified by Benne and Sheats, seem to be fairly common to problem-solving groups. Of course, the leader or any group member may fill several of these roles as the group develops effective shared leadership.

Maintenance Roles

The second category of roles is that of *maintenance roles.* Benne and Sheats identify five common maintenance roles.[4] These roles are related directly to the group's climate, that is, to the general atmosphere that determines members' reactions to the group as a whole. They include the *encourager,* who is supportive, acceptive, and reinforcing of others in the group; the *harmonizer,* who is able to reduce tension and resolve conflict when the discussion becomes "heated"; the *gatekeeper,* who controls channels and constructively promotes fairness and equality of opportunity to participate; the *compromiser,* who values group cohesion highly and thus models for the group a willingness to listen to and consider opposing opinions and to modify personal opinions when appropriate. Additional roles include the *standard-setter,* who works to establish consensus procedures; and the *comedian,* whose role is to provide relaxation, a sense of humor, and release of tension.

Again, as with task roles, these maintenance roles may be fulfilled by several persons, each of whom is concerned with one or more roles. But, it is not unusual to find one person to whom the group looks for leadership in just one of these maintenance roles. Whether the roles are shared or not, it is important that the roles be fulfilled.

Whatever the role, and whether it is task or maintenance, the smooth and productive operation of groups depends in no small way on the quality of role-taking by members of the group.

Status and Identity

A third issue to be confronted is **status** and **identity** in the group. Recognition and attention from a group is related to identification. If the individual's participation is to be sought by the group, the individual must be known as a person with a *particular identity.*

Name two groups to which you belong. How does your identity and role differ in the two groups?

The point was made earlier (chapter 3) that we have many selves, and we do not reveal the same self to all groups in which we have membership. One self is revealed in one group, while other selves are revealed in other groups. Further, our perceptions of ourselves are not always the same as the group's perception of us. The kind of identity the group assigns to us is directly related to the role expectations and functions its members have in mind for us. Because we soon learn that "who we are" in the group (identity of self as perceived by others) is important to our functioning in that group, we are concerned with the kind of identity we have in the eyes of our colleagues. When we enter a new group, we often attempt to establish identities that will enable others to "know" us and that will make us useful and wanted in the group.

Some identities carry higher status than others. When the status of each member is equal to that of all other members, communication is generally about equal among the members of the group; and when one or perhaps two persons achieve higher status than the other members of the group, communication generally takes place between equals or flows downward from higher status to lower status. Rarely do those of lower status initiate a significant number of messages to those in higher status. Higher-status individuals normally initiate messages more often than those at lower levels.

Who we are, as perceived by the group and by ourselves, is an important issue in small-group functioning. Who we are in terms of knowledge, attitudes, communication skill, listening skill, popularity, position, age, reputation, and power is the issue of identity and status—an issue that must be resolved by every individual in the group, as well as the group, before the group can function effectively.

Affection

Liking and disliking were discussed in chapter 6 as important elements in interpersonal communication. Hence, it is important in the small group. Personal emotions are very much a part of one's participation in a small group. Interpersonal attraction or unattraction are powerful elements in groups, but the issue of affection of liking usually is not resolved until the issues of *belonging, control, role taking,* and *identity* have been resolved. Schutz suggests that the development of affection is usually the last phase in the development of an interpersonal relationship.[5] After persons have encountered each other, and defined each other and their relationship, bonds of affection can develop.

The importance of affection as a factor in group functioning lies in the fact that you determine whether, and to what extent, you will permit bonds of affection to develop. If you develop a dislike for members of the group, experience too little affection, or refuse to allow the development of affection, you may decide to be "standoffish" and to maintain an emotional distance between yourself and the others. On the other hand, if you develop close, emotional relationships with others in the group, you will find the group satisfying and your behavior will be productive. When an individual resolves the affection issue, a significant obstacle to group productivity is removed. Also, the leader should remember that liking and affection are related to the amount of interaction in a group. Therefore, it is wise to plan activities that encourage more interaction among members of the group. The greater the group's interaction, the greater the affection in the group.

Cohesiveness

Cohesiveness refers to the feeling of closeness or tightness within the group. A group with high cohesiveness shares a great number of values and behaviors. Each member has a feeling of "belonging." But cohesiveness goes beyond belonging—it connotes strong commitment so that the desire to stick together is quite strong. Without cohesiveness, groups tend to shatter under pressure and threat. With cohesiveness, group members stay together and "stick it out," even in the face of adversity and conflict.

If you wanted to increase the cohesiveness of a group, you would want to increase each person's commitment to the group, and each one's desire to continue the relationship. You will recall again from chapter 6 that we identified factors related to maintaining interpersonal relationships: inclusion, control, affection, and the mutual satisfaction of needs. In the small group, these factors translate into accepting one into the group rather than leaving the person an outsider; demonstrating affection for and interacting with a person so as to develop a closer relationship; giving the person equal influence with others in the group; and interacting with the appropriate emotional tone. If these things are continually done by the members of the group toward a new member and toward each other, the group's cohesion will be strong. Cohesiveness at its best will produce a bonus effect for the group. This bonus effect we call synergy, or the ability of a group to produce better results than members of the group could produce working individually. Cohesiveness could have a negative effect only if taken to an extreme in which "groupthink" developed.[6]

Social Climate

All of these people issues—belonging, role taking, status and identity, affection and cohesiveness—combine to create a **social climate** for the group. Probably nothing is more directly related to the success or failure of a group than its social climate. A healthy interpersonal climate within a group is a tremendous enabling factor for the success and productivity of the group. Con-

Cohesiveness is important to the functioning of the small group.

versely, the group caught in a morass of pathological interpersonal behaviors finds it almost impossible to accomplish its tasks and reach its goals. An unhealthy interpersonal climate in a group is counterproductive to its functioning.

Understanding of and Sensitivity to Group Processes

A final issue is the individual's **understanding of and sensitivity to group processes.** If you are to be a productive group member and find group work satisfying, you must be able to cope satisfactorily with the group situation. To do that, you must have a knowledge of the factors that operate in the group process—that is, factors relating to the individual (belonging, identity and status, role taking, and affection) and factors related to the processes of group discussion and problem solving.

Issues Related to the Group

The following four issues are no less important to group productivity than are the issues of individuals (**socioemotional climate**), but they are group task issues and they must be resolved by the group rather than by individuals. We shall consider four task issues: (1) leadership skills, (2) decision-making skills, (3) problem-solving skills, and (4) participant skills.

Group customs, goals, personal attributes—all affect group leadership and group processes.

Leadership Skills

Leadership skill—the first issue facing the group—has been defined as:

> Interpersonal influence, . . . through the communication process, toward the attainment of a specified goal or goals. Leadership always involves attempts on the part of a *leader* (influencer) to affect (influence) the behavior of a *follower* (influencee).[7]

The situation, customs of the group, goals, and personal attributes all affect leadership. At the beginning of a discussion, the problem must be defined, interest and concern generated, and procedures and tasks identified. Later in the discussion, arguments may need to be cooled and resolved, or other problems may arise, creating needs for other leadership influences.

Leadership varies from group to group. One group may require **permissive leadership,** in which the leader acts as a central point for communication exchange. In another group, **democratic leadership,** with its reliance upon guiding the group, is most effective; and in yet another group, a more directive authoritarian type of leadership may be needed.

Democratic Leadership or Authoritarian Leadership

There has been much debate over authoritarian leadership and democratic leadership. Some writers claim advantages and disadvantages for each, while others opt for democratic leadership only.

Democratic leadership is no more nor less active than authoritarian leadership. A democratic leader does not sit back passively, doing nothing, while the group members achieve the goal. In fact, the passivity of the leader is independent from the style of leadership—authoritarian or democratic.

Authoritarian leadership is characterized by decisiveness through or by the leader; democratic leadership delegates decisions about goals and means for achieving goals to the members of the group. Although leaders seldom fall totally into one category or the other, they do tend, generally, to keep control of decision making or to facilitate decision making by the group.

Being a democratic leader involves more than letting the members vote. Voting does *not* by itself make a group democratic. Voting is often used by the authoritarian leader to make the group appear democratic. Members "vote" for the leader's authoritarian decisions in order to "prove" their loyalty, to avoid punishment, and to make themselves eligible for awards. When the authoritarian leader has the power to reward, it is amazing how popular that leader's ideas and methods are with members of the group. In the absence of the leader, however, the situation may be quite different. One of the weaknesses of authoritarian leadership is that cooperation, participation, and commitment may be perfunctory—pure sham.

Genuine democratic leadership finds its essence in honest interpersonal relationships—in real and free transaction among all members of the group. Things that disturb members of the group get on the agenda. Interpersonal conflicts, contradictory goals, antagonism toward the leader—in the democratic group, these and other dissatisfactions are dealt with rather than swept under the rug and defined as inappropriate for the group's deliberation. If all these things can be talked about in a group, the group may not always *appear* to be efficient. Some may see the democratic group as confused and inefficient; the slowness of democratic decisions and of "consensus reading" may be mistaken for inefficiency. The speed of action of authoritarian groups is easily mistaken for efficiency. The appearance of honest discussion when it is really lip service, of hard decision making when it is only verbal conformity, and of action when it is nonparticipative capitulation may suddenly manifest itself as failure and sham. On the other hand, the working out of conflicts in the democratic group, *although time consuming,* makes consensus possible and results in a strong personal commitment by group members that motivates them to implement group decisions.

The democratic leader assists the members in their functions. Characteristically, this kind of leader listens, offers information and advice, respects each member's ideas and input, and works to develop healthy and mature communication within the group.

Effective leaders work at solving task problems as well as at solving the group's interpersonal problems. An effective leader maintains high morale and increases group cohesion, facilitates the development of liking and involvement, and carries out specific task functions. Often the effective leader introduces new ideas and calls attention to problems; assists the group in clarifying and defining goals; and opens the meeting and starts the discussion. The leader's main obligations during the meeting are to (1) adhere to the agenda; (2) aid in structuring procedures or in adhering to procedures that facilitate the group's orderly functioning; (3) develop a productive socioemotional climate by discouraging polarization, hostility, and attacks on personalities and encouraging respect, openness, liking, and task involvement; and (4) be aware of the group's progress so as to keep members aware of both progress and problems. When necessary, the leader summarizes progress, makes transitions from one step to another or from one agenda item to another, and focuses the group's attention on special group problems. Although there are other responsibilities and duties of leaders that vary with the type of group or the objectives of the group, these are the most important general functions. With shared leadership, however, group members help fulfill various leadership functions.

Emergent and Shared Leadership

The most effective leadership is that which emerges from the situation itself. If the situation needs strong and direct leadership, then a strong and direct person will be the most effective leader. If a group needs peacemaking and attention to the socioemotional climate, then a person who is a socioemotional leader will be most effective.

Socioemotional leaders are concerned with the climate of the group. Such a leader is sensitive to the needs of each member of the group and is skillful in meeting those needs, in fostering a climate of liking, and in developing trust and healthy communication in the group. Socioemotional leaders tend to be encouraging, supportive, and impartial.

Task leaders focus on the problem to be solved. They know that the quality of the solution or action taken by the group is directly dependent on the quality of the problem-solving process. Accurate definition and analysis of the problem is necessary; adequate data is essential; the discovery and testing of all possible solutions is important; and the plans for implementing the solution must be carefully drawn. The task leader keeps the group "on track" in terms of accomplishing everything necessary for the emergence of a good solution to the problem.

Groups differ from each other in their needs; some groups need socioemotional attention while others need task attention. Emergent leadership fits the needs of the group as those needs emerge. This approach to leadership suggests that, at any given time, any member in the group may serve some leadership function. Leadership, consequently, may be shared by the leader with various group members. Not all of the group members are leaders, but particular leadership needs may be noticed and satisfied by an individual member. *No one person, not even the best leader, can supply all the leadership needs for every group all the time.* That is because there is no absolute set of qualities that guarantees effective leadership for all situations. Emergent leadership is, then, leadership that responds to the needs of a specific group, and it may be shared at times with members of the group. The authoritarian leader may desire to retain as much power as possible while the democratic leader encourages the development and emergence of various types of leaders—persons with special skills who assume leadership in problems when their contribution is needed.

Phillips and Erikson, small group experts, have identified some of these special skills that are common to many groups. Leaders having these special

Good group decisions result from free and accepted participation by all members of the group.

skills might emerge in a shared-leadership situation. They include the front man, the expediter, the game leader, the wisdom purveyor, the idea man, and the inspirational leader.[8]

The *front man* is a person who possesses extraordinary skills in dealing with the public or outside organizations and groups. This person is a liaison with the outside—a channel of communication with others outside the group whose support or contribution is needed.

The *expediter* is the one who is expert at problem solving within the group. This person knows where the group is, where it ought to be, why it is not getting there, and what ought to be done to solve the problems and move toward the goal. The member who expedites the group's problem-solving function is generally the task leader.

The *game leader,* according to Phillips, is opposite to the expediter. Skilled in providing cathartic experiences, the game leader tells jokes, introduces anecdotes, or brings feelings into the open. This person is conscious of climate and process, and maintains the group's sense of humor and perspective. The same leader serves in the role of socioemotional leader.

The *wisdom purveyor* is just that—a man or woman who, by reason of experience, age, or longevity in the group, can provide historical data relative to the group's past trials and errors. This person provides objective and constructive historical data, rather than the negative "We've never done it that way!" or "We've tried it, and it won't work!"

The *idea person* is creative and imaginative. It is important that any group have as many viable alternatives as possible. The idea person is an expert in brainstorming whose contribution to the group can be invaluable. In most groups, there is a need for someone who can help the group recover its enthusiasm and excitement when boredom and discouragement set in. This is the person who—with help from the game leader—gets the group through its low times.

Can you explain fully what shared leadership is?

Finally, there are various persons who are leaders for the group, who serve in their own areas of expertise. They do not attempt to lead in every area of the group's activity, but in their own areas they contribute unique skills and experiences.

In democratic groups, these and other leadership roles emerge so that leadership is shared according to need and expertise. It is not difficult to understand the tremendous advantage that a group gains through shared leadership. Few single leaders have the skill and capability to perform all the roles that need to be performed in a productive and successful group.

Leaderless Groups

All of us have participated in leaderless groups, perhaps without knowing it. The bull session has no designated leader; the five persons who discuss an office problem during coffee-break form a leaderless group; and buzz groups or committees during class sessions often have no designated leader. There is a clear distinction between a leaderless group and a leader*ship*less group. No group can function efficiently without leadership; but in the leaderless group there can be excellent leadership without a designated, formal leader. The effective leaderless group is one relying entirely on **shared leadership.** Leadership functions are so widely shared and diffused throughout the membership that no individual can be accurately designated as leader. Whoever has the skills needed at a particular moment contributes leadership at that time. The leaderless group can operate effectively only if the needed leadership skills are present within the membership.

Decision-Making Skills

Decision making—a second issue in the small group—should not be confused with problem solving. In small-group discussion there are many decisions to make: decisions on what problems are to be tackled, when they are to be placed on the agenda, how they are to be handled, how much participation is wanted, what action the group should be taking, when discussions should be stopped, whether a topic is germane to the discussion, and what goal the group should be seeking. A group decision is nothing more than several individuals' decisions that coincide to allow a choice to prevail. Each member of the group is constantly involved in making personal decisions. Some decisions, however, must necessarily be made by the group, either by having the chairperson or another individual make them or by allowing the group as a whole to make them. Group decisions fall into two categories: those having to do with group

Figure 8.1 Leader-group relationship in decision making.

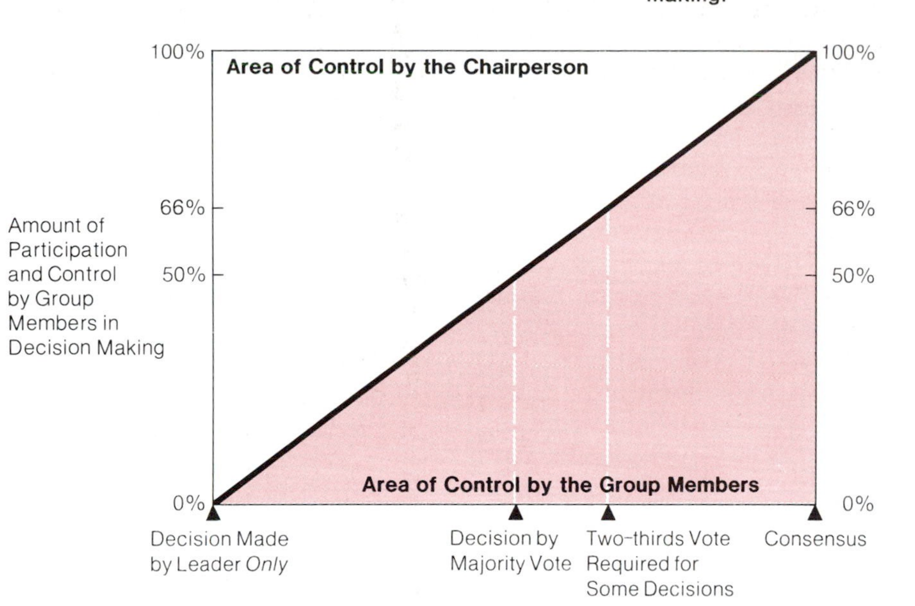

process, that is, the establishment or modification of procedures for dealing with the task at hand; and those related to the task, that is, the fundamental decisions necessary to reach the group's specific objective.

Group decisions may be made by authority (the chairperson or one or two dominant members of the group), by majority vote, or by consensus. Group decisions made by a single individual and then forced upon the members by manipulation, persuasion, or the influence of raw power usually have the effect of destroying group decision-making ability and morale. The single exception may be the conference situation in which it is clearly understood that the chairperson has the responsibility for making the decisions and the group serves consultative, advisory, and sounding-board functions. Studies have shown that some 60 percent of business and professional people who participate in regular staff conferences said that the actual decision making did not occur in the conference, but was made by the chairperson at a later time.[9] This procedure for making decisions may be satisfactory when the climate, policies of the organization, and procedures are clearly understood and accepted. When that is not the case, autocratic decision making can have disastrous effects upon the group. Figure 8.1 illustrates the leader-group relationship in decision making.

Two other methods for making decisions are more satisfying to the group—consensus and majority vote. **Consensus** occurs when everyone in the group agrees to the decision; the strength of consensus lies in the group's total support of the decision. There is a danger in relying on consensus, however: group members could be pressured to capitulate so that consensus can be achieved. This will result in a false consensus, and is ultimately detrimental to the group.

True consensus is the result of careful and effective interpersonal communication. When consensus can be achieved, it is the best decision-making procedure. When it cannot be achieved, the group must pay the price of delayed action while attempts at understanding, persuasion, and integration are made, or it must rely on majority vote to resolve differences and make decisions.

The one-person one-vote, majority-rule procedure has been the foundation of our democratic process. The **majority-vote method** may be used if it is sufficient that only a majority of the group be involved in the decision. Majority vote permits the group to arrive at a decision even though some individuals are not in agreement, and it reduces the time necessary to arrive at a decision when there are different opinions. One of the major weaknesses of making decisions by majority vote is that it tends to force division and polarization, thus leaving some members uncommitted to the policy or action. According to Phillips, this system is satisfactory only for final decision in the small group. Before such final decisions are made, issues must be raised and proposals devised. These phases include decisions that are better made through consensus.[10] It would seem, however, that at whatever level the decisions are made, true consensus is the method of greatest merit; and, when the situation requires all of the group's resources and the fullest cooperation of all members, consensus is the only satisfactory decision-making procedure.

Problem-Solving Skills

A third issue related to the group is **problem-solving ability.** Problem solving is composed of six steps: (1) definition and analysis of the problem, (2) establishment of criteria or standards for the solution, (3) discovery of possible solutions, (4) evaluation of each solution, (5) selection of a solution, and (6) implementation of the solution.[11]

Definition and Analysis

When a problem is encountered, there is an awareness of a goal and a barrier to that goal. The first step in problem solving includes the specific identification of the goal and the obstacles to it. The best way to understand a problem is to analyze it thoroughly: define the problem; discover its qualities, characteristics, and elements; compare it to other problems; and study its relationship to other entities and ideas.

Included in this first phase of group problem solving is the clear specification of the problem—the **phrasing of the question.** It should usually be phrased in the form of an open-ended question that is neither too narrow nor too broad. Open-ended questions do not restrict the number of choices to two.

"Should the voting age be lowered to eighteen?" offers only two alternatives and is therefore too narrow for effective problem solving through discussion. Equally detrimental to discussion is the question that is phrased too broadly. "What should be done about voting?" is so broad that almost any topic may be discussed. A narrower, yet not unduly restrictive question could be, "What is the best voting age requirement?" Once the problem has been phrased, the group needs to check agreement on the meanings of the terms in the question as well as of the terms that are apt to be used in the discussion.

Other aspects of the first step in problem solving are **fact finding** (What are the facts? What are the available statistics? What are the opinions of experts? Are there similar situations?); identification of causes of the problem (Why are conditions as they are? Which are symptoms and which are causes?); and consideration of the relative impact of each cause. This opening phase of problem analysis is usually guided by the chairperson, who calls attention to the problem, reviews or asks members to review its background, and generally encourages a full discussion of the nature of the problem.

Establishment of Criteria for a Solution

The second step in problem solving is the **establishment of criteria** that the solution must satisfy. No one proposes answers or solutions without a frame of reference (a set of criteria) in mind. But the group cannot function effectively in solving the problem if each member operates with a personal set of criteria. Nor can the group operate efficiently if the criteria or standards for the solution are poor in quality or not clearly understood by the group. It is important that the group give attention to the establishment of relevant and important criteria that solutions must satisfy.

Criteria are used to judge the adequacy of something. In the problem-solving group, the proposed solution to the problem is judged. How can we tell whether a proposed solution is a good solution or not? Each of us can go through that evaluative process by applying criteria to the solution, that is, by testing the solution to see if desirable results will be achieved and undesirable ones not achieved. We have, in fact, a set of standards or characteristics to which the solution must conform. In this second step, the group sets out, and agrees to requirements a solution must meet before it is adopted. These criteria will, at a later time, be used to evaluate proposed solutions and to select the best solution. Time spent by the group in discovering and agreeing to a clear set of criteria is time well spent in the problem-solving process.

Discovery of Possible Solutions

The third step in problem solving is the **discovery of possible solutions.** This phase should be the most permissive, free, and uncritical period of the discussion. One of the biggest mistakes in group discussion is evaluating, criticizing, and judging each solution as soon as it is offered—often before it has been adequately explained, and certainly before all other possible solutions have been identified. Brainstorming is highly productive in this step of problem solving.

Evaluation of Solutions

Step four is **evaluating and testing each solution.** Evaluation is done in terms of the criteria established and in terms of other decisions that may now be made such as: Should the present system be modified? Should the present system be discarded and an entirely new approach taken? Are there one, two, or three criteria of such high priority that satisfying them is more important than satisfying *all criteria?* Evaluating the proposed solutions leads naturally to the next step, the selection and testing of one specific solution.

Selection of a Solution

Arriving at the best solution is tantamount to reaching a decision. During these steps of problem solving, evaluation, judgment, and debate (in the best sense of these terms) occur. Focusing on one solution is a *critical step* in problem solving and should be done as carefully and with as much agreement as possible. The advantages, disadvantages, cost, ease of implementation, and chances of success for the accepted solution should be carefully considered.

Implementation

The final step in solving any problem is **implementation or "taking action"**—doing something. The best solution to the problem is doomed to failure if it is *not* properly implemented. Too many groups make decisions and then drop the matter, assigning no one to carry out the solution. Decisions that are carefully made require too much effort to be dropped just because a chairperson and the group do not perceive that implementation is a necessary part of problem solving.

A simple list of steps for solving problems is no guarantee that the problem will be solved. Groups do not move mechanically and rigidly through the steps; sometimes they jump from one point to another. They discover in evaluating solutions that an important criterion was overlooked earlier and must be added; or they discover that the "perfect solution" is not among their list of possible solutions and so they decide to modify the criteria. In general, however, the best problem solving follows a logical plan of attack. Some things are naturally antecedent to others—that is, establishment of criteria must come before the evaluation of any solution. Problem solving is not magical. It requires the best of interpersonal communication skills and the best of thinking skills. A group's understanding of the rational approach to problem solving is an important element in small group discussion.

What are the steps to be followed in logical problem solving?

Planning for Productive Meetings

How many formal meetings have you attended in the past month? Count the meetings in which you have been a participant during the past two weeks. You will probably agree that those meetings which were subject to systematic planning were the most successful. When planning a meeting several concerns should be addressed: need for the meeting; goals of the meeting; the agenda; who should participate; and facility selection, reservation, and preparation.

A well planned meeting is more likely to achieve its goal.

Need for the Meeting

Our society has become so meeting oriented that we frequently forget to ask the most basic question: Is there really a need for this meeting? Frequently there are alternatives to a meeting that might better achieve the short- or long-range objectives, be more acceptable to the participants, be more economical, be more suitable for the solicitation or dissemination of relevant information, and result in better decisions or solutions.

Goals of the Meeting

Earlier in the chapter we discussed different types of groups. One of the types discussed was problem-solving groups. While determining meeting goals or objectives, you should keep in mind that some problems cannot be completely solved in one meeting or in a restricted amount of time. Just as in an interview or a speech, the communicator must set realistic goals or expectations. Goal setting must take into consideration a range of variables, including available time, personnel, budget restraints, the group's power or authority to implement decisions, and other variables germane to the specific problem or issues at hand.

Agenda

Once the goals of the meeting have been established, an agenda should be developed. The agenda is a plan of action for the group to follow. In many ways it is similar to an outline used by a speaker or a set of carefully selected questions used by a skillful interviewer. It could be considered a road map for the leader to follow. Without a road map or an agenda it might be rather difficult to know where the group is going or when the group has arrived. Pursley and Watson have listed eight items to be included in an agenda:

1. The purpose of the meeting
2. The date and location of the meeting
3. The time to begin and end the meeting
4. Objectives (goals)
5. Topics for discussion with reasonable time frames for each
6. Brief minutes from previous meetings when appropriate
7. Announcements
8. Materials necessary to bring to the meeting[12]

Tropman suggests that an agenda should be structured by using the "rule of thirds." This approach suggests the following structure:

1. Use the first third of the meeting to discuss business and simple topics
2. Use the middle third of the meeting to discuss the most difficult tasks
3. Use the final third of the meeting to discuss easy topics[13]

Agendas can be useful instruments for maximizing the effectiveness of a group and keeping the group on track. For best results, agendas should be distributed to participants ahead of time. Having the agenda prior to the meeting will help participants successfully face both the individual and group issues discussed earlier in this chapter. The bottom line is that each participant will have a maximum opportunity to know what to expect during the meeting and to arrive better prepared.

Participants

Solicitation of personnel is sometimes not under the meeting planner's control. When it is, however, the meeting planner must consider the backgrounds of the participants; the number of participants; and participant competencies, experience, availability, and communication style.[14]

Depending upon the issues at hand and the meeting goals, planners must consider the consequences of participants having similar as opposed to diverse backgrounds, beliefs, and values. For example, suppose you were pulling a group together to organize a new religious youth group, political party, or ball team. Would you want participants to have identical or varied spiritual or political or athletic experience? What difference would it make?

If time was important to the problem-solving process, would you be better off to increase or reduce the number of participants in a group discussion session? What would be gained and what would be lost by limiting the number of participants selected? What specific communication competencies would you look for in the persons you would select to participate in a problem-solving session in your dormitory wing? As you think back about the task and maintenance roles operant in small groups, consider the communication competencies and communication styles needed to make the roles functional.

Facilities

Proper selection, reservation, and preparation of the meeting room can mean success or failure for a meeting. In selecting a room for a meeting, one might consider the environmental impact of the facility on the group participants. The size, location, convenience, freedom from distraction, lighting, ventilation, and decor are just a few of the basic concerns to be considered.

Most organizations require a considerable amount of paperwork to be processed to reserve a room. If you're the curious type, check on the paperwork needed to reserve the room where your communication class meets. Generally, facility requisitions must be processed through the department that coordinates room usage. The form will probably need at least three signatures. In addition, the requisition may need to be sent to several other departments, including security, maintenance, and housekeeping. A slip up at this point can mean you don't have the appropriate furniture, lights, access, air conditioning/heating, refreshments, or a clean room. Even worse, you might find another group in the room who did the appropriate paperwork.

In addition to selecting and reserving a room, it is important to prepare the room properly. Our attention is closely related to the comfort and satisfaction of our surroundings. The meeting planner should attend to every detail ranging from adequate leg and elbow room to extra bulbs and projectors for audiovisual equipment. Notepaper, pencils, drinking glasses, chalk, and erasers are just a few of the essentials. The essentials may differ with each meeting you plan, but preparation for each meeting is essential. It will generally be embarrassing to both the planner and the participants when the one essential for the meeting is forgotten or omitted. The best advice is to plan early, plan thoroughly, and don't take anything for granted. Many successful group leaders and meeting planners have learned the hard way to respect Murphy's law. Murphy's law is especially appropriate in terms of room selection, reservation, and preparation. Murphy's law says "Whatever can go wrong will go wrong."

Participant Skills

You will undoubtedly be a participant in dozens of conferences, committees, and other small groups for every *one* in which you are the leader. It is easy to take a participator's responsibilities for granted—not only to fail to prepare for participation but also to develop an attitude of indifference toward your responsibility to the group. Committee members can be productive only when they take sufficient time to prepare adequately for the subject on the agenda.

It is unfair to impose on the time of other group members if you are not prepared to contribute constructively. Preparation on the topic, then, is one of the duties of the productive participant. Other duties or characteristics, as identified by experts on discussion, include:

1. an attitude of respect and open-mindedness toward others,
2. a favorable attitude toward flexible, permissive interaction,
3. an awareness of communication barriers,
4. an understanding of group processes,
5. an ability and willingness to speak to the point,
6. an ability to listen effectively,
7. an ability to think logically and analytically, and
8. a desire to cooperate and to conciliate in order to reach group goals.[15]

Several of these skills or characteristics have been treated in previous chapters. The traits identified by experts as most important for participants in group communication are, for the most part, those traits necessary for effective intrapersonal and interpersonal communication.

Summary

This chapter has presented a description of small-group communication. The nature, characteristics, and definition of the small group have been discussed. We have noted that although not every assemblage of people constitutes a group, the major types of small groups include primary groups, educational groups, casual groups, support groups, and problem-solving groups. Major issues related both to the individual and to the group were discussed.

Most of the business of society is carried on in small groups. In committee meetings and conferences in church, school, government, and business organizations, decisions are made and problems are solved that permit people to integrate and live cooperatively. No responsible individual can escape from or ignore small-group participation; and no group, if it is to be productive, can operate satisfactorily if its members are ignorant or unskilled in interpersonal communication. Each of us is challenged to increase our understanding of the process and to improve our skills as participants in small-group problem solving. The skills we have discussed that have to do with intrapersonal and interpersonal communication are needed in the small group.

You are probably already participating in several small groups of various kinds—educational, support, and problem solving; and in these groups, you have an excellent opportunity to observe what we have discussed in this chapter. You can bridge the gap between reading about phenomena and observing them as you make the transfer from your textbook and communication class to the outside world.

Questions and Exercises for Review

1. How does a problem-solving group differ from an educational group?
2. What is cohesiveness in a group and what is its effect on small-group process?
3. Contrast democratic and authoritarian leadership.
4. How does group size affect group process?
5. What are some of the things a successful meeting planner does that an unsuccessful planner might overlook or take for granted?

Key Terms and Phrases

group
aggregation
primary groups
casual groups
educational groups
panel-discussion group
symposium
forum
support groups
problem-solving groups
agenda
synergy
belonging
taking a role
task roles
status
identity
cohesiveness
groupthink
social climate
understanding of and sensitivity to group processes
socioemotional climate
permissive leadership
democratic leadership
authoritarian leadership
shared leadership
decision making
consensus
majority-vote method
problem-solving ability
phrasing of the question
fact finding
establishment of criteria
discovery of possible solutions
evaluating and testing each solution
arriving at the best solution
implementation or "taking action"

For Further Reading

Barker, Larry L.; Wahlers, Kathy J.; Watson, Kittie W.; and Kibler, Robert J. *Groups in Process: An Introduction to Small Group Communication,* 3d ed. Englewood Cliffs, New Jersey: Prentice Hall, Inc., 1987.

Barlow, S. et al. "Leader Communication Style: Effects on Members of Small Groups." *Small Group Behavior* 13 (November 1982): 518–31.

Becker, S. L. "Directions of Small Group Research for the 1980s." *Central States Speech Journal* 31 (Fall 1980): 221–24.

Dewey, John. *Logic: The Theory of Inquiry.* New York: Holt, Rinehart & Winston, 1938.

A good text if you are interested in the Dewey reflective thinking and logical problem-solving procedure.

Likert, Renis, and Likert, Jane G. "A Method for Coping with Conflict in Problem-Solving Groups." *Group and Organization Studies* 3 (December 1978): 427–34.

Phillips, Gerald M. *Communication and the Small Group.* Indianapolis: The Bobbs-Merrill Co., 1973.
A readable and comprehensive treatment of the small group process.

Tannenbaum, Robert; Weschler, Irving R.; and Massarik, Fred. *Leadership and Organization.* New York: McGraw-Hill Book Co., 1961.
If you are interested in reading more on leadership, you will find this book an interesting one.

Tubbs, Stewart L. *A Systems Approach to Small Group Interaction.* 3d ed. Reading: Addison-Wesley Publishing Co., 1988.
This book does a good job of relating group interaction to contemporary systems theory.

Notes

1. George C. Homans, *The Human Group* (New York: Harcourt Brace Jovanovich, 1950), 1.
2. L. P. Bradford and D. Mial, "When Is a Group?" *Educational Leadership* 21(1963): 147–51.
3. K. Benne and P. Sheats, "Functional Roles of Group Members," *Journal of Social Issues* 4, no. 2 (1948): 41.
4. Benne and Sheats, "Functional Roles," 41.
5. William C. Schutz, *The Interpersonal Underworld* (Palo Alto, Calif.: Science and Behavior Books, 1966), 21–23.
6. Janis Irving, *Victims of Group Think: A Study of Foreign Policy Decisions and Fiascoes* (Boston: Houghton-Mifflin, 1972).
7. Robert Tannenbaum, Irving R. Weschler, and Fred Massarik, *Leadership and Organization* (New York: McGraw-Hill Book Co., 1961), 24.
8. Gerald M. Phillips and Eugene C. Erikson, *Interpersonal Dynamics in the Small Group* (New York: Random House, 1970), 83–85.
9. Martin Kriesberg, "Executives Evaluate Administrative Conferences," *Advanced Management* 15 (March 1950).
10. Gerald M. Phillips, *Communication and the Small Group* (Indianapolis: The Bobbs-Merrill Co., 1966), 7.
11. This problem-solving sequence originated with the work of John Dewey, *How We Think* (New York: Heath Publishing Co., 1910).
12. M. G. Pursley and K. W. Watson, "How To Plan and Hold a Meeting," *CITIBUSINESS,* (August 1983): 33–34.
13. J. E. Tropman, *Effective Meetings: Improving Group Decision-Making.* (Beverly Hills, Calif.: Sage, 1980).
14. This material was adapted from "Planning and Conducting Meetings" in *Groups in Process: An Introduction to Small Group Communication* by Larry L. Barker, et al. (Englewood Cliffs, N.J., 1987), 221–31.
15. Major Herman Farwell, "An Evaluation of a Television Method of Teaching Group Process" (MA thesis, University Park: Pennsylvania State University, 1964).

Part 3

Public Communication

Public communication is the next logical extension of the communication process—after intrapersonal and interpersonal communication. As interpersonal communication fulfills individuals' needs as they relate to other individuals, so public communication permits a society to fulfill societal needs. Public communication is the tool through which society's work is done. There has never been a time in recorded history when public communication was not used to accomplish society's work. We have made great progress in education, business, government, religion, and entertainment through public communication. Today, of course, our public communication is not limited to face-to-face situations; we have virtually worldwide public communication through the mass media of radio and television. *There has never been more public speaking in the world than there is today.* Public speech consumption per person is at an all-time high. We do not know how many speeches are given in the United States each year, but a conservative estimate by one group puts the figure at five hundred thousand.

Part 3 of this book focuses on this important communication process—public communication. In this part we will consider the three major components of any public communication situation: the speaker (chapter 9), the audience (chapter 10), and the message (chapter 11); and then we will discuss in detail the two basic types of public communication—informative speaking (chapter 12) and persuasive speaking (chapter 13).

Focus

The Components of Source Credibility

Sources of Credibility

Credibility Before the Speech

Credibility through Speech Content

Credibility through Vocal Delivery

Credibility through Body Use and Appearance

Modes of Delivery

Impromptu

Memorized

Extemporaneous

Manuscript

Prompters

Three Characteristics of Effective Delivery

The Speaker

The speaker is an important variable in the public communication situation. The same speech given to the same audience by two different speakers will produce different outcomes. We call this speaker effect "ethos" or source credibility, and that is the topic of this chapter. We identify three components of source credibility (trustworthiness, expertise, and dynamism). Next, we investigate four sources of credibility: what is known about the speaker before the speech; credibility established by means of the speech content; the speaker's nonverbal vocal behavior and visual signals sent by the speaker through physical activity.

Students of communication have long noted that *who* says something is often as important in communication effectiveness as *what* is said. Common sense and experience also tell us that the perceived character of the speaker is one of the factors affecting an auditor's response to a message. The vividness of the speaker's personality; the speaker's sincerity, power, status, and expertise; the awe, admiration, trust, and affection of the audience for the speaker—these and other factors are important speaker-related variables in public communication.

Students of communication and practitioners of the art have made careful observations and have suggested several behaviors—vocal, physical, and logical (i.e., decisions the speaker makes and reveals to the audience)—that are believed to be related to this general factor, *the speaker's influence.*

The general factor (influence of the speaker) has many labels, including **ethos,** *prestige, status, image,* and **source credibility.** Whatever label is used, however, it is apparent that the impact of a message depends in part on who the sender is. Consciously or unconsciously, listeners react personally to the speaker. E. M. Griffin illustrates the importance of source credibility to his students in a persuasion class by presenting the following series of famous quotations.

1. Give me four years to teach the children and the seed I have planted will never be uprooted. (Mao Tse-tung)
2. The fear of ideas makes us impotent and ineffective. (Martin Luther)
3. There is always room for a man of force and he makes room for many. (Joseph Stalin)
4. There is only one grade of men; they are all contemptible.[1] (Billy Graham)

As you can see, each quotation is attributed to a famous person; however, the men listed above did not say these things. Griffin explains that while some students receive the form that links the statement about training children to Mao Tse-tung, others receive a different sheet that credits it to Martin Luther. Once the students indicate the amount of agreement with each item, they are asked whether their attitude was affected by who stated the idea. Interestingly enough, most students maintain that the source of the idea had no influence upon them. In fact, many contended that they didn't even notice the name. Upon totaling the overall results, however, Griffin says he "almost always finds that there is more agreement with the idea if it comes from Luther than if it originates with Mao Tse-tung."[2]

In this day of communication saturation, audiences—both student and nonstudent—demand that speakers be worth listening to. They expect a speaker to know the subject, accept responsibility for what is said, and be sincere and trustworthy. In short, audiences today, perhaps more than ever before, stand ready to confer or deny credibility to the speakers claiming their attention.

Charisma can be a powerful part of a speaker's ethos.

The Components of Source Credibility

Within the last few years, a number of researchers have attempted to determine empirically the specific dimensions of source credibility. These independently conducted investigations have generally shown similar results. The findings suggest that receivers judge three relatively independent dimensions of source credibility that determine the influence potential of any given speaker for a given audience on a stated topic at a stipulated time. Specifically, these studies indicate that audience members evaluate a speaker along three lines: (1) **"trustworthiness"** or "safety" (goodwill, intentions, predictability, honesty, and integrity), (2) **"expertise"** or "competence" (qualifications, intelligence, judgment, experience, and firsthand knowledge), and (3) **"dynamism"** or charisma (energy, liveliness, likability, and attractiveness).

Of course a speaker desires high credibility. As speakers, we want to be perceived as intelligent, capable, and informed. A speaker wants to be believed—to be seen as honest and sincere. A speaker wants to be liked—to be seen as a person of **goodwill,** warmth, and affection. You will recall that these factors were identified as important factors in interpersonal communication in Part 2, and now we see that they are important characteristics in public speaking also. *Expertise, trustworthiness,* and *dynamism*—these are the components of credibility. When a speaker is evaluated highly in these factors, that speaker can be effective in public communication.

In your generation you have witnessed how one can achieve source credibility—and how one can lose source credibility. Revered speakers in virtually every vocation have seen their credibility diminished, and in some cases stripped, overnight. In 1987 and 1988, electronic preachers whose organizations influenced Christianity world wide, suffered multi-million-dollar deficits and extensive cutbacks to their "outreach" efforts following disclosures of sexual improprieties and in some cases money mismanagement. Aspiring presidential candidates and Supreme Court hopefuls saw life-time dreams and hard-working political organizations disintegrate as the handling of sensitive issues failed to meet the credibility demands of the various publics. Questions of integrity, communicator intent, consistency, and honor permeated the electronic media and devastated the audience-perceived speaker credibility of leaders in religion, politics, law, and the military.

Can you identify and explain the three components of source credibility?

If a speaker is evaluated low in one or more of the dimensions of credibility, that speaker will find it difficult to be effective in public communication. We have come to know that situation well, too, and our popular term for it is **credibility gap.** A credibility gap has a negative effect on public speaking. But what can speakers do or say that will cause the audience to perceive them as trustworthy, competent, and dynamic?

Notice that we used the word *perceived.* Credibility has to do with what the audience *perceives* the speaker as being. Regardless of the speaker's knowledge, prestige, experience, and motivation, it is what the audience believes the speaker to be that determines credibility. Credibility, then, can change from audience to audience and from situation to situation.

Sources of Credibility

Where does an audience get the information it uses to determine credibility?

There are three general sources of information from which an audience determines the credibility it gives to a speaker: (1) things known about the speaker before the speech is given, (2) personal information the speaker reveals through the content of the speech (verbal communication), and (3) information communicated through the manner in which the speech is delivered (nonverbal communication). Let us look more closely at these three areas.

Credibility Before the Speech

Most speakers come into the speaking situation with some credibility level already established. If the audience has heard of the speaker or has known of the speaker in any way, a certain level of credibility already exists. For example, if the President of the United States were to come to your speech class to talk with you, a certain level of credibility would exist before either of you entered the classroom. In other words, a speaker's reputation for honesty, friendliness, warmth, experience, position, intelligence, judgment, and so forth is one source of information used to determine credibility.

For example, imagine that each of the speakers listed below is scheduled to speak at your college. How credible is each one? Is the credibility of each influenced by dimensions of trustworthiness, expertise, dynamism, or combinations of these dimensions? Assess each name below and then compare your opinion with classmates.

Ronald Reagan	Dr. Ruth Westheimer
Mikhail Gorbachev	Col. Oliver "Ollie" North
Jimmy "The Greek"	Michael Jackson
Pope John Paul III	Jim Bakker

Extrinsic Credibility

The speaker's reputation, or information about the speaker, detached from the speech that is given, is called **extrinsic credibility.** Information about the speaker may concern more than intelligence or personality; it may identify whom the speaker represents. If the speaker is president of General Motors or Chrysler Corporation and is going to give a speech on how auto pollution has been exaggerated, we may suspect the speaker's motives. Credibility in this instance relates to a source other than the speaker. This illustrates how the source of a public message is not always just the speaker; it may also be an organization, a government, a church, or a business. Especially in these days when almost everything is handled through organizations, the organization's image or credibility rubs off onto the speaker representing it.

In short, anything the audience knows about the speaker before the speech, including reputation, job, sponsoring organization, and so on, becomes a source of information to determine source credibility. This is true whether the information is received by means of direct contact, news media, billboards, or the telephone.

The introduction of the speaker constitutes yet a second source of prespeech information. There has probably been more research on how introductions influence credibility than on any other variable related to credibility. A number of experiments have been made concerning the same speech by the same speaker, but with different introductions on each occasion. These experiments show that varying the introductory remarks about the speaker changes credibility and increases or decreases persuasiveness or attitude change. In one study, for example, the speaker gave the same speech (juvenile delinquents ought to be treated more leniently) to three groups of high school students. Once he was introduced as a juvenile court judge, once as an ordinary citizen, and once as a person with a criminal record as a juvenile delinquent. His credibility was highest, of course, when he was a judge, and there was more attitude change, too.[3] The introduction of a speaker can be especially important in establishing credibility when the speaker is not known by the audience. The speaker can be "humanized" (made likable and human) or accorded status (offices, honors, titles, and accomplishments can be identified) by the introduction.

Can you explain clearly what extrinsic credibility is?

Credibility through Speech Content

Intrinsic Credibility

Information revealed in the speech itself constitutes a third means by which credibility emerges. The speaker makes conscious selections of illustrations, arguments, anecdotes. Through these selections of speech content the speaker reveals the self. This **self-presentation** is the rhetorical counterpart of self-disclosure in interpersonal communication. The process of the speaker revealing private information through the speech is directly related to credibility. The credibility resulting from the self-presentation is called **intrinsic credibility.** The speaker's *extrinsic credibility* (that brought with the speaker before the speech began) is modified by and integrated with the speaker's intrinsic credibility. Other writers have divided extrinsic and intrinsic credibility into three categories: initial credibility, derived credibility, and terminal credibility. Initial credibility is essentially the same as extrinsic credibility. Derived credibility refers to that credibility the speaker earns during the presentation and thus may be equated with intrinsic credibility. Terminal credibility is essentially the combination of a speaker's extrinsic and intrinsic credibility. Every speaker, through self-presentation, enhances or diminishes the level of credibility assigned at the beginning of the speaking situation. In addition to self-presentation, the speaker can enhance intrinsic credibility by establishing common ground, being thoroughly prepared, and demonstrating a good sense of humor.

Establish Common Ground

The establishment of **common ground** between the speaker and the audience is one thing a speaker can do to enhance intrinsic credibility. You may recall that this same phenomenon is an important part of the acquaintance process in informal dyadic communication. Also, you may recall from our previous discussion that liking and interpersonal attraction tend to accompany similarity of traits, attitudes, values, and interests. The same relationship holds true between common ground and credibility in public speaking. When an audience perceives that the speaker is "like it"—has the same values, interests, and attitudes; shares habits and activities; and is sympathetic to its point of view—the audience identifies the speaker as standing on the same ground with it. Thus credibility is enhanced.

Be Prepared

Preparation is another factor that establishes credibility. Audiences easily spot sloppy preparation. If the speaker does not care enough about the audience and the speaking situation to prepare carefully and thoroughly, the audience often takes offense. Poor preparation is an indication of a lack of sincerity, a failure to accept the responsibility that goes with public speaking. Thorough preparation enhances credibility and obvious inadequate preparation diminishes it.

The speaker's information should be up-to-date. It should be accurate and authoritative. Reasoning should be clear and persuasive, and evidence of high quality should be used as needed. Examples selected should be relevant and understandable. The speaker's language should be appropriate to the audience. These should be the concerns in preparing the speech; credibility is enhanced when the speaker has done the necessary homework.

Sense of Humor

Speakers reveal themselves through humor, in both the type of humor they use and their **"sense of humor"** or attitude toward themselves. Jokes or stories that belittle others or have a vicious and demeaning undertone can have disastrous effects on what the audience thinks of the speaker. Sick or cruel humor does not reveal a person of goodwill and kindness. On the other hand, if the humor is wholesome or directed at oneself, it can have a strong positive effect on credibility. Research indicates that it may not always increase understanding or attitude change, but it often does affect the audience's liking for the speaker.

When a speaker reveals a good sense of humor, the audience sees a person of balance—a person who is not tied up by a *high ego;* one who does not position oneself above others; and one who does not take oneself too seriously. Through these verbal messages, or the absence of them, a self is presented that affects the speaker's credibility.

Credibility through Vocal Delivery

The fourth source of information used by an audience to determine credibility is the speaker's physical nonverbal behavior. In public communication, we call this *delivery.* The audience receives information about the speaker as the "self" through vocal and body communication, that is, through delivery.

The voice, which reflects the speaker's attitudes, feelings, and inner states, can be controlled and developed to reinforce verbal messages. Some of the major elements in **vocal delivery** are force, pitch, rate and rhythm, quality, articulation and pronunciation, and conversational style.

The primary function of the voice in delivery is to help the speaker communicate effectively. The speaker must be heard and understood. Also, the speaker must be pleasing. These are essential objectives of the effective speaker. The eight elements listed above help make the objectives become reality.

Little communication occurs if the audience cannot hear the speaker. Receivers should not have to strain, turn their heads, or cup their hands behind their ears to hear. Nothing is more distressing to listeners than to strain to catch a few words now and then. The weak-voiced, mumbling speaker greatly impairs communication effectiveness. To be heard requires adequate and sustained vocal loudness and projection. The speaker must adjust volume to the size of the room and should always project to the last row of the audience. Some speakers are careless about adjusting their voices to the particular speaking situation. They may be speaking too loudly or too softly for the size of the room or for the "atmosphere" of the situation.

Delivery affects an audience's perception of the speaker's credibility.

Force

Force is conditioned by psychological state. Excitement, depression, fear, and other attitudes or emotions can decrease the speaker's sensitivity to vocal delivery. Speakers frequently fail to realize they are speaking too loudly or too softly or with inhibition. Effective speakers learn to be aware of the psychological state of the audience and to compensate accordingly in the vocal delivery. In an intense communication situation a speaker will often increase the volume to match the intensity of the situation. Indeed, increased volume can be used effectively to call attention to the idea or for emphasis, but undue loudness born of intense emotion may detract from the message and become irritating to the listeners. We do not communicate well when we shout at each other. Sheer loudness may cause the listener to focus on the volume and lose the message. Many of us tend to increase the loudness of our voices as the validity and strength of our argument decreases, unaware that a message that did not get through when sent in an adequate conversational tone will do no better when it is shouted.

On the other hand, some persons speak too softly. They seem to have no feeling, emotions, nor awareness that anyone is seated in the audience beyond the first row. They go on and on at a low level of intensity. Is it any wonder that they are not granted high credibility?

Pitch

Pitch refers to the location of a tone on a musical scale and is determined by the frequency of sound vibrations per second. A speaker who uses only one pitch speaks in a monotone voice. Although few of us speak in a monotone, many persons—especially in public speaking—tend to restrict their range of pitch so that their voices are monotonous. The effective speaker constantly uses a variety of pitches in order to reinforce meaning and to add color to the speech.

Pitch is our interpretation of the frequency of the sound. If the vibratory pattern is slow, the pitch of the sound is lower; hence, the higher the frequency of vibrations, the higher the pitch. People normally have a pitch range (distance between highest pitched and lowest pitched tones) of one and one-half to two octaves. Although a speaker may use a wide variety of pitches, there is a habitual basic pitch level that is characteristic of much of that person's speaking. It is the basic pitch level to which one refers when saying of a person: "He has a high-pitched voice," or "Her voice is unusually low pitched." The male voice is usually about an octave lower than the female voice, with the average habitual pitch of the male voice at about 250 cycles per second, or very close to middle C.

An inappropriately high-pitched speaking voice may result from imitation or habit. It may also result from tension caused by fatigue, stage fright, anger, or frustration. It is possible, although sometimes quite difficult, to change the habitual basic pitch of one's voice.

Pitch is important in the effective transmission of speech. Through pitch the speaker adds color and meaningful reinforcement to the words of the message. Appropriate use of pitch can clarify meaning, secure and hold attention, and help to build imagery and interest in the speech.

Rate and Rhythm

Both **rate and rhythm** are significant elements in vocal delivery. A rapid delivery can suggest to the audience that the speaker is rushing to get through rather than calmly seeking to send a message.

When we say that speech is "too fast," we are not referring so much to the rate of pronouncing the words as we are to the rapidity of the ideas and points, although it is possible for a speaker to pronounce words so rapidly that carelessness in diction and articulation, makes words unidentifiable. The brain can process identifiable words at three or four times the speed at which they are spoken. The problem occurs when new or difficult ideas, meanings, or content require that the listener take time to let the message "soak in." It is not unusual that the public speech especially, with new information and new ideas put together compactly, demands that the speaker talk slowly enough to allow the listeners to absorb the message. Most college students have had the unfortunate experience of listening to a rapid-fire, jet-speed, fifty-minute lecture by a professor who has to cover all the material "today."

Research evidence on speaking rate indicates that when the material is easily understood or is of average difficulty, the normal speaker need not worry about speaking too fast; but when the speech is composed of material that is difficult to understand, the speaking rate must be reduced. Many students have experienced the problem of a too rapid delivery in mathematics classes. The professor did not pronounce the words rapidly, but moved from one step in the formula to the next, and then to the next, before the students had time to *understand* what was said.

One can also speak too slowly, and once listeners become bored with too little information they may decide to tune out the speaker. Studies show that changes in rate of speaking and in rhythm are associated with attitudes and emotional states. Faster rates, shorter comments, and more frequent pauses are associated with anger or fear, while slower rates and drawn-out speech are associated with grief and depression.[4] Duration—the temporal length of sounds and silences in speech—is also related to the mood of the speaker.[5] This special factor in rate is used to create the drawl of the stereotyped cowboy. In order to project clearly and accurately, a speaker usually increases the duration of sounds as well as the intensity of volume.

Quality

Quality is an element in vocal delivery that is difficult to define. When you hear the same note on a musical scale played with the same degree of loudness on a trumpet and on a violin, the difference you hear between the two is in the quality of the two tones. Just as we recognize the tones of a violin as different in quality from the same tones of a trumpet, so we recognize an individual voice as distinctive from other voices because of its quality. **Voice quality** refers to the subtle blending of elements into a unique voice. We speak of voices as being clear, husky, harsh, nasal, gutteral, falsetto, sonorous, hard, soft, shrill, warm, twangy, penetrating, syrupy, and honeyed.

Quality is determined, in part, by the size, shape, flexibility, and condition of the vocal folds, resonators, and the entire vocal mechanism. It is also affected by the speaker's emotional and physical states. A voice of clarity, richness, resonance, and strength depends on a certain favorable physical and emotional state of the speaker—being able to breathe properly and to use the nasal and mouth cavities for maximum resonance, and avoiding unnatural tensions in the speaking mechanism. As noted in the chapter on nonverbal communication, the voice is a mirror of the inner person. If confidence, hostility, openness, and affection are related to source credibility, as studies have shown them to be, then voice quality is an important element working for or against the public speaker.

Articulation and Pronunciation

Precision in articulation and accuracy in pronunciation are important factors in being understood. The organs most essential to clear diction are the tongue, teeth, lips, jaw, and velum, all of which are used in varying degrees to help us speak clearly and distinctly. The process of articulation by which we modify vocalization to create individual sounds in almost unending combination is the unique step that makes intelligible speech possible. Without articulation and pronunciation, we could not produce intelligible speech. We could only vocalize.

The presentation of new information may require the speaker to talk slowly and deliberately.

Articulation refers to the formation of individual speech sounds, and pronunciation refers to the fitting together of these sounds into words. Articulatory problems are of four types: sound substitutions, sound distortions, sound omissions, and sound additions. Young children often substitute one easy-to-make sound for a more difficult sound. *Rabbit* sometimes becomes "wabbit," and *run* becomes "wun." A child of one of your authors substituted the *y* sound for *l* for a period of a few months; once, when he saw the Christmas lights spanning the main street at each intersection in the little town of Lakin, he excitedly exclaimed, "Yook at the yights in Yakin!" Although such substitutions may be understandable and expected in a four-year-old child, when an adult persists in substituting *th* for *s* or *w* for *r,* it becomes a handicap to communication effectiveness. Similarly, sound distortions, adversely affect one's ability to present an effective message.

Problems of omission and addition of sounds are even more common in adult speech than are distortions or substitutions. These problems relate directly to **pronunciation** and are often a speech habit. An extremely rapid rate of speaking sometimes causes omissions; in many cases it is sheer carelessness that ingrains the habit. Sloppy diction is often the result of habitual omissions (*probly, cuz, libary, doin', goin', sord*) and habitual sound additions (*elum* for *elm* and *filum* for *film* and *stastistics* for *statistics*). Some articulatory problems may have physical causes. These as well as some other articulary problems are best handled by trained speech therapists; but when habit, imitation of a poor model, or carelessness causes the problem, *you* can do something about it.

Correct pronunciation closely matches a standard, but there are various standards that may be used. Heinberg has identified them as the majority standard (used by the majority of the people of the country); the regional standard (acceptable in a given region); the audience standard (pronunciation used by one's audience); an authoritarian standard (imposed by some officially sanctioned group); and the cultured speaker standard (pronunciation used by those persons of prestige who engage frequently in public communication).[6] This fifth standard is probably the best for use in a college speech class, as expressed by the editors of the Merriam-Webster dictionaries: "At present all cultivated types, when well spoken, are easily intelligible to any speaker of English, and there is a very large percentage of practical identity in the speech sounds used."[7] The function of most dictionaries is to present the pronunciations currently prevailing in the best usage and not to attempt to dictate what that usage should be. Suggested pronunciations in dictionaries are periodically revised to reflect the observed changes in pronunciations.

Poor articulation and pronunciation can reduce the speaker's credibility. For this reason, you should check your articulation and pronunciation and, if need be, embark on an improvement program.

Conversational Style

The purpose of public communication—to transfer a message as effectively as possible—can best be accomplished through a fluent, **conversational style** of delivery. Rather than delivering the message in dramatic, oratorical, or any other odd or unique style, the speaker should deliver the message in a style that harmonizes articulation, pronunciation, quality, pitch, rate, rhythm, and all other voice elements into a warm, personal style as might be found in the best of informal conversations. The aim is for listeners to feel that you are *talking with them*—not performing for them, lecturing to them, or demonstrating your beautiful oral communication skills, but communicating with them. Your interest, enthusiasm, concern with the listener, and sincerity must show in your vocal delivery. Superficiality is never an adequate substitute for sincerity. Oratorical gymnastics cannot satisfactorily replace a live, melodious, well-projected vocal delivery.

Conversational delivery is appropriate in almost any kind of speaking situation, from an intimate, dyadic interchange to a formal lecture or televised address or sermon. Effective speakers learn to use a conversational style in public speaking. Occasionally, someone will have an image of public speaking in which physical and vocal delivery is characterized by trite and rigid behaviors ranging from shouting to whispering dramatically, to lowering the pitch and speaking in pear-shaped tones (without harshness, thinness, or nasality). Such delivery interferes with the message rather than aiding it, and the usual result is either a jerky, bombastic, exploding delivery or another essentially nonfluent style.

"Conversational style" does not mean an unrehearsed, rough, rambling manner of speaking. "Rambling" is *not* a characteristic of effective and enjoyable conversation. A rambling, bumbling delivery can be as disastrous in a public speech as the glib, mechanistic delivery or the bombastic delivery. Rambling is a barrier to communication. The public speaker who wanders from the message, who verbalizes notions that fleet through the mind, and who gets lost in the message will soon lose the audience. Rambling and mumbling are not characteristics of an effective conversational style of delivery. The fluent, conversational speaker, whether preacher, teacher, politician, or lecturer, makes listening easy and enjoyable. The speaker who advances ideas smoothly, confidently, clearly, and positively, stands a better chance of getting the desired audience response than does the speaker who is hesitant, jerky, and rambling. Effective vocal delivery enhances the effectiveness of public communication.

Credibility through Body Use and Appearance

In addition to auditory cues, visual signals are sent by the speaker through physical activity. The body is used as a communication transmitter in at least four ways: eye contact, facial expression, gestures, and movement.

Eye Contact

Eye contact is essential for effective public speaking. When the speaker avoids the audience by *not* establishing eye contact, the audience feels uneasy, embarrassed, suspicious, and generally negative toward the speaker, whether in social conversation, a small group, an interview, or in a televised lecture. If the speaker looks at the floor, out the window, at the ceiling, or past the listener, it is difficult for the listener to maintain the kinds of attitudes that enhance receptivity. When eye control is established with the listener, the speaker not only communicates more directly but can also watch the reaction of the auditors so as to be sensitive and alert to feedback. The speaker can then pick up the signs of doubt and misunderstanding or the signs of acceptance.

Facial Expression

Facial expression is extremely important as a conveyor of attitudes and emotions, as you will recall from the chapter on nonverbal communication. Through facial expression a speaker can show interest and enthusiasm for the message; listeners can hardly be expected to be interested in a subject in which the speaker is not interested. An emotion or communication apprehension may cause an inexperienced speaker to hide a positive personality behind a lifeless mask. Then negative or inhibited attitudes that betray the intended message may be conveyed to the audience.

Gestures

Gestures are used to reinforce the verbal message, and the speaker who acquires the ability to use them freely, naturally, and effectively enhances communicativeness. Gestures can be used to punctuate thought and emphasize meaning, to help create clear pictures, to reflect attitudes, to identify and delineate ideas, to break up stiffness and awkwardness with physical animation that releases the warmth and humanness of the speaker, and to relax the mind from the tensions produced by physical rigidity. Gestures that seem natural, spontaneous, and suitable to the speaker are an important asset to the public speech.

Facial expression is an important conveyor of attitude.

Body Movements

Body movements are also used to reinforce or contradict verbal messages. The slumped speaker conveys dejection; the lax, sloppily postured speaker conveys indifference; the tense speaker conveys fear—all of these postures and body messages are received by the listeners and act to negate the verbal message. Again, as shown in the nonverbal communication chapter, body movement is important in communication, especially in the public-speaking situation. As with gestures, effective body movement not only reinforces the verbal message but also helps the speaker to achieve poise and freedom of expression through physical activity that releases the pent-up-energy.

For several years, speakers were instructed on precisely how to stand, how to gesture, and what facial expressions to use. The position of the hands for expressing various emotions was illustrated; the placement of the feet to convey resistance or other impressions were carefully prescribed. All such instructions were stated in rules. Today, we believe that such standardization is undesirable, since no two speakers or receivers are identical. You must develop your own skills in bodily communication to meet your specific personality characteristics. Rather than memorizing artificial positions of the feet or hands for the expression of a given emotion, each speaker must allow bodily communication to spring from inner feelings associated with the message. In addition, each speaker should embark on a self-improvement program aimed at discovering and eliminating frantic, distracting movements, gestures, and postures that contradict and intrude on the message. Shifting of the feet, repetitive and meaningless facial movements, arms folded across the chest, rocking to and fro, leaning on the podium, and other distracting bodily communication should be replaced by comfortable, positive physical communication.

Personal Appearance

Personal appearance is another important aspect of nonverbal communication in delivering the speech.

We are beginning to realize that a person's credibility can be influenced as much by nonverbal as verbal self-presentation. A recent newspaper article referred to several attorneys who double as wardrobe consultants for trial cases. The attorneys contend that "the right clothes (and hair, makeup, demeanor—overall appearance, in fact) makes an impression because judges and juries are only human and take everything—including appearance—into consideration in evaluating the argument of each side."[8] One lawyer who specializes in domestic trials such as divorce, alimony, or child custody contends that when the clients are not asked to testify, the jury gets an impression of them by looking at them, never hearing them speak. These patterns are also appearing in rape trials where the victim is counseled to wear clothing which will not help the defense attorney or the jury find justification for the crime. What we are seeing is a deliberate effort by lawyers to help their clients fit the image being portrayed.[9] Some are also orchestrating their own nonverbal presentation. One attorney said, "I basically adopted that 'dress-for-success' look as my basic costume six or seven years ago."[10] Another says he dresses for each particular stage of a long trial. His change of attire ranges from a conservative business suit at the start to a blazer and pink shirt several days into the proceedings. At the conclusion of the trial he would wear a dark suit for his final arguments.[11]

It is not necessary for us to appreciate the inordinate impact of the human body's appearance, movement, or dress on the communication process. It is essential, however, that we as communicators recognize this aspect of the process and take the ethical and appropriate encoding and decoding actions.

Body communication is an important and inescapable part of public speaking. Before a word is spoken, the audience is sizing up the speaker, forming opinions about the way the speaker looks, walks, is dressed, and stands. Listeners mark points for or against the speaker on the basis of posture, poise, and physical appearance (attracted or not attracted); they see the speaker as warm or cold, as sincere or insincere, as intelligent or unintelligent. These perceptions and evaluations are derived, in part, from what each listener sees—from reception of the nonverbal messages sent by the speaker.

How is self-presentation (intrinsic credibility and nonverbal delivery) like self-disclosure?

Modes of Delivery

Delivery has been a major topic in this chapter on the speaker. We now expand this discussion to include specific modes of delivering a speech. The five ways of delivering a speech are impromptu, by memory, extemporaneous, by reading a manuscript, and by prompters.

Impromptu Delivery

In **impromptu delivery,** the speech is presented with little preparation, perhaps spontaneously. Most of us have given such speeches. They are usually short—perhaps no more than one or two minutes long. Sometimes we are asked to report on the convention we attended, or to explain what action was taken on an issue in a meeting we attended; and we may find ourselves giving a ten-minute speech for which we've had no opportunity to prepare. To be organized, fluent, and adaptive in impromptu speaking is a valuable skill and asset.

Impromptu delivery has at least one advantage—spontaneity. You may recall that spontaneity was discussed in chapter 6 when we were considering supportive and defensive communication. Spontaneity in speaking has a positive effect on listeners. It is seen as honest, open, and nonmanipulative. There is something genuine and nondeceptive about spontaneity. The disadvantage of impromptu speaking, however, is that since one has no opportunity to collect evidence or organize ideas, effective reasoning may not be easy to produce. Impromptu speaking is usually used in more informal situations.

Memorized Delivery

Memorized delivery is a second way of delivering a speech. Usually the speech has been carefully prepared, written out, and then committed to memory. Memorized speeches can be among the worst or the best of speeches. Very often a memorized speech is poor because spontaneity in thought as well as in verbal and nonverbal behavior is lost. The natural effective qualities of human communication—qualities of facial expression, movement, and vocal expression—are lost, and mechanical, disjointed behavior often results. Besides this handicap, the flexibility and adaptability of extemporaneous or impromptu delivery is taken away since one ignores feedback as the memorized speech continues. Adjustment to the audience is virtually impossible. Moreover, one always runs the risk of forgetting part of the speech.

There are sometimes certain topics or arguments that demand such careful presentation, or that have been given so many times by a speaker that memorized delivery is a natural and effective mode. These instances are quite rare for most of us, and few of us are capable of handling the memorized mode as effectively as we can the extemporaneous delivery.

Extemporaneous Delivery

The third mode of delivery is extemporaneous. Notes, although not required, are often used in extemporaneous speaking. **Extemporaneous delivery** has the advantages of being planned while at the same time spontaneous in its wording and expression of ideas. The organizational pattern has been established, and essential points as well as supporting materials have been carefully selected, but the wording and expression of content occur spontaneously as the speech is given. Minimal notes may help one recall points of the speech or enable one to give statistics precisely, but the speaker is free to adjust and adapt delivery and ideas as needed.

Manuscript Delivery

Manuscript delivery is the fourth mode to which we call attention. Preachers, executives, broadcasters, politicians, and other professionals often use manuscript delivery. Speakers who are often quoted in the press frequently use manuscript delivery so that the entire speech is written out and the wording and content precisely controlled. The chief disadvantage of manuscript delivery is that effective use of gestures, eye contact, and general physical behavior is frequently inhibited. Also, spontaneity is lost. Finally, it is difficult to adapt the message to audience feedback. Nevertheless, manuscript delivery is widely used today in public speaking.

Prompters

Prompters are the answer to the demands of the information age. As satellite television, teleconferencing, and industrial applications of videotaping increase, speakers in virtually every profession are finding increasing demands and opportunities to speak on-camera. Frequently the speeches are too long to memorize and are inappropriate for on-camera scripts. Three uses of prompters have emerged to solve these problems for speakers. The first use involves the standard cue card. Cue cards are generally 14″ × 22″ strips of poster board with copy written large enough to be read from a distance of eight to twelve feet. The card is held by the floor manager or an assistant. As one line is read, the card is immediately replaced with a new card containing the next line of the script. The cards enable the speaker to maintain eye contact with the audience while delivering what is essentially a manuscript speech.

A second use of prompters involves the use of cue cards to outline the sequence of main points, topics to be covered, jokes, and so on. Johnny Carson, for example, presents his monologue from an outline appearing on a series of cue cards. Although his jokes are memorized, the cue cards are used to remind him of the proper sequence. Cue cards used as outlines need not be held next to the camera lens as they are for scripted speeches. Rather, the cards can be positioned off-camera within easy view of the speaker.

The teleprompter, a third prompting device, enables the speaker to maintain maximum eye contact while reading continuous copy. This is accomplished by means of a closed-circuit vidiocom camera that scans the speech text, and a television monitor and mirror system. These instruments are mounted on a studio camera within view of the speaker. The script, which appears to the speaker on the face of a one-way mirror, is invisible to the camera and thus to the audience, and is out of the way of the camera technicians. The obvious advantages of the teleprompter are: (1) the speaker can read the lines and still look straight into the camera, (2) the speed of the moving copy is

Teleprompters are examples of modern day technology that can enhance eye contact in the public speech while utilizing a manuscript.

variable and can be controlled by the prompter operator, (3) any normally typed script can be run immediately on the prompter, and (4) last-minute manuscript changes can be made without complications.

All forms of prompters require careful scripting and directing. The speaker will normally receive thorough instructions from taping personnel and it is imperative that these directions be followed completely.

Three Characteristics of Effective Delivery

We have discussed delivery rather extensively in this chapter because it is the means by which the speaker is revealed. Delivery also has an enormous impact on credibility. We have identified the components of vocal and bodily delivery, but the final point to which we should call attention in this chapter is that there are three objectives or characteristics of effective nonverbal communication in the public-speaking situation: (1) vocal and physical delivery should *not* draw attention away from the message; (2) vocal and physical delivery ought to be energetic and to communicate enthusiasm to the audience; and (3) one's nonverbal communication ought to reveal the speaker in command of the speech situation—confident and at ease in the role.

If delivery calls undue attention to itself, it detracts from the message and acts as "noise" in the situation. Being overly dramatic, for example, can mask the content for some listeners. Similarly, if one's delivery communicates boredom, fear, or lethargy, rather than enthusiasm and concern, the audience may see no reason for being concerned or enthused. And if the speaker is ill at ease and lacks confidence, the audience may be ill at ease too, and lack confidence that anything worthwhile will occur. The audience can relax and listen to the message when the speaker controls the speaking situation with confidence, ease, and poise that communicates to the audience "all's well"—this speaker knows what he or she is doing and enjoys doing it.

Can you describe the five modes of delivery and give the advantages of each?

Summary

This chapter has focused on the speaker as an important influence on outcomes in public communication. Although we know that the speaker is but one element in the dynamic public-speaking situation, and even though we know the speech and the audience influence the speaker, yet the speaker can, by appropriate behavior, be an influence in shaping the outcomes of the communication situation. It has been noted that *who* the speaker is, as perceived by the audience, is a powerful variable in public communication. Further, we have identified the major dimensions used by listeners to define the speaker: trustworthiness, expertise, and dynamism. Finally, we investigated the relationship between delivery and the speaker's ability to influence the communication outcome. We have clearly shown that delivery is directly related to credibility.

The speaker can increase personal influence over communication outcomes by practicing and using proven delivery principles. One area, then, with which you may want to be concerned is your delivery—your nonverbal communication to the audience. The principles we discussed in chapter 5 apply as well in the public-speaking situation as they do in small group and interpersonal communication situations. As a public speaker, your feelings, attitudes, and psychological states will be communicated via the same channels that carried those messages in the interview situation, in social conversation, or in intimate interaction.

Of course, in most instances, the speaker brings along an "image." The speaker's authority, experience, power, reputation—in short, all that the audience knows about the speaker—influence the audience's judgment of speaker credibility. Character, expertise, likableness—these are the foundations of source credibility.

As these characteristics are developed by you through your interaction with others, you acquire the "raw stuff" out of which credibility is made.

Questions and Exercises for Review

1. What are other terms for course credibility?
2. What are the three major components of source credibility?
3. Where does the audience get the data it uses to ascribe credibility to a speaker?
4. What are the advantages and disadvantages of each of the five modes of delivery?
5. What are desirable outcomes or characteristics of effective delivery?

Key Terms and Phrases

- ethos
- source credibility
- trustworthiness
- expertise
- dynamism
- goodwill
- credibility gap
- extrinsic credibility
- self-presentation
- intrinsic credibility
- common ground
- preparation
- "sense of humor"
- vocal delivery
- force
- pitch
- rate and rhythm
- quality
- voice quality
- articulation
- pronunciation
- conversational style
- eye contact
- facial expression
- gestures
- body movements
- personal appearance
- impromptu delivery
- memorized delivery
- extemporaneous delivery
- manuscript delivery
- prompters

For Further Reading

Andersen, Kenneth E., and Clevenger, Theodore, Jr. "A Summary of Experimental Research in Ethos." *Speech Monographs* 30 (1963): 63–67.

This is a classic summary of research findings related to ethos, and it is one of the most cited references in the literature of the field.

Aronson, E., and Golden, B. W. "The Effect of Relevant and Irrelevant Aspects of Communicator Credibility on Opinion Change." *Journal of Personality* 30 (1962): 135–46.

An investigation of which aspects of credibility enhance persuasion and which do not.

Benjoy, Joseph W. "The Credibility of Physically Attractive Communicators: A Review." *Journal of Advertising* II (1982): 15–24.

Griffin, E. M. *The Mind Changers: The Art of Christian Persuasion.* Wheaton: Tyndale House Publishers, Inc., 1983.

Haiman, F. "An Experimental Study of the Effects of Ethos in Public Speaking." *Speech Monographs* 16 (1949): 190–202.

An interesting experiment on ethos.

Harms, L. S. "Listener Judgments of Status Cues in Speech." *Quarterly Journal of Speech* 47 (1961): 164–70.

An interesting study of how we judge a speaker's status from nonverbal cues.

McCroskey, J. C., and Jensen, T. "Measurement of the Credibility of Mass Media Sources." *Journal of Broadcasting* 19 (1975): 169–80.

Focuses on how to measure the credibility of mass media sources. Credibility applies to sources as well as to speakers.

Notes

1. E. M. Griffin, *The Mind Changers: The Art of Christian Persuasion* (Wheaton, Ill.: Tyndale House Publishers, Inc., 1983), 117

2. Griffin, *Mind Changers,* 117.

3. Herbert Kelman and Carl Hovland, "Reinstatement of the Communication in Delayed Measurement of Opinion Change," *Journal of Abnormal and Social Psychology* 48 (1953): 327–35.

4. Dean C. Barnlund, *Interpersonal Communication: Survey and Studies* (Boston: Houghton Mifflin Co., 1968), 529.

5. Grant Fairbanks and LeMar W. Hoaglin, "An Experimental Study of the Durational Characteristics of the Voice During the Expression of Emotion," *Speech Monographs* 8 (1941): 85–90.

6. Paul Heinberg, *Voice Training for Speaking and Reading Aloud* (New York: Ronald Press Co., 1964), 256–59.

7. By permission. From *Webster's New International Dictionary, Second Edition,* © 1959 by G. & C. Merriam Co., Publishers of the Merriam-Webster Dictionaries.

8. Rita Rouse, "Lawyers Say Justice is Not Blind to Clothes Worn for Court." *Tulsa World* 13 January 1984, 14-A.

9. Rouse, "Lawyers," 14-A.

10. Rouse, "Lawyers," 14-A.

11. Rouse, "Lawyers," 14-A.

Focus

The Audience

A second component of public speaking is the audience. It is an important element since the audience ultimately determines the success of the speaker. In this chapter, we consider the role of the audience in the public communication situation, the definition of an audience, types of audiences, and audience analysis. Audience analysis is the primary topic in this chapter and it is discussed in detail. We consider audience analysis before the speech, during the speech, and after the speech. We identify the kinds of information we need to discover about an audience; we discuss how environmental factors can affect an audience; and we stress the importance of being attentive to audience feedback during the speech so that the speaker can adapt to the audience.

The Role of the Audience

What is the role of the audience in the communication process? Is it one of passive acceptance in which the communicator does something to the audience, with or without its consent? Such a concept is commonly held by the general public and is thought to be the model commonly used by those in advertising and public relations. This concept of the audience emphasizes one person's exploitation of others. To view the audience in this way—as a passive mass of individuals waiting to be told what to think and what to do—is to view the communication process as a one-way street. This linear concept of the communication process suggests that the speaker need only push certain verbal buttons to gain the desired response. The idea of the powerful communicator being able to change either the attitudes or the behavior of the respondents at will lacks convincing support from research. Some situations, however, appear to create the circumstances that do successfully result in the exploitation of audiences. These situations are mainly created and controlled by the communicator and require more time, energy, ingenuity, and resources than are ordinarily available for almost any legitimate communication situation. Such "communication circumstances" raise serious moral questions and are not our primary concern in this chapter.

Communication research seems to support a far different view of the role of the audience than that as recipients in a one-way or linear communication process. Recent research shows public communication to be a two-way transaction between communicator and audience in which each party is actively engaged, and in which both communicator and audience give and get something in return. The role of the audience in the communication process is not a passive one. The audience actively engages in the speech act by reacting to the speaker and the speech, often affecting the speaker's message from moment to moment. This transactional concept of the role of the audience suggests that the audience and speaker mutually influence each other. The fact that the audience exerts influence on the speaker and the speech is evidence of the importance of the audience as a variable in the communication process. The transaction between the speaker and audience is dynamic and complex and presents every speaker with the challenging responsibility of knowing and understanding the audience.

The primary responsibility of any speaker wishing to communicate ideas to others is to discover the nature of those to whom the message is directed. Discovering the nature of an audience, its wants and needs, its attitudes and beliefs—in short, all there is to know about it—is essential to effective and successful communication. In speech communication, this discovery process is referred to as **audience analysis.**

More than two thousand years ago, Aristotle recognized the importance of audience analysis when he observed that a speech was composed, or grew out of, the interaction of three elements: the speaker, the subject, and the persons addressed. He added that of these elements it is the persons addressed—

the audience—that determines the speech's end or object. Aristotle's pronouncement still holds true today. When all is said and done, the end result of the speech, its success or failure, is determined primarily by the audience; although, as we have seen in chapter 9 the speaker may also exert an influence. But if there is any one element more important than the other two elements, it is the audience, for its members grant or deny the speaker's request. This clearly suggests that if speakers wish to be effective, they must (1) analyze the audience, and (2) adjust and adapt themselves and their ideas to the audience. The audience, then, is the single most important element for the speaker to consider in the public-speaking process.

Can you explain the role of the audience in the public-speaking situation?

What Is an Audience?

The chief features of an **audience** are (1) it has a specific purpose, (2) it meets at a predetermined time and place, and (3) it has a standard form of polarization and interaction. The specific purpose, of course, is to attend to the message of a speaker. In the more common forms of public address—the President's state of the union message, political rallies, Sunday sermons, and lectures—the audience is aware of the **time and place** the speech will occur. Perhaps the most unique qualities of the audience are polarization and interaction. **Polarization** is the quality that makes a group of persons into an audience; it introduces direction and purpose into an otherwise unorganized group. Polarization occurs when the individual members of a group direct their attention to a common object—the speaker—rather than to each other. When the members of an audience consciously accept their roles as listeners and the role of the speaker as speaker, the audience is polarized. Without polarization, there is merely a group of individuals devoid of structure. The people in a subway terminal at rush hour, hurrying to various trains, or those in an airport, waiting the arrival or departure of flights, lack polarization; hence they are not audiences.

In the audience there are two significant forms of interaction present at all times (but at varying levels): (1) that among individual members of the audience and (2) that between the audience and the speaker. The interaction among the individual members of an audience is manifested most overtly during those moments just prior to and after a speech. There is a great amount of concerted social activity present during these pre-speech and post-speech periods. Open greetings, handshakes, and pats on the back are common during these periods. Depending on the nature of the audience, the speaker, and the occasion, hostilities as well as pleasantries may well occur. The speaker who has carefully analyzed an audience can rather accurately predict the kind of social interaction that will take place within the audience. Careful observation of the audience during this pre-speech period can provide the observant speaker with invaluable information about the audience. Such analysis may allow the speaker to adjust to the immediate mood of the audience and the occasion. The interaction of audience members during the actual speech is often more

Concerted social activity.

subtle. The intensity of interaction during the actual speech depends primarily on the degree of homogeneity or group feelings that exists within an audience. Audiences of high homogeneity tend to reinforce and intensify their feelings and responses toward the speaker and the speech. The higher the degree of **audience homogeneity,** the more predictable is the interaction and response of the audience.

The speaker who addresses an audience of high-level homogeneity can anticipate reasonably unified behavior from the individual members during the speech; if the audience shares a common ground or sense of togetherness, the members will tend to react in the same manner to the message. On the other hand, the speaker who addresses an audience of low homogeneity (possessing little common ground or sense of togetherness) is likely to find the behavior of that audience unpredictable. The lower the degree of homogeneity, the more uncertain we are as to how the audience will interact or what the response to the message will be. It is this behavior, however, that is the basis of interaction between the speaker and the audience. The way in which the audience is reacting to the speaker and the message is the only key for determining the immediate success or failure of public communication.

The audience, by virtue of its behavior, exerts considerable control over the speaker's message from moment to moment throughout the speech. This process of interaction between the speaker and the audience is a continual one. The speaker who is aware of and adjusts to the audience greatly enhances the chances for effective communication.

The beginning speaker is primarily concerned with analyzing the audience in a formal speech setting, a setting in which the individual members of the audience have willingly chosen to attend the speech. Such a setting suggests that the speaker will be able to determine the general nature of the audience by virtue of interest in the subject, the occasion, and/or the speaker. From this point of view, we can define the audience as an assembled group of individuals who typically meet at a predetermined time and place for the specific purpose of seeing a speaker and hearing the message.

Types of Audiences

Unfortunately, not all audiences have the same degree of purpose and direction toward the speaker and the message as does the formal audience. Hollingworth gives a useful classification of audiences based on the degree of their organization or orientation toward the speech situation.[1]

The first audience in Hollingworth's classification is the **casual audience.** Such an audience would not be called an audience at all by some persons, since such audiences lack any consistent, strong common focus. Sightseers wandering about a museum, occasionally listening to an explanation of some ancient relic, are illustrations of this audience type. Such audiences display little or no homogeneity and have little speaker-listener orientation or polarization. The primary challenge to the speaker facing a casual audience is to get their attention, that is, to try "to make an audience out of them."

Distinguished from the casual audience is a second type that Hollingworth refers to as *passive* or partially oriented. The **passive audience** is best characterized as being disinterested. Partially oriented audiences are found in many college classrooms, social organizations, and perhaps most typically in the after-dinner audience. The primary challenge to the speaker is to create interest in the listeners.

A third type of audience is the **selected audience.** It is composed of individuals who have gathered for some common and known purpose. Usually the individuals in this audience have been especially invited to attend a closed or semiclosed meeting because they are known to have previous interest in the subject to be considered. The speaker normally has the attention and interest of the selected audience. The first task, then, is to make an impression on them.

Fourth is the **concerted audience,** which has an active purpose, with sympathetic interest in a mutual enterprise, but with no clear division of labor or rigid organization of authority. The concerted audience has a high degree of orientation toward the speaker and the purpose. Graduate seminars, specialized training groups, and some political meetings are examples of concerted audiences. The primary task of the speaker is to persuade these audiences and to direct action.

A fifth and final type is the **organized audience**—the college band in formation, for example. The members of these groups are completely oriented toward the speaker or leader. In such an audience, the labor is fixed and the

What type of audience is this?

lines of authority clearly demarcated. The speaker enjoys considerable control over the organized audience. The speaker's challenge is simply to guide the specific action of the audience.

The speaker's task is illustrated in table 10.1, Hollingworth's summary of a speaker's responsibilities at various audience levels.[2] The types of audiences identified by Hollingworth are not absolute, mutually exclusive types. The truth is that you may find some persons fitting into several of these types—all in the same audience. But nevertheless, the classification schema is useful when a speaker is analyzing the type of audience to be addressed. One can think in terms of the audience as a whole—or in terms of the degree of "concertedness" or of "passiveness" in the audience as a whole. If the speaker, by using the taxonomy of types of audiences, can better understand an audience and thus perceive how to adapt to the audience and how to move the audience toward an orientation more favorable to the speaker's purpose, then it is a worthwhile aid to audience analysis. Most persons who do much public speaking easily recognize the types of audiences that Hollingworth describes. You may recognize one or more of these audiences when you give a speech in class.

Can you identify and differentiate the types of audiences?

Only through careful analysis will the speaker be able to determine the predisposition of the audience toward the subject, occasion, and speaker. Audience analysis is a continual process and is essential to the preparation, delivery, and evaluation of the effectiveness of the speaker and the message. Audience analysis, then, must take place three times—before the speech, during the speech, and after the speech. Let us consider pre-speech audience analysis.

Table 10.1 Speaker's responsibilities at various levels of audience orientation. (From *The Psychology of the Audience*, by H. L. Hollingworth, © 1935. Reprinted by permission of the American Book Company.)

Pedestrian Audience	Passive Audience	Selected Audience	Concerted Audience	Organized Audience
Attention	. . . . .	. . . . .	. . . . .	. . . . .
Interest	Interest	. . . . .	. . . . .	. . . . .
Impression	Impression	Impression	. . . . .	. . . . .
Conviction	Conviction	Conviction	Conviction	. . . . .
Direction	Direction	Direction	Direction	Direction

Pre-Speech Audience Analysis

Pre-speech audience analysis is the essence of speech preparation. No facet of message preparation, whether it be conducting research, structuring the speech, or practicing the delivery, should be considered independently from the audience to which the speech will be given. As the opening chapters have stressed, communication consists of evoking a response from a receiver. While preparing a speech, it is important that the speaker have a constant mental image of the audience. Audience analysis consists of asking oneself (1) What do I know about the group of people who will listen to this speech? and (2) How can I use that knowledge to increase the probability of achieving my goals?

Approaches to Audience Analysis

Audience analysis is a unique blending of informal, demographic, and purposive analysis. Informal audience analysis is the process of collecting general information by means of direct and indirect personal experience, general questions about the audience, program format, physical setting, and expected image. Two traditional approaches to audience analysis are the *demographic approach* and the *purposive approach*. **Demographic audience analysis** consists of gathering as much information as possible about the demographic characteristics of the audience, such as age, sex, political preference, socioeconomic status, religion, and the like. **Purposive audience analysis** is concerned with the strategies a speaker uses to achieve the goal with a certain audience.

It is evident that demographic data in itself is of little use to a speaker. The value of collecting information about the age, sex, and socioeconomic status of an audience is limited to the speaker's ability to draw inferences from that information about the values and attitudes that will affect the outcome of the communication. If one's goal is to convince the school administration of the

Audience acceptance aids the speaker.

need to spend funds for additional campus parking, a detailed analysis of the religious affiliations of the audience is probably of little use. Knowledge of the occupations and economic status of the audience, however, might be helpful in predicting its predispositions toward the topic. For another speaker whose speech purpose is to win support for stricter abortion laws, knowledge of the audience's religious beliefs might be more helpful than any other demographic data that could be collected. Thus it is suggested that the speaker combine the two traditional forms of audience analysis with informal audience analysis. The speaker should consider relevant general and demographic data within the context of the particular speech purpose.

Informal Audience Analysis

The availability of detailed, scientifically collected statistical data on which to base an audience analysis is extremely rare. More often a speaker must draw inferences about the audience on the basis of informal observations and analysis. Direct personal experience with an audience is surely the best source of an informal analysis. The minister who speaks to the same congregation every week knows most members of the audience personally and can make many intelligent generalizations about the members' attitudes, values, and predispositions. Classroom teachers are often heard to label certain classes as liberal or skeptical or fun-loving. These inferences are based on several hours of informal, direct interaction and are probably sound examples of audience analysis. When a person is a longtime member of a group, audience analysis is almost intuitive. That person knows from direct experience what "goes over" with that audience—what would be boring, what arguments would seem logical, and what appeals would spark an emotional response.

When a speaker does not have such direct personal experience, it is useful to find out as much as possible about the audience by asking others. Any outside speaker will have some sort of contact with the audience—usually the program chairperson who issued the invitation. A speaker who questions this person about the audience should not be apologetic, for the questions will show interest and seriousness about speech planning. One thing a speaker should always try to ascertain is how much knowledge the audience has of the topic. A medical professional invited to speak to a women's club on AIDS might mistakenly assume that the members were uninformed. This speaker might prepare a general speech in oversimplified layman's terms, only to arrive at the meeting and discover that the speech was part of a series on health issues and that the audience had been hearing speeches, reading books, and holding discussions on this topic for months. A speaker should also seek information about the *format* of the program: What is the time limit? Is a question-and-answer period following the speech desired? Will the audience be finishing a large meal? Is the speech the main event of the program or will the speech be between a glee club performance and the annual election of officers?

Sometimes a speaker needs information about the *physical setting* and should feel free to ask if the audience will be seated at tables or in rows of chairs. The speaker should certainly ask for an estimate of the size of the audience and may want to check on the availability of a lectern, a microphone, a blackbroad, or equipment for showing slides or films. Some speakers are very adaptable and have no trouble speaking in a third-grade classroom, using an upside-down wastebasket as a lectern, when they had expected a large lecture hall. However, if there are some aspects of the physical setting that will affect the speaker's efforts, these factors should be checked in advance.

There is another aspect of general information about the speech situation that a speaker should include in the informal analysis. The speaker should have some understanding of the speaker's image held by the audience: Is the speaker seen as an expert? Does the audience have any misleading ideas about the speaker's qualifications? Often one can get cues about perceptions of one's image by talking to one or more members of the audience. Certainly, knowledge of this expected image can be an important factor in preparing a speech. If the image that the audience has is approximately correct, the speaker should probably adjust to audience expectations. Audiences have some ideas about what a foreign exchange student or a doctor or a school principal is like. Audiences also expect certain behavior from women speakers or from younger speakers. As long as the image reflects general cultural standards, the speaker is wise to adjust to the image. On the other hand, no speaker should try to project a misleading image. A cardinal rule of communication effectiveness is, "Be Yourself." Speakers who try to borrow images that work for others usually meet with disastrous results.

Demographic Analysis

In addition to informal audience analysis, the speaker will often ask questions or seek information about demographic characteristics of the audience. A few of these demographic factors are considered in this section.

Age

It is a good idea for a speaker to try to find out the age range and average age of the audience. While the generation gap is often exaggerated, there is no doubt that communication among different age groups is difficult and complex. Disraeli is credited with the statement, "If a man's not a little liberal when he's twenty, there's something wrong with his heart. If he's not a little conservative when he's fifty, there's something wrong with his head." Although we can all think of many exceptions, the generalization that younger people are more liberal and older people are more conservative is basically valid. The generalization is more applicable if we use the terms *liberal* and *conservative* to represent basic world views rather than specific political ideologies. Younger people are frequently more idealistic, more impatient, and more optimistic than older people, who tend to be more pragmatic, cautious, and pessimistic. Most middle-aged and elderly people have a substantial stake in the institutions of society. They are understandably reluctant to change those institutions, often at the expense of property, status, and difficult personal adjustments, unless they are sure that the changes are definite improvements. Teenagers and young adults, also understandably, are outraged at corruption, injustice, and imperfections in institutions and are eager to try various reforms. They are discouraged by the response of their elders who say, "We've tried that before."

In addition to adjusting speech content to the age level of the audience, a speaker must make certain adjustments in style of presentation. A study by Kausler and Lair showed that younger people can gain information from a faster rate of presentation than can older people.[3] It seems that, in general, older people also prefer a slower, more deliberate style of speaking and younger people prefer a faster livelier pace. A speaker with a predominantly older audience may need to use a slower rate of delivery and a clear, step-by-step development of points. With a more youthful audience, the speaker could use a faster rate of delivery (although of course the speaker must be intelligible) and could use various patterns of organization, as long as there is a coherent progression of ideas.

Sex

Many psychological studies have reported that men and women are different in more than the obvious ways. The feminist movement has refocused attention on the nature of these differences, many of which were culturally created; for example, society taught women that they ought to display certain attitudes, such as being emotional, submissive, and home oriented.

Several researchers, including Franklin Knower and Thomas Scheidel, reported that their research results indicated that women were more prone to

The demographic characteristics are important to audience analysis.

change their attitudes, less impressed with logical arguments, and less effective in influencing other women than were their male counterparts.[4] These studies generally reported that women were more persuadable than men and that women retained significantly less speech content than did men.[5] More recent research indicates that if the previous research was true, it was primarily true of men and women at the time the research was conducted. While research reported in 1977 indicated that studies of classroom speech evaluations showed differences between the sexes, more recent research has raised serious questions regarding the validity of many of the traditional stereotypes. Current research reflects a changing status of women and suggests that perhaps many of the earlier conclusions regarding gender differences resulted from researchers confusing levels of interest expectation or knowledge with sex differences.[6] Judy Pearson's discussion of gender research observed that "although it has been determined that women are more easily persuaded than men, many of these studies have been questioned on methodological grounds. It appears, however, that feminine individuals may be more easily persuaded than masculine individuals and that psychological sex roles have more predictive value than biological sex."[7]

So where does the variable "sex" fit into audience analysis today? First, one should consider the female population of every audience. Just as one should consider the elderly, youth, poor, and other constituencies, careful attention must be given to the question, "Are the results of my speech in any way dependent upon my recognition of the number, age, or general characteristics of the female population of my audience?" If the women in the audience are regulated or motivated by the traditional female steroetypes or role expectations, your failure to recognize and adapt accordingly might be detrimental to your desired results. Perhaps Ross was correct when he observed that in modern America, male-female distinctions "are often less meaningful than the attributions people (men or women) make about gender roles. An assessment of masculinity, femininity, and androgyny (the reflection of both male and female characteristics) may provide a better measure of sex-role adaptability."[8]

The American culture is certainly undergoing many changes in its sexual stereotypes and any generalization should be regarded with caution. Moreover, certain subcultures (perhaps, for example, many groups of artists, or highly educated people, or urban dwellers) may make fewer sex role distinctions than the general culture does.

Socioeconomic Status

The United States does not have a rigid class system based on birth and family background. However, occupation, income, education, and family history combine to form a characteristic labeled *socioeconomic status.* Many studies have examined differences among socioeconomic groups. According to one major finding, cultural deprivation in lower socioeconomic groups is especially great in the area of language development. In fact, what appeared to be evidence of lesser intelligence in the lower socioeconomic groups has been related to the inability of those groups to cope with intelligence tests that tended to be culturally weighted toward middle class experiences and vocabularies. There is no need to cite research to prove that members of culturally deprived classes are often frustrated and angry. They are bitter and suspicious toward members of higher socioeconomic groups who appear to have blocked their progress.

When a speaker addresses an audience of a lower socioeconomic status, it is wise to remember that they are not necessarily inferior to the speaker in intelligence, although they may be deficient in middle-class vocabulary and language. The speaker should omit words and phrases that are unusual or that are used "to impress" in a pompous manner. The speaker need not change a personal style of speaking—attempting, for instance, to inject "ghetto talk" through the use of slang expressions. As explained in the discussion of image, this would be unnatural and insincere; however well intentioned, it would be obvious. When in doubt with any audience, it is better to talk a bit above them, as long as one seems concerned and sincere, than to appear to talk down to them. The late Robert Kennedy quoted a line of poetry by Aeschylus in an Indianpolis ghetto on the night of Martin Luther King's assassination. He did not say the quotation in Greek, nor did he refer to "that well-known phrase of Aeschylus'." Consequently, the audience did not see a rich politician trying to impress them with his education. They heard a concerned man who wanted to share a thought that was meaningful to him.

Religion

At earlier points in American history, knowledge of an audience's religious makeup might have been the most valuable information a speaker could have. One could say with some certainty that Baptists did not drink alcoholic beverages or that Catholics were opposed to artificial methods of birth control. Today, *religion,* at least institutionalized religion, seems to have less direct influence on the specific attitudes of individuals. Many Christian denominations seem to accept more diversity of belief and behavior; and the ecumenical as well as the charismatic movements are breaking down rigid doctrinal differences among denominations. Contributing further to this change is the rapidly growing electronic church that ministers to people over the radio and television. While traditionally we have focused the religion aspect of audience analysis on denominational affiliation, today this limited focus is inadequate. Our contemporary world is a pluarlistic, complex mosaic. During past centuries the world missionary efforts were from West to East. Christians of many religious denominations went as missionaries to Africa, Asia, and the Orient. In recent years, however, the movement has begun to move from the opposite direction as well—from East to West. Today, members of one's audience might be associated with the Hare Krishna movement, Zen Buddhism, the Black Muslims, Bahaism, Transcendental Meditation, or Yoga. Hindu temples and Muslim mosques have been erected in several of our major cities and thousands have been converted to these various religious movements in the past two decades.[9] A *U.S. New and World Report* article entitled "America's Cults Gaining Ground Again" quotes researchers who believe that some of the stronger cults will "become part of the commonplace religious scene . . . and likely . . . win acceptance, if not respectability," within the next decade or two. Their current strategy is to move into smaller communities, where their influence is less diluted than it is in larger cities, and begin to make a major impact on everyday life.[10] The important point for communication is that the trend is toward a more personal set of religious beliefs that one may or may not practice within the context of a given church or religious organization.

There have been many studies of the traits, attitudes, and values of persons of the Pentecostal, Catholic, Protestant, and Jewish faiths. These studies have served to break down some stereotypes. Many stereotypic generalizations however seem to apply only to doctrinaire and active members of those denominations. Hence, it is not very helpful for a speaker to know that the audience is 90 percent Catholic unless further information is acquired about what "being Catholic" means to the audience.

It is important to remember the point made earlier that demographic data about an audience is helpful only if it can be used by a speaker to help achieve the speech objective. Facts about age, sex, socioeconomic status, and religion may help to draw inferences about *some* audiences in terms of their predispositions on *some* topics. These predispositions, classified as audience values and audience attitudes, are inherent components in purposive audience analysis.

Can you identify at least two types of demographic data and tell what we know about each from research?

Purposive Audience Analysis

With purposive audience analysis one asks, "By what arguments, materials, and strategies can I adapt to the audience's position so as to accomplish the purpose of my speech?" To what about an audience's position does a speaker wish to adapt? It is the audience's *position on the thesis of your speech* that you as the speaker must know, adapt to, and use to move them to your thesis or to accomplish your speech purpose, be it to inform, persuade, or entertain. The audience's position on the thesis or speech topic is represented by its values and attitudes. These predispositions toward your topic, toward you, toward strategies and procedures, toward institutions, persons and practices to which you might refer in the speech—all these predispositions and more, constitute one's values.

Audience Values

An evaluative predisposition that deals with institutions, broad philosophical concepts, or styles of behavior is called a value. To say, "Family life is good" expresses a value, but so does a negative statement such as "Cheating is bad," because both statements are evaluative.

Some generalizations about an audience can be made on the basis of the values of the society in which the audience lives. An extensive study by Steele and Redding classified traditional **American values** into core categories and secondary categories.[11]

Core Categories

1. Puritan and pioneer morality: the tendency to view the world in moral terms as good or bad, ethical or unethical
2. Value of the individual: the primacy of individual welfare in governmental and interpersonal relationships
3. Achievement and success: the primary desirability of material wealth and success; the secondary desirability of success and achievement in vocations, professions, social service, and so forth
4. Change and progress: the widespread belief that society is progressing and developing toward better things and that change is an index of progress
5. Ethical equality: the ideal of spiritual equality for all in the eyes of God; closely related to equality of opportunity promised in part by free public education
6. Effort and optimism: obsession with the importance of work. Hopeful, optimistic effort will cause all obstacles to yield.
7. Efficiency, practicality, and pragmatism: higher regard for practical thinkers and doers than for artists or intellectuals

Secondary Categories

1. Rejection of authority: freedom from restraints by government or society
2. Science and secular rationality
3. Sociality: getting along, making contacts
4. Material comfort
5. Quantification: tendency to equate value with size or numbers
6. External conformity: adherence to group patterns
7. Humor
8. Generosity and considerateness
9. Patriotism

The reader will probably agree that the majority of Americans do hold many of these values. Yet it is evident that a common set of values does not lead to agreement among all members of a society. Values are such general statements that they often cause conflict when applied to specific issues. For instance, the values of the individual and the values of practicality and progress may conflict over an issue such as whether the government should be allowed to tear down family homes so a new highway can be built. Because of the many natural contradictions among values, it is usually not very helpful to have a listing of an audience's values unless one also has some estimate of the hierarchy on which the values would be ranked if they came into conflict. Rokeach's scheme for the ranking of beliefs can be modified to show two levels of values, as shown in figure 10.1.[12]

Core values are those so central to a person's belief system that to change one of those values would amount to a basic alteration of self-concept. **Peripheral values** are an individual's more or less incidental beliefs that can be easily changed. For example, you may have a *core value* that killing another person is wrong; and a *peripheral value* that you prefer to avoid stepping on (killing) a small ant.

Whenever two values come into conflict, the one closer to the core is most likely to determine an auditor's response. Therefore a speaker should try to draw intelligent inferences about an audience's core values and stress those in the speech. Suppose one has an educational innovation which one would like a school to adopt. In speaking to the school board the speaker might stress the values of practicality, efficiency, and local control of education. In speaking to the teachers the more idealistic values of progress in education might be stressed. It is important to note that the speaker is not assuming that teachers are impractical or that school board members do not care about educational progress. No doubt everyone in both audiences values all the concepts mentioned here. In a limited speech, the speaker makes the decision to stress those values that are probably closer to the core in each audience.

Figure 10.1 Different levels of values.

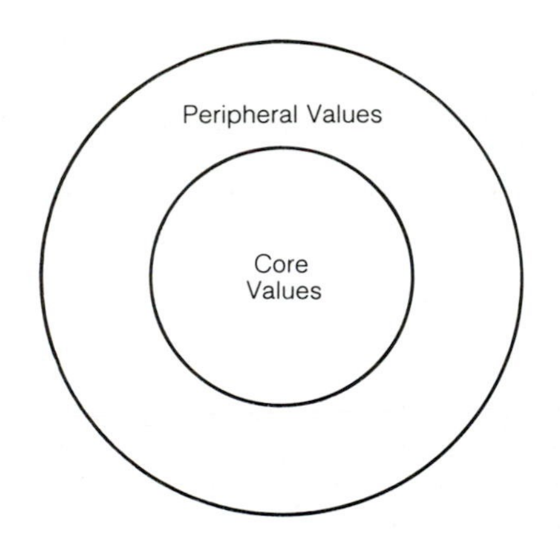

A second way that the speaker can use values to analyze an audience is by trying to forge new links between issues and values and strengthen or weaken existing links. Perhaps an audience has linked the issue of spending money on the space program to the values of patriotism, scientific progress, and achievement. A speaker who wishes to cut back spending on the space program can try to link the issue to other values such as economy, humanitarian values (in terms of other priorities), and the value of human life (stressing danger to astronauts). All of these new values are common ones and perhaps some members of the audience hold them as core values. If the speaker convinces the audience that these new issue-value links exist, they may change their opinions.

Audience Attitudes

Probably the most valuable information for any speaker is a knowledge of **audience attitudes** toward the topic. If the central idea of the speech were stated as a single declarative sentence, it would be possible to have each member of the audience indicate a personal initial position along a continuum like the one shown in table 10.2.

If, either through a formal survey or through inferences based on other audience data, a speaker is able to decide where the majority of the audience would be placed on such a continuum, the audience can be categorized as neutral, hostile, or favorable.

The Neutral Audience

An audience may indicate lack of opinion on a topic for one of three reasons. (1) It may be *indifferent*. A women's church group may be neutral on whether turbine-powered engines should be allowed in the Indianapolis 500 simply because it doesn't care enough about the issue to form an opinion. (2) It may be

Table 10.2 Audience attitude continuum

Strongly Disagree	Disagree	No Opinion	Agree	Strongly Agree

uninformed. A certain audience may be highly concerned about medical standards but still have no opinion about the adequacy of osteopaths' training because it has no background or information on the topic. (3) It may be *undecided.* An audience of heart specialists may be well informed and much concerned about the risks involved in transplanting a baboon heart into a human being; but the doctors may believe that the potential for life outweighs the risk of death. These same doctors may state that they have no opinion on the moral or religious implications of the procedure. Such an audience is often called a "committed neutral audience." It is evident that a speaker's strategies would vary considerably among the three types of neutral audiences.

Attention is the speaker's prime concern with the *indifferent neutral audience.* The great danger is that the audience will "tune out" as soon as it hears the topic. As explained in chapter 2, each person has an elaborate filtering system that leads to attending those stimuli that are seen as related to one's own self-concept. When an auditor seems to be saying "So what?" that person is really saying "What's it to me?" The speaker with an indifferent neutral audience should use vivid examples, humor, novelty, suspense, and all the other techniques designed to gain attention, but the use of personal references is the most valuable aid. The speaker should make liberal use of the pronoun *you.* The major goal is to show the audience that it is directly involved in the speaker's topic.

With the *uninformed neutral audience,* the speaker takes on the role of educator. An error frequently made in speaking to this kind of audience is the use of technical terminology that the group doesn't understand. While you should not overestimate the specific knowledge of such an audience, neither should you underestimate its general intelligence. Any audience resents a speaker who seems to talk down to them. The speech to an uninformed audience must be didactic in effect but not pedantic in tone.

The *undecided neutral audience* is treated much like the hostile audience, which will be discussed next. To win agreement from this type of audience, one must tip the balance so that arguments on the speaker's side of the issue outweigh those on the other side. A study by Sears and Freedman suggests a promising strategy for influencing an undecided audience. They found that people who thought they were hearing new arguments on an issue were more likely to change their opinion toward those arguments than people who heard the same arguments but were told that they were hearing a summary of points they had heard earlier in the experiment.[13] This shift in opinion was especially marked among those who had indicated uncertainty about their original position. This study would seem to suggest that the speaker with an undecided audience should present new evidence or arguments on a topic or appear to be presenting arguments that the audience had not heard before.

The Hostile Audience

The speaker facing an unfavorable audience must be extremely sensitive and diplomatic in approach. An overly zealous attempt to win over the audience to the speaker's viewpoint can work against the purpose of the speech. First, as with the indifferent audience, there is the risk that the hostile group will tune out the speaker. The discussion of selective perception in an earlier chapter explained that people perceive only what they want to perceive. Thus Democrats may refuse to really listen to the arguments of a Republican candidate, or a group of angry workers may be convinced that management can say nothing that is worthy of their attention, or persons of one religious persuasion may find it totally ludicrous to listen to arguments of a different persuasion. The second danger is that a hostile audience *will* listen to a speech and that something in the content or presentation will make them even more hostile toward the speaker's position—a phenomenon known as *boomerang effect*. To minimize either of these dangers, adjustments must be made in the speaker's immediate goals, the speech content, and the presentation.

Recognizing that on any important topic the process of attitude change is a slow one, the speaker should be reasonable in the goals set for any one message to a hostile audience. If one strongly disagrees with the position that the legal age of drinking should be lowered, it is very unrealistic to expect that the same person will come to agree strongly with that position as the result of a speech. It is far more realistic to hope that the listener will disagree less strongly or perhaps adopt a neutral position. If this realistic approach is taken, the speaker will avoid asking the members of the audience to commit themselves to a specific course of action—if they cannot accept the speaker's specific solution, they will tend to reject the entire message. With a hostile audience, one should offer several options for consideration. Rather than urging auditors to join an alien cause or donate money to the campaign of a candidate they are known to oppose, the speaker should ask them to think about the points raised in the speech and suggest sources for more information. An excellent example of setting realistic goals for a hostile audience is the campaign promoting halfway measures for smokers. Many smokers who would reject a message urging them to stop smoking will consider smoking fewer cigarettes or a smaller portion of each cigarette.

Once the speech purpose has been restricted to a manageable task, the speaker can begin to structure the speech content in a way that will win acceptance from the hostile audience. The most useful technique in such circumstances is known as *the common ground approach.* The speaker should stress the issues and values common to both the speaker and the audience. Often a speaker and a hostile audience will agree on ends but not on means. For instance, a speaker who advocates building a waste disposal site near a

The hostile audience presents a challenge to the speaker.

community would be wise to stress at the outset of the speech: "All of us are interested in providing adequate waste disposal in the safest and least threatening manner possible." The hostile audience is psychologically set to disagree and argue with the speaker. The most important thing the speaker can do is break down this set and present material with which the audience is inclined to agree.

With all hostile audiences, speakers should rely heavily on logical proof and complete evidence. If possible, quotations should be used from authorities with whom the audience identifies. A speaker must be cautious in the use of emotional appeals with a hostile audience. Such an audience tends to see any obvious effort to arouse emotions as a trick by the speaker to cover up for the lack of a sound case.

By far the greatest challenge for the speaker with a hostile audience is to *establish personal credibility*. Because the audience rejects the speaker's position, there is a tendency to reject the speaker as a person as well. If the speaker can win some level of personal acceptance and respect, there is a good chance that the speaker's position will at least be considered by the audience. All of the techniques mentioned so far can help to build a speaker's credibility. Taking a realistic stand on the topic and building common ground will help to portray the speaker as a reasonable person and to foster audience identification. Relying on logical proof and solid evidence makes the speaker appear intelligent, thorough, and knowledgeable. In addition, the speaker must be cognizant of any aspect of appearance, dress, or language that may be offensive to the audience. The general tone of delivery should be sincere and direct.

If speakers use humor, they might try to direct it toward themselves. It is often a good idea for speakers to disassociate themselves from the more extreme and objectionable proponents of their viewpoints by stating directly what they do not approve. For instance, a student arguing for more student participation in the governing of universities might tell a hostile audience, "I am not in favor of students determining faculty promotions or granting their own degrees. I do not want to do away with all administrators." Then as the speaker goes on to talk about the additional sources of personally desired student input and student power, the audience may be listening to the speaker as an individual distinct from any stereotype. The speaker, the speech, and the audience are variables that interact—that become intertwined into one process. Speakers who can apply their knowledge and skills to the speech and to the particular audience can more easily accomplish their purposes. The late Norman Thomas, four times the Socialist party's presidential candidate, spent most of his career addressing audiences who were hostile to his cause. An authoritative summary of the strategies for coping with hostile audiences is offered in Thomas's observation:

> Some things you do not do unless you are intent on failing. You don't insult your audience, but you may kid it; you don't patronize it or talk down to it; you don't apologize to it for your convictions; you don't whine about being "misunderstood"; you don't beg for favor. You assume and may occasionally appeal to an audience's spirit of fair play, its sporting instinct, its desire to know what you think. You seek a point of contact—sometimes by sharp challenge to arouse attention, sometimes by beginning with partial agreement with what you assume is majority sentiment and then on that basis developing your divergence in thinking. You try—but not too often or too hard—to appeal to your audience's sense of humor even in divergence of opinion. If the facts warrant it, and you have led up to it, you may denounce specifically and vigorously ideas and actions with which large sections of your audience have been in accord. But be sure of your facts and be very sparing in imputing to your opponents base motives. In the minds of some men, honest, well-supported denunciation may stick and bring forth later fruit.[14]

What advice could you give a speaker who will address a hostile audience?

The Favorable Audience

The speaker who discovers that the majority of the audience is favorably predisposed toward the topic is very fortunate. Such an audience is not without challenges though for the speaker who wishes to have optimal influence on the audience. The main goal of the speaker with a favorable audience is to *reinforce and intensify the positive attitudes* that it holds and to try to move those who agree with the speech to a point where they will *act* on their beliefs. In trying to make positive attitudes more vivid and intense, the speaker can rely heavily on emotional proof. The favorable audience is likely to respond to moving examples, strong value appeals, and emotion-laden language. Unlike the hostile audience, who sees a speaker's use of emotion as a substitute for logic and evidence, the favorable audience tends to accept emotional appeal

Attention is polarized in this audience, but what is its attitudinal orientation?

as the legitimate extension of logical arguments to which it has already agreed. It is equally evident that a favorable audience will not challenge a speaker's credibility as much as a hostile audience will. The favorable audience seems to reason, "If he's on our side, he must be a nice guy." Consequently, this kind of audience is likely to be more tolerant of idiosyncracies and imperfections in the speaker's presentation. Even so, the speaker should not be totally indifferent toward the personal impression made.

While logical argument need not play as central a role with a favorable audience as it does with the neutral and, especially, the hostile audience, a solid rational structure should be the basis for all speeches. There are two uses of reasoning and evidence that are uniquely suited for a favorable audience. In both cases, the speaker assumes the role of "coach." First the speaker must try to move the audience from passive agreement to overt action. In direct contrast to the vague and varied solutions offered the hostile audience, the favorable audience requires specific direction. The speaker should tell members of the audience what organizations they can join, what public leaders to write, what projects they can volunteer to help with, where they can send money. Often people strongly agree with a proposition and leave a speech hoping that "the scientists will do something about the environment" or "the President will straighten out our economy" or "Congress will help the poor people." With complex problems and a society where sources of power seem farther and farther removed from the individual, it is a real challenge for a speaker to make

Regardless of the thoroughness of the speaker's preparation, unforeseen problems can occur.

a favorably disposed audience aware of their own power to bring about change. Suggesting alternatives for specific action calls for creativity and knowledge on the part of the speaker. The speaker should be as specific as possible, giving addresses and phone numbers and passing around sign-up sheets.

Make Use of Opinion Leaders

The speaker's second "coaching" job for a favorable audience is not unlike the role of a communication teacher. The speaker should train the members of the audience to persuade others. Much opinion change takes place through informal *opinion leaders* who gain their information from a speech or the mass media and pass it on to personal acquaintances. It should be assumed that some members of the audience are opinion leaders. The speaker should use dramatic examples and graphic statistics that are likely to be remembered and quoted to others and should urge members of the audience to talk about the issues to other people. Ministers often ask committed members of their congregations to bring a friend to church next Sunday. Speakers at political rallies try to extend their influence by asking partisans to talk to their friends and neighbors.

To summarize pre-speech audience analysis, it can be said that the speaker should gather informal data both directly and indirectly. The speaker should consider general questions about the audience, program format, physical setting, and expected image. Demographic data offers much useful information for planning a speech. However, this data is useful only insofar as the speaker can relate it to the speech purpose. Purposive analysis, including knowledge of an audience's general values and specific attitudes, is directly helpful in adjusting speech content so that a speaker has a high probability of meeting these goals.

Environmental Factors Affecting the Audience

Operating in every public situation are environmental factors that tend to affect audience attention, interest, and comprehension. These environmental factors can be placed into three main categories: (1) physical setting, (2) competing stimuli, and (3) audience size and proximity.

Physical Setting

As pointed out earlier in this chapter, one aspect of careful pre-speech analysis is to determine the physical setting in which the speech is to take place. Discovering how the audience will be seated, the anticipated size of the audience, and available facilities (i.e., chalkboard, and audiovisual equipment, microphone, lectern, etc.) will minimize the problems a speaker might face. Regardless of how carefully one analyzes the physical setting for the presentation, certain unforeseen problems are bound to occur during the speech. Characteristic of these unforeseen problems are power breakdowns that cause the microphone to go dead, the motion picture or slide projector to quit, and the air conditioning or heat to shut off—all of which can be extremely unpleasant and distracting to an audience. The speaker who "panics" only adds to the distraction. A simple acknowledgment of the problems (not a lengthy apology) will serve to ease the tension for both the audience and the speaker. The capable speaker will simply adjust to the problem and carry on. Amazingly, the audience will often forget its discomfort too.

Dealing with Competing Stimuli

Competing stimuli, such as the screaming of a siren, noisy traffic, lawnmowers, the roar of a passing jet, or the slapping of window blinds, present the speaker with a series of frustrating problems. Such stimuli are bound to distract even the most intent listeners. If the competing stimuli are only momentary, the speaker can adjust to them by increasing volume so that the message can be heard above the disturbance. If the speaker is completely "drowned out," it would be futile to continue; here, the best procedure is simply to acknowledge the interruption and begin again as soon as possible. It is even possible to make such competing stimuli work in the speaker's favor, as in the case of the individual who was delivering a highly controversial speech to a rather hostile audience. Midway through the speech he was interrupted by the screaming of a number of police sirens passing by just outside the auditorium. Noting that the audience was completely distracted by the sirens, he commented, "I knew this talk was going to be controversial, but I had no idea it would be this controversial." The audience laughed in appreciation of his ability to adust to the interruption and perhaps became even less hostile toward the speaker.

The Proximity of Auditors

What would you do if your audience was seated in a scattered manner?

The size of an audience and the physical proximity of its members have a definite effect upon the individual auditor. Communication research indicates that as the size of the audience increases, the intellectual functioning of its members decreases.[15] The larger the audience, the more apt auditors are to be distracted.

The size of an audience will determine, in part, the mode of presentation. With smaller audiences, presentation of a speech will be informal. As the size of the audiences increases, the formality of the presentation will increase. With large audiences, the elevation of the speaker above the floor level increases prestige and often gives added influence to the ideas. Dispensing with the platform for smaller audiences induces a stronger rapport between speaker and audience, which is conducive to more effective communication.

The proximity of the speaker to the audience is an important consideration in public speaking. As the distance between the speaker and the audience increases, the interaction between the two decreases. Generally, the closer the speaker and the audience, the more personalized the message appears to be.

Placement of individual auditors, and their proximity to one another, provides additional concern for the speaker. The closer the auditors are to one another, the stronger the interaction among them. Close physical proximity tends to cause the members of the audience to conform to acceptable standards of behavior—and seems to produce a feeling to togetherness. Dissension among individual auditors is decreased as they come physically closer together.

The speaker must be aware of the environmental factors operating during the speech and the effects they have on the audience. The ability to cope with and adjust to the unexpected are necessary prerequisites for a successful speaker. The beginning speaker should try to be in command of the situation at all times. Once command is lost, the speaker's ideas have lost their power. This means that successful speakers must be able to adjust and adapt both themselves and the message from moment to moment throughout the speech.

Audience Analysis and Speaker's Adaptation during the Speech

Through pre-speech audience analysis, the speaker carefully constructs the message to insure maximum attention, interest, comprehension, and acceptance by the listeners. As the speaker approaches the audience and prepares to begin the speech there are two concerns: (1) What effect will my speech actually have on the audience? and (2) What effect will the audience have on me? Will the speaker be successful in attempts to gain the listeners' attention, maintain interest, ensure understanding, and gain the acceptance of ideas? No amount of preparation or pre-planning can absolutely ensure how a particular audience will react to a speaker or to the speech, or, for that matter, how the speaker will react to or be affected by the audience. The speaker must, throughout the entire speech, be constantly analyzing the behavior of the audience and adjusting or adapting to listener behavior. If the speaker wishes to intensify or modify the behavior of the audience, then the speaker must intensify or modify his or her own behavior. This transactional process is carried on by the exchange of messages between the speaker and the audience. Feedback, a concept discussed in chapter 6, is an important part of the transactional process.

Use of Feedback

As you will recall, feedback describes a kind of reciprocal interaction between two or more events, in which one activity generates a secondary action which, in turn, redirects the primary action. In applying feedback to the speaker-audience communication process, the following elements can be seen: the speaker generates the initial activity, the speech; the secondary action is the reaction by the audience to the speaker and the speech. The redirection of the primary action, the modified speech, takes place as the speaker adjusts and adapts to the reaction of the audience. This process is a dynamic and continual one. The speaker, in front of an audience, generates a course of action, visually and verbally, then modifies or intensifies communication behavior in terms of the audience feedback that is received. **Audience feedback** is used to describe the effect on the speaker of the auditors' responses, the consequent reinforcement or modification of the speaker's own communicative behavior, and its subsequent effect upon the auditors.

The concept of feedback in public speaking asserts that a speaker, in order to be a successful communicator, must adapt and adjust to the responses of the audience during the actual presentation of the speech. The obvious questions then are: How does a speaker determine when an audience is responding? What kinds of responses are there? What do they mean? and How does a speaker reinforce or modify behavior accordingly? Let us examine some cues (audience responses) that can be measured and/or observed in an audience and make some practical suggestions as to how the speaker can interpret and react to them.

Be Concerned with Attention, Interest, and Comprehension

The prerequisites for accepting a speaker's ideas are attention, interest, and comprehension. These, then, are the variables of audience behavior we are most interested in measuring and/or observing. These during-the-speech responses fall into three categories: physiological processes measured by electronic devices; the listener's continual self-reporting of responses by using electrical or mechanical switches or other devices; and the listeners' behavior during the speech, which the speaker can observe. This third type is the most important in a typical public speaking situation.

Observe Audience Behavior

Observable audience behavior is of the most practical value to the speaker for speech analysis during the course of the speech. This observable behavior, in the form of overt physical movement, provides the speaker with cues from which the audience's response to the message can be inferred. On the basis of this information, the speaker adjusts and adapts communication behavior in an attempt to modify or intensify the auditors' behavior. Such analysis is based on the assumption that, within a particular culture, fairly uniform connections exist between the physiological, mental, and emotional states of an individual. For example, an auditor who is fidgety or searching through her purse is thought to be paying little, if any, attention. The auditor "slouched" down in a chair with eyes closed is looked upon as being totally uninterested. The auditor who sits, apparently paralyzed, staring out the window is considered to be off in a personal little world. A look of puzzlement, accompanied by the shrugging of the shoulders, is often interpreted as total lack of comprehension. Icy glares and the biting of lips are assumed to signal anger. Of course, not all observable behavior is negative. The speaker is generally rewarded by approving nods of heads, warm smiles, and applause, all of which can be interpreted as positive reinforcement. The auditor who follows every move of the speaker and "hangs on every word" is naturally thought to be deeply interested in what is being said. The list of inferences predicting internal states by their external manifestations is virtually endless. One hypothesis is that auditors manifest their internal states in observable physical behavior. Numerous studies that indicate strong relationships between observable behavior and inner states have been referenced earlier in this chapter.

Use Multi-Behavior Indicators

The speaker should be cautioned that sometimes inferences can be wrong, especially if they are based on specific acts of only one or two auditors. The auditor who appears to be off in a personal little world may indeed be concentrating on the speaker's message. The slouching auditor may also be in deep concentration. The smiling face that was taken for positive reinforcement may reflect pleasure that has nothing to do with the speech content or the speaker. Reading audience response behavior with accuracy will improve as the speaker gains experience and learns to rely on *several* cues from *several* auditors. Regardless of the hazards that do exist, observable audience behavior remains the most sound, practical, and immediate basis a speaker can use for determining the impact of the message.

What is the speaker's responsibility to a "dozing" audience?

The speaker must adjust and adapt behavior in order to modify or intensify the behavior of listeners. If the audience's behavior (falling asleep, staring out the window, talking, fidgeting, etc.) indicates that it is inattention or disinterested, the speaker will certainly wish to modify listener behavior. There are numerous ways in which a speaker can accomplish this goal during the speech. Perhaps the most effective technique is to become more assertive in delivery. The speaker can be physically assertive. It is difficult to listen to a speaker who is "buried" behind the podium, who is inanimate—in short, who exhibits poor nonverbal delivery. Effective delivery, incorporating physical movement and appropriate gestures, may well be the stimuli needed to evoke attention and interest from the audience. When the audience appears to be straining to hear, the problem can be corrected simply by raising the volume of the voice. If the speaker perceives, through audience cues, that listeners do not comprehend the message, the speaker should not continue to lead them rapidly through a maze of perplexing facts and figures, but stop, check the delivery rate, and perhaps slow down. More often, however, the audience is simply unable to grasp the meaning of the ideas. If this is the case, the speaker must "re-explain," or reiterate, the ideas. The use of internal summaries (periodic summations of information) will add greatly to the clarity of a speech. The perceptive speaker will prepare these internal summaries in advance and, based on audience cues, use them as needed.

Audience Feedback Can Reinforce You as Speaker and Stimulate You

Reinforcing responses are just as important as negative cues. An audience may nod in agreement and smile happily, and the speaker will be reinforced and proceed with greater confidence than before. The importance of perceiving observable behavior and accurately reading audience cues cannot be overemphasized. The success or failure of the speaker's presentation may well depend on the speaker's ability to interpret audience behavior and adjust accordingly. The adage "practice makes perfect" is nowhere in communication more applicable than in the speaker's ability to interpret accurately an audience's observable behavior. The beginning speaker who maintains an attitude of awareness toward the audience has already taken the first step toward improving the ability to read audience cues.

Post-Speech Audience Analysis

The most common and informal means of **post-speech analysis** is based on immediate, overt audience response. Applause, questions, compliments, and criticism from audience members all help the speaker gauge personal speaking effectiveness. Attitude questionnaires, interviews with audience members, and follow-up studies are excellent sources of data for such an analysis, but are impractical in a great many speech situations. Many seminar programs include brief evaluation forms to be completed and left with a monitor. Direct observation of audience behavior is another indicator of speech effectiveness. If the speaker asked them to sign up for a project, how many actually signed up? If the speaker asked audience members to investigate a topic further, how many read books, talked to other people, or listened to more speeches on the topic? Like the previously mentioned techniques, this behavioral analysis presents several practical problems. Moreover, the speaker must be cautious in attributing changes in audience behavior directly to the speech. If, however, the audience adopts a course of action substantially different from similar groups who were not exposed to the speech, it is reasonable to assume that the message played some role in influencing behavior.

Post-speech audience analysis can take a number of different forms. Plays, movies, night club acts, advertisements, and some speeches are often field tested on selected audiences. Post-speech data is analyzed to revise the messages for their final presentations. The nonprofessional speaker can make use of a similar technique by trying out a speech on friends, roommates, families, and others to see how an audience actually reacts.

When a speaker regularly addresses the same audience, the post-speech analysis serves a different function. Teachers and ministers are able to plan long-range strategies. They seek regular feedback on their audiences' comprehension and acceptance of message content and also try to assess their own personal appeals as speakers. Through this process they are able to clarify or reiterate concepts and adapt future presentations with greater effectiveness. The student who is assigned several speeches in a class should seek similar feedback since the same audience will be addressed frequently.

The speaker addressing an audience only once might assume that post-speech analysis is not important. On the contrary, such analysis provides the only means of determining what effect, if any, the speaker had on the audience. While the speaker may never speak again to that audience on that topic, any information gained about the strategies used is helpful. Every speech experience, if evaluated, adds to the speaker's repertoire of skills and understanding of audiences, and forms a basis for more sophisticated and sensitive audience analysis in the future.

Summary

In summary, the audience is the single most important variable in public communication because it ultimately determines the success or failure of the speaker and the speaker's message. Audience has been defined as an assembled group of individuals who meet at a predetermined time and place for the specific purpose of seeing a speaker and hearing a message. Audience analysis is the process of collecting information about an audience and using that information to draw inferences about the best way to achieve the purpose of one's speech. Before the speech the speaker should try to determine the relevant demographic characteristics of the audience, its general cultural values, and its specific attitudes toward the speaker and the topic. These data should be used in selecting materials, arranging ideas and materials, and in presenting the message. During the speech the speaker should be sensitive to feedback, especially that manifested in observable behavior. Recalling those interpersonal principles discussed in chapter 6 the effective speaker will establish a dynamic communication situation while adjusting and responding to the messages sent nonverbally by the audience. Following the speech, the speaker should seek some measure of speech effectiveness. At each of these "check points" the speaker should use the information to adapt both physical behavior and the verbal message to the audience.

Questions and Exercises for Review

1. What is the role of an audience?
2. What is an audience?
3. Name and compare five types of audience.
4. What demographic data does one need for audience analysis and what does such data tell a speaker?
5. What is the relationship between environmental factors affecting an audience and during-the-speech adaptation?

Key Terms and Phrases

- audience analysis
- audience
- time and place
- polarization
- audience homogeneity
- casual audience
- passive audience
- selected audience
- concerted audience
- organized audience
- demographic audience analysis
- purposive audience analysis
- American values
- core values
- peripheral values
- audience attitudes
- audience feedback
- post-speech analysis

For Further Reading

Clevenger, Theodore, Jr. *Audience Analysis.* Indianpolis: The Bobbs-Merrill Co., 1966.
A small book that is quite readable and interesting.

Hollingworth, H. L. *The Psychology of the Audience.* New York: American Book Company, 1935.
An old-time classic that, in many ways, was far ahead of its time.

Holtzman, Paul D. *The Psychology of Speaker's Audiences.* Glenview, Ill.: Scott, Foresman and Co., 1970.
An exceptionally fine treatment of audience analysis.

Kennedy, Patricia S. and O'Shields, Gloria H. *We Shall Be Heard: Women Speakers in America.* Dubuque, Ia.: Kendall/Hunt, 1983.
This anthology explores the contribution of significant women speakers in critical periods of American history since 1828.

Minnick, Wayne C. *The Art of Persuasion.* New York: Houghton Mifflin Co., 1968.
An excellent resource for "applying what is known about human behavior in general to a specific audience in order to anticipate or evaluate its response to a particular persuasive communication."

Neuman, W. R. "Television and American Culture: The Mass Medium and the Pluralist Audience." *Public Opinion Quarterly* 46 (Winter 1982): 471–82.
A good treatment of the pluralistic audience concept.

Oliver, Robert T. *The Psychology of Persuasive Speech.* New York: Longmans, Green and Co., 1957.
A review of psychological principles and their adaptation to the persuasive speech situation.

Ross, Raymond S. *Understanding Persuasion Foundations and Practice.* Englewood Cliffs, N.J.: Prentice-Hall, Inc., 1985.
Good discussion and comparison of speakers who are rhetorically sensitive (RS), noble selves (NS), and rhetorical reflectors (RR).

Seamond, John T. *Tell It Well: Communicating the Gospel Across Cultures.* Kansas City: Beacon Hill Press, 1981.
A case study of persuasive techniques across cultures.

Notes

1. H. L. Hollingworth, *The Psychology of the Audience* (New York: American Book Co., 1935), 19–32.

2. Hollingworth, *Psychology of the Audience,* 25.

3. Donald H. Kausler and Charles V. Lair, "Information Feedback Conditions and Verbal-Discrimination Learning in Elderly Subjects," *Psychonomic Science* (1968): 193–94.

4. Franklin H. Knower, "Experimental Studies in Changes in Attitudes: A Study of the Effects of Oral Arguments in Changes of Attitude," *Journal of Social Psychology* 6 (1935): 315–47.

5. Thomas Schiedel, "Sex and Persuasibility," *Speech Monographs* 30 (November 1963), 353.

6. Raymond S. Ross, *Understanding Persuasion Foundations and Practice* (Englewood Cliffs, N.J.: Prentice-Hall, 1985), 113.

7. Judith C. Pearson, *Gender and Communication* (Dubuque, Ia.: Wm. C. Brown Publishers, 1985), 328.

8. Ross, *Understanding Persuasion Foundations,* 113.

9. John T. Seamond, *Tell It Well: Communicating the Gospel Across Cultures* (Kansas City: Beacon Hill Press, 1981), 19.

10. "America's Cults Gaining Ground Again," *U. S. News and World Report,* 5 July 1982, 37–41.

11. Edward Steele and W. Charles Redding, "The American Value System: Premises for Persuasion," *Western Speech* 26 (1962): 83–91.

12. Milton Rokeach, "Images of the Consumer's Mind On and Off Madison Avenue," in *Speech Communication,* ed. Howard Martin and Kenneth Anderson, 256–62. Reprinted from *ETC: A Review of General Semantics,* Vol. XXI, no. 3, by permission of the International Society for General Semantics.

13. D. O. Sears and J. L. Freedman, "Effects of Expected Familiarity with Arguments upon Opinion Change and Selective Exposure," *Journal of Personality and Social Psychology* 2 (1965): 420–26.

14. Norman Thomas, *Mr. Chairman, Ladies and Gentlemen. . . .* (New York: Hermitage House, 1955), 116.

15. M. Deutsch, "An Experimental Study of the Effects of Cooperation and Competition Upon Group Process," *Human Relations* 2 (1949): 199–231.

Focus

Step 1: Selecting the Topic

Step 2: Determining the Purpose

Step 3: Considering the Audience

Step 4: Organizing and Outlining the Speech

Three Major Parts of a Speech

Patterns of Arrangement

- *Motivated Sequence*
- *Time Sequence*
- *Space Sequence*
- *Topical Pattern*
- *Logical Patterns*

Psychological Ordering of Arguments

- *Primacy-Recency*
- *Climax-Anticlimax*

Transitions

Phrasing Main Points

Step 5: Gathering Supporting Materials

Step 6: Giving the Speech Impact through Language and Style

Step 7: Preparing to Handle Questions

Rationale for Fielding Questions

Guidelines for the Question-Answer Session

Special Techniques for Fielding Questions

The Message: Steps in Speech Preparation

In this chapter, we are concerned with the speech itself. We study the speech in terms of the steps followed in preparing the public communication message. Those steps involve: (1) selecting the topic; (2) determining the purpose; (3) considering the audience; (4) organizing the speech; (5) gathering supporting materials; (6) giving the speech impact through language and style; and (7) preparing to handle questions.

One of the key elements in public communication, along with the speaker and the audience, is the message. Of these three elements, it is the message that has received the most attention and study throughout our historical attempt to understand public communication. This chapter will look at the message from the standpoint of the steps the speaker must follow in order to prepare the speech.

Although we will consider individual elements of public messages as steps in preparation—selecting the subject, determining the purpose, gathering materials, organizing the speech, giving attention to language and style, and preparing to feld questions—we must remember that these elements are not perceived by the receiver as discrete units. Rather, spoken public messages are perceived as one unit; various elements interact to produce the impact on the auditor. The public speech, if it is to be effective, must have a structure that unifies the individual elements we shall discuss.

Messages of all types have an internal structure. Painting, musical compositions, computer programs, plays, and speeches, too, have an internal structure, which means that they can be analyzed or broken into parts—there is an arrangement of elements into specific relationships. Speeches, like musical compositions, are highly structured, with the basic elements combined to produce an effective public message. The major elements composing a public speech are purpose, materials, organization, and style. The first topic to be considered, and the first step in speech preparation, is selecting a topic.

Step 1: Selecting the Topic

The selection of the speech topic is directly related to the success of the speech. For any speaker, even for you as a speaker in your communication class, reputation will be determined in part by the quality of the message. Of course, the speaker, the audience, and the occasion enter into the public speaking situation and have an effect on the outcome of the speech; but the content of the speech is extremely important. Good speech content alone can achieve high interest from the audience. This is especially true when the speech deals with an issue that affects the audience directly.

What are your favorite topics?

Don't make topic selection more difficult than it is. Topic selection can be made manageable by following three basic principles. First, *select a topic in which you are knowledgeable.* You will normally be expected to research any speech topic, but researching a known subject puts you hours ahead. Secondly, *select a topic in which you are interested.* Low interest level in a speech topic will make the assignment a drudgery to you during preparation and to the audience during presentation. Do us all a favor by listing the many things in which you have knowledge and interest, and select from that list. Thirdly, *select a topic that will interest your audience.* The more interest your audience has in your topic, the easier it will be to hold their attention during the speech. Audiences are interested in topics that: relate to their needs (think in terms of Maslow's hierarchy of needs); satisfy felt needs (think in terms of Monroe's

Your world is full of interesting speech topics.

need-satisfaction framework); are timely or new (think of the rapidly growing age of information technology and how it relates to your audience); focus on controversy or conflict of opinion (think of the different values related to nuclear energy, conservation, consumerism, America's role overseas, etc.).

Frequently the beginning speaker has difficulty relating these three principles to a first speech assignment. A list of subject categories follows (subtopics could be listed for each category):

1. Personal experience
2. Domestic affairs
3. Education
4. Science
5. Business and labor
6. Religion
7. Politics
8. Environment
9. Sports
10. Entertainment

How many subtopics can you think of for each listed category?

Once you have selected a subject, you must narrow the topic until it can be handled appropriately in the allotted time. The key to effectively narrowing a topic is to keep the following in mind: speech occasion; knowledge, comprehension and interest levels of the audience; amount of time allotted for your speech; the expectations of your audience; and your speech purpose.

Step 2: Determining the Purpose

The purpose of communication is to win a response. The speaker who has not determined what responses to elicit is almost certain to wander along in a disorganized manner and to talk about irrelevant details. It is therefore necessary for the speaker to have a **general purpose** for the speech.

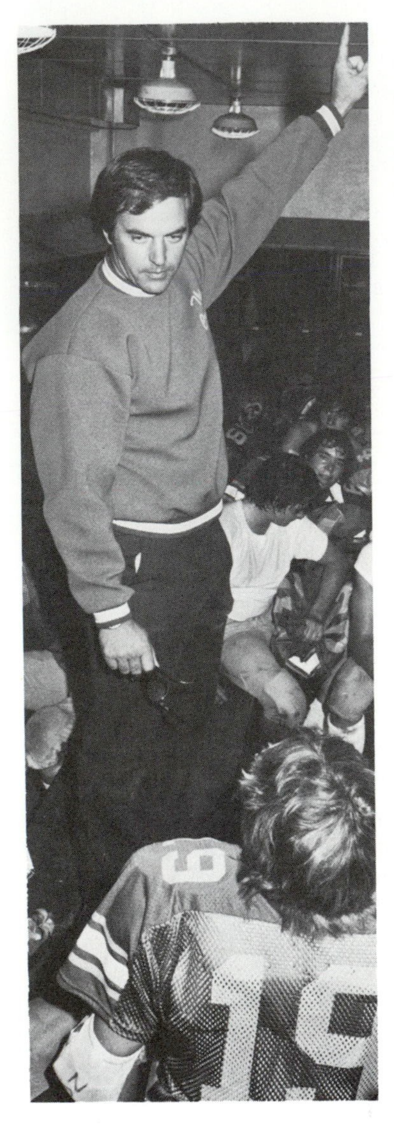

Pep talks are persuasive speeches.

Responses sought from public speeches are not identical. The after-dinner speech, the classroom lecture, the political campaign speech, and the sermon all seek different responses. Each speech has a different purpose. Writers on public speaking have identified three general speech purposes: to inform, to persuade, and to entertain. The informative speech seeks comprehension or understanding; the persuasive speech seeks attitude change and change in behavior or action; and the entertaining speech, which is not discussed, seeks enjoyment.

Every year, thousands of conferences are held in which speaking to impart knowledge plays a major role. People translate technical and research information into usable directives. Experiences and events are described, definitive meanings are probed, and things and events are interpreted so as to point out their implications.

A second type of general purpose is to persuade. Persuasive speeches can be classified as speeches that affirm propositions of fact, propositions of value, and propositions of policy. *Propositions of fact* offer the truth of existence, legality, or causality. In such a speech, the speaker seeks to prove that the proposition of fact espoused is, in reality, true. The purpose goes beyond helping the audience to understand an event, process, or concept. The purpose is to seek approval and acceptance of the "fact." With any proposition of fact, the speaker asks the audience to accept a specific assessment of reality. In order to accomplish this, the speaker must present knowledge about the fact that is to be accepted or rejected, identify appropriate standards to be used in making the judgment, and apply the standards to the data. Propositions of fact may deal with past fact (did John Doe commit this act?), present fact (persons are now in training to become professional arsonists), and future fact or propositions of prediction (college enrollment will decrease next year).

A second kind of persuasive speech focuses on *propositions of value*. Values shape the goals of collective human action and guide personal thought and behavior, and hence there are times when a speaker wishes to persuade the audience that a proposition of value has merit. Such speeches are sometimes called speeches of inspiration. Often, the speaker attempts to reinforce values already held by the audience; most commencement speeches are of this type, as are many sermons. There are also occasions, political and nonpolitical, when the speaker seeks to change values, intensify commitment to a value, or formulate a value. In all such speeches, the proposition of value is concerned with rightness or wrongness, goodness or badness, justice or injustice, or with wisdom or foolishness. It does not seek to establish the existence or reality of an act, event, or object as does the proposition of fact; instead, it seeks to pronounce a judgment as to the *worth* of the act, event, or object.

The third type of persuasive speech deals with a *proposition of policy*. A proposition of policy is concerned with a proposed course of action. When a public speech urges the listeners to vote to approve a school bond, it is a proposition of policy. When abortion legislation is proposed, a proposition of policy is being urged.

Regardless of the nature of the proposition or the type of persuasive speech, there must be one—and only one—general purpose for the speech. Within the speech, however, one may entertain and inform as a *means* to persuasion. Nevertheless, one guiding purpose should undergird the entire speech.

Beyond the general purpose, one must define a **specific purpose** for the speech. The specific purpose is the general purpose stated, in terms of the subject, for the specific audience to which it is directed. The specific purpose identifies the precise response the speaker desires from the audience. It is usually a single, concise clear statement that delineates precisely what the speaker wants the audience to do, feel, believe, understand, learn, or enjoy. The following examples illustrate general and specific purposes:

Subject: The salesman's use of nonverbal communication
General Purpose: To inform
Specific Purpose: To have the audience understand the salesman's use of nonverbal cues to derive useful information about the customer
Subject: Student loans
General Purpose: To persuade
Specific Purpose: To get the members of the audience to write to their representatives in Congress urging approval of proposed legislation supporting student loans

The specific purpose must be selected in terms of audience analysis, speaker's objective, available time, and the occasion. It is the focal point toward which all comments, arguments, and supporting materials are directed.

Step 3: Considering the Audience

In chapter 10 we considered the importance of the audience in the speech situation. We observed that any speaker wishing to communicate ideas to others dare not ignore the receivers; rather, the wise speaker attempts to know the audience. Through careful audience analysis, the speaker discovers the important characteristics of this specific audience that will interact with the speech topic and purpose and with the speaker. It is important that the speaker discover the audience's wants, needs, attitudes, beliefs, and values that are likely to be important in this speech situation. How does the audience feel about this proposition? Are they of the same opinion? Are they divided in opinion? Are they polarized and highly ego-involved? What is their knowledge level on this topic? Are they educated? highly verbal? generally receptive to new ideas? emotional?

Once the speaker has carefully analyzed and learned as much as possible about the audience, the acquired information must be used in constructing the speech. That information is important to selecting the specific purpose for this audience. It tells the speaker what to expect from the audience. This information guides one in determining the organizational pattern of the speech in selecting supporting materials, and in giving the speech impact and style for this audience. If you do not recall what we have learned about audience analysis, you may want to review chapter 10.

Step 4: Organizing and Outlining the Speech

Organization is integral to most of the experiences of the normal individual. From architecture to feelings and thoughts, the average person tends to accept form and reject the formless, to accept harmony and reject dissonance. Humans are organized in eating, sleeping, working, and playing. In fact, we react to material presented in a disorganized manner by rejecting it or organizing it according to our own systems—our own prejudices. No phenomenon of life, animate or inanimate, appears to the normal individual as completely devoid of order. Such form or structure is equally a part of the public speech—from the most basic form of introduction, body, and conclusion to the more sophisticated forms of sequence of ideas. When our plans follow habitual organized patterns, we are more satisfied, more receptive, and freer from frustration. So it is in the public speech. Effective organization can reduce frustration for both the receivers and the sender. When the speech is unorganized, listeners tend to lose interest, to become confused, and to become resentful of the imposition upon their time. Quintilian stated:

> . . . speech, if deficient in that quality *arrangement,* must necessarily be confused and float like a ship without a helm; it can have no coherence; it must exhibit many repetitions, and many omissions; and, like a traveler wandering by night in unknown regions, must, as having no stated course or object, be guided by chance rather than design . . . just as it is not sufficient for those who are erecting a building merely to collect stone and timber and other building materials, but skilled masons are required to arrange and place them, so in speaking, however abundant the matter may be, it will merely form a confused heap unless arrangement be employed to reduce it to order and to give it connexion and firmness of structure. . . .[1]

Organization seems to be an extremely important and pervasive phenomenon in human existence. Edward Sapir has written that even such highly personal activities as breathing fall into categories of polite and impolite and therefore become *organized physiological responses.*[2]

Learning is another area in which order and organized patterns play a strong role. Learning involves the perception of patterns, and authorities in learning psychology are giving increasing emphasis to the importance of this organizing function. Research indicates that learning is painfully slow when organization is not present. Inasmuch as a public speech is a learning situation, organization is imperative.

Organization is helpful to the speaker, for it facilitates clarification of ideas and the development of the speech into a meaningful cohesive unit. It aids the receivers because it permits them to understand the message more easily. Wheeler and Perkins investigated the relationship between learning and organization and report these findings: (1) the more easily recognized the plan of arrangement, the more quickly learning takes place: (2) the longer the content to be learned, the more necessary orderly arrangement becomes; (3) when orderly arrangement is expected but fails to appear, confusion is created; and

Keep your audience in mind as you organize your speech.

(4) learning is most effective when the orderly arrangement is as explicit as possible and is deliberately explained to the learner at the beginning.[3] Later studies—Darnell's for example—have shown that manipulating organization even at the level of a sentence makes a difference in comprehension.[4] Clearly, organization is an important variable in the public speech.

The Three Major Parts of a Speech

At the simplest level, an effective speech has an introduction, a body, and a conclusion. The introduction is an important part of the speech: first impressions, first perceptions, and first judgments exert an unusual amount of influence on subsequent behavior. There is much to be accomplished in the opening remarks of a speech.

Three studies of introductions and conclusions of public speeches indicate that the average length of the introductions was 8.00 percent, 8.55 percent, and 9.00 percent of the total length of the speech.[5] On the basis of these descriptive studies, the introduction appears to occupy about 9.00 percent of the speech's total length. From the same studies, eleven frequently used kinds of introductions were identified: reference to subject, reference to audience, reference to occasion, a quotation, reference to current events, historical reference, an anecdote, startling statement, a question, humor, and personal reference. Humor, personal reference, and reference to the occasion are all used in Adlai Stevenson's opening remark for his concession speech in 1952: "A funny thing happened to me on the way to the White House."

Some of the objectives of the speech introduction can be accomplished through the remarks made by the person introducing the speaker. This person can aid greatly in tuning the audience so that its attention is on the speaker and the speech. An effective introduction enhances the speaker's credibility, reveals the nature of the topic, and creates in the audience an expectancy and readiness for the speaker. To accomplish these objectives it is often necessary for the introducer to relate to the audience the speaker's experience, background interests, and qualifications for the topic at hand. Further, the introducer may need to increase the audience's interest in the subject by showing why the topic is of particular interest and how it is related to their needs and wishes.

The second major part of the speech is the body, or substantive part, with which the remainder of this chapter deals.

The third basic part of the speech is the conclusion. Having developed and supported an idea, the conclusion should serve the purposes of summarizing and stimulating the audience to make the response sought by the speech. The studies by Miller, Hayworth, and Runion show that conclusions averaged 5.40 percent, 5.10 percent, and 9.12 percent of the total length of the speech.[6] The most frequently used conclusions are the challenge, the quotation, the summary, a vision of the future, the appeal, the inspiration, advice, the proposal of a solution, the question, and reference to the audience.[7]

Patterns of Arrangement

There are several ways to arrange the major points of the body of the speech so as to give the ideas and materials a structure, pattern, or pleasing relationship. Insofar as research findings are concerned, many different patterns may be equally satisfactory. To help you learn to use various structures of organization, the following patterns are presented. The first pattern was introduced by Alan Monroe in 1935. His **motivated sequence** pattern has long been popular with many speakers because of its flexibility and ease of adaptation to multiple general speech purposes, including speeches to entertain, inform, convince, stimulate, and actuate. The remaining patterns can be either adapted to the substructure of the motivated sequence or used as the primary speech pattern. Some are probably better suited to a particular speaker, to particular listeners, and to specific purposes than are others; but the effective public speaker must be acquainted with all these patterns in order to select the most appropriate one.

Motivated Sequence

The motivated sequence pattern is popular because of its easy adaptation to communication demands ranging from presentation of informative reports to persuasive efforts including sales, ministry, corporate advocacy, public relations, pep talks—a range of persuasive speech situations. Its practical utility is based on the premise that there is a high degree of uniformity in the thinking processes of most listeners. You will readily see the similarity between the following outlined steps and the sequence of behaviors most people use in making a decision or buying a product or service.

The motivated sequence consists of five basic steps:

1. Attention: the process of creating audience interest
2. Need: the development of the problem by demonstrating political, social, economic, spiritual, or institutional inadequacies and injustices
3. Satisfaction: the proposal of a solution or plan of action designed to alleviate the problem or injustice outlined in the need step
4. Visualization: involves painting a verbal picture of how one's world will look after the plan or "satisfaction step" is adopted or rejected
5. Action: a specific request or challenge to implement the solution explained in the "satisfaction step."[8]

Although all five steps are used for a persuasive speech, only the first three steps are developed in the speech to inform. The final two steps are optional and seldom developed in depth. Also, in the speech to inform, the need step becomes a need for information as opposed to a problem requiring a solution. The satisfaction step becomes the body of the speech or the unit of information the speaker wants to present rather than the solution to a problem.

Time Sequence or Chronological Pattern

A second method of organization is to begin at a certain point in time, and then move forward in a **chronological pattern.** All human experience can be organized in terms of time. From accounts of travels and the day's events to recipes, information can be organized according to a time sequence. Children who have never considered "organization" find it easy to recount the events of a party chronologically with a series of "and then" transitions.

When time-order patterns are used, you may move forward from a chosen point in time (or backwards, in some rare instances), but if you jump haphazardly from date to date, disregarding the natural sequence, your audience will be confronted with a confusing picture.

Space Sequence

A third method of organizing material uses a spatial pattern. Speech topics such as geography, flood control, football strategy, and plans for an urban renewal program often necessitate the use of a **spatial pattern** of organization. In the space sequence, material is arranged in terms of physical location, moving from east to west, north to south, from the center to the outside, clockwise, and so forth. Space is the element that relates each point to all other main points. The weather report on television, for example, is frequently arranged in a spatial pattern.

Outline a speech topic, using the time-order pattern, and then organize the same topic again using a space-order pattern.

Topical Pattern

Some subjects fall into topics or categories that are parts making up the whole. Neither space nor time unifies these main points, but the fact that they are each and all members of the same family—parts that are related inasmuch as they do combine to make the whole—serves to unify them. For example, financial reports may be given in terms of assets and liabilities or income and expenses. A talk about the national goverment may be divided into three main areas—discussion about the legislative, the executive, and the judicial branches of government. The **topical** arrangement is one of the most widely used forms of organization. In fact, some speakers make the mistake of relying entirely on this one pattern, and they use this pattern even when it is less effective than another pattern would be.

Logical Patterns

The patterns of arrangement identified as **logical patterns** include problem-solution, cause-effect, analogy, induction, and deduction. Actually, all patterns of arrangement are "logical" (otherwise they are not *patterns*), but the term *logical patterns* as used here is related to argument, debate, and rational persuasion.

The *problem-solution pattern* has two major points—the problem and the proposed solution or solutions. Similarly, the *cause-effect* method of organizing a speech has two main points—a description of factors that represent the *cause* and a prediction or identification of the subsequent *effect*. Speeches on farm surpluses, the rising cost of living, and cancer lend themselves to a cause-effect or problem-solution pattern of organization.

The inductive and deductive patterns of arrangement are also logical methods of organizing material. Although every pattern of arrangement can be classified as either inductive or deductive, we shall treat these patterns separately.

The *inductive pattern* of organization moves from specific examples or instances to the conclusion that the examples dictate. It is reasoning from the specific to the general, from examples to the generalization that can be appropriately drawn. We learn early to use the inductive pattern in reasoning and probably use it daily throughout our lifetimes.

Following is a hypothetical example of the inductive pattern.

Example 1: Federal Program A required thirty cents of each dollar for administrative costs, while a similar state program in state Z required twelve cents of each dollar for administrative costs.

Example 2: Federal Program B required thirty-six cents of each dollar for administrative costs, while similar state programs in states, W, X, and Y cost fourteen, twelve, and sixteen cents of each dollar for administrative costs.

Conclusion or inference drawn: therefore, it is evident that federal programs are more costly than similar state programs.

It should be noted that the number of examples used—one or many—depends upon the quality of the example and the nature of the item being generalized. If we are attempting to make a generalization about the effect of jumping off a ten-story building on the jumper, one example may be quite enough to warrant a conclusion. Generally, however, more than one example is required in order to win belief or acceptance of the conclusion from the audience.

A second method of organizing ideas—*the deductive pattern*—is opposite to the inductive pattern in that the reasoning moves from the generalization to the specific instance. The generalization is already accepted by the listener, and so the deductive pattern involves showing that the specific instance or issue is a member of the family of the larger generalization. Hence, if the specific instance is included in the generalization in all essential ways and the generalization is already accepted as true, then the specific instance may also be accepted as true. This method of argument often labels, classifies, or categorizes the specific example or situation at issue. Following is a hypothetical example of the deductive pattern.

Conclusion (Relative to the statement at issue): This specific animal is a dog.

Accepted Generalization: Dogs are animals having characteristics A, B, C, D, E, and F.

Application of the tests to see if this specific animal fits into and only into the generalization: This animal does have the characteristics A, B, C, D, E, and F.

Conclusion: This animal is a dog.

It is not uncommon for a public speaker to want to relate a specific problem to a commonly accepted generalization. The important requirement is to discover the essential tests that must be satisfied in order to make the specific instance "like those in the generalization."

Inductive and deductive patterns of organization are often used by attorneys in legal summations, by senators or congressmen in legislative speeches, and by research scholars in talks before scientific groups who demand rigorous, logical procedures. These patterns may seem somewhat difficult to follow and thus may be poorly suited to audiences of a lower educational level.

The *analogy*—another logical pattern—consists of comparing two similar examples in which the audience knows what is true of one example and must accept it as being true of a second example *if* the second example is exactly like the first in all essential aspects. This "truth" about the second example is the point at issue—the conclusion that one wants the audience to accept. The known and accepted truth of the first example, and likeness of the two examples, constitute the main points of this pattern of organization.

Whatever pattern of organization is used, that pattern and *only* that pattern must be used for that level of breakdown or analysis. For example, if the topic is *transportation* and four main points are used, all four points must be related according to a *single principle* governing that pattern of organization.

Through verbal cues, and sometimes visual devices, good speakers make their organization clear to the audience.

Subject: Transportation

Correct Topical Pattern	Incorrect Mixed Pattern Topical and Spatial
I. Automobiles	I. Automobiles
II. Planes	II. Planes
III. Ships	III. Transportation in Alaska
IV. Trains	IV. Transportation in Nigeria

At the secondary level, when another *unit* or *whole* is broken into parts, another pattern of arrangement may be used. For example, although the first-order breakdown of the body of the speech above uses a topical pattern, one might use a time-sequence pattern to discuss automobiles.

I. Automobiles
  A. 1890–1919: Age of Discovery
  B. 1920–1935: Age of Competition
  C. 1936–1965: Age of Power and Speed
  D. 1966– ?: Age of Ecological Adaptation
II. Air Planes
  A. What would you list here?
  B.

Psychological Ordering of Arguments

The two remaining patterns may not be so much *standard* patterns of organization as they are **psychological ordering of arguments.** They are the primacy-recency method of arranging arguments and the climax-anticlimax arrangements of arguments.

Primacy—Recency

A factor to consider when arranging arguments or main points of a speech is the order in which the arguments should appear. In the time-order arrangement, the points are made according to the sequence of their occurrence; but with many of the other patterns of organization, one could select which argument or point should be made first, second, third, or last. Considerable research has been done to test how the position of an argument (first, last, or in the middle) is related to persuasion or attitude change. Some findings point to a **law of primacy,** that is, to a principle stating that materials placed first in a message have a greater impact on an audience than subsequent materials. Other findings seem to support a **law of recency:** some arguments, news stories, and explanations seem to have a greater effect if they are presented last.[9] On the other hand, propaganda studies have shown that the nation getting its message across first has a great advantage; and in studies of advertising, the first one with a message seems to have a better position.

One explanation of the strong effect of "first" arguments or presentations in propaganda campaigns, political campaigns, and advertising campaigns is that these communications in the "real" setting—the field or naturalistic setting—are often the *only side of the argument actually received.* The individual—especially if uninformed or not already holding an opinion—will get the one side (the first presented) and then become closed minded to the issue. We are often prone to avoid issues or information contradictory to our view of the world. Thus, in the real world, selective exposure tends to increase the impact of primacy. If one can guarantee exposure to both sides, then primacy may not have as great an advantage, the exception being when the same speaker presents contradictory material. In that instance there is reason to believe that the material presented first has more influence.

The evidence *available* does not allow us to make absolute statements relative to whether the first or last order is most influential *in every instance.* But we know a few situations in which first is best, and some where last may be best, and we know that the middle is seldom, if ever, best.

Climax—Anticlimax

The ordering of arguments within a particular pattern of arrangement (topical pattern, spatial pattern, etc.) may also be related to the saliency or importance of the arguments or topics. One could arrange three unequal arguments in a **climax pattern,** that is, from weakest to strongest; or one could arrange them in an **anticlimax pattern,** that is, from strongest to weakest. Minnick reviews some studies on this issue and explains contradictory findings in terms of the laws of learning. He states that when an audience has little interest in the speech topic, it may be wise to place the strongest argument first. Or if one is presenting *pro* arguments and *con* arguments and one wants the thesis (pro argument) accepted, the pro arguments should be presented first.[10] It may also be that the source credibility of the speaker is related to climax-anticlimax ordering of arguments. Some persons suggest that the speaker with low credibility, or a speaker unknown to the audience, should place the strongest arguments first.

Although we have little concrete evidence to guide us on this issue, it appears that the climax order is often best.

Transitions

In addition to determining the best pattern to follow in organizing the speech, one must give special attention to the transitions. **Transitions** provide the linkages that enable the audience to see the pattern being used, to move with the speaker from one main point to another, from one subpoint or supporting point to another, and from the introduction into the speech. It is always good practice to plan transitions from point to point and include them in the outline. Table 11.1 includes some commonly used transitions that signal relationships between ideas.

Phrasing Main Points

The main points of the speech should be carefully worded so as to give the speech emphasis and clarity. Supporting materials, discussed next in this chapter, constitute the bulk of the speech; but the major thrust of the message is conveyed by the main points—the foundation or framework upon which details are fitted. Effective public speakers phrase main points carefully so that they are clearly understood and easily remembered. Four characteristics should be evident in the phrasing of main points: *vividness, conciseness, immediacy,* and *parallelism.*

Main points stated in vivid, attention-getting words and phrases stand out clearly and can be remembered easily. Similarly, main points that are concise rather than rambling and cumbersome increase the clarity of the speech. Thirdly, main points that appeal directly to the immediate concerns of the receivers enhance the effectiveness of the speech. And finally, whenever possible, a uniform type of sentence structure and similar phraseology should be used for all main points made.

Table 11.1

To Signal an Addition	
moreover	and
in addition	furthermore
also	

To Signal Place	
beyond	inside
over	to the right
under	nearby
opposite to	adjacent to

To Signal Time	
first, second	later
next	now
finally	the next day
meanwhile	subsequently

To Signal Comparison	
likewise	in comparison
similarly	

To Signal Results	
thus	accordingly
hence	therefore
because of this	so
as a result	conse-quently

To Signal Contrast	
however	but
nevertheless	on the other hand
yet	on the contrary
still	notwithstanding
in contrast	otherwise

To Signal an Example	
for example	namely
for instance	specifically

To Signal an Explanation	
in other words	simply stated
that is	in fact

Connectors—words linking independent statements to each other; sentence combining

To Signal a Contrast: although

To Signal Time Relationships: while, when, after

To Signal Cause/Effect: since, because

To Signal an Addition: besides

To Signal Space Relationship: where

An example can be effectively indicated by a pointed finger or an extended hand.

Step 5: Gathering Supporting Materials

Gathering supporting materials involves approaching the topic from a scholarly perspective. The first step is to carefully search your own knowledge of the topic. With the speech topic clearly in mind, ask yourself five basic questions: (1) What do I know from seeing or hearing about this subject? (2) What do I think or believe about this subject? (3) What feelings are aroused in me in connection with this subject? (4) What purposes do I have in mind as I prepare on this subject? (5) How much time am I willing to spend in preparing this subject?

The second step is to search for materials outside yourself. Some of this search might be through personal interviewing. Most frequently, however, speech research will involve extensive use of library resources. As you research your subject, use the following criteria in selecting materials: (1) Is this material relevant? (2) Is it current? and (3) Is it accurate, fair, and reliable?

Major sources for researching topics are included in the following list. Most school libraries have reference librarians who welcome the opportunity to assist you in acquiring maximum benefit from these sources.

1. *Bibliographic Index:* A cumulative bibliography of bibliographies. An excellent place to begin when you don't know where to begin.
2. *Matlon's Index to Journals in Communication Studies through 1979.* An excellent beginning place if your speech relates to any area of communication.
3. The current *Index to Journals in Education* (CIJE). This index covers more than seven-hundred publications of periodical literature in the field of education.

Gathering supporting materials.

4. Other scholarly sources include: *Communication Abstracts, Resources in Education, Humanities Index, Education Index, Dissertation Abstracts, Psychological Abstracts, Sociological Abstracts,* and *Index to Religious Periodical Literature.*
5. Guides to periodicals, newspapers, and popular journals include three sources: *New York Times Index* (the master key to the news since 1851); *The Times Index;* and *The Reader's Guide to Periodical Literature* (probably the most frequently used index for speeches of social or political importance).
6. *Books in Print* is occasionally useful to the student who wants to extend speech preparation beyond the book references found in card catalog and microfiche systems.
7. Additional useful information can be gleaned from yearbooks, documents and reports, *Facts on File,* government depository libraries, collections of quotations and biographies, ERIC, and computer sources.

These are major sources of materials. Numerous supporting materials are available from one's own knowledge and experiences as well as from the library and other sources.

The kinds of **supporting materials** include explanations, figurative and literal analogies, hypothetical and factual illustrations, specific instances, statistics, testimony, restatement, and visual aids. Sometimes two or more of these types of supporting materials best serve certain purposes. Figurative analogies, comparisons, and hypothetical illustrations for example, are especially useful to make ideas clear and understandable; specific instances, statistics,

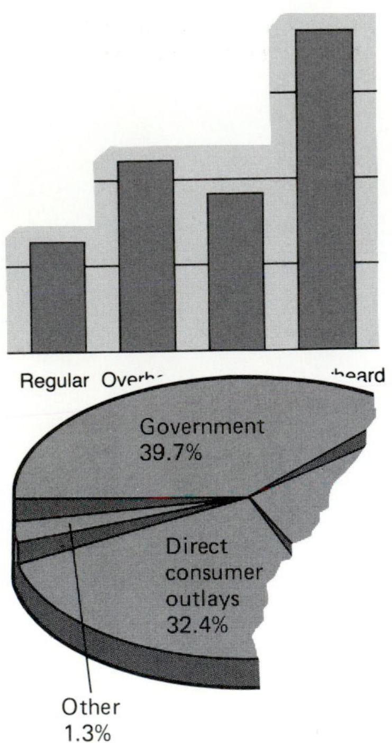

Bar graphs and pie charts are two common types of supporting materials.

and testimony, on the other hand, are more useful as evidence to gain belief, or to persuade. Literal analogies and factual illustrations serve both purposes effectively.

Explanations are expository statements clarifying the meaning of a term or setting forth the relationship between parts—seldom adequate when used alone. It is better to follow the explanation with comparisons or illustrations. One should also remember to keep explanations simple, short, and accurate.

Analogies are comparisons of two things similar in certain essential characteristics and therefore judged to be similar in other characteristics. Analogies are of two kinds: figurative and literal. A **figurative analogy** compares things in different classes: for example, the eye with a camera or a thermostat with communication feedback. A **literal analogy,** on the other hand, compares things of the same class: for example, Cadillacs with Lincolns, Indianapolis with Wichita, or Purdue with Ohio State. Literal analogies are used as evidence to prove points, but figurative analogies are primarily used to clarify points.

Illustrations are detailed examples or instances. If the example is not explained or detailed, but merely referred to or pointed to, then the example is a *specific instance* and its usefulness is primarily that of establishing proof. If, however, the example is explained through the revelation of details, then it is an illustration. Illustrations may be real (factual) or they may be hypothetical. **Factual illustrations** may serve to establish proof, while **hypothetical illustrations** are useful to clarify meaning.

Statistics are figures that summarize *many instances* and indicate relationships among phenomena. They enable one to summarize a large amount of data quickly and to interpret a mass of specific occurrences or instances. Hence they are useful as evidence in a persuasive argument.

Statistics may sometimes be difficult for audiences to comprehend; therefore the relationship or comparison represented in the statistics should be clearly identified and explained. Also, statistics should be translated into immediately understandable terms. Large numbers can be stated in round numbers, and comparisons can be used. Pie or bar graphs can be quite helpful in making statistics understandable.

Testimony is the verbatim reporting of a person's opinion or conclusion. First hand testimony is one of the primary forms of evidence (supporting material) used in courts of law. In speeches, the testimony of authorities is quoted by the speaker. Testimony can be used both for clarity and for evidence to establish proof. It must meet two essential tests: (1) The person who made the statement must be qualified to make such a statement. Is the source an authority by virtue of skills, training, recognition, and reputation? (2) The testimony must be acceptable and believable to the audience.

Restatement is the reiteration of an idea in different words. Repetition is the process of saying again an idea in the same words previously used. Restatement and repetition do not constitute evidence, but they often have a persuasive effect not unlike the piling up of evidence. The utility of reiteration

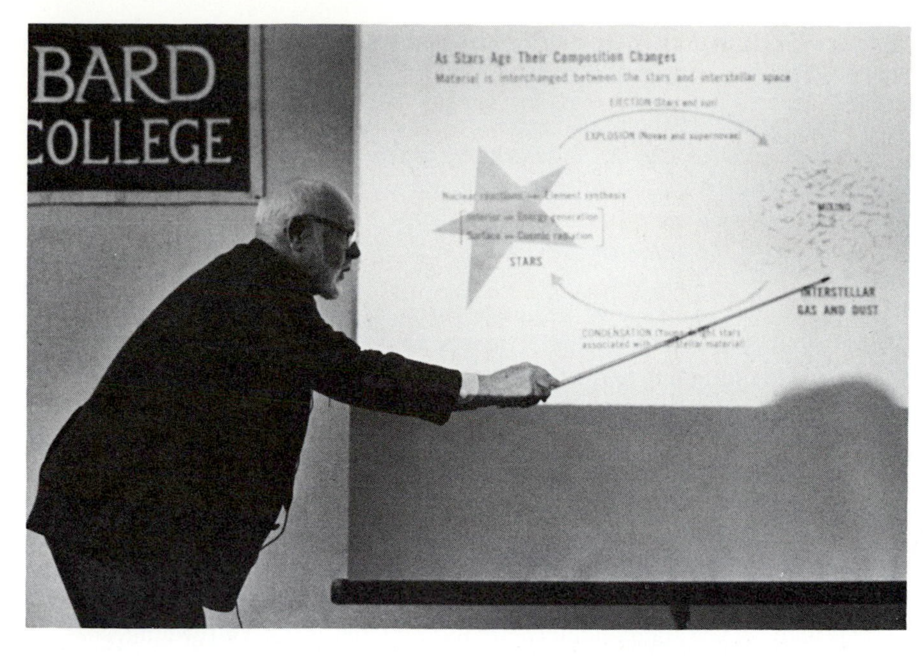

The use of visual aids can enhance communication.

and repetition is amply demonstrated by the profits resulting from these persuasive tactics when they are used in advertising. Reiteration and repetition in public speeches serve the purpose of clarifying and recalling patterns of arrangement and patterns of development. Initial summaries, during-the-speech summaries, and end-of-speech summaries are examples of useful repetition and reiteration used to enhance understanding through constant clarification.

A final form of material is visual aids. **Visual aids,** although they are not verbal supporting material, can enhance the reception of ideas and can communicate information. Visual aids include charts, diagrams, maps, pictures, simulated models, and real objects. Demonstration speeches rely upon the use of visual aids, but other kinds of speeches may also profit from their use. It is important that one consider carefully the *purpose* of the visual support when choosing visual aids. Sometimes a simple diagram is better for the purpose of clarifying than the real object. If one wanted to explain the parts of the heart, for example, a simple diagram or a large walk-through model might be preferable to a real heart. Actual equipment and objects are not necessarily better than other types of visual aids, although in some instances only the real object is capable of adequately fulfilling the objective in mind.

A speaker who uses visual aids should remember three important rules: (1) do not stand between the listeners and the visual aids; (2) use only visual aids that are *relevant* since complex and irrelevant detail will function as noise and counteract any positive effect; and (3) be sure the visual aid is of a size and in a position to be clearly visible to the entire audience.

Step 6: Giving the Speech Impact through Language and Style

Another variable in the public speech is language. Effective use of language, the words selected, the arrangement of the words, and the development of specialized functions for the arrangements all contribute to the force of the message and even more to clarity. The theme to follow in language and style is: *Make it fit the audience!* It is wise to always take the audience's perspective.

The use of one type of language throughout the speech results in monotony and destroys the listener's interest. Long and involved sentence structure becomes fatiguing to the listener. A **written style** rather than an **oral style** in public speaking seems artificial to the listener, and excessive use of slang is tiresome and deadly. The best public-speech language is as direct as possible.

The effective public speaker works continually for a better understanding and appreciation of words. English-speaking societies have more than one-half million words available to them; and the average individual has a vocabulary of about ten thousand, about two thousand of which are used in habitual patterns of conversation. The average college student recognizes sixty thousand words and can use approximately twenty thousand. Robert Browning, considered by many persons to have had the most extensive usable vocabulary of all English writers, used some thirty-five thousand different words in his writings. The task for the effective public speaker is to expand the vocabulary (conversational and general) and to acquire new understandings about *how best to use* that vocabulary—that is, how to *select words,* and how to *arrange words into effective sentences.*

Microcomputers are making it easier for speakers to engage in "word management." Some software packages currently hold more than 50,000 words and provide multiple functions including thesaurus, dictionary, and spelling checker. Many software packages also allow the user to add words not currently in the Thesaurus.

To become aware of the many possibilities from which the most forceful or effective word can be chosen, the student of public speaking must study dictionaries and the words used by others. Dictionaries attempt to record all the words used in speech, but they do not create or prescribe words; they only record how a word has been used in the past. While the use of some words is so narrow that only one definition is required, other words have several meanings that require numerous definitions.

Just as everyone has two sets of manners, informal and formal, so there are two levels of language, informal and formal. Informal language style abounds on television and radio as well as in the movies. So persuasive is this influence that a *mass language* has evolved in the United States. This level of language sacrifices *precision* in word usage to clichés, jargon, euphemisms, and worn-out metaphors, all of which have one common characteristic—

impression. When the effective public speaker speaks to an audience, it is important not to fall into the patterns of mass language style. "Cool," "turkey," "neat," "straight," "state of the art," "for sure," and "get down" are examples of clichés—words or phrases robbed of their effectiveness and meaning through overuse.

In addition to vague words and clichés, ineffective speaking is sometimes characterized by the use of jargon—the technical language of a profession. The lawyer who uses "whereas" and "therefore" too often in a public speech is using jargon. In contracts, these terms may be necessary to provide for contingencies, but they are deadly to an audience. Similarly, the college professor who uses "it would seem," "it is not unreasonable to say," or "it might be considered helpful" in a public speech will be considered affected by the audience. This language may be appropriate for the scientific journal, but it is jargon in the public speech and may create suspicion and rejection in the minds of the audience.

Another way to look at words is in terms of their concreteness and abstractness. Concrete words refer to specific things that can be seen, felt, smelled, or experienced, while abstract words are signs or symbols for ideas, concepts, or relations that are not "sensed" directly. Everyday language is a mixture of both, and although both types of words are essential to communication, too many abstract words in the public speech can cause problems. Inexperienced public speakers tend to avoid concrete words; they do not realize that concrete words increase attention and clarity.

Words are also classified as popular and learned, that is, simple and monosyllabic words as compared to more vague and polysyllabic words. The common reference to this classification system is: "He uses big words" or "You can understand what he says; he doesn't use those big words." Following are some examples of popular words and their learned counterparts:

Popular	**Learned**
round	circular
thin	emaciated
fat	corpulent
brave	valorous
king	sovereign
book	volume

A style that uses popular words tends to be clearer and more direct than a style containing learned words.

Concrete and abstract words are *not* synonymous with popular and learned words. Concrete and abstract words are classified according to criteria different from those used to classify popular and learned words. The concrete-abstract classification is based on the referents of words, while the popular-learned classification is based upon the level of usage. In deciding which words to use, one must be guided by the need for clarity, the tone desired in the speech, and the expectations of the audience. Although one should generally use popular, concrete, and simple words, there are situations when the nature of the topic and the audience demand a higher level of language usage. In studies conducted by Brooks, Emmert, and Adrian, it was found that the effect of congruency of language usage (upon source credibility, for example) between speaker and listener varied acccording to perceived-role relationship and the expectations of the audience.[11] Students accorded higher *credibility* to professors whose public-speaking language usage was moderately congruent with the students' language usage than they did to professors whose public-speaking language was highly congruent with their own language usage. Students *expected* professors to use language a little differently than they themselves did. The use of learned words by professors did not decrease their source credibility. A positive relationship between language usage congruency and retention was found in the studies.

As the studies we have cited show, it is difficult to make hard, absolute rules about using language, but George Orwell suggested six rules that generally serve to improve one's public speaking, especially if rule six is kept in mind.

1. Never use a metaphor, simile, or other figure which you are used to seeing in print.
2. Never use a long word where a short one will do.
3. If it is possible to cut a word out, always cut it out.
4. Never use a passive phrase where you can use an active one.
5. Never use a foreign phrase, a scientific word, or a jargon word if you can think of an everyday English equivalent.
6. Break any of these rules rather than say anything outright barbarous.[12]

In addition to these suggestions concerning language, you should recall and apply those understandings gained from chapter 2 on using language in communication. The public speaker must remember that it is people, not words, that mean; that it cannot be assumed that everyone else "speaks my language"; that it is a dynamic, complex world from which we are abstracting with a limited vocabulary; that language is always a calculated risk; and that feedback should be used to check on the message received and to guide further messages.

Not only must the speaker pay attention to the words selected, the words must be organized and arranged in the way most likely to convey the intended meaning, feeling, or attitude to the audience. A large vocabulary permits speakers to be specific, vivid, affective, and accurate if they can also put words together into effective phrases, clauses, and sentences. Although oral style permits more latitude in structuring sentences and in expressing ideas than does the standard written style, speakers who make grammatical errors (such as

The effective speaker prepares to handle questions.

incorrect verb tense or disagreement in number between subject and verb) must recognize that many audiences will hold them acccountable and will not accord them the desired credibility.

Step 7: Preparing to Handle Questions

"Does anyone have a question? No? OK, thank you for listening." Was the speaker competent? successful? Another speaker confessed, "I'm really not much of a speaker, so after I make a few opening remarks, I open up for questions." Strangely enough, the audience frequently leaves this second speaker saying they have heard a good speaker. Was the second speaker competent? successful?

Both situations are similar to a "fourth down punt" effort. The first speaker has failed to make the potential yardage by **fielding questions,** and the second speaker has failed to gain the results available through carefully planned discourse. While there are exceptions, a competent communicator will generally opt to achieve a predetermined purpose by means of an effective presentation of ideas, arguments, or appeals and then try for additional points with an effective period of speaker-audience interaction. Therefore, let's discuss the process of fielding questions. Included in this section is a discussion of: a rationale for fielding questions, guidelines for the question-answer periods, and special techniques for fielding questions.

Rationale for Fielding Questions

The objectives one wishes to achieve through a question-answer session may include one or more of the following:

1. to further the specific speech purpose
2. promotion of audience involvement in the communication process
3. clarification and/or extension of information, arguments, or proposals
4. defense and refutation
5. enhancement of speaker credibility and rapport

To further the specific speech purpose. Regardless of whether the speaker's general purpose is to inform, persuade, or entertain, the specific purpose is based on the speaker's perception and analysis of the audience. Since perception is always limited, audience analysis is at best an educated inference. And because public speaking is linear, it is reasonable to conclude that we will experience "noise" in any speaker-audience context.

Remember, the objective of public speaking is not simply to follow an outline from beginning to end or to complete a communication assignment, but to "win a response." Just as the fourth down represents a last chance for a first down, the question-answer session represents a last head-to-head opportunity for the speaker to accomplish the goal for which he has brainstormed, researched, and practiced. Like the fourth-down situation, the question-answer period is not the time to fumble the ball. The effective communicator approaches the question-answer portion of a speech as thoroughly as the speech itself.

Promotion of audience involvement. In the opening chapter we indicated that the audience functions primarily as receivers and responders. We further explained that "whereas the audience members 'may' communicate with the speaker, the speaker does most, if not all, of the speaking." The question-answer period helps to maximize the limited "transactional potential" of the public-speaking situation. Although every "sighted" speaker can strive to "read" nonverbal messages or responses from the audience, the question-answer process is the only opportunity to verify, clarify, and interact on a level approaching interpersonal communication.

Even in very large audiences, speaker-audience interaction can be achieved with limited control by placing microphones in aisles or in the hands of assistants throughout the audience and allowing audience members to ask questions or offer personal responses. Additional speaker control can be achieved by equipping the speaker to walk out among the audience, select respondents, and perhaps lead the respondent with appropriate questions. Careful planning and training of assistants is essential for the ongoing success of these techniques.

Clarification or extension of information, arguments, or appeals. Feedback was defined earlier as that "integral part of the human communication process that allows the speaker to *monitor* the process and to *evaluate the success* of an attempt to get the desired response from the receiver." If the desired response is understanding, the question-answer session gives the speaker an opportunity to evaluate speaker effectiveness. If the questioner obviously does not understand what was explained and illustrated, the speaker now has an "overtime" opportunity to use additional forms of clarifying support material—including explanation, factual or hypothetical illustration, analogy, specific instances, testimony, and restatement—to achieve the desired understanding.

If the desired response of the speaker's specific purpose is audience belief or actuation, the question-answer session again gives the speaker an opportunity to assess effectiveness. Argumentation and persuasion are extremely complex processes. What appears rational and feasible to one person might appear fallacious and reckless to another. Two persons might respond similarly to an issue on an attitude scale. However, their ego involvement on that issue as well as their latitude of acceptance (or willingness to consider other positions) and latitude of rejection (or predisposition to reject other positions) might vary considerably.

During the question-answer session it is essential that the speaker assess the level of understanding or acceptance in as non-defensive a manner as possible and then proceed systematically with corrective measures.

Defense and refutation. In chapter 7 we discussed how interpersonal conflicts could be categorized according to the level of intensity-controversy, competition, and combat. The same division of categories is appropriate for interpersonal conflict during the question-answer process. Knowing the level of conflict between speaker and audience member will help to determine response strategy and tactics. If the two parties are at the controversy level, the differences may relate to values, policies, or facts. Resolution may still be possible through the rational development of evidence and reason. If the controversy is competitive, however, the speaker is faced with one or more audience members who have come with personal hidden or declared agenda. The speaker may need to adopt a win-lose, lose-win, lose-lose, or win-win strategy.

Enhancement of speaker credibility and rapport. In chapter 9 we observed that audiences today, more than ever before, "stand ready to confer or deny credibility to the speakers claiming their attention." All three dimensions of source credibility—safety or trustworthiness, expertise or competence, and dynamism—increase or decrease with the speaker's handling of audience questions. Intrinsic, or derived credibility, are enhanced in direct proportion to the speaker's ability to meet audience expectations. One of the authors had the privilege of working with a group of nuclear engineers who had been charged with the responsibility of designing and building a nuclear plant for a large public utility company in the Midwest. Due to growing community apprehension, the engineers had been asked to present speeches and slides to interested community groups, as well as appear in special hearings and participate in mediated interviews. The engineers were selected on the basis of their technical knowledge of nuclear energy. Following a speech, prepared by

Controversy in a public-speech situation may relate to different values, policies, facts, or even hidden agendas.

the public information department, the nuclear engineers were frequently expected to field questions. Because the engineers were able to read the speech and comment on technical information displayed on slides, they were generally perceived as credible on the competency or knowledge component of source credibility. Too often, however, they were drawn by sometimes hostile audience members, hearing attorneys, or media interviewers into areas other than their own expertise. When this happened, the engineers were frequently perceived as not having the expertise to build a nuclear plant in the community's backyard. Also, when the engineers appeared uncertain about responding to specific questions, audience-perceived dynamism, safety, and competency declined.

The training requested by the utility company was designed to (1) help nuclear engineers recognize a questioner's intent; (2) determine what should be done with the question (i.e., answer it or refer questioner to appropriate source); (3) adapt to different kinds of audiences including friendly civic groups, attorneys for official hearings and media personnel capable of editing out essential parts of an answer.

Although extensive local and national training was used, the powerful utility giant was not able to respond effectively to the numerous questions and arguments generated primarily by one female "environmentalist" from a small neighboring community. The nuclear plant was scrapped before it reached ground level. Could the use of effective question-answer techniques have saved the project? Certainly not by itself. When the stakes are high, however, competent speakers take advantage of every credible means of clarification and persuasion in a given situation.

Guidelines for the Question-Answer Session

This section will outline preparation strategies, basic techniques for fielding questions, and wrap-up courtesies for the question-answer session.

Preparation strategies. The speaker can best prepare by doing the following: knowing the informational needs of the audience, identifying complex as well as controversial areas within the speech, and understanding the basic type and cultural context of the target audience. Also, it is essential to determine whether there are peripheral points that may not be central to the speech but are of interest to certain members of the audience.

Preparation tactics used by successful speakers have included brainstorming and discussing lists of potential questions with peers or key interested persons, preparation of "blackbooks" containing potential questions, and question-answer rehearsal sessions.

A representative of the previously mentioned utility company had been scheduled for several weeks to speak to a Tuesday morning civic club. He was given the prepared slides and the blessing of the utility company. Nothing unusual. Then on the weekend prior to the breakfast, Three Mile Island became a household phrase. The speaker appeared, gave his speech, showed his slides and concluded by asking "Are there any questions?" Twenty hands reached for the sky. The words, "What happened at Three Mile Island?" filled the room.

The speaker responded, "It's funny you would ask." He then turned on his projector and proceeded to show slides describing the Three Mile Island incident. The utility company had done its weekend homework.

Basic techniques for generating and fielding questions. First, make a smooth transition that communicates warmth, appreciation, interest, and openness. Next, adopt question-answer techniques most appropriate for a particular style of speaking, speech topic and purpose, type of audience, and speech situation. Third, in the unlikely event that no one asks a question promptly, it is helpful to be ready with one or two planted questions. Ask one or two persons to ask specific questions supplied by you. These confederates should be asked to wait several seconds and then ask their questions if others have not responded. Planted questions should normally be ones which have been carefully

Select three techniques you can use in your next speech if you have questions from the audience.

selected and thoroughly researched. Several specific techniques will be discussed later in this chapter. The following, however, are techniques appropriate for a broad range of question-answer situations.

1. Recognize and compliment or thank the questioner.
2. Analyze the question and questioner's intent and then paraphrase the question.
3. Respond to the audience rather than to the questioner.
4. Develop an effective "impromptu" procedure for organizing the response.
5. Relate the answer back to specific points in the speech.
6. Keep answers brief, succinct, and cogent.
7. Carefully monitor the nonverbal messages being sent and received.
8. Ask the questioner if your response answered the question, and quickly move to the next person preferably in another part of the audience.
9. Field questions from different sexes, age groups, etc. and parts of the room.
10. Be gracious but remain firm and in control.

Wrap-up courtesies for question-answer sessions. Finally, how does one conclude the question-answer process? First, it is important to know when to stop. The speaker should be sensitive to the time constraints of any speaking engagement and carefully read the signals from various members of the audience. An effective way to close is to again preview the major ideas discussed in the speech, present a previously prepared concluding statement, and welcome informal discussion after the meeting if appropriate.

Special Techniques for Fielding Questions

Due to the potential impact some of the basic techniques listed above can have on the communication process, we want to expand on some of them here. Although the first two are basic in nature, they may also be considered special techniques.

Recognizing and complimenting the questioner. Recognition of the questioner should not be taken for granted. The questioner should be recognized by name, when possible. To do so is both courteous and a powerful motivator. Any recognition should be as specific and personal as the situation will allow. Recognition by name, however, is probably the most personal, powerful, and motivating recognition you can make. Other techniques include recognition by color or style of clothing, location in the room, or perhaps an object the questioner is wearing. Recognition of a person in the ways listed above is often perceived as a direct or indirect compliment. Complimenting can also be done by responding, "That's an excellent question," "I'm especially glad you asked that question," "Your question is an important one—it's one which I considered myself," or "That's a very timely question."

Determining the questioner's intent. Is the questioner asking for additional information, clarification of a specific point in the speech, or for the sake of argument or contention? Effectiveness at this point calls for skill in listening for the kind of question being asked. Is the question open, closed, leading, or perhaps loaded? Is the question really a question or is it a carefully camouflaged statement?

Once the question and intent is understood, it should be paraphrased. Fetzer and Vogel list four valid reasons for repeating or paraphrasing the question:

1. Once the speaker has given the floor to the questioner, the speaker must take this power and authority back.
2. The speaker has the obligation of making sure that all members of the audience have heard the question.
3. This repeating or paraphrasing of the question makes the "ownership" of the question a total audience concern. The speaker is not talking to one person but to the entire audience.
4. By repeating or paraphrasing the question, the speaker is allowing more time to think about a proper response.[13]

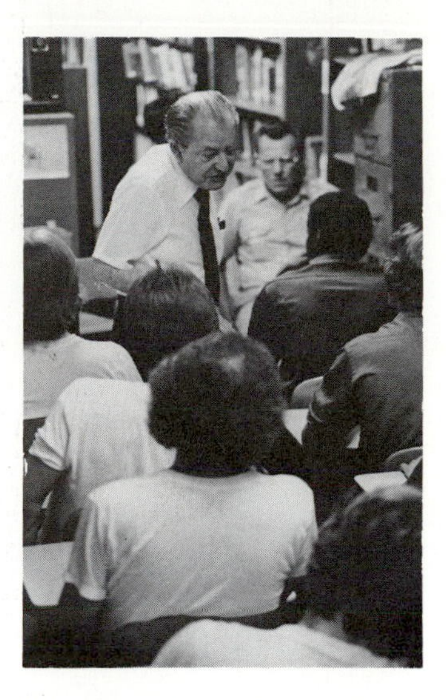

It is essential to determine whether there are peripheral points which may not be central to the speech but are of interest to certain audience members.

If the questioner is asking for additional information or clarification, the speaker should be able to provide it. If not, it is generaly best to acknowledge that the speaker doesn't have the desired information, but will be happy to get it for the questioner. If the speaker does attempt to provide the desired information, combining several of the following techniques should be helpful.

—properly acknowledge the questioner
—paraphrase the question
—explain why the information is important to the audience and how it relates to the speech
—make a clear, succinct, preliminary summary of points to be covered
—develop each point with explanation, illustration, analogy, examples, statistics, or other appropriate forms of support
—conclude with a final summary
—ask the questioner if the question has been answered
—call for another question from another part of the room

If the questioner is disputing a point made in the speech, a more persuasive response might be necessary. There are numerous approaches available depending on the friendly or unfriendly relationship between the speaker and the questioner. During any speaker-audience conflict situation, the speaker is generally well advised to keep the exchange on a rational and impersonal basis. When justifying or defending a position made during the speech, the speaker should attempt to establish a position and diminish the impact of the opposing point of view. Basically, the speaker should answer objections in an orderly and systematic manner. Included in the response should be (1) a statement of the questioner's claim; (2) a carefully stated objection to the claim; (3) evidence in the form of examples, statistics, illustration, analogy, or testimony; (4) a clear statement of the significance of the rebuttal.

Respond nonverbally. In chapter 5 we indicated that as much as 93 percent of the impact of a message may be nonverbal. When responding to a questioner, one should be especially sensitive to the use of the voice, touch, gestures, facial expressions, and the control of space and time. Most of us enjoy seeing a speaker smile. The smile tells us the speaker likes us. We also appreciate spontaneity, warmth, and enthusiasm in the vocal delivery.

Occasionally one encounters a hostile audience member. In this case, several nonverbal response techniques are available, including vocal, spatial, and time dominance. When an audience member raises his voice, it is frequently wise for the speaker to reciprocate. When the interrogator stands and leans forward, the speaker may offset the territorial invasion by standing and taking a step forward when possible. If the questioner becomes intimidating, it is generally best for the speaker, to assume that the audience is somewhat embarrassed and will be supportive of the speaker who is firm but reasonably tolerant towards the questioner. During rare, critical situations there are numerous power responses available to the speaker, including moving toward or standing next to the questioner, gently resting a hand on the questioner's shoulder (male to male), refusing to yield to the questioner's interruptions, and demanding to be allowed to answer question one before going to a second or third question hurled in rapid succession by the same questioner. Essentially, we are saying the speaker should be strong and forceful, and yet as gentle and diplomatic as possible. The speaker should welcome feedback from the audience, but not become intimidated or manipulated by a small segment of the audience.

Summary

In this chapter we have considered the major steps in speech preparation: selecting the topic, determining the purpose, considering the audience, organizing, gathering supporting materials, considering language and style, and preparing to handle questions. Once again, we should remember that these elements in the speech are not isolated from the total public-speaking process; they are an integrated part of the dynamic and complex phenomenon of public communication. The speech, the speaker, and the audience exert influences upon each other and upon the total process. The effective public speaker is aware of the fact that all elements interact to affect each other and is therefore concerned with and alert to the many forces involved. Although the speaker is careful to plan as intelligently and accurately as possible, it is important to remain flexible and open to feedback and correction.

In understanding the concepts discussed in this chapter, it may be helpful to observe and identify these phenomena in real public communication situations. Does the speaker use an identifiable pattern for arranging ideas? What is the pattern? Has the speaker selected materials to which the audience responds appropriately? And were the materials appropriate to the purpose? If it was a persuasive speech, did the speaker use a climax or anticlimax order? Where was the strongest argument placed? Was the speaker prepared for audience interaction? As you come to recognize these and other elements in public communication, you can use them in your own speeches.

Questions and Exercises for Review

1. What purposes can public speeches have?
2. Name and explain the six patterns of arrangement discussed in this chapter.
3. When should the strongest argument in a speech be given first among the arguments used in the speech?
4. Name, define, and give an example of at least four kinds of supporting material one might use in a speech.
5. How can a speech be given impact through language and style?
6. How can questions be answered so as to motivate additional questions?

Key Terms and Phrases

general purpose
specific purpose
motivated sequence
chronological pattern
spatial pattern
topical pattern
logical pattern
psychological ordering of arguments
law of primacy
law of recency
climax pattern
anticlimax pattern
transitions
supporting materials
explanations
analogies
figurative analogy
literal analogy
illustrations
factual illustrations
hypothetical illustrations
statistics
testimony
restatement
visual aids
written style
oral style
fielding questions

For Further Reading

Biesecker, Thomas D., and Parson, Donn W. "Characteristics of the Message." In *The Process of Social Influence*. Englewood Cliffs, N.J.: Prentice-Hall, 1972, 271–370.
An excellent review of experiments focusing on the effects of message variables on attitude change.

DeVito, Joseph A. *The Elements of Public Speaking*, 3d ed. New York: Harper & Row Publishers, 1987.
Appendix A includes several general guidelines for asking and answering questions.

Downs, Cal et al. *The Organizational Communicator.* New York: Harper & Row Publishers, 1977.
Provides five guidelines for answering questions.

Festinger, Leon. *A Theory of Cognitive Dissonance.* Evanston, Ill.: Row Peterson, 1957.
The classic presentation of the theory of cognitive consistency.

Fetzer, Ronald, and Vogel, Robert. *Designing Messages.* Chicago: SRA, Inc., 1982.
Concise and useful treatment of message design.

Miller, Edd. "Speech Introductions and Conclusions." *Quarterly Journal of Speech* (April 1946): 181–83.
An old article, but one of the few discussions of types of introductions and conclusions.

Tandberg, Gerilyn. *Research Guide in Speech.* Morristown, N.J.: General Learning Press, 1974.
An excellent overview of available resources and techniques for gathering speech materials.

Notes

1. H. E. Butler, trans., *The Institutio Oratoria of Quintilian* (Harvard University Press, 1950), vol. 3. bk 7: 2–3.

2. Edward Sapir, "The Unconscious Patterning of Behavior in Society," in *Selected Writings of Edward Sapir in Language, Culture, and Personality* (Berkeley, Calif.: University of California Press, 1951), 545.

3. Raymond H. Wheeler and Frank T. Perkins, *Principles of Mental Development* (New York: Thomas Y. Crowell Co., 1932), 292–96.

4. Donald K. Darnell, "The Relation between Sentence Order and Comprehension," *Speech Monographs* 30 (1963): 97–100.

5. See: Edd Miller, "Speech Introductions and Conclusions," *Quarterly Journal of Speech* (April 1946): 181–83; Donald Hayworth, "An Analysis of Speeches in Presidential Campaigns from 1884 to 1929," *Quarterly Journal of Speech* 16 (1930): 35–42; and Howard L. Runion, "An objective Study of the Speech Style of Woodrow Wilson," *Speech Monographs* 3 (1936): 75–94.

6. Miller, "Speech Introductions and Conclusions"; Hayworth, "Speeches in Presidential Campaigns"; and Runion, "Speech Style of Woodrow Wilson."

7. Miller, "Speech Introductions and Conclusions."

8. Douglas Ehninger et al., *Principles and Types of Speech Communication,* 9th ed. (Glenville, Ill.: Scott, Foresman and Company, 1982), 144–66.

9. See, for example, R. Ehrensberger, "An Experimental Study of the Relative Effectiveness of Certain Forms of Emphasis in Public Speaking," *Speech Monographs* 12(1945): 94–111; P. Tannenbaum, "Effect of Serial Position on Recall of Radio News Stories," *Journalism Quarterly* XXXI (1954): 319–23; D. Berlo and H. Gulley, "Some Determinants of the Effect of Oral Communication in Producing Attitude Change and Learning," *Speech Monographs* XXIV (1957): 10–20.

10. Wayne C. Minnick, *The Art of Persuasion* (New York: Houghton Mifflin Co., 1968), 261–62.

11. William D. Brooks and Philip Emmert, "The Effect of Language Usage Congruency Upon Credibility, Attitude Change, and Retention" (Paper delivered at the National Convention of the Speech Association of America, Los Angeles, December 28, 1967); William D. Brooks and Paula J. Adrian, "Language Usage Congruency and Academic Achievement" (ms., the University of Kansas, 1966); and Paula J. Adrian, "A Study of the Relationship Between Language Usage Congruency and Perceived Ethos" (Master's thesis, University of Kansas, 1967).

12. George Orwell, "Politics and the English Language," in *Shooting an Elephant and Other Essays* (New York: Harcourt Brace Jovanovich, 1960).

13. Ronald Fetzer and Robert Vogel, *Designing Messages* (Chicago: SRA, Inc., 1982), 245.

Focus

Finding and Selecting Information

Finding Information

Adapting Information

Checking for Overload

Positioning the Message

Giving Impact to the Speech

Structure

Clarifying Information

Developing Positive Attitudes toward Information

Using Visual Aids

Planning for Questions

Informative Speaking

This chapter treats six topics that are important to effective informational speaking. They are (1) finding and selecting information; (2) adapting information; (3) giving the speech impact; (4) clarifying information; (5) using visual aids; and (6) planning for questions. The theory and principles related to these topics are identified and applied.

If the average reader tried to catch up with one year's output of learned publications in the sciences, it would take about fifty years, reading twenty-four hours a day, seven days a week.[1] Neil Postman and Charles Weingartner illustrate the knowledge and communication explosion as follows:

> Imagine a clock face with 60 minutes on it. Let the clock stand for the time men have had access to writing systems. Our clock would thus represent something like 3,000 years, and each minute on our clock 50 years. On this scale, there were no significant media changes until about nine minutes ago. At that time the printing press came into use in western culture. About three minutes ago, the telegraph, photograph, and locomotive arrived. Two minutes ago: the telephone, rotary press, motion pictures, automobile, airplane, and radio. One minute ago, the talking picture. Television has appeared in the last ten seconds, the computer in the last five, and communication satellites in the last second. The laser beam—perhaps the most potent medium of communication of all—appeared only a fraction of a second ago.
>
> It would be possible to place almost any area of life on our clock face and get roughly the same measurements. For example, in medicine, you would have almost no significant changes until about one minute ago. In fact, until one minute ago, as Jerome Frank has said, almost the whole history of medicine is the history of the placebo effect. About a minute ago, antibiotics arrived. About ten seconds ago, open-heart surgery. In fact, within the past ten seconds there probably have been more changes in medicine than is represented by all the rest of the time on our clock. This is what some people call the "knowledge explosion." It is happening in every field of knowledge susceptible to scientific inquiry.[2]

The knowledge explosion and our highly developed technology make the constant communication of information necessary. In this chapter, we are concerned with informative speaking, one of our most used types of speaking. For most of us, it is and will continue to be our primary type of public speaking. As a college student, you are surrounded by informative speaking and you participate as an informative speaker. In the "world of work" you will have numerous occasions to engage in public communication both as a producer and consumer of messages. Many of these occasions will involve informative speaking, generally identified as "presentational speaking" in the business world. Gerald Goldhaber has outlined a number of such occasions as they occur in organizational settings and categorized them as internal and external activities.[3]

Informational communication is that communication in which new knowledge is accepted by an audience as true or plausible. In Part I of this book, we discussed the individual's communication system. We explained that we come to know our world primarily through our senses. But we also pointed out that we come to know our world through language (verbal and nonverbal). Through language, the symbolic process enables us to learn about the world by means of someone else's sensory experiences. This is essentially what is happening in informative speaking. We acquire knowledge (sometimes factual, sometimes evaluative; sometimes opinions and sometimes feelings), but it is knowledge another has and shares with us.

Table 12.1 Common Public Organizational Communication Activities

Internal Activities	External Activities
Supervisory or department head meetings	Goodwill speeches
Suggestion systems	Commercial speeches and advertising
Organization-wide meetings (boss talks, jobholders' meetings)	Political speeches
Union meetings	Lobbying
Grapevine	Civic and social club presentations
Social functions (picnics, holiday parties, awards banquets, etc.)	Convention and conference presentations
Oral technical reports and presentations	Formal public speech (special occasion)
Training programs	Television and radio interviews
Orientation sessions	Testimony before legislative bodies
Briefing and information sessions	Addresses to stockholders

Part 3 of this text focuses on public communication. We have examined the three major components of public speaking in detail: the speaker, the audience, and the message. Now we will put these three components together in the informative speech situation. Since we have already discussed audience analysis, how the speaker may enhance credibility, and the various elements to be considered in message preparation, we will give our attention in this chapter to six problem areas that relate directly to informative speaking. As we investigate each of these, we will be concerned, of course, with audience analysis, speaker analysis, and message organization. The suggestions we make relative to these six problem areas relate as well to the speaker, the audience, and the message.

Finding and Selecting Information

You cannot give an informative speech unless you have information to give. There is no greater asset for informative speaking than "knowing the subject." But how do you come to "know" a subject?

Finding Information

The sources of information are what you already know (all your experiential history concerning that topic) and what you acquire additionally through reading and talking with others. The first category is the more important. But information stored in your memory is not always readily available. Generating information from your **experiential history** can be aided by applying to your subject a list of topics that can help you recall information or by exploring areas in which you seek information. You could, of course, just "think about the subject" and hope ideas pop into your head; but the use of a set of topics that can be applied to virtually any subject will provide you with a systematic way of recalling information stored in your memory. This technique has been called a Topical System for Generating Thoughts.[4] You may find the following **topical system** helpful in recalling information or discovering areas of new information.

1. What is the *spatial* relationship of this thing?
2. Is the concept of *time* importantly related to this?
3. What is the *form* or shape of this?
4. What is the *substance* of this?
5. What is the *size* or *quantity* of this?
6. Does this move, or what is its *activity*?
7. Does this *change* rapidly? slowly? How does it change?
8. Does this have *power* or *energy*?
9. Can this *harm* or *help* other things?
10. Why is this thing *desirable*?
11. What *causes* this, or does it cause anything?
12. What *correlations* exist between this and other things? What things accompany it; or what things are never found with it?
13. Is this practical or *workable*? Is it feasible?
14. How is this *similar* to other things?
15. How is it *dissimilar* to other things?

Select a topic for an informative speech, and apply the questions on this page in order to discover information you possess on that topic.

It is possible—quite helpful, in fact—to ask these questions about any subject you have selected for a speech. Not all of these questions will apply to every subject, but there will be at least some that apply to the subject you have selected. Thus, if you check through this list of topics, you will systematically discover the areas of your subject in which you have the greatest knowledge and the areas in which you may need to seek information.

Figure 12.1 illustrates the many subjects within one's personal field of experience or awareness. Select one subject and begin asking questions from the topical system. Some questions are obviously more appropriate for some subjects than for others, but you can see how the topic questions can get you started in the right direction.

By gathering more material than you need, from your own knowledge and from other sources, you can select the most interesting illustration, the hardest-hitting statistic or evidence, and the most relevant example. The quality of

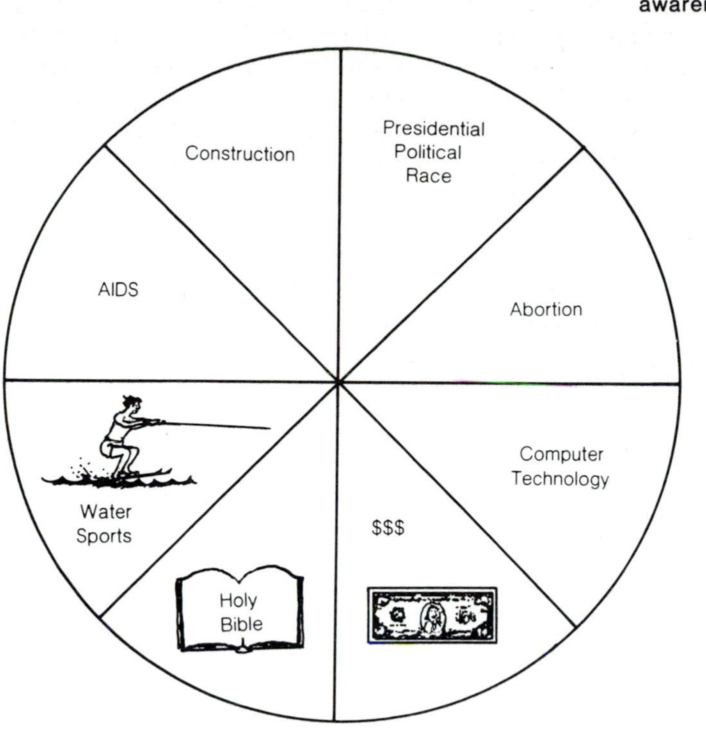

Figure 12.1 Personal field of experience or awareness.

your speech will go up if you have enough material to permit you to be selective; if you have barely enough material, you will have to use all of it. Also, when you get into the speaking situation, you may find that you need more examples or data on a given point. It is a good feeling to have more than enough material instead of running short.

In chapter 10 we provide a rather comprehensive list of indexes and abstracts to assist you in your search for information. At this point we would only caution you regarding two things: (1) the fact that information is in print does not make it fact, and (2) don't let your search for information become an end unto itself. Keep your speech purpose in front of you at all times and collect only that information that is relevant to your speech purpose.

Selecting information. After you have used the topical system to generate as wide a variety of information as possible, your next task is to decide what you will use for your particular speech. Since it is impossible to say everything that can be said on a subject, what few things should be included in your speech? What information will be the most effective? Three guidelines can help you in this selection of material: (1) the audience, (2) the topic itself, and (3) you, the speaker.

The audience is a primary concern when selecting material or information for a speech.

The *audience* is a primary concern when selecting material or information for a speech. We stressed this point in chapter 10 when we considered the audience and again in chapter 11 in our study of the message. The four questions that you must answer in order to select the most enlightening information on a particular subject for a particular audience are

1. What does the audience already *know* about this subject?
2. How interested are they in this subject?
3. What is their attitude toward this subject?
4. Which materials will best build a common ground between the audience's experiences, perceptions, and attitudes and your own?

Consideration of these four questions will permit you to select the most significant information for the audience. You will want to add to their knowledge rather than tell them what they already know; you will want to use material that relates to their interests; and you will want to use material "common to their ground," that is, material relevant to and consistent with their attitudes, values, and experiences.

The topic itself is the second guideline to be used in selecting information. The questions you must ask yourself are (1) Are there aspects of this subject that are so important they must be discussed? (2) Are there aspects of this subject that should not be discussed? and (3) Does this subject lend itself better to certain types of materials than to other types, to visuals better than to statistics, or to examples better than to cause-effect scientific explanation?

The *speaker* is the third concern in selecting material for the speech. Ask yourself: (1) Do I have an extrinsic credibility gap? (2) Will the material I am selecting enhance each of the three components of intrinsic credibility (trustworthiness, expertise, and dynamism)? Although these concerns are essential for successful persuasive communication, they are also critical to your success in "persuading" the audience to listen to your "informative" speech. (3) Have I successfully coped with communication anxiety so that I can present myself and my ideas to my own personal satisfaction?

These three guidelines, that is, the audience, the topic, and the speaker, are important aids in selecting the best information to include in the speech.

Using the topic you selected for applying the questions on page 301, write out answers to the four questions on page 306.

Adapting Information

Checking for Overload

Having generated as much information about your topic as possible and having considered how much of this information to use, you must make sure that you do not overload the audience. Do not present too many main points or too much information in general. Overload confuses, tires, and usually results in the audience "turning off the speaker." The outcome, of course, is that the audience doesn't really gain knowledge; it retains little of the information you present. Verner and Dickinson report:

> In a lecture given by a brilliant scholar with an outstanding topic and a highly competent audience, 10 percent of the audience displayed signs of inattention within fifteen minutes. After eighteen minutes one-third of the audience and 10 percent of the platform guests were fidgeting. At thirty-five minutes everyone was inattentive, at forty-five minutes, trance was more noticeable, then fidgeting; and at forty-seven minutes some were asleep and at least one was reading. A casual check twenty-four hours later revealed that the audience recalled only insignificant details, and these were generally wrong.[5]

I expect all of us have experienced audience situations similar to that described by Verner and Dickinson. Hopefully, *we have experienced it as a member of the audience* rather than as the speaker. Although there can be several reasons for audience inattention and failure to retain information, one reason is communication overload. No speech should have as many as twelve or fifteen main points. Research demonstrates that people can handle only a limited amount of information.[6] Probably few speeches should contain more than three or four main points, and the supporting material in each subpoint should consist of a similar number of items. Educational researchers and scholars often call this process **chunking.** It means that people can process information if it is broken into chunks and these chunks are broken into smaller chunks. Using that principle, the speech should have no more than three or four main points; each main point would be broken into no more than three or four subpoints; and each subpoint would be supported by no more than three or four pieces of sustaining material. There is no magic number, but the objective is to avoid overloading the listener with information. **Information overload** becomes counterproductive because little or nothing is retained by the listener who is bombarded with too much information.

Positioning your Message

Perhaps one word more than any other can be said to have charted the course of advertising during the past decade. That word is "positioning." **Positioning,** according to Al Ries and Jack Trout, authors of *Positioning: The Battle for Your Mind,* "is the first body of thought that comes to grips with the problems of getting heard in our overcommunicated society."[7] Although positioning is central to marketing, selling, and persuading, it is also an essential concept for successful informative communication.

Consider that annually 30,000 books and 10 million tons of newsprint are published. Add to this the fact that 98 percent of all American homes have at least one television (a third have two or more), and that the average American family watches television seven hours and twenty-two minutes a day and you have what might be described as "a traffic jam on the turnpikes of the mind."[8] If you want your audience to listen to the information you have just found, you will have to work at it.

Positioning as we are describing it, starts with a message. But positioning is not what you do to the message, but rather what you do in the minds of your audience. In other words, you must position the message in the minds of the audience. The point is simply this: just because you have three points on your outline doesn't mean they will be attended to or retained in your audience's minds. The listener must say internally, "of all the stimuli demanding my attention right now, this message is the most essential."

Positioning involves five steps: (1) capturing audience attention; (2) creating rapport with the audience; (3) creating topic significance; (4) establishing topic relevance; and (5) making it more important to listen to your speech than to attend to several thousand stimuli available to the listener both internally and externally. Monroe has called this last step "pointing,"[9] By **pointing** he refers to the process of making the listener believe that the message is important and relevant to the listener's well-being. Positioning occurs primarily in the introductory portion of the speech or argument. It involves explaining, illustrating, and using other appropriate forms of support that demonstrate how the informative message about to be presented will personally benefit the listener.

Giving Impact to the Speech

Impact in an informative speech is the result of appropriate structure, clarity of information, and positive attitude on the part of the speaker.

Impact in an informative speech is the result of appropriate structure, clarity of information, and the speaker's positive attitude.

Structure

In chapter 11 we discussed speech structure. One pattern of arrangement, you will recall, is the motivated sequence. We have just covered the steps of the motivated sequence under positioning. The satisfaction step of the motivated sequence represents the body of the speech and essentially involves three parts: presummarizing, detailed information, and a final summary.

Presummarizing, sometimes called **proactive emphasis** or message forecasting, occurs after you have captured the audience's attention, created rapport, established topic significance, and positioned the speech as essential information for the listener. Presummarizing is telling the audience specifically what two, three, or four points you will cover in the informative speech. If you were discussing your communication department, you might presummarize by saying: "In the few minutes we have together, I will discuss the three divisions of our communication department: telecommunications, organizational communication, and drama."

After forecasting the points to be discussed, you would then begin the *detailed development*—sometimes called **coactive emphasis**—by repeating the first point, telecommunications, and develop the point with necessary subpoints and forms of support. For example, you might choose to discuss the telecommunications faculty, curriculum, and facilities. Once the telecommunications point was developed, you would move to organizational communication and finally to drama. After discussing each of the three divisions of the body of the speech, you would (following the motivated sequence) give a final summary or repetition of the main points discussed.

The *final summary,* sometimes referred to as **reactive emphasis,** is ordinary repetition, except that you should try to be creative enough to take it out of the ordinary.

Pointing to an important idea adds emphasis.

Proactive emphasis includes previewing, presummarizing, highlighting, and forecasting message components you want the audience to remember. These techniques help the listener to rehearse ideas, and rehearsal of ideas is related to retention of information. One study found that 86 percent of listeners retained a piece of information when it was preceded by "Now get this," but only 53 percent retained it when no proactive statement was made.[10]

It should be pointed out that proactive emphasis can be "stated," that is, communicated, nonverbally as well as verbally. One can pause, use vocal force or inflection, use a gesture, or vary one's behavior by other nonverbal means to "point to" or "highlight" what is to come.[11]

Coactive emphasis includes transitions, direct statements relating the idea to other ideas in the speech, statements showing relationships, and statements relating the idea to other ideas with which the listener is familiar. All of these techniques result in the idea being "rehearsed" and given significance rather than standing alone in a "one-shot pass" through the mind.

Clarifying Information

The next concern in presenting the informational speech is clarity. Clarity is the prime objective in informational speaking. Our goals are understanding and new knowledge—not change of attitude or persuasion.

Clarity is an interesting quality. Whereas ambiguity, bias, and distortion frequently find their way into persuasive speeches, clarity is an integral part of the message when the speaker's purpose is to inform. Perhaps one key to clarification is the adoption of the now well-known KISS principle:

Keep
It
Simple
Stupid

Again, as with recalling information and selecting information to be used, there are guidelines that can help in achieving clarity in informational speaking:

1. Point to the actual object (demonstrate).
2. Use analogy (compare to something the listener understands).
3. Refer to quantity (use statistics).
4. Visualize (create a mental picture).
5. Contrast.
6. Define.
7. Illustrate by examples (real or hypothetical).
8. Be specific rather than general.
9. Be concrete rather than abstract.

Good visuals can also clarify. And they appeal to our affective responses. When the verbal message is accompanied by a congruent or supportive visual message, several effects are usually achieved. Clarity is enhanced; impact is increased; emotional and attitudinal orientations are motivated; and persuasiveness is often improved. The strong effects of using more than one medium to send a message are well documented by research. For example, Linkugel and Berg state:

> Studies conducted at Atlanta show that when knowledge was imparted to a person by telling alone, the recall three hours later was 70 percent, and three days later, only 10 percent. When imparted by showing alone, the knowledge recall three hours later was 72 percent, and three days later, about 35 percent. A marked improvement. But does this mean that we should stop speaking and just show pictures? Obviously no. When both telling and showing were the teaching tools. . . .The recall three hours later was 85 percent, and three days later, 65 percent. This should emphasize that recall increases markedly by using both speech and pictures.[12]

Seiler reported from his experimental study:

> The results of the statistical testing indicated that attitude change and the rating of the speaker's credibility were significantly greater when visuals were used than when visuals were not.[13]

Other researchers have found the same relationships between the use of visual aids with verbal messages and retention. In fact, the evidence is strong not only in regard to retention and credibility but also in regard to comprehension, communicativeness, attention, reduction of speaker anxiety, message clarity, and attitude change.[14] Clearly, the use of visual aids can have a desirable affect on the communication of information. For that reason, we will discuss how to use visual aids toward the end of this chapter.

Developing Positive Attitudes toward Information

Exhibit positive attitudes toward your information. An audience is imitative. In fact, we all are imitative of one another. We have observed this reciprocity phenomenon in other chapters, and we have observed it especially in its relation to affective behavior. This same principle is of concern at this point as it relates to giving impact to information. If a speaker exhibits certain attitudes toward the information presented to an audience, then the audience is motivated to have similar attitudes toward that information. We know that the attitudes we have toward information—how important we think it is, how exciting it is to us, how relevant it is, and so forth—have a great deal to do with how we perceive information, process it, and remember it. Therefore, if you reveal positive attitudes toward your information—if you as a speaker exhibit enthusiasm toward your material, if you are intimately involved with it and if you view the information as important—the audience will be motivated to have similar attitudes; and those attitudes give impact to the information and increase the probability that it will be retained by the audience. If the speaker is excited by the information the excitement may become contagious and the audience get excited too. It is possible to overdo it, of course, and a word of caution is in order. One's own attitudes and orientation toward the information must be genuine. Don't try to fool your audience! You must remember that the audience and its response is your primary concern rather than your own involvement with the topic. Stated another way, do not allow your involvement with the information to overrun or entirely mask out your concern with the audience. It is possible for one to become so engrossed in the information itself that the audience is ignored entirely. Don't let that happen! Let your orientation toward the material be revealed to the audience as you communicate *with the audience.*

Before leaving this first principle of how to give impact to information, we need to note that the converse is also true—that is, when a speaker cares little about the speech, exhibits no excitement, enthusiasm, nor commitment to the information delivered, then the audience is likely to feel the same way. If the speaker doesn't care, why should the audience care?

Using Visual Aids

Anything that appeals to the visual sense is a **visual aid.** The most frequently used visual aids are (1) objects, (2) models, (3) chalk or grease boards, (4) pictures or charts, (5) slides and overhead or opaque projections, and (6) videotape or motion picture films.

Objects. The authors have seen objects ranging from alarm clocks to caskets used as visual aids. The most common informative speech in which objects are used as visual aids is the demonstration speech. Since objects used as visual aids are usually small, many persons in a large audience are not able to see them well. Therefore it is better to use objects as visual aids when the audience is small and located near the speaker. In fact, most demonstrations are given to a small audience, often to no more than a half-dozen or dozen persons.

Models. When the object itself is too large to bring into a room and use in a speech, when the object is too complex to illustrate the principle being discussed, when one wants to explain an abstract process by adding the visualization of it, or when one wants to support and amplify the verbal message, models are the most appropriate visual aid to use. Models include such things as a model car, a model engine, or a model building. Therefore these models are subject to the same problems as objects, that is, it may be difficult for them to be seen by members of a large audience in an auditorium. Models should probably be used for only small audiences, such as a normal classroom.

Chalk or grease board. One of the easiest visual aids to use is a chalkboard. One can be found in almost every classroom. Convention centers and hotels have them available for small meeting rooms. And a large number of

The most common informative speech in which objects are used as visual aids is the demonstration speech.

conference rooms in business and industrial buildings are equipped with portable chalkboards. The chalkboard can be a highly effective visual aid, but it can also be easily misused. A common error is to write too much on the chalkboard—to write one's speech as it is given. Also, one can write so illegibly that it works against communication rather than for it. It becomes "noise." A third common problem is that some persons face squarely into the board and talk into it as they write or draw. The audience sees only the back of the speaker's head and hears only the faint echo off the chalkboard. A final weakness in the use of a chalkboard is the temptation to use it in an impromptu manner. As with impromptu speaking, control and effectiveness are usually lost. Visual aids ought to be as carefully planned and purposefully used as the verbal message. Here are some guidelines to consider in using the chalkboard: (1) Put the material on the board before beginning the speech, if possible. (2) Write or draw on the board for only a few seconds at a time. (3) Either face part of the audience as you draw, or draw for a couple of seconds and *then speak as you face the audience.*

Pictures, drawings, or charts. These constitute the most widely used type of visual aid. They are inexpensive, easily obtained, and easily meshed with the verbal message. Little wonder these visual aids are so effective. Pictures should be big enough to be seen. Drawings should be in bold, clear lines. In fact, "line drawings" executed with clear, bold lines are often better as visual aids than realistic drawings of the person, building, or other item. Lettering and drawings should be large, and contrast should be used (black on white, or if you use colors, don't use light green on medium green, for example). Charts include bar graphs, pie graphs, maps, organization charts, and various other "organizing" charts that show relationships, linear or chronological steps or sequences, and chains of command. The important points to keep in mind about using charts is to keep them simple, clear, and attractive—and to remember that *charts always need to be interpreted.* They don't speak for themselves as well as pictures, models, or real objects do.

Slides, projections, and computer graphs. The slide presentation has almost taken over as *the* visual aid in informative or presentational speaking in the business-industrial conference setting. Slides or projections are also commonly used for travel talks and in professional conventions. They are especially valuable because they usually can be seen easily and they facilitate explanation and focusing—that is, they are good "attention-getters." The major drawback to their use has been their preparation. Not everyone is expert at making slides or transparencies, although the skill can be easily acquired if one takes the time to do so. Slide photographs are easily available, of course, and some organizations (universities, schools, and businesses) have specialists who provide such services for speakers.

The overhead projector is also popular because it can be used in a room that does not need to be darkened, and the speaker can easily write, draw, or point during the talk.

Graphics software has recently changed the world of visual aids for the public speaker, especially in the business and professional arena. The quotation below describes the cover story in a recent *PC Magazine.*

> . . . as with everything they touch, PCs and software have changed the way you can produce graphics. While you once might have spent hours cutting and pasting charts together or relied on production houses or art departments to create the graphics for those charts, you can now use graphic software to produce charts yourself, saving hours and dollars in the process.[15]

Graphics computer software makes it possible for those with access to PCs to design transparencies and slides quickly and tastefully. For many of us transparencies have a special appeal. Prepared properly, they can be used in a wide range of circumstances. Available software makes it possible to create text of varied sizes, charts, graphs, banners, and other items with amazing ease.

Where greater visual sophistication and message impact is preferred, the speaker will want to consider transferring graphics from the computer disk or from floppy disks to slides. Probably the highest quality and most professional output will be achieved by using 35mm color slides. These slides are capable of producing high-resolution, crisp, colorful images.

In addition to transferring graphics to slides and transparencies, graphics can be transferred directly from the computer screen. Some student speakers may also want to investigate the use of visuals through the interaction of the compact disk and video tape.

A recent study conducted by 3M Corporation and the University of Minnesota found slide shows to be perceived as the most professional form of presentation.[16]

Films and videotapes. Films and videotapes are probably used more in instructional settings than in other informational speaking situations. This is also true of the videotape recorder. These particular visual aids are unlike the other visual aids we have discussed because they dominate the speaker. The speaker says a few words and starts the film. From then until it is stopped, the film takes over. This does not make films ineffective. Rather, they can be most effective, but they dominate the speaker entirely and are consequently outside the scope of our interest in the informational speech.

As a summary of our consideration of visual aids, the following guidelines should help you to make the most effective use of visual aids: (1) show the visual aid *only* when you're talking about the point it demonstrates; (2) keep your attention primarily on the audience; (3) explain and make effective use of visual aids; (4) be sure the visual aid can be seen; and (5) keep visual aids clear, neat, and attractive.

Planning for Questions

Recall that in chapter 11 we emphasized the use of a question-answer session to further your specific speech purpose, promote audience involvement, and clarify information. Since your purpose is to inform, you should take time now to determine what areas of your speech will most likely generate questions and prepare yourself to handle those questions competently. You should also review, at this point, several specific techniques for generating questions from the audience as well as appropriate response techniques.

Summary

In this chapter we have considered six major topics that are directly related to informational communication. We have suggested using a list of topics—topics that apply to almost any subject—as a means of systematically generating and selecting information with the audience, topic, and yourself as speaker in mind. Adapting information to account for message overload and message position was our second concern. Thirdly, we looked at three methods of giving your speech impact: structure, clarification, and positive attitudes toward information. Fourthly, we discussed how to achieve clarity and how to use visual aids. Finally, we reiterated the importance of careful planning for questions from your audience.

Questions and Exercises for Review

1. What is the *knowledge explosion?*
2. What is the *Topical System for Generating Thoughts?*
3. Information must be selected and adapted to the ___, ___, and ___.
4. What is information overload and how does it affect the listener?
5. List at least five techniques for giving clarity to information.
6. Ideas on information can be given impact by applying what two principles?
7. Name three ways one can emphasize an idea.
8. What is the advantage in using visual aids in informative speaking?
9. How does the motivated sequence adapt to the informative speech?
10. What can the speaker do to assure himself of herself of spontaneous and quality questions?
11. Name some direct and some indirect methods of complimenting the questioner.

Key Terms and Phrases

experiential history
topical system
chunking
information overload
positioning
pointing
presummarizing
proactive emphasis
coactive emphasis
reactive emphasis
visual aid

For Further Reading

Donce, Frank E.X. "What Do You Mean Presentational Speaking."*Management Communication Quarterly* 2 (1987): 260–72.
A commentary on the similarities and differences between public speaking and presentational speaking.

Miller, G. A. "The Magical Number Seven, Plus or Minus Two: Some Limits on Our Capacity for Processing Information." *Psychological Review* 63 (1956): 81–97.
A summary of the research on "chunking" and the difficulty of handling improperly organized information.

Nelson, W. "Topoi: Functional in Human Recall." *Speech Monographs* 38 (1970): 121–26.
An application of the classical use of Topoi (a topic list) to information recall.

Tacey, William S. *Business and Professional Speaking,* 4th ed. Dubuque: Wm. C. Brown Publishers, 1983.
An excellent book for adapting informational speaking to the business or professional selling.

Notes

1. Louis Martin, "Science Is Polluted by Printed Words . . . Billions," *Chicago Tribune,* 7, June 1970.

2. Neil Postman and Charles Weingartner, *Teaching As a Subversive Activity* (New York: Delacorte Press, 1969), 10.

3. Gerald Goldhaber, *Organizational Communication,* 4th ed. (Dubuque: Wm. C. Brown Publishers, 1986), 325.

4. See, for example, John F. Wilson and Carroll A. Arnold, *Public Speaking as a Liberal Art,* 2d ed. (Boston: Allyn & Bacon, 1968), 115; and R. P. Hart, G. W. Friedrich, and W. D. Brooks, *Public Communication* (New York: Harper & Row, 1975), 184.

5. C. Verner and G. Dickinson, "The Lecture: An Analysis and Review of Research," *Adult Education* 17 (1967): 90

6. See, for example, G. A. Miller, "The Magical Number Seven, Plus or Minus Two: Some Limits on Our Capacity for Processing Information," *Psychological Review* 63 (1956): 81–97; and G. Mandler, "Organization and Memory," in K. W. Spence and J. T. Spence, eds., *The Psychology of Learning and Motivation,* vol. 1. (New York: Academic Press, 1967).

7. Al Ries and Jack Trout, *Positioning: The Battle for Your Mind* (New York: McGraw-Hill Book Company, 1981).

8. Ries and Trout, *Positioning.*

9. Douglas Ehninger et al., *Principles and Types of Speech Communication.* 9th ed. (Glenview, Ill.: Scott, Foresman and Company, 1982), 156.

10. R. Ehrensberger, "An Experimental Study of the Relative Effects of Certain Forms of Emphasis in Public Speaking," *Speech Monographs* 12 (1945): 94–111.

11. Roger Wilcox, *Oral Reporting in Business and Industry* (Englewood Cliffs, N.J.: Prentice-Hall, 1967), 110–11.

12. W. Linkugel and D. Berg, *A Time to Speak* (Belmont, Calif.: Wadsworth, 1970) 68–69.

13. W. Seiler, "The Effects of Visual Materials on Attitude Change, Credibility, and Retention in a Persuasive Message Presented on Video Tape" (Ph.D. diss., Purdue University, 1971), 54.

14. See, for example, C. F. Hoban and E. B. Van Ormer, *Institutional Film Research* (University Park: Pennsylvania State University, 1950); G. L. Gropper, "Learning from Visuals: Some Behavioral Considerations," *AV Communication Review* XI (Summer 1963): 75–95; R. M. V. Travers, *Research and Theory Related to Audio-Visual Information Transmission* (U.S. Department of Health, Education, and Welfare, Office of Education, 1964); and W. Severin, "The Effectiveness of Relevant Pictures in Multiple-Channel Communication," *AV Communication Review* XV (Winter 1967): 386–401.

15. Cheryl J. Goldberg and Gerard Kunkel, "Charting a Course through Graphics Software," *PC Magazine* (1987): 113.

16. Robin Raskin, "Producing Quality Output: When Only the Best Will Do," *PC Magazine* (1987): 289.

Focus

A Code of Ethics

Reasoning: The Starting Point of Persuasion

Deductive Reasoning

Inductive Reasoning

Toulmin's Inferential Pattern of Reasoning

Basic Underlying Premises of Persuasion

Erosion and Deterioration—Entropy

Change Is Threatening

Attitudes, Beliefs, and Values Vary in Strength

Reinforcing Attitudes Versus Changing Attitudes

Psychological Orientations and Information-Processing Habits

Psychological Factors in the Persuasive Speech

Cognitive Consistency and Cognitive Dissonance

Maslow's Hierarchy of Needs

Ego-Involvement

Specific Emotional Appeals

Persuasive Speeches to Reinforce or Actuate

Strategies for Increasing Social Cohesion

Strategies for Intensifying Values or Beliefs

Strategies for Increasing Resistance to Persuasion

Build Self-Esteem

Bolster the Belief Structure—Anchoring

Inoculate

Persuasive Speeches to Reverse Attitudes or Behavior

The Common Premise Strategy

The De-Anchoring Strategy

Persuasive Speaking

In this chapter, a code of ethics is introduced. This code of ethics outlines a set of general principles appropriate for a range of communication situations. Three reasoning patterns of importance to persuasive speaking are discussed. In addition, five premises about persuasion are identified. These premises are the guidelines used to create strategies for persuading specific audiences on specific topics. Much of the experimental research in persuasion has grown out of these five premises.

Psychological factors, including cognitive consistency, personal needs, ego-involvement, and emotional appeals, are discussed.

Finally, this chapter focuses on two types of persuasive speeches—the speech to reinforce attitudes or beliefs, and the speech to change attitudes or beliefs. Different strategies are presented for each type.

Our ability to achieve our goals depends to a great extent on our ability to interact with others in such a way as to cause them to cooperate with us. None of us can exist—let alone achieve our goals and fulfill our needs—without others. Therefore a portion of our communication is concerned with attempts to influence or persuade others. One way we do this is in face-to-face public communication situations. So extensive is our society's use of persuasion that we would be remiss if we did not give it special consideration in our study of public communication. As a receiver, each of us engages daily in persuasive communication. If we are to be better "consumers" of persuasion, we need to understand it clearly. And, of course, most college-educated persons, by virtue of the level of position college graduates hold, frequently find themselves initiators of persuasive communication. There is no escaping persuasion. We are each involved in it. Occasionally, someone raises a question about the role of persuasion in society. Some have said that any attempt to influence another (that is, to persuade another) is unethical and dehumanizing. Our position on this question is stated as follows:

> . . . no matter how "evil" these terms may sound, we as people in a complex society have little choice but to understand persuasion, and to use it effectively. For every persuader of the ilk of George Lincoln Rockwell or Adolf Hitler, there are mass mobilizers like Mahatma Ghandi and Jesus Christ. . . . It is our very simple-minded belief that if you do not choose to influence, if the word *strategy* gets stuck in your throat as you attempt to utter it, or if you believe that human beings are capable of *not* influencing one another (either intentionally or unintentionally), you should retreat from human society. To forsake persuasion and the techniques for making it effective might be to forsake some of your deep-seated beliefs and to insure that the world will progress (or regress) without the benefits of *your* views, *your* concerns, and *your* ideas.[1]

We are in the midst of influences. We are dependent upon influencing and being influenced. *Mutual influencing is the work of society.*

Whether we are persuading or being persuaded, we are dealing with efforts to change persons. One does not attempt to persuade someone to believe something strongly or to behave in some way when that person already believes it or already behaves in that way. Persuasion is the attempt to *change* another, that is, to change an attitude, a belief, or a behavior.

The goal of persuasion ranges along a continuum from a very slight change to a radical change—one of reversal or complete turnaround in attitude or behavior. Sometimes the persuader seeks a change as slight as simply *strengthening an attitude or belief.* Sometimes the persuader wants to *activate a belief,* that is, to influence listeners to put their already existing belief into action. And sometimes the goal is to reverse a belief or behavior. We are going to investigate those types of persuasive efforts in this chapter; but first we will consider some basic premises about persuasion, persuaders, and persuadees.

We have already investigated the major variables that relate to the speaker, message, and audience in chapters 9, 10, and 11. Now we are going to apply those variables in combination with the persuasive speaking situation. We will be looking at several variables more deeply than we did in those three chapters. Sometimes we will be looking at phenomena from different perspectives. Our focus is on the total process of persuasion. We will consider six broad topics: (1) a code of ethics; (2) reasoning: the starting point of persuasion; (3) basic underlying premises of persuasion; (4) psychological factors in the persuasive speech; (5) persuasion to reinforce or actuate; and (6) persuasion to reverse attitudes or behavior.

A Code of Ethics

Prior to accepting our role as persuasive communicators in today's complex society, it is essential that we confront the issue of "ethical responsibility." The centrality of ethics to the study of communication was demonstrated in 1982 when the Speech Communication Association selected "Communication, Ethics, and Values" as the theme for its convention. Frank Dance's presidential address that year focused on ethics and was titled "This Above All."[2] The following year Kenneth Andersen, in his presidential address to the same organization, proposed "A Code of Ethics for Speech Communication." The goal of his address was to set forth a series of ethical standards, a set of moral articles, which, when taken together, would constitute an ethical guide for individuals as they communicate.[3] Andersen's tenets in a generalized, hierarchical order starting with the most basic are abbreviated as follows:

Article one: Accept a proper burden of responsibility for the communication activity in whatever position you find yourself in a particular interaction.
Article two: Act so that the potential effectiveness of all future communication is enhanced.
Article three: Act to maximize individual freedom of choice and responsibility while enhancing the quality of the society as a whole.
Article four: Act so that the respect of each participant for self and for the other is maximized.
Article five: Act to improve communication ability and understanding.
Article six: Enforce the code upon self and upon all others.[4]

While these articles do not provide a set of specific injunctions capable of guaranteeing absolute rights and wrongs for every situation, they do outline a set of general principles to draw upon as we face specific communication situations. Two specific strengths of Andersen's code include making ethics (1) the responsibility of both the sender and receiver, and (2) applicable to every context or level of human communication.

Table 13.1 Propaganda Devices

1.	Name Calling	5.	Plain Folk
2.	Glittering Generalities	6.	Card Stacking
3.	Transfer	7.	Bandwagon
4.	Testimony		

Ethical communication has been a central issue for propagators of persuasive messages in politics, preaching, advertising, management, and yes even science, for years. So powerful are the means of persuasion, observes Wayne Minnick, that "in the hands of evil, heedless, or ignorant men, they may be used to induce an audience to act in ways that are unwise or unjust."[5] If Minnick is correct, then to engage in persuasive communication bears an awesome responsibility. Minnick would question whether all of the "available means of persuasion are fit for decent men to use."[6]

Communicators engaged in persuasion have traditionally adopted one of two views concerning ethics: they have judged ethics in terms of the end sought by the persuader, or they have judged persuasion according to the means used by the persuader. Unfortunately, life "in the fast lane" makes it difficult to judge the ethics of every communication in every situation by these views. In an attempt to identify questionable propaganda techniques, the Institute for Propaganda Analysis published seven allegedly spurious modes of persuasion which it identified as "propaganda devices."[7] The implication was that these devices (see table 13.1), which frequently make us believe and do what we would not believe or do under less passionate circumstances, should not be used by an ethical communicator.

Careful examination would indicate that several of the propaganda devices are common to our everyday diet of persuasive appeals. Minnick suggests that Name Calling occurs even in church where attendees are labeled saint or sinner.[8] Is it wrong, some would ask, to recognize men as "men of peace" or "men of war"? Should we label political, business, and religious leaders who engage in cheating, lying, and graft?

After careful examination of the ethics issue, Minnick concludes that an advocate must be careful to ensure that all use of discourse is highly ethical. To accomplish this noble feat, he suggests the following guidelines.

> First, he must reject out of hand all frauds, deceptions, concealments, and specious arguments—modes of persuasion that are intrinsically unsound. Second, he must cultivate the capacity for careful investigation and judicial investigation and judicial and reflective deliberation of controversies and problems. He must endorse only those positions whose truth claim merits his advocacy. He must use methods that are intrinsically sound as a criterion of his own choices. Finally, having assured himself as well as he can of the soundness of his position, he may use ethically neutral methods (suggestion, emotional excitation, and the like) in ways which are consistent with and can be defended by reliable evidence and sound reasoning.[9]

Reasoning: The Starting Point of Persuasion

The first step in preparing a persuasive message involves the process of reasoning. Reasoning, the foundation of advocacy, is the process of moving from data or evidence to a conclusion. There are several ways in which we reason, but we will be concerned with the three most common patterns: deductive reasoning, inductive reasoning, and Toulmin's pattern of reasoning.

Deductive Reasoning

Imagine that while conversing with a new student, named Matt, you express the rather common perception that "Plutonians are rednecks." To your amazement, the student becomes irate—almost violent—and reports to you that he is Plutonian and proud of it. Each of us has no doubt experienced either the personal embarrassment or irate response suggested in this interaction. There are relationships between conclusions and supporting premises, and when we encode messages, we must be careful that we really intend the implications contained in our statements. Similarly, when we decode messages we need to be aware of the logical implications in the message. In other words, we must check the validity of the reasoning. Reasoning is concerned with the connections and relationships between and among ideas. It is concerned with the movement from fact to fact, from fact to inference, and from inference to conclusion.

Deductive reasoning is sometimes studied in terms of Aristotle's categories of syllogism and enthymeme, two terms which describe so much of the processes of reasoning and persuasion. The **syllogism** is a formal pattern of reasoning used to apply a generalization to a specific case. The **enthymeme** is a truncated rhetorical adaptation of the syllogism, a rhetorical syllogism. Let's take a moment to discuss and illustrate each of them. When the example about Plutonians is outlined in its full form, as in table 13.2, it is a syllogism. In truncated form, as in table 13.3, the syllogism becomes an enthymeme. In the syllogism, the Major Premise states the generalization, "All Plutonians are rednecks." The Minor Premise relates a special case or class to the generalization: "Matt is a Plutonian." From the two premises, the conclusion follows: "Therefore Matt is a redneck."

In the enthymeme no major premise is given, but an implied premise dictates the conclusion regarding Matt. The same is true for the appropriateness of Pluto to serve specific roles in society, for example, club treasurer. Whereas the syllogism is generally associated with "universals," the enthymeme, or "rhetorical" syllogism is satisfied to let its proof be understood. Where the syllogism will draw its conclusion from a Major Premise (or universal application) and a Minor Premise (or specific application), the enthymeme might draw its conclusion from general opinions, stereotypes, or even prejudices. The enthymeme, or "partial syllogism," is based less on certainty and more on "probability." Aristotle explains that the "brevity of the enthymeme makes it easier to follow than the full syllogistic statement and hence better adapted to popular argument."[10]

Table 13.2 Examples of categorical syllogisms

Major Premise	Minor Premise	Conclusion
All Plutonians are rednecks.	Matt is a Plutonian.	Matt is a redneck.
All dogs have four legs.	Borke is a Dog.	Borke has four legs.
Ex-cons are untrustworthy.	Pluto is an ex-con.	Pluto is untrustworthy.
All men are mortal.	Socrates is a man.	Socrates is mortal.

Table 13.3 Examples of Enthymemes

"Once a Plutonian redneck, always a Plutonian redneck."
"Socrates must share the inevitable fate of all men."
"Atlanta is not a virgin, because she strolls through the woods with young men."
Hermagoras
"Since abortions involve willful destruction of life, it's my position that physicians should not perform them."

You will seldom hear a formal syllogism in either interpersonal communication or in public speeches; they are found more often in debate and logic textbooks. Rather, in interpersonal communication and in public communication, the syllogism usually appears in the form of the enthymeme—a telescoped or abbreviated syllogism. But it is possible to construct the syllogism that is implied in a particular enthymeme. The premise in a deductive line of reasoning is often omitted because the listeners are familiar with the implied premise and can easily supply it mentally. Persuaders generally capitalize on unstated premises. In everyday persuasion, communicators frequently appeal to unquestioned authorities, imply stereotypes, and employ cultural truisms. The informal nature of the enthymeme allows communicators to take verbal and pictorial shortcuts.

Inductive Reasoning

In **inductive reasoning,** as with deductive reasoning, we are attempting to reach a conclusion. However, we approach it from a direction opposite that used in deductive reasoning. Rather than moving from a general statement to a particular case as we do in deductive reasoning, we move from particular cases to the generalization.

In inductive reasoning, one moves from specific items of information (evidence) to a logical conclusion (generalization). For example, if the cost of diamonds has increased at the rate of 5 percent per year for the past ten years, there is reason to conclude that the cost of diamonds next year will probably be 5 percent higher than they are this year. Deductive reasoning is concerned with the "inevitability" of conclusions, but inductive reasoning is concerned

Figure 13.1 Thinking processes involved in logical argument, based on Toulmin's inferential pattern of reasoning.

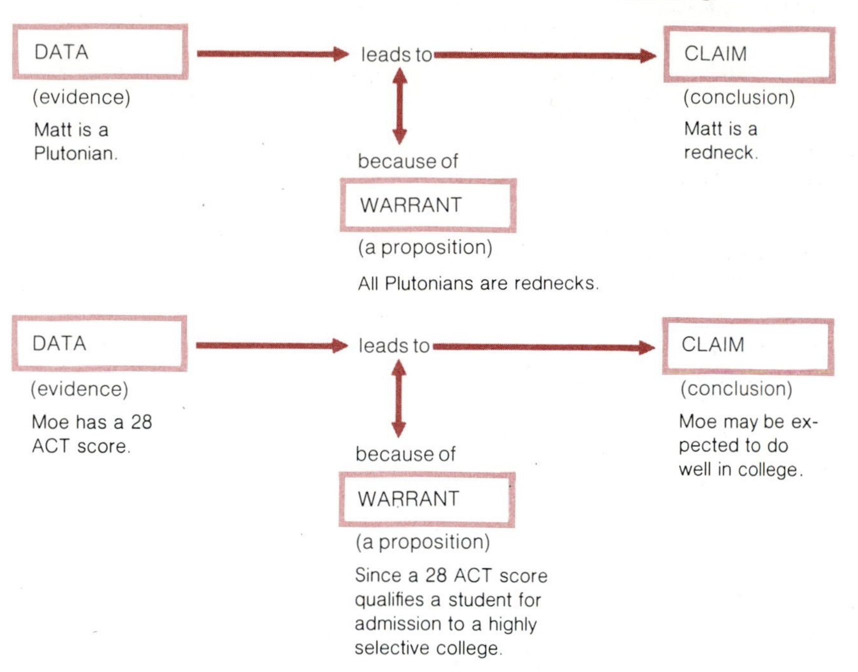

with the "probability" and "reliability" of conclusions. Deductive reasoning tends to be more absolute, while inductive reasoning allows for relative conclusions, that is, for *probably true* conclusions.

Toulmin's Inferential Pattern of Reasoning

A third pattern of reasoning is **Toulmin's inferential pattern.** Stephen Toulmin, a British mathematician, says that we infer from data to a claim through the use of a warrant. By **data,** he means evidence such as examples and instances; by **claim,** he means conclusion; and by **warrant,** he means a general proposition.

Toulmin illustrates well the dynamics of the thinking processes involved in logical argument.[11] According to Toulmin, argument grows out of information (data) leading to an inference or conclusion (claim), but between the two is a process of thought that permits the claim to follow from that data. That step he calls the warrant. The warrant is a bridge-like statement spelling out the legitimacy of moving from data to claim. Toulmin's view takes into account the role of the receiver when encountering a so-called logical argument from a sender. As figure 13.1 illustrates, the claim that the sender wants the receiver to accept grows out of data and is made acceptable by each warrant.

Figure 13.2 Examples of Toulmin's inferential pattern of reasoning.

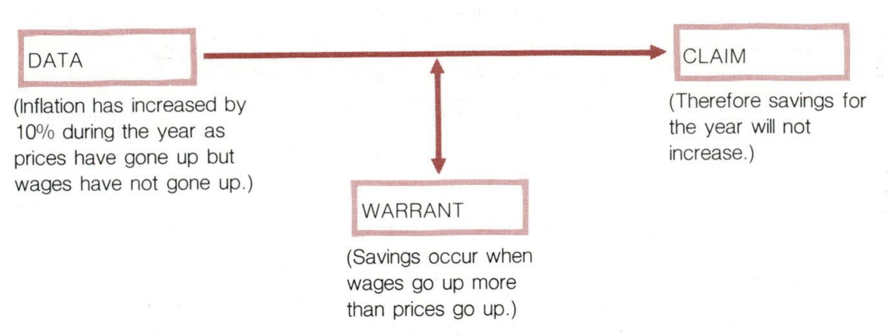

By using the same examples employed earlier, it is apparent that the premises and conclusions are outlined differently, but the elements are still present. The premises may be stated or simply implied. Whether stated or not, however, it is important for both the message sender and message receiver to have a clear understanding of each component of the persuasive message.

When one believes the data and accepts the reasoning process as valid, the claim is warranted. The warrant is the statement that identifies precisely how and why the claim is appropriate. As can be noted from the example in figure 13.2 the warrant does not stand on the "main proof line," that is, from data to claim. It may seem incidental to the argument, but it is quite important to the receiver because it establishes the legitimacy of the claim and thus provides a psychological linking of data and claim.

Toulmin adds even more to the process. He points out that the general proposition, or warrant, may be given support (called **backing**) to strengthen the likelihood of the claim's being warranted and, consequently, accepted. Materials that constitute the backing component are less direct, as evidence, than are the materials (evidence) that make up the data on the main proof line. Backing consists of materials that are limited to enhancing the acceptability of the warrant. When the warrant is accepted at face value, no backing is necessary. When the warrant is weak or questionable, however, backing (warrant support) is essential. Even with the backing for the warrant, it's still possible that you or I would not yet accept the claim. We might think the conclusion was too all-encompassing—too rigid and absolute.

Even with the best of warrants, regardless of their backing, one may be aware of "exceptions to the case." This introduces Toulmin's fifth component, **reservation.** The reservation component, sometimes called *rebuttal,* identifies exceptions to the warrant. Frequently, special conditions or circumstances relevant to the claim will affect the force of either the warrant or the claim. When one says that a specific act will occur "unless. . . .," one is getting ready to

Figure 13.3 Complex example of Toulmin's inferential pattern of reasoning.

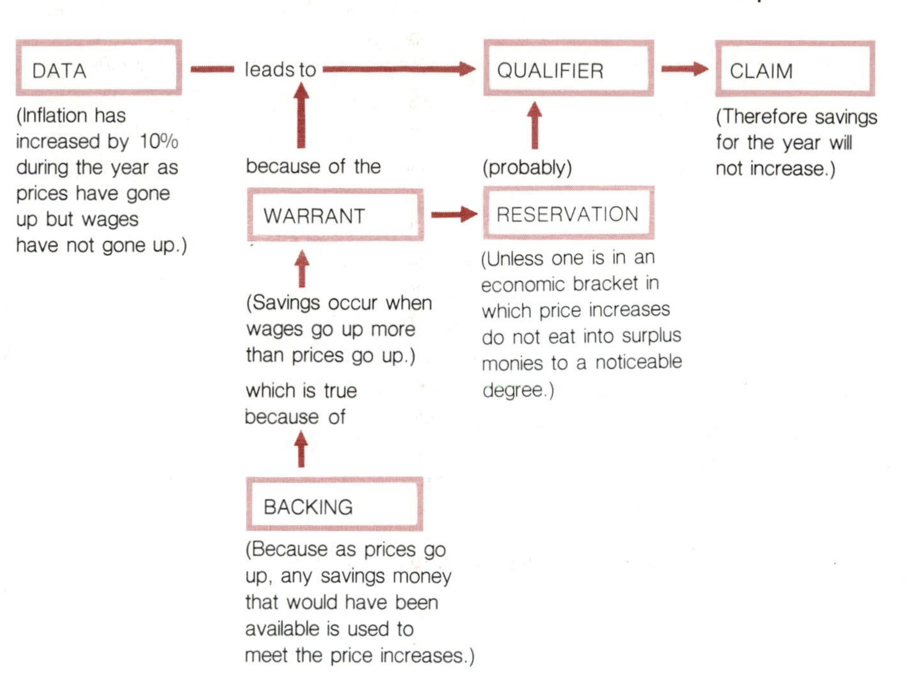

state the reservation portion of the Toulmin unit of proof. Ehninger and Brockriede have identified three kinds of reservations applicable to certain types of proof:

> (a) An intervening or counteracting cause may completely or partially block the main proof line. (b) Special circumstances in the factual context surrounding the specific relationship between evidence and claim may not conform to the general relationship expressed in the warrant. (c) Counterproofs may have greater validity or force than the proof under consideration.[12]

The final component of the Toulmin unit of proof is the **qualifier.** Qualifiers allow for the validity of the conclusion. It is important any time either the data or the warrant is to any extent less than certain. Qualifiers are worded in many ways: possibly, probably, at the .05 level of confidence, almost certainly, my educated guess is, and there is a 30 percent chance of rain. The diagram in figure 13.2 reflects these additions to the line of reasoning.

In figure 13.3, Toulmin's warrant represents a premise already accepted. If, however, more explanation or evidence is needed to understand and accept the premise, then support is there. The support data are specific statistics falling within the warrant and relating to it so that the conclusion ("savings will not increase this year") is acceptable. In order that the conclusion not be too absolute, a qualifier is added—that is, "*probably* savings will not increase this year."

Basic Underlying Premises of Persuasion

Before you can prepare a persuasive speech intelligently, you should be aware of what is known about persuasion or the factors related to persuasion. In this section, basic premises relative to persuasion are identified. These premises are the guidelines we use in creating strategies for specific audiences on specific topics or propositions.

Erosion and Deterioration—Entropy

Things tend to wear out, erode, or deteriorate. It is rather easy for us to see the truth of this premise as it applies to physical objects. The new $12,000 automobile—or the $85,000 Rolls Royce, for that matter—shows wear and deterioration all too soon. In a few months, the car is worth only a fraction of the original purchase price because it has deteriorated. Restoration ranges from tune-ups to new tires to rust-out repair within a few months after the purchase of a new car. And collectors of antique and classic cars are aware of the fact that virtually every piece of an old auto has to be "restored." No car remains in its new condition forever. Neither does any other object, of course. It seems that almost everything once brought into full existence is then in the process of wearing out. This process is called entropy.

Entropy, or the deteriorating process, applies to things other than objects. You can make your room spotlessly clean and in a few days do it all again. Kitchen duties and household chores have to be repeated and repeated because everything is continuously getting soiled, wearing out, or coming apart. One has to constantly restore, revitalize, repair, re-clean, and re-create.

This same phenomenon applies to persons and organizations in regard to attitudes, beliefs, and commitments. These things weaken and erode, too. For individuals, as well as for society's institutions and organizations, it is necessary to restore and reinforce if deterioration is to be prevented. We see this restoration and reinforcement task accomplished in many ways every day. It ranges from R and R (rest and rehabilitation) programs for the military to the coach's half-time pep talk.

Almost all of this rebuilding of beliefs, attitudes, and commitment is accomplished through communication—persuasive communication to sustain attitudes, to get us to put into practice what we believe, and to "keep the faith!" This premise—that everything we construct, including our attitudes, tends to weaken and deteriorate—is the basis for the persuasive speech to reinforce, which will be discussed later in this chapter.

Change Is Threatening

A second premise important to an understanding of persuasion is that **change is often threatening.** We have discussed the phenomenon of change earlier in this text. We have observed that change is always occurring. The first premise—that everything wears out—is merely a restatement of the fact that everything changes. Change means that our perceptual world is less valid *unless we adjust to the change.* Sometimes it seems that just when we think we understand our world and have things under control, change comes along; and sometimes the

Change is often threatening.

change is so great that adapting to it is difficult. Adapting to change is a challenge, and when the change has to do with our values and beliefs rather than with selecting a brand of toothpaste or learning to drive a car, the change is even more of a challenge. In fact, change can be threatening to us. When we engage in persuasion to change attitudes or behavior, we do well to remember this. The premise that change can be threatening is a foundation stone for the persuasive speech to reverse attitudes or behavior, also discussed later in this chapter.

Attitudes, Beliefs, and Values Vary in Strength

The third premise relative to persuasion is that *one's attitudes, beliefs, and values vary in strength or importance.* This—the salience or prominence of the attitude or value to be changed—is one of the most important variables to consider when planning a persuasive speech. Rokeach contends that beliefs are hierarchical, that is, that some beliefs are foundations for other beliefs and that some beliefs are more intensely held than are other beliefs.[13] Figure 13.4 illustrates the hierarchical levels according to strength of the belief.

Level I beliefs are one's most *basic,* prominent beliefs. Level II beliefs are intermediately *strong.* And Level III beliefs are *peripheral.* Peripheral beliefs are less ego-involving than are strong or basic beliefs, and are more easily changed. Persuasive attempts to reverse basic beliefs are threatening to the listener and may elicit hostility.

Another aspect of the hierarchy of beliefs or values, in addition to variation in prominence, is that peripheral beliefs are often anchored by strong beliefs, and strong beliefs are anchored by basic beliefs. In other words, peripheral beliefs grow out of strong beliefs, and strong beliefs grow out of peripheral beliefs. For example, a basic belief such as, "Hygiene is important to

Figure 13.4 Hierarchy of beliefs.

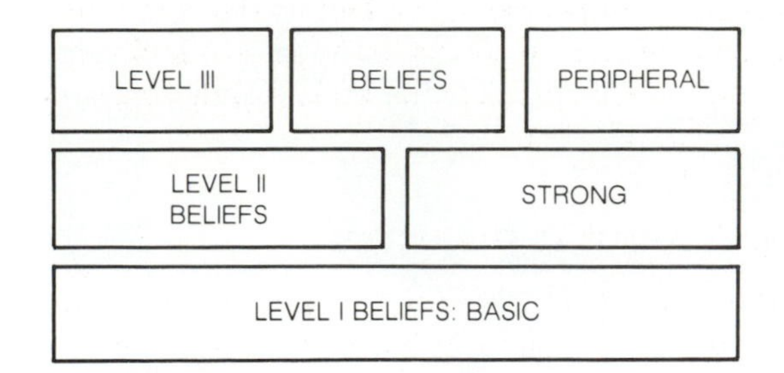

good health," may lead to a strong belief, "I should brush my teeth," which may lead to a peripheral belief, "I will buy Brand X toothpaste." It would probably be easier to persuade one with this belief structure to change brands of toothpaste than to persuade that person to cease brushing teeth.

The hierarchical relationship of beliefs has another implication. Because beliefs or values are tied to or anchored in other beliefs or values, when a basic belief is uprooted, then other beliefs—strong and peripheral, for example—may come tumbling down too. Sometimes it is necessary for the persuader to point out the hierarchical ties of beliefs so that the consistency or inconsistency comes into the awareness of the receiver.

Identify and explain five basic premises related to persuasion.

As we move down the hierarchy from peripheral through strong to basic, the need for social reinforcement of our beliefs (the first premise) probably decreases because we are much more ego-involved with basic beliefs than with peripheral beliefs; that ego-involvement provides intense initial and continuing salience to the belief.

Reinforcing Attitudes versus Changing Attitudes

The fourth premise is that *the persuasive objective can range from reinforcing a belief or attitude to reversing it, and the difference between these two extremes is significant in terms of planning the persuasive strategy.* We discussed this premise in the introduction to this chapter and need not repeat that discussion here, but it is an important premise in persuasion.

Psychological Orientations and Information-Processing Habits, and their Relation in Persuasibility

A fifth premise is that *an individual's psychological orientation and habits of responding to and processing information are related to persuasibility.* Research has demonstrated that open-mindedness, closed-mindedness, authoritarian personality, dogmatism, and degree of self-esteem are related to persuasibility.[14] Some personality characteristics or psychological orientations apparently do not permit free, logical, and open reception of new or different information and do not permit objective considerations of persuasive messages.

Psychological Factors in the Persuasive Speech

Next we want to consider some selected **psychological factors** that can affect the audience. The psychological factors we will discuss grow out of our chapter 11 coverage of the fifth and sixth steps of speech preparation—gathering supporting materials and giving the speech impact.

Cognitive Consistency and Cognitive Dissonance

Psychological structure—the organized set of cognitions people have about themselves, others, and the world—is an important element to consider in persuasive speaking. The principle of **cognitive consistency** suggests that one's psychological structure is composed of an integrated and organized set of cognitions relative to the person, object, or event with which one is concerned. If new information that is inconsistent with cognitions presently held enters one's awareness, one will experience cognitive disonance. **Cognitive dissonance** refers to the disruption of one's organized cognitive and psychological structure and the subsequent production of disequilibrium. The theory suggests that the person who experiences such dissonance feels compelled to make an adjustment between the ongoing cognitive structure and the new information so that equilibrium and harmonious integration of all the cognitions can be reestablished. People are continually striving for consistency and harmonious relationships among thoughts, beliefs, values, and behaviors. When inconsistency occurs and one becomes aware of it, psychological tension is produced and the person is thereby motivated to change actions, attitudes, values, or beliefs to create consistency again. Osgood, Festinger, Heider, Tannenbaum, and others have conducted research and written about cognitive dissonance, balance theory, or the principle of congruity and its relationship to persuasion.[15] The implication for persuasive speaking is that persuasion is more likely to occur when dissonance is experienced by the one being persuaded; and since dissonance results from an awareness of contradictory or inconsistent cognitions, the task of the persuader is to present information that makes the one being induced aware of contradictory conditions already held, or to create dissonance by giving new information that is inconsistent with the cognitive structure held.

The creation of cognitive dissonance does not necessarily mean that the one being persuaded will accept the solution proposed by the persuader. It does mean, however, that the person experiencing psychological tension will seek to restore equilibrium. Acceptance of the persuader's proposed change is of course one way of doing so. The person may also choose not to believe the persuader; to rationalize by saying, "It applies, but not to me"; to become angry at the persuader and repress the information; or to accept some change other than that proposed by the persuader. To help the person change in the

Figure 13.5 Maslow's hierarchy of needs.

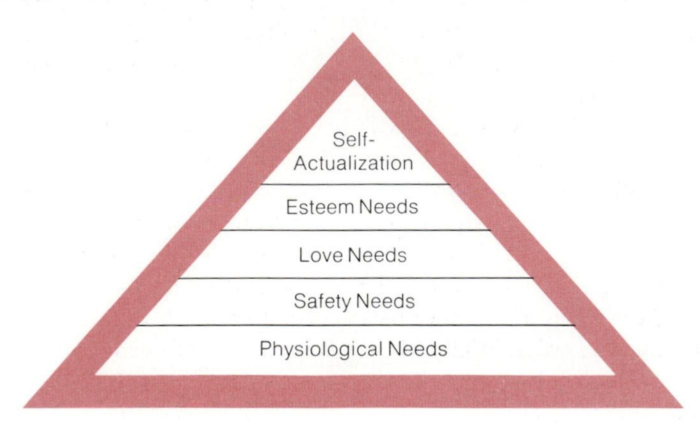

direction advocated, one might want to consider the relative strength or importance of each of the inconsistent cognitions and attempt to argue for a change that is more salient to the individual than is the cognition to be rejected. One way of doing this is to consider personal needs as if they were in hierarchical order.

Maslow's Hierarchy of Needs

Maslow believes that our basic needs can be placed into five broad categories: (1) physiological needs, (2) safety needs, (3) love needs, (4) esteem needs, and (5) the need for self-actualization.[16] The hierarchy is arranged with the most basic and demanding of needs (physiological) at the bottom and the least basic and demanding (self-actualization) at the top, as shown in figure 13.5. **Physiological needs** are necessary for physical survival. They include the need for food, drink, shelter, and sex; avoidance of injury, pain, discomfort, disease, or fatigue; and the need for sensory stimulation. In America, the physiological needs are generally satisfied routinely so that most persons are seldom preoccupied with them. Physiological needs, consequently, do not generally motivate Americans as strongly as do needs that are further up in the hierarchy. *If physiological needs are not satisfied, however, they are stronger in their motivation than any higher needs.* Persons with empty stomachs probably care less about esteem or self-actualization than persons with full stomachs.

Safety needs focus on the creation of order and predictability in one's environment. They include preference for orderliness and routine over disorder; preference for the familiar over the unfamiliar; desire for tenure, for savings accounts, insurance, police and fire departments, welfare plans, social security, and armed forces. When one's safety is threatened, love, esteem, and self-actualization needs tend to lose their motivating power.

Love needs are of two types: love and affection between husband and wife, parents and children, and close friends; and the need for belonging—for identifying with larger groups (church, club, work organization, etc.). When these needs are not met, feelings of rejection and isolation result, with subsequent feelings of mistrust and suspicion toward others.

Esteem needs refer to the desire for reputation, prestige, recognition, attention, achievement, and confidence. Most sociologists believe that esteem needs are powerful motivators in America.

Maslow's highest need is **self-actualization**—the fulfillment of one's capabilities and potentialities. An example of such motivation is the pianist who desires to be as great a pianist as possible. Self-actualization needs take on strong motivating power when other more basic needs have been fulfilled.

A word of caution is in order. While Maslow's hierarchy of needs can be a useful tool for the persuader, it is precisely that—a tool. We should be aware that because people differ culturally, psychologically, and physically, as well as in many other ways, they may not necessarily respond according to the same hierarchical order. People might also be driven by several needs simultaneously and by needs not recognized by Maslow. Maslow's hierarchy of needs does, however, provide a useful starting place for identifying the drives operating within an audience.

Can you identify the level of need (using Maslow's hierarchy of needs) stressed in a speech you read or heard?

In persuasion, the greater the congruence between the belief or action advocated and the felt need of the persuadee, the higher the probability that persuasion will occur. If a speaker makes a listener aware that a listener-held belief is at odds with an important listener need, dissonance will result; and if the speaker's proposed solution resolves the problem for the listener, then the speech is psychologically valid.

Ego-Involvement

A third psychological element to consider in persuasive speeches is **ego-involvement.** As Sherif, Sherif, and Nebergall state:

> It is one thing to change a person's . . . preference for one brand of candy over another. It is another thing to try to change the person's commitment to the value of the family, to his religion, to his politics, to his stand on the virtue of his way of life. The latter commitments and stands are ingredients of his self-picture—intimately felt and cherished in his own eyes. As such, the latter are among his ego-involved attitudes. The term involvement in our approach refers to the arousal of such attitudes.[17]

Ego-involved attitudes are derived from values. Information that is inconsistent with an ego-involved attitude will, of course, create more tension or dissonance than will information inconsistent with a peripheral or non-ego-involved attitude. For this reason, ego-involvement is an important element to consider when a speaker is concerned with the creation of cognitive dissonance. The more ego-involved the listener is with a topic or value, the more likely it is that dissonance will be created when another ego-involved value or belief is shown to be inconsistent with the first value.

Can you identify two issues in which you are highly ego-involved and two in which you have relatively low ego-involvement?

Thus if two values, two beliefs, or two behaviors of a person (or an audience) are shown to be inconsistent, dissonance will be greater if those values, beliefs, or behaviors are prominent or *salient*—that is, if the person has high ego-involvement with both values, beliefs, or behaviors. Of course, if they are peripheral beliefs (preference of toothpaste, for example), little dissonance will be created. The speech may not have much psychological pull or persuasiveness with the listener.

Specific Emotional Appeals

Emotional appeal is another psychological factor in public speaking. So, attention to an audience's feelings (affective or emotional state) can be an important factor in the psychological appeal of a speech.

Strong appeals to certain emotions or psychological states can be made through language and supporting materials. Three pairs of emotions—or six psychological states—are offered here as examples of psychological and emotional appeals that can be observed in public speeches. Understanding these appeals is advantageous not only to the public speaker but also to the receiver of public communication. It may well be that the major value of understanding the phenomenon of psychological appeals lies in the fact that it enables the "consumer" of public speaking to *participate* in the transaction in a more rational manner. Our discussion of the theoretical explanation of emotional appeals and how they may be used via language and supporting materials is based, in part, upon material presented in lectures given by Paul Brandes.[18]

Some emotions seem to be dichotomous. Examples of such pairs are pride and pity, affection (or love) and anger (or hate), and fear and its opposite, the absence of fear (security). These bipolar emotions can constitute strong persuasive appeals. A more detailed discussion of each of these pairs follows.

Pride and Pity

An appeal to *pride* results in the creation of a feeling of high self-esteem. In the public speech, one normally appeals to the audience's pride, or self-esteem. The primary technique used in public communication to appeal to the listener's pride is the compliment, which may be used directly or indirectly. An audience may be directly complimented in terms of its intelligence, sophistication, educational level, social position, possession of power or wealth, and potential abilities and skills. Probably no technique has a longer history of use in our attempts to influence others through emotional appeal than the pat on the back—the soft-soaping, sweet-talking, complimenting behavior. Untold millions of dollars worth of products are sold by telling people directly how great they will be after they have used the advertiser's product.

Courtesy of American Greetings Corporation.

There is some evidence to indicate that "accidental" or unintentional appeals are more effective in persuading the receiver than are recognized, purposeful attempts. Consistent with this position is the explanation that *indirect compliments* to an individual or audience are even more effective in appealing to pride than are direct compliments. These indirect compliments are not easy to plan or to carry off, but they are powerful in their effect. Communicating an awareness of a problem the audience has is an indirect compliment, for example. Similarly, referring to audience members by name is an indirect compliment. Association of the speaker with persons the audience knows and holds in high esteem is an indirect compliment and an appeal to the audience's esteem. Allowing the audience to participate through humor or through the interchange in a question–answer process also constitutes an indirect compliment. Finally, humility on the part of the speaker is an indirect compliment that recognizes the corresponding worth and esteem of the audience. Studies of the public speaking of former President Lyndon B. Johnson show his rather extensive use of humility.

The opposite of pride is *pity*. The speaker may use pity in several ways. When one attempts to create pity for oneself, the goal might be audience sympathy for the speaker. Secondly, a speaker may appeal for pity for the theme of the speech. Finally, the speaker may appeal to pity for the audience and the terrible condition and mistreatment they have experienced. Some cues by which the emotional appeal to pity can be identified include remarks such as, "I'm a poor person; I don't have the money to buy this election"; remarks about one's unfortunate physical appearance; remarks about not being appreciated, not being understood, or being mistreated or unfairly treated; about being denied rights and falling from greatness. Such "poor mouthing" is an appeal to pity.

Affection (or Love) and Anger (or Hate)

Appeals to *affection* result in adoration, identification, and sharing. Such appeals are projected by family relationships, "overcoming" difficulties, shared struggle or tragedy, and reminiscing. Speakers who make references to their wonderful spouses, the children at home, or the kids for whom they bake cookies or with whom they play baseball are making appeals to affection, intentional or unintentional. Similarly, the political candidate who appears publicly with spouse, family, or children appeals to affection. Reference to tragedies or struggles that the speaker has shared with the entire audience or with individual audience members constitutes an appeal to affection. We have witnessed on television some very tender and affectionate moments between a losing political candidate and loyal workers following concession of defeat, just as we have witnessed the emotional experience of the loser offering congratulations to the winner. Reminiscing, whether in interpersonal communication or public speaking, appeals to affection.

Anger and hate grow out of injustice and to disappointment and frustration. Speakers make emotional appeals by using name-calling, appeals to prejudice and making direct reference to injustice, frustration, and hopeless situations.

Fear and Security

Fear is one of the few emotional appeals to be extensively investigated by behavioral research scholars in speech communication. Theoretically, the major fears among adults are (1) fear of not having food, shelter, and health; (2) fear of loss of freedom; (3) fear of not developing one's talents, and of not living a fulfilled life; and (4) fear of the unknown. Threat to survival has been the fear most deeply researched by behavioral scientists.

From the many experiments that have been done on fear appeals by communication scholars and psychologists and from the reports made on those studies in communication and psychology journals, we have generally concluded that mild fear appeals are the most effective emotional appeals in public speaking. They seem to be more effective than either strong or weak fear appeals. Apparently, weak fear appeals don't move receivers enough, and strong appeals either paralyze people into inaction or, for some other reason, have a boomerang effect of *not* producing change at all. Despite the questions yet unanswered about fear appeals, fear remains one of the commonly used emotional appeals in public speaking. Such appeals are made by calling attention to a problem, to costs, to a successful solution—and by proposing a change.

Cognitive dissonance, basic needs, ego-involvement, and emotional appeals are factors that operate to give the speech psychological validity for the listener. Attention to these elements can be highly beneficial to the speaker as well as to the auditor.

Now we are ready to consider two specific types of persuasive speeches—the speech to reinforce beliefs or attitudes and the speech to change beliefs or attitudes.

Can you analyze a speech in terms of the emotional appeals discussed in this chapter?

Persuasive Speeches to Reinforce or Actuate

This type of persuasion focuses on public communication aimed at getting us to give to the United Fund, the Blood Bank, and to religious or other charitable organizations; on communication aimed at getting us to buckle seat belts; and on communication aimed at getting the football team "psyched up" for the game. Every organization, and society-at-large, has a need for this kind of persuasive communication. The values and objectives of society and organizations must be defended against the gradual erosion and weakening that occur. Values, beliefs, and behaviors need to be reinforced constantly, strengthened, and reaffirmed. This is accomplished through communicative rituals and public communication that inspires or stimulates. Keynote addresses, political party rallies, church services, sales meetings, conventions of professional organizations—all are examples of this type of persuasive communication.

There are at least three strategies possible for persuasion aiming to reinforce or sustain attitudes and behavior. They are (1) **increase social cohesion,** a feeling of togetherness; (2) **intensify values and beliefs;** and (3) prepare listeners to be able to **resist later persuasion counter to their attitudes and beliefs.**

Strategies for Increasing Social Cohesion

Over time, the bonds that draw persons together in an organization can also weaken. Relationships and meanings come to be taken for granted. Sometimes the feelings of unity and closeness weaken to the point where they almost disappear. That is the time for persuasion aimed at renewing those feelings of closeness in relationship, that is, social cohesion.

President John Kennedy faced such a situation in regard to the need for a renewed feeling of unity between the United States and its European allies when he took office. He toured Europe, speaking to the people of various nations to rekindle their feeling of unity. The zenith of his tour occurred in West Berlin. There, speaking to thousands amidst cheering, clapping, and flag waving, he rekindled the feelings of unity and culminated his speech with, "Ich bin ein Berliner!"—"I, too, am a Berliner!" There was an emotional outpouring from the audience, a strong expression of the unity they felt as a result of that speech and that statement.

Social cohesion is increased through the use of such strategies as reminding the audience of its commonalities and the salient values tying that particular group together.

Social cohesion is increased through the use of such strategies as the following: (1) reminding the audience of its commonalities; (2) reminding the audience of the salient values tying that particular group together; (3) recalling those events, places, and instances of the past that have meaning for the organization; and (4) re-identifying the common antagonists or enemies. Whether it's the Kennedy speech in Berlin, the "I Have a Dream" speech of Martin Luther King, Jr., before a quarter of a million persons in front of the Washington Monument, the minister's inspirational sermon to the congregation, Knute Rockne's "Get one for the Gipper," or President Ronald Reagan's attempt to win nonpartisan support and approval relative to U.S. policy in El Salvador and the Middle East, one or more of these four strategies are in evidence.

Strategies for Intensifying Values or Beliefs

A second objective this type of public communication may have is to restrengthen and intensify values or beliefs. This public communication is clearly "in-group" communication. The feeling of unity may be strong, but some belief or value has slipped and needs to be rebuilt or re-intensified. There are six strategies that appear to be effective in accomplishing this objective.

The **"carrot-and-stick" strategy** is often used in this situation. The carrot is all the good things that come from maintaining the value or belief, and the stick is all the bad things that will result from giving up this value or belief. It is a strategy of maximizing contrasts. It is a matter of the forces of good versus the forces of evil, of juxtapositioning opposite emotions, with all the positive and good linked to the value to be reinforced and all the negative and

Persuasive communication—convention style.

bad linked to *not* maintaining the value or belief. The receiver is "enticed" by the carrot to retain the belief and "threatened" by evil if the value is not retained.

A second strategy is to infuse the belief with emotion so as to breathe life and fire back into the belief. This is often accomplished through emotional language and strong visualization. The **creation of mental pictures** can give life and power to an abstract value or belief. This strategy makes use of emotion-laden meaning. The wonderful results of holding to this value are visualized by means of word pictures, as are the terrible results of not holding fast to the value.

Another strategy we see used in this kind of persuasive public speaking is that of **simplifying the value or goal.** It would be foolish for a speaker who wishes to inspire the audience to go into a complicated discussion of the goal, to work at explaining the complexity of the issue, or to drag out long lists of factual evidence. The audience will respond by re-intensifying its commitment to the goal or value more readily if the speaker *simplifies the goal* and expresses the value succinctly. In fact, the ultimate value simplification is to make the value or goal into a slogan.

A fourth strategy is the use of **strong, emotion-laden nonverbal communication** in connection with the verbal message and the situation. American flags, symbols, spotlights, and dramatically decorated speaker's platforms are examples of common nonverbal messages. Again, the emotional aspect of inspirational persuasive communication is evident. Even the speaker's nonverbal communication will be emotional and strong in effective speeches to reintensify values or goals.

Infusing a belief with emotion.

Another way of intensifying a value or belief is by **audience participation.** If you overtly "act out," that is, express your belief or commitment to a value, the value or belief is more intensified than if you just passively run it through your head. The evangelist who wishes to "rekindle" the commitment of a congregation, or the cheerleaders who wish to "pep up" the students, wisely involve them in overt action. They have them stand, clap, yell, sing, and so forth.

The sixth and final strategy for re-intensifying and sustaining an organization's identifying values and beliefs is the use of **ritual communication**—public ritual. This strategy is simply to formalize a message so as to quickly identify the value or belief. These messages are ritualized in form and very often stylized in their expression. Through this vehicle—this public ritual—all the members of a group "speak as one." The expression of the value is clearly *not* just the speaker's or the leader's, but *the voice of all.* This is the essence of public ritual. Because public ritual is a strategy for re-intensifying values or beliefs, it deals with emotions and feelings that are connected to patterned public expression. As the mouthpiece of the audience, the speaker simply expresses or echoes what the audience is feeling. Such speeches are sometimes referred to as *echoic speeches.* The spokesperson for a group, appearing at a special congressional hearing as a representative of that group, gives an echoic speech.

How can a speaker intensify an audience's commitment to selected values or beliefs?

Another example of public ritual communication is the *ceremonial speech.* The funeral sermon, the eulogy, the dedication speech, the nomination acceptance speech, and numerous other speeches that articulate and symbolize a "collective message" are examples of ceremonial speeches utilizing public ritual. They sustain a society's or an organization's values.

Strategies for Increasing Resistance to Persuasion

A third possible objective that persuasive communication to reinforce attitudes may have is that of helping the receivers to withstand future persuasion. The concern is not primarily to increase cohesion or to re-intensify a value, but to prepare the audience for someone who will try to *reverse* its attitude or belief. There are three basic strategies that can help accomplish this objective.

Build Self-Esteem

Persons of low **self-esteem** seem to be vulnerable to persuasion, so if you can help persons to increase their self-esteem, they will be less susceptible to persuasion. How can a person's self-esteem be improved? Apparently, one of the best ways is to **provide the person with a "success experience" relative to a belief or behavior.** The research of Kelman, Stukat, Gelfand, Mausner, and Block and others is quite convincing concerning the effects of this strategy.[19] A person who has had a successful experience with a behavior will be more resistant to persuasive attempts to change that behavior. The strategy is unusually effective if the person witnesses the simultaneous failure of one who will try to change the person's attitude or behavior at a later time. But even without the failure of the antagonist, the success experience builds self-esteem and thus increases the person's resistance to counter persuasion. Reminding the audience of the benefits that have come to them because of this new behavior and telling them they are wise to have accepted their belief are examples of this strategy. Alcoholics Anonymous and drug rehabilitation centers have found this manner of improving self-esteem to be one of their most productive strategies.

Bolster the Belief Structure—Anchoring

A second strategy by which resistance to persuasion can be increased is to **strengthen a person's particular belief.** This can be accomplished by increasing commitment to the belief and by anchoring the belief.

Commitment to a belief can be increased by having listeners verbalize their belief. McGuire's research indicates that writing the belief or writing positive statements about the belief increases the person's resistance to subsequent counter persuasion.[20] Public verbalization of a belief is even more effective. Perhaps the inconsistency and the reluctance for a public admission of error is too great for us to reverse a belief we have publicly stated. Of course, the most effective commitment strategy of all is *public behavior* in support of a belief. *Actions do speak louder than words*—that is, behavior linking one to the belief is a stronger commitment than public verbalization of the belief. Kiesler's research shows this strategy as powerfully effective.[21]

Anchoring beliefs is the other major strategy by which beliefs are made more resistant to change. When an attitude, belief, or behavior is tied to other attitudes or beliefs, it is more resistant to persuasion than if it is not tied to other beliefs. As we pointed out earlier in this chapter, beliefs often grow out of other beliefs—basic beliefs give rise to strong and peripheral beliefs. When the relationships among beliefs are clarified and emphasized, that whole cluster of beliefs is strengthened. Each member of the **belief cluster** has support, and an attack on one of the beliefs is less successful when the person is aware of that belief's tie-in to other salient beliefs—the attack is less effective because the belief attacked is anchored.

Again, McGuire identifies three ways by which beliefs can be anchored: (1) tie the belief to other beliefs important to the individual; (2) tie the belief to a highly salient value; and (3) tie the belief to an individual whom the person holds in high esteem.[22]

We now turn to the third and final strategy for increasing resistance to persuasion—inoculation. The three—build self-esteem, bolster the belief structure, and inoculate—are effective ways of helping believers stay believers.

Inoculate

Inoculation is a strategy that is analogous to medical immunization. As with medical immunization, the person is given the ability to "fight off" the attack. There are three ways by which this may be done: (1) by forewarning; (2) by providing counter-arguments; and (3) by identifying weaknesses in the opponent's arguments.

Forewarning is one of the easiest ways to inoculate against coming persuasive attempts. Just to point out that persuasion is coming causes the person to rally defenses—strong arguments, materials, and experiences available—against the impending attack.

Providing counter-arguments is another form of immunization. The arguments of the opposition are identified and offsetting counter-arguments are given to the listeners. The listener will recall the counter-arguments when the attack comes and use them to resist the opponent's persuasive efforts.

A third procedure for inoculating is *to identify weaknesses in the arguments that will be used by the opponent and then destroy those arguments.* The best procedure is to give the opponent's arguments a little shot of the disease and let the listener pick out the weaknesses and create personal refutational arguments. *If the listener is capable of doing it, this is the best way.* If the listener, alone, is not capable of capitalizing on the opponent's weaknesses, then the refutational arguments and attack must be prepared by the persuader and presented to the listener.

Through inoculation, the bolstering of beliefs, and the strengthening of self-esteem, resistance to coming persuasion can be increased.

Explain how beliefs may be anchored so that the individual can resist persuasion more easily.

Persuasive Speeches to Reverse Attitudes or Behavior

We turn now to the second major type of persuasion—the most difficult of all—reversing attitudes or behavior. In the previous section of this chapter, we have been concerned with persuasion to reinforce attitudes and to strengthen resistance to other persuasion. Now we are concerned with overcoming resistance to change—we want to alter beliefs, change attitudes, and reverse behavior. In these instances, the persuader is at odds with the audience. The persuader's objective is to the audience so it will accept the persuader's attitude or belief, or behave in a prescribed way. We know from our five basic premises that change is threatening to people. This means that sometimes there is hostility toward the persuader. At the least, there is some degree of resistance that must be overcome.

We are going to discuss two strategies that can be effective in overcoming resistance and hostility to persuasion. These are the common premise strategy and the de-anchoring strategy.

The Common Premise Strategy

The **common premise strategy** consists of (1) identifying a premise (a value or a belief) that is salient for the listeners; (2) showing that you, too, hold that premise (it is a common premise); and (3) revealing that the premise is the basis of, or is at least consistent with, the thesis of your persuasive speech. William Kunstler is a well-known attorney who defended the Chicago Seven. (The Chicago Seven were among those accused of illegal acts performed to protest the Vietnam War and were also said to be involved in Civil Rights incidents.) He used the common premise strategy in a speech to an audience of Penn State students by telling the story of William Penn and his run-in with the law in London. When Parliament passed a bill that prevented Penn from preaching in his church, Penn got around it by preaching in the street. But he was arrested and charged with inciting a riot. When asked whether he pled guilty or not guilty, Penn said that he wouldn't plead either way unless he knew the nature of the indictment, and that meant he had to know what law he had broken. There was no law on which to base the indictment and the judge could not provide one. Without one, Penn would not enter a plea, but kept on pressing for his rights. Finally, the judge ordered him gagged and bound.

Kunstler attempted to establish a common premise by opening his speech with that story, and tying it to the Chicago Seven trial, in which one of the defendants was bound and gagged in the courtroom.

Kunstler's common premise strategy made use of some principles of persuasion we identified earlier in this chapter—beginning the speech on common ground and initially withholding the thesis or proposal.

The common premise strategy argues essentially from analogy, and such a strategy has been a well-known and respected persuasive strategy since the era of classical Greece.

The De-Anchoring Strategy

A second strategy for overcoming resistance to persuasion is **de-anchoring.** We identified anchoring beliefs as a strategy for inducing resistance to persuasion. Now our objective is the opposite. If the belief to be changed can be detached from other beliefs, it will be cut loose from the internal support derived from belief clusters and will be more susceptible to change.

The first thing you would do to put this strategy into practice is to discover what beliefs are likely to be called to mind by listeners when the belief you want to change is discussed. Having discovered these beliefs, you must show that they are unrelated to the belief in question, that the belief in question is inconsistent with them, that inconsistency exists among the beliefs in the cluster, or that the entire cluster is inconsistent with other belief clusters. The anchoring effect will be nullified by any of these means, and the belief to be changed will be cut loose from supporting beliefs. Hart and others say of this strategy:

> To use such an approach effectively, the persuader obviously must know which underlying attitudes are holding the target belief in place. Sometimes, such knowledge is difficult to obtain. In fact, at times, listeners themselves are unaware of the feelings which anchor a given target belief. In such a situation simply pointing out these anchoring beliefs and then arguing against them, a

> persuader has relatively little trouble in subsequently "cutting loose" the target belief. . . . For example, an advertisement recently appeared in many campus newspapers which asked for contributions to the East Pakistani Relief Fund. Instead of beginning with the "Help an Orphan" approach, the ad asserted and developed the following points: "We can well understand why you might refuse our plea. After all, giving has become impersonal and involuntary; we've lost the ability to be shocked by man's inhumanity to man; and we've all got our own problems." By thus reckoning directly with the "opposition's" point of view, the creators of the appeal were in a position to alter anchoring beliefs.[23]

With the de-anchoring strategy, you confront head-on the major arguments (beliefs) the audience is apt to raise against the proposal. Once these are refuted and discredited, the belief to be changed stands alone.

Summary

This chapter has focused on a code of ethics, three types of reasoning, five basic premises of persuasion, and several psychological factors that were identified and discussed. The principles and psychological factors were then applied to two kinds of persuasive speeches—those aimed at reinforcing and sustaining attitudes, beliefs, and behaviors, and those aimed at changing attitudes, beliefs, and behavior. Various strategies that utilize one or more of the principles identified through research were proposed and explained as means to reinforce or change attitudes. Among those were strategies for (1) increasing social cohesion, (2) intensifying values and beliefs, (3) increasing resistance to persuasion, (4) building self-esteem, (5) bolstering a belief by anchoring or by inoculating, (6) using a common premise approach; and (7) a de-anchoring strategy.

Questions and Exercises for Review

1. How does your code of ethics relate to your persuasive speaking?
2. What is the significance of *belief hierarchies* for the persuader?
3. Identify and explain three factors that make people more resistant to persuasion.
4. Explain the theory of cognitive dissonance. How can you apply it in persuasive speaking?
5. Name people's basic needs according to Maslow. What is their hierarchy, and what is the implication of the hierarchy for persuasive speaking?
6. What is the "carrot-and-stick" strategy?
7. Differentiate echoic speeches from ceremonial speeches.
8. How do anchoring beliefs and de-anchoring beliefs relate to persuasion?

Key Terms and Phrases

deductive reasoning
syllogism
enthymeme
inductive reasoning
Toulmin's inferential pattern of reasoning
data
claim
warrant
backing
reservation
qualifier
entropy
threat of change
psychological factors
cognitive consistency
cognitive dissonance
physiological needs
safety needs
love needs
esteem needs
self-actualization
ego-involvement
social cohesion
intensify values and beliefs
resist later persuasion
counter to attitudes and beliefs
"carrot-and-stick" strategy
creating mental pictures
simplifying the value or goal
strong, emotion-laden nonverbal communication
audience participation
ritual communication
self-esteem
provide a "success experience"
relative to a belief or "behavior"
strengthen a belief
anchoring beliefs
belief cluster
inoculation
common premise strategy
de-anchoring strategy

For Further Reading

Andersen, K. *Persuasion: Theory and Practice.* Boston: Allyn & Bacon, 1971.
An excellent review and interpretation of persuasion research and its application.

Bostrom, Robert N. *Persuasion.* Englewood Cliffs, N.J.: Prentice-Hall, Inc., 1983.

Brembeck, Winston L., and Howell, William S. *Persuasion: A Means of Social Influence.* Englewood Cliffs, N.J.: Prentice-Hall, Inc., 1976.

Cronkhite, G. *Persuasion: Speech and Behavioral Change.* New York: The Bobbs-Merrill Co., 1969.
Another excellent book that summarizes and applies the findings and theories of persuasion.

Goffman, E. *Interaction Ritual, 1965.* New York: Doubleday & Co., 1967.
A very readable treatment of the role of ritual in communication.

Griffin, E. M. *The Mind Changers: The Art of Christian Persuasion.* Wheaton, Ill.: Tyndale House Publishers, Inc., 1983.

Janis, I. L., and Fishback, S. "Effects of Fear-Arousing Communications." *Journal of Abnormal and Social Psychology* 48 (1953): 28–92.
An excellent summary of the fear-appeal research.

Laird, A. W. "Persuasion: A Tool of Courtroom Communication." *Psychology: A Quarterly Journal of Human Behavior* 19 (1982): 50–57.

Miller, Gerald R. "Studies on the Use of Fear Appeals: A Summary and Analysis." *Central States Speech Journal* 14 (1963): 117–25.
An excellent review of fear appeal research.

Minnick, Wayne C. *The Art of Persuasion.* Boston: Houghton Mifflin Co., 1968.

Seamond, John T. *Tell It Well: Communicating the Gospel Across Cultures.* Kansas City: Beacon Hill Press, 1981.

Sherif, C. W.; Sherif, M.; and Nebergall, R. E. *Attitude and Attitude Change.* Philadelphia: W. B. Saunders Co., 1965.
The work of the authors concerning ego-involvement and attitude change is thoroughly presented in this highly readable book.

Smith, Mary Ann. *Persuasion and Human Action.* Belmont, Calif.: Wadsworth Publishing Co., 1982.

Toulmin, Stephen. *The Uses of Argument.* Cambridge, England: Cambridge University Press, 1958.

Notes

1. Roderick P. Hart; Gustav W. Friedrich; and William D. Brooks, *Public Communication* (New York: Harper & Row, 1975), 255.

2. Frank E. X. Dance, "This Above All," SPECTRA XVIII (December 1982): 3–5.

3. Kenneth E. Andersen, "A Code of Ethics for Speech Communicaton," SPECTRA XX (January 1984): 2. Reprinted from SPECTRA by permission of the Speech Communication Association.

4. Andersen, "A Code of Ethics," 2–3.

5. Wayne C. Minnick, *The Art of Persuasion* (Boston: Houghton Mifflin Co., 1968), 279.

6. Minnick, *Art of Persuasion,* 279.

7. C. R. Miller, *Propaganda Analysis* (Institute for Propaganda Analysis, I, 2 November 1937), 1–3.

8. Minnick, *Art of Persuasion,* 283.

9. Minnick, *Art of Persuasion,* 287.

10. Donald L. Clark, *Rhetoric in Greco Roman Education* (New York: Columbia University Press, 1957), 119.

11. Stephen Toulmin. *The Uses of Argument* (Cambridge, England: Cambridge University Press, 1958).

12. Douglas Ehninger and Wayne Brockriede, *Decision by Debate* (New York: Dodd, Mead and Co., 1970), 106.

13. M. Rokeach, *Beliefs, Attitudes, and Values* (San Francisco: Jossey-Bass, Inc., Publishers, 1968).

14. See, for example, H. Simons, "Persuasion and Attitude Change," in L. Barker and R. Kibler, eds., *Speech Communication Behavior* (Englewood Cliffs, N.J.: Prentice-Hall, 1971), 227–48; R. Nye, *Conflict Among Humans* (New York: Springer Publishing Co., 1973); and Ithiel deSola Pool; F. W. Frey; W. Schramm; N. Maccoby; and E. B. Parker, eds., *Handbook of Communication* (Chicago: Rand McNally & Co., 1973).

15. See A. R. Cohen, "Communication Discrepancy and Attitude Change: A Dissonance Theory Approach," *Journal of Personality* 27: 386–96; Leon Festinger, *A Theory of Cognitive Dissonance* (Evanston, Ill.: Row Peterson, 1957); Fritz Heider, *The Psychology of Interpersonal Relations* (New York: John Wiley & Sons, 1958); C. E. Osgood, "Cognitive Dynamics in the Conduct of Human Affairs," *Public Opinion Quarterly* 24(1960): 341–65; and P. Tannenbaum, "Attitudes Toward Source and Concept as Factors in Attitude Change Through Communications" (Ph.D. diss., University of Illinois, 1953).

16. A. H. Maslow, *Motivation and Personality* (New York: Harper & Row, 1954), 80–92.

17. Carolyn W. Sherif; Musafer Sherif; and Roger E. Nebergall, *Attitude and Attitude Change* (Philadelphia: W. B. Saunders Company, 1965), vi.

18. Paul D. Brandes, professor of English and Chairman of the Speech Division at the University of North Carolina at Chapel Hill, gave a series of classroom lectures in 1964 at Ohio University that set forth this theoretical framework concerning emotional appeals in public speaking.

19. H. C. Kelman, "Effects of Success and Failure on 'Suggestibility' in the Autokinetic Situation," *Journal of Abnormal and Social Psychology* 45 (1950): 267–85; K.G. Stukat, *Suggestibility: A Factorial and Experimental Study* (Stockholm: Almquist and Wiksell, 1958); D. M. Gelfand, "The Influence of Self-Esteem on the Rate of Verbal Conditioning and Social Matching Behavior," *Journal of Abnormal and Social Psychology* 65 (1962): 159–65; and B. Mausner and B. Block, "A Study of the Additivity of Variables Affecting Social Interaction," *Journal of Abnormal and Social Psychology* 54 (1957): 250–56.

20. W. J. McGuire, "The Nature of Attitudes and Attitude Change," in G. E. Lindzey and E. Aronson, eds., *The Handbook of Social Psychology,* vol. 3 (Reading, Mass.: Addison-Wesley Publishing Co., 1969), 136–314.

21. C. A. Kiesler, *The Psychology of Commitment: Experiments Linking Behavior to Belief* (New York: Academic Press, 1971).

22. McGuire, "Nature of Attitudes and Attitude Change," 1969.

23. R. P. Hart; G. W. Friedrich; and W. D. Brooks, *Public Communication* (New York: Harper & Row, 1975), 254.

Glossary

Abstraction process The process of using selected stimuli rather than all of the stimuli received to identify, classify, and stand for the whole

Accidental happenings Interactions with others or occurrences in relation to self that are not intentional or not created by self

Accuracy in communication One variable in inducing cooperative behavior and managing conflict satisfactorily

Acquaintance process The process of persons coming to know each other

Action language Gestures, posture, facial expression not used exclusively as substitutes for words

Adjustive techniques Techniques for reducing hostility; e.g., physical aggression, verbal aggression, rationalization

Affection Liking or love

Agenda Goals to be attained or tasks to be achieved by either a group or an individual

Aggregation A collection of a large number of individuals that does not qualify as a group

Alienation Separation; disliking; aloneness

American value Values held by a majority of Americans

Analogical message Nonverbal messages; feelings and emotion messages

Analogies Comparisons of two things, similar in certain essential characteristics

Anchoring beliefs Beliefs related or tied to the belief under attack or in question

Anomia Unwillingness to communicate

Anticlimax pattern Placing major or strongest point or argument first

Applicant's character Personal behavior, honesty, etc.; of importance to an interviewer

Appropriate emotional tone One of Argyle's five relationship factors

Appropriate responsiveness or inclusion One factor important to the maintenance of friendship

Arbitration Allowing a third party or outside party to make the decision resolving negotiation

Arriving at the best solution Fifth and penultimate step in problem solving

Articulation The formation of individual speech sounds

Assigned roles Roles given to one by others; roles forced on one

Assumed roles Roles one takes by one's own choice

Audience Persons receiving a message

Audience analysis Process of acquiring data about an audience for the purpose of understanding the audience

Audience attitudes Attitudes held by a significant number of audience members

Audience feedback Response behavior of the audience to the speaker or source, mostly nonverbal communication in the face-to-face speaker-audience situation

Audience heterogeneity The degree of difference among the audience members

Audience homogeneity The degree of sameness among the audience members

Audience participation One strategy for intensifying values or beliefs

Auding Third stage of the listening process in which meaning emerges

Auditory fatigue Temporary hearing loss caused by continuous exposure to sounds of certain frequencies

Authoritarian leadership Characterized by decisiveness through or by the leader

Backing Support for the warrant in Toulmin's inferential pattern of reasoning

Being ignored Being denied access to another person; a dominant causal factor of alienation

Belief cluster A group of beliefs that are interrelated

Belonging Feeling of being accepted by the group or the other person

Body movements Used to reinforce or contradict verbal messages

Brainstorming Free, open thinking without restrictions, evaluations, or judgments made on the ideas produced

"Carrot-and-stick" strategy Offering reward and punishment

Casual audience An audience that lacks any consistent, strong common focus.

Casual group Coffee group, bull session, social group

Cessation Agreeing not to resolve a combat; one end to conflict

Channel Means by which message stimuli move from source to receiver, i.e., light waves, sound waves, etc.

Characteristics, reputation, and intentions One situational factor related to trusting

Chronological pattern One way of organizing the major points of the body of the speech

Chunking Breaking information into smaller chunks so that it can be processed more easily

Claim The conclusion in Toulmin's thought procedure

Climax pattern Sending the major argument or most important message last

Closed questions Those limiting the answer to yes–no, enumeration, naming, etc.

Coactive emphasis Relating an idea to another known idea

Cognitive consistency Agreement or fitting together of ideas or cognitions

Cognitive dissonance Disagreement or antitheticalness between cognitions

Cohesiveness Sticking together; the feeling of closeness or tightness within a group

Combat Action against one's opponent with the intent of harming or destroying that opponent

Common ground Having the same values, interests, and attitudes; one way of enhancing intrinsic credibility

Common premise strategy Starting with a premise that all accept or agree to

Communication apprehension Fear of communication

Communication confidence How we view ourselves as communicators as manifested in our attitudes toward communication situations

Communication is adaptive Adjusts to cope with change so as to fulfill its purpose

Communication is continuous Has no beginning and no end but is ongoing

Communication is dynamic Characterized by ever-changing relationships among its parts

Communication is systemic The parts or variables in communications when they are interrelated and working together

Communication is transactional Each communication event is unique, as it is defined and created by two or more unique persons

Communication networks The wheel, circle, Y, chain, etc.—patterns for organizing and controlling the flow of messages

Communicators Those things involved in information reception, perception, processing, and transmission

Competition Striving for nonsharable goals

Competitive goals Two or more persons desiring the same goal when only one can obtain the goal

Completing The process whereby one "fills in" missing data to complete the picture, sentence, i.e., the message, to the person's desired message

Concerted audience One with a clear and single purpose or orientation

Conflict management Attempting to resolve conflict

Congruent goals Goals that are sharable; two persons can have the same goal and both attain it together

Connotative meaning A person's "own" meaning for a word based on that person's feelings, experiences, and associations related to the word

Consensus Agreement by all

Content of the messages One variable in conflict management

Controversy A disagreement or argument perceived by the parties as resoluable to at least the partial satisfaction of both

Conversational style Unaffected, natural, as when one talks with another informally

Core values The deepest most important values one has

Covert sequence Placing interview questions in the most advantageous places in the interview

Creating mental pictures One strategy for intensifying values or beliefs

Credibility Influence within the source; *see* ethos

Credibility gap A difference in the image or ethos projected publicly and revealed at another time or in another place

Cultural communication Communication between persons of different cultures

Data Facts, opinions, evidence

Dating A way of realizing that everything changes over time; $Bill_{1965}$ is not $Bill_{1981}$

De-anchoring Destroying beliefs anchoring the belief one wants to change

Decision making Decisions involving procedures and subject matter

Deductive reasoning Reasoning *from* a generalization *to* a specific conclusion.

Delayed feedback The kind of feedback received in mass communication: letters, phone calls, etc.

Democratic leadership Based on respect for each individual and control by individuals freely

Demographic audience analysis Analysis using age, sex, income, religion, place of residence, etc.

Demographic exchanges Exchanging demographic information with another person, characteristic of the first four or five minutes of the initial interaction situation.

Denotative meaning Objective meaning; meaning given in a dictionary

Differential goals One cause of conflict

Digital message Verbal messages; intentional, controlled messages

Direct feedback Purposive; originated by the receiver and sent directly to the source

Directive structure Structuring or planning so as to control the development and direction of the event—the opposite of an indirective approach or a nondirective approach; one structure for an interview

Discovery of possible solutions Third step in problem solving

Dominance One factor important to the maintenance of friendship

Dyadic communication Two-person communication

Dynamism Energy, strength, attraction exerted by a speaker or source; one of the elements of ethos or credibility

Educational group A group whose purpose is to instruct or learn

Ego-involvement Degree of importance of a value to the self

Emotional state *See* psychological state

Enthymeme A syllogism in which one of the premises is implicit

Entropy Tendency for things to wear out, erode, or become disorganized

Entry phase The initial exploratory stage of an interpersonal relationship

Establishment of criteria Second step in problem solving

Esteem needs Reputation, prestige, recognition, and achievement needs

Ethos Source credibility; image; influence in communication residing in the source

Evaluating and testing each solution Fourth step in problem solving

Experiential history The experiences you have had; one source of information

Expertise One dimension of source credibility; competence, qualifications, intelligence, and so on.

Explanations Statements clarifying the meaning of or relationship of things

Expressive actions Unintentional, constantly adaptive, responding to feelings and needs of the moment

Extemporaneous delivery Speaking without notes or with notes in which ideas are worded sketchily, but organizational pattern is planned and supporting materials are carefully pre-selected

External feedback Feedback received via the receptors of hearing, seeing, feeling, tasting, and smelling

Extrinisic credibility Reputation of a speaker; or remarks about the speaker—things outside the speech itself

Eye contact A way of communicating more directly and being sensitive to feedback

Facial expression Facial movements to convey meaning

Fact finding Part of opening phase of problem analysis

Factual illustrations Detailed examples that are real

False masks Looking like something you are not

Feedback Return signals from a receiver to the source

Fielding questions Answering questions from the audience

Figurative analogy Two unlike things are compared; two things from different classes are compared in terms of likenesses

Filtering The process whereby a person blocks out information so that the message is more acceptable

Force Strong projection of the voice

Forum A discussion in which the audience directs questions and enters into the discussion of the topic

"Four-minute barrier" The point at which information exchange patterns shift or change in the acquaintance process, usually about four minutes into the process

Full, free communication One variable in conflict management; one interview structure

Fully sharable goals Congruent goals; goals that may be possessed by both parties to the conflict

Funnel sequence One interview structure; moving broad, general questions to narrow, specific questions

General purpose of speech The overriding objective sought: to inform, to persuade, or to entertain

Generation gap Characterized by difficulties in communication between parents and high school or junior high school children

Gestures Communication by the hands, arms, shoulders

Goodwill Positive feelings and evaluation of another

Group Three or more persons (usually few in number) who communicate with each other over a span of time with a common purpose

Groupthink The group's members *not* thinking independently but going along with the group

Hearing Physical process of receiving sound waves

Heterophily Differences between persons

Homophily Likenesses or similarities of persons

Hostility Disliking; opposite of affection

Hypothetical illustrations Fictional detailed examples

Identifying and recognizing The second stage of listening in which patterns and familiar relationships are recognized and assimilated

Identity Being recognized as having membership in the group and as having a place or role in the group

Illustrations Detailed examples or instances; one kind of supporting material

Immediate feedback Feedback such as is possible in face-to-face communication

Implementation or "taking action" The final step in problem solving

Impromptu delivery Speaking "off-the-cuff," without preparation

Inclusion *See* appropriate responsiveness

Independent goal A goal that either individual can win or lose regardless of the cooperation or participation of the other

Indexing A way of "mentally" realizing that person 1 is not peron 2; they are different persons

Indirect feedback Nonpurposive and unintentional feedback

Inductive reasoning Reasoning from specific examples, i.e., from data to a generalization

Informational interview An interview that has the purpose of giving or receiving information

Information overload More information than the system can process

Information processing The use of the central nervous system, the brain, and the hypothalamus to receive, interpret, evaluate, and store information from the outside environment; i.e., perceiving, thinking, and remembering

Initial contact phase The first minutes of the acquaintance process

Inoculation Giving the audience an "immunization shot" against subsequent persuasion

Integrative resolutions Answers that bring disputants together in mutual satisfaction

Intensify values and beliefs One strategy for persuasion aiming to reinforce or sustain attitudes and behavior

Internal feedback Feedback received from within one's self

Interpersonal attraction The liking of one person for another

Interpersonal communication One or more persons engaged freely and directly with each other in overt and covert transmission and reception of messages

Interpersonal trust Relying on or having confidence in another person

Intimacy One factor important to the maintenance of friendship

Intimate distance Under twelve inches

Intrapersonal communication Takes place within the individual; thinking; communication with self

Intrinsic credibility Things revealed during the speech; the speaker's verbal and nonverbal messages that project an image

Inverted funnel sequence One interview structure; moving from closed, specific questions to broad, open questions

Johari window A pictorial model depicting understanding of self and others

Law of primacy The principle that the first in a series of anything is a stronger stimulus than following items in the series

Law of recency The last argument (most recent) or message will be best remembered and most influential

Leading questions Questions indicating what the exact answer should be

Levels of communication Intrapersonal, interpersonal, and public; each builds on the preceding level, with intrapersonal being the most basic level

Listening The total process of hearing, identifying, and auding, i.e., of receiving sound waves, wording and recognizing them, and assigning meaning

Literal analogy Both things compared belong to the same class

Logical pattern One following the scientific process step-by-step; e.g., problem-solution, cause-effect

Long-term memory Ability to store and recall data over an extended period of time

Loudness or softness One type of vocal qualifier

Love needs Affection needs

Majority-vote method Arriving at a decision without consensus

Manuscript delivery Reading a speech

Marital communication One situation in family communication, characterized chiefly by intimacy and the comparative permanence of the relationship

Maslow's hierarchy of needs Physiological, safety, love, esteem, and self-actualization needs

Mediation Enlisting a third party or outside party to help in negotiation

Memorized delivery Each word of the speech is memorized and recalled as the speech is given

Message An idea, concept, emotion, desire, or feeling one wishes to share with another; or, any verbal or nonverbal behavior used to evoke meaning

Mirror questions Restating a comment of the other person in question form; the question "mirrors" the other person's statement

Motivated sequence A five-step organizational pattern that is based on psychological "need" steps

Movement A type of action language characterized by pace, length of stride, and walking posture—all of which vary with the emotional state and personality of the individual

Nature and quality A situational factor that can affect trust

Negative feedback Feedback that indicates the message has not been received correctly or not accomplished its objective

Negative self-concept Low self-esteem; poor concept of self

Negativism A general attitude of distrust and hostility; an adjustive technique for reducing hostility

Negotiation A trading process between contestants

Neurological inhibition An ability of the neural system (the brain and its network) to block out incoming stimuli

Noise Any physical, physiological, psychological, or semantic distortion or interference with a message

Nondirective structure One in which the interviewee controls content, pace, and general procedure

Nonsharable goals Goals that one person wins entirely while the other person loses entirely

Nonverbal communication Communication other than words: tone of voice, gesture, etc.

Nonverbal feedback Facial expression, posture, gestures, etc.

Object language Meanings attached to material things, to objects

Opening, body, and closing The parts of the interview

Open questions Those allowing the respondent to answer in any way he or she chooses

Optical illusion A trick in perception whereby our eyes "see" a real thing in a false way (two curved lines as straight, for example)

Oral-auditory rehearsal Repetition or practice

Oral style Way of communicating unique to oral speaking

Organizational communication Persuasive communication carried out by a person or persons representing an organization

Organized audience Highly motivated audience needing only someone to direct them, e.g., military unit or athletic team

Panel-discussion group A group of four to six participants and a chairman who carry on a public conversation

Paralanguage Intonation, stress; i.e., "how" one says something that conveys anger, joy, or the "real" message rather than the words that are spoken

Passive audience Partially oriented audience; captive listeners

Perception The process by which stimuli are turned into information

Perceptual differences One cause of conflict

Peripheral values Values less important or less salient

Permissive leadership The leader acts as a central point for communication exchange

Personal appearance An important aspect of nonverbal communication in delivering a speech

Personal zone Private or intimate distance; area immediately around one's self; 1½ to 3 feet

Personality differences One cause of conflict

Persuasive interview An interview whose purpose is to modify the beliefs or attitudes of another

Phrasing of the question The first phase of group problem solving

Physical aggression An adjustive technique for reducing hostility

Physiological needs Food, shelter, sex needs

Pitch Frequency of vibration of vocal cords; a type of vocal qualifier; one element in vocal delivery

Pointing Making that point or topic appear important or relevant

Polarization When the members of a group direct their attention to a common object—the speaker—rather than to each other

Positioning Arranging ideas so as to give emphasis to one

Positive feedback Feedback that indicates the message has been received correctly

Post-speech analysis Analysis after the speech

Posture One type of action language

Power A major factor in interpersonal communication

P-O-X balance theory Heider's theory of how two person's liking or disliking each other affects their expected likings or dislikings of other objects, persons, etc.

Preparation One way of enhancing speaker credibility

Presence of a third person A situational factor related to trust; trust is greater if no third party is involved

Presummarizing Preview of the speech given by the speaker

Presymbolic communication Usually thought of as animal communication; communication that does not utilize symbols, and hence cannot refer to the past or the future

Primary group First group; family

Prisoner's dilemma A competitive goal situation, i.e., I win and you lose, automatically, or vice versa

Proactive emphasis Presummary; forecasting

Probing questions Secondary questions that dig deeper into answers to previous questions

Problem-solving ability Moving from defining and analyzing the problem all the way through implementation of the solution

Problem-solving group Group whose purpose is to solve some problem or accomplish some task

Process Characterized by many parts working together as a system; i.e., it is dynamic (relationships among parts constantly change), adaptive (it adjusts to changes in the environment), and is continuous (never stops and had no beginning)

Process of speech communication The working together of many variables or parts in order to exchange meanings and feelings among persons

Prompters Use of cue cards or teleprompter in speaking on-camera

Pronunciation The fitting together of sounds into words

Provide "success experience" relative to belief or behavior One way of improving self-esteem and increasing resistance to persuasion

Proximity Nearness in distance between persons; a factor in interpersonal attraction

Psychological factors Factors that appeal to listeners on the basis of psychological needs rather than logical ones adding evidence and reasoning

Psychological pattern of ordering arguments A pattern based on any one of several psychological sequences; i.e., need-satisfaction, dissonance-dissonance reduction, and others

Psychological state The existence of some emotional state that predisposes one to respond in one way rather than some other way

Public communication An audience or public receives (public speaking or mass media) primarily and the source sends primarily

Public distance Used for public seaking, acting, certain business situations

Purposive actions Intentional overt and identifiable by either the listener or talker

Purposive audience analysis Analyzing an audience in terms of the purpose of the speech

Qualifier An allowed exception to the claim or conclusion in Toulmin's procedure

Quality What makes a voice distinctive; one element in vocal delivery

Quintamensional sequence Uses one question in each general area of a survey interview

Rate and rhythm Speed of speaking and of presenting ideas

Rationalization Process of providing invalid reasons for one's objective or value; an adjustive technique for reducing hostility

Reactive emphasis Reviewing

Receivers The five senses

Reciprocal scanning The process of strangers "sizing up the other"

Reference group A group in which one has membership or to which one wishes to belong

Referent The thing for which a symbol stands

Releaser concept When one aspect of a stimulus situation automatically triggers a certain behavior as a response, the behavior is "released" by that specific stimulus

Reservation The exception element in Toulmin's pattern of reasoning

Resist later persuasion counter to attitudes and beliefs One strategy for persuasion aiming to reinforce or sustain attitudes and behavior.

Restatement Reiteration of an idea in different words

Rewards A factor in interpersonal attraction; we like those who reward us and dislike those who punish us

Rhetoric Persuasion

Ritualized communication Characterized by being carried on via a pattern or formula

Role expectations Expected behavior as defined by that role

Role playing Behaving so as to imitate the role of another

Role pressures One cause of conflict

Safety needs Desire for order, security, tenure, etc.

Selected audience One whose members have been "selected" or invited while other persons were not invited

Selective perception The eyes (or other sense organ) choose some stimuli from among hundreds of stimuli and focus or attend to those selected

Self-actualization Realizing one's fullest development in terms of his or her capabilities and highest desires and values

Self-concept A person's idea of himself or herself; a person's answer to "Who am I?"; one's perception of self

Self-disclosure Revealing one's self to another; sharing information about one's self to another

Self-esteem Pride or worth of one's self

Self-fulfilling prophecy Behaving in accordance with how one has defined oneself

Self-presentation Revealing one's self by presenting, i.e., as a public speaker

"Sense of humor" One way of presenting a self, which affects speaker credibility

Sensory deprivation Condition in which the amount of information received is too limited for us to "fill in" sufficiently enough to make sense of it; a severe limitation of stimuli

Sensory intaking Process of receiving stimuli

Sequencing patterns of questions Ways of structuring the interview; e.g., funnel sequence

Sharable goals Goals that two or more persons can all obtain

Shared-goals resolution A solution providing for both persons or all persons involved to have the goal

Shared leadership That leadership distributed among several persons

Short-term memory Information retained only briefly

Significant others Includes parents, brothers, sisters, peers, and any other persons for whom we have esteem and who have influence and power over us.

Silence as communication Meaning conveyed by silence

Simplify the value or goal One strategy for intensifying values and beliefs.

Social climate The interpersonal climate within a group

Social cohesion A feeling of sticking together; a desire to be supportive of the group

Socioemotional maturity One area of concern for an employer interviewing an applicant

Social isolation Being alone; out of contact with others

Social zone Area comfortable for social activity; not too close and not too distant; 4½ to 8 feet

Socioemotional climate Affective conditions in the group

Source credibility *See* ethos

Space as communication Meaning attached to spatial distance

Spatial pattern A pattern based on spatial relationships; i.e., near or far, north or east, or west or south, etc.

Speaking rate versus listening rate We listen faster than we can speak

Specific purpose of speech The general purpose stated in terms of the subject and specific audience

Speech communication The process by which information, meanings, and feelings are shared through the exchange of verbal and nonverbal messages

Spread register Lengthened intervals between pitches

Squeezed register Shortened intervals between pitches

Standardized interview Every question is set as to wording and sequence and no alteration or change is permitted

Statement of fact or description Based on reporting objective data

Statement of inference An interpretation from objective data

Statement of judgment A valuing of something; bad or good, etc.

Statistic Mathematical representation of a relationship; i.e., percentages, frequencies, etc.; one kind of supporting material

Status Ranking or position in the group

Status differences One cause of conflict

Stereotyped role One so commonly known that its expected behavior is clear and not necessarily relevant to the role needed in the situation

Stress A factor in interpersonal attraction; anxiety and stress motivate us to seek and be attracted to others

Strengthening belief Strategy by which resistance to persuasion can be increased

Strong emotion-laden, nonverbal communication One strategy for intensifying values and beliefs

Structure cooperative action One variable in conflict management

Support group A type of therapy group

Supporting materials Types of information including explanations, analogies, illustrations, specific instances, testimony, and visual aids

Supportive listening A type of reinforcing and therapeutic listening

Syllogism A formal pattern of reasoning used to apply a generalization to a specific case

Symbol That which is used by the brain to represent a stimulus when the stimulus is absent; words are important symbols for us

Symbolization Process of assigning an event or phenomenon to a symbol that will stand for that event or phenomenon so that the event or phenomenon can be retrieved from memory

Symposium Two to four speakers, each of whom gives a prepared presentation to an audience

Synapse A junction in a neural network where "new" electrical impulses give a "boost" to incoming messages or inhibit them by not firing or opening the pathway

Synergy The benefit derived from members working in a group that exceeds their possible individual contributions

Tactile communication Communication by touch or feel

Taking a role Filling the numerous task and maintenance roles in a small group

Task roles Formal and informal roles that need to be filled if the group is to accomplish its task

Tempo Rate or speed of speaking; one type of vocal qualifier

Territoriality Idea that living things stake out or need to claim a territory as theirs

Testimony Verbatim reporting of a person's opinion or conclusion; one kind of supporting material

Therapeutic groups Groups that have cathartic and positive influences on their members

Threat of change The premise that change is threatening is a foundation stone for the persuasive speech intended to reverse attitudes or behavior

Time and place One of the chief features of an audience

Time as communication Assignment of meaning based on time, i.e., late, early

Time pattern A pattern of organization or arrangement based on time, i.e., past, present, future

Topical pattern Method of organizing speech material by topic or category

Topical systems Systems consisting of lists of topics; one way of generating information

Total destruction One end to conflict

Total victory One end to conflict

Toulmin's inferential pattern of reasoning Consists of data, warrant, support for warrant, qualifiers, reservations, and claim

Transactional communication That in which each person defines the other and himself or herself *uniquely* for that relationship

Transition Move from one point to another

Transmitters Organs used in sending messages

Trustworthiness The degree to which the audience is willing to rely on the speaker, to believe the speaker

Tunnel sequence One interview structure; uses series of questions that are *all* open or *all* closed

Understanding of and sensitivity to group processes Knowing the factors that relate to the individual and to the processes of group discussion and problem solving

Unjust treatment A factor in interpersonal attraction; e.g., if we harm another, we tend to develop a dislike for that person

Use of quotation marks A reminder that the meaning we have for a word is an abstraction and can be different from the meaning someone else has.

Value differences One cause of conflict

Values and beliefs Intensifying values and beliefs is one strategy for persuasion aimed at reinforcing attitudes and behavior

Verbal aggression Attack upon another with words; an adjustive technique for reducing hostility

Verbal feedback Feedback in words; contrast "nonverbal feedback"

Visual aids Objects, models, chalkboard, pictures, slides, etc.

Vocal delivery All vocal aspects of speaking; force, pitch, rate, etc.

Vocal differentiators Crying, laughing, or breaking—factors applied to verbal messages

Vocal identifiers *Uh-huh* or *huh-uh;* meanings of yes or no

Vocal qualifiers Paralanguage elements, such as pitch, tone, tempo

Voice quality Set of characteristics that give a voice its unique identification

Warrant The belief that data are valid and, thus, that the claim is warranted

White noise A din of noise that masks out messages

Withdrawal Leaving the scene—a difficulty in handling hostility

Written style That way of using words and patterns of words that is unique to writing

Photos

Chapter Openers

1: © 1988 Ken Olson; **2:** © Michael Siluk; **3:** © Carolyn A. McKeone; **4:** Owen Franklin/Stock Boston; **5:** © Cleo Freelance Photo; **6,7:** © Steve Takatsuno; **8:** © James L. Shaffer; **9:** © Steve Takatsuno; **10:** © Michael Siluk; **11:** © Alan Carey/The Image Works; **12:** © Cleo Freelance Photo; **13:** © James Ballard.

Page 6: Museum of Modern Art, Film Stills Archive/Frost Publishing Group; **page 7:** © Cleo Freelance Photo; **page 9:** © David Wells/The Image Works; **page 27:** Rollin Kocsis; **page 28:** Harriet Gans/© The Image Works; **page 35:** © 1988 Ken Olson; **page 45:** © Alan Carey/The Image Works; **page 46:** © Allen Ruid; **pages 48,49:** © Jean-Claude Lejeune; **page 50:** © Alan Carey/The Image Works; **page 64:** Tony O'Brien/Frost Publishing Group; **page 65:** © Allen Ruid; **page 68:** Lionel Delevingne/Picture Group; **page 69:** Frank Siteman/EKM Nepenthe; **page 70:** © James L. Shaffer; **page 82:** © Richard Anderson, 1988; **page 83:** Bob Daemmrich/© The Image Works; **page 84:** © Robert Kalman/The Image Works; **page 85:** © Jean-Claude Lejeune; **page 90:** Frank Siteman/EKM Nepenthe; **page 95:** © Steve Takatsuno; **page 107:** Emil Fray; **page 109(top):** © Jean-Claude Lejeune; **page 109(bottom):** Rick Smolan; **page 110:** © Jean-Claude Lejeune; **page 118:** Alan Carey/The Image Works; **page 126:** © Jean-Claude Lejeune; **page 128:** © James Ballard; **page 130:** Alan Carey/The Image Works; **page 132:** © 1988 Ken Olson; **page 138:** © James L. Shaffer; **page 139:** Rick Smolan; **page 146:** David Strickler; **page 152:** Michael Hayman/Corn's Photo Service; **page 154:** © Steve Takatsuno; **page 158:** © James Ballard; **page 161:** P. Strange, United Nations/Frost Publishing Group; **page 169:** © James L. Shaffer; **page 171:** Mark Antman/The Image Works; **page 181:** © Bob Daemmrich/The Image Works; **page 183:** © Jean-Claude Lejeune; **page 184:** Alan Carey/The Image Works; **page 187:** Dwight Cendrowski; **pages 189,193:** © George W. Gardner/The Image Works; **page 194:** © Michael Siluk; **page 197:** Mark Antman/The Image Works; **page 203:** © Patsy Davidson/The Image Works; **page 215:** UPI/Bettman; **page 220:** Brad Bower/Picture Group; **page 223:** © Jean-Claude Lejeune; **page 226:** © James L. Shaffer; **page 230:** Rick Browne/Picture Group; **page 238:** © James L. Shaffer; **page 240:** Frank Siteman/EKM-Nepenthe; **page 245:** © Bob Coyle; **page 253:** © James L. Shaffer; **page 255:** © 1988 Ken Olson; **page 256:** Frank Siteman/EKM-Nepenthe; **page 269:** © James L. Shaffer; **page 270:** John Maher/EKM-Nepenthe; **page 273:** © Howard Dratch/The Image Works; **page 278:** © Bob Daemmrich/The Image Works; **page 282:** © Jean-Claude Lejeune; **page 283:** David Strickler; **page 285:** © Howard Dratch/The Image Works; **page 289:** James L. Shaffer; **page 292:** © Michael Siluk; **page 295:** Bill Powers/Frost Publishing Group; **page 306:** © Jean-Claude Lejeune; **page 309:** Billy Graham Evangelical Assn./Frost Publishing Group; **page 310:** © Howard Dratch/The Image Works; **pages 313,329:** © James L. Shaffer; **page 335:** Courtesy of American Greetings Corp.; **page 338:** © Jean-Claude Lejeune; **page 339:** Las Vegas News Bureau; **page 340:** Rick Smolan.

Name Index

*Pages with a *t* denote a table in the text: pages with a *n* indicate a footnote at the end of each chapter.

Subject Index